The Development of Modern Industries in Bengal

Bengal's traditional industries, once celebrated worldwide, largely decayed under the backwash effects of the British Industrial Revolution in the first half of the nineteenth century. Although colonial ambivalence is often cited as an explanation, this study also shows that a series of new industries emerged during this period.

The book reappraises the thesis of India's deindustrialisation and discusses the development status of the traditional industries in the early nineteenth century, examines their technology, employment opportunities and marketing and, finally, analyses the underlying reasons for their decay. It offers a study of how traditional industries evolved into modern enterprises in a British colony, and contributes to the broader discussion on the global history of industrialisation.

This book will be of interest to scholars of Indian economic history as well as those who seek to understand the widespread effects of industrialisation, especially in a colonial context.

Indrajit Ray is Professor in the Department of Commerce at the University of North Bengal, India.

Routledge Explorations in Economic History
Edited by Lars Magnusson, Uppsala University, Sweden

For a full list of titles in this series, please visit www.routledge.com/series/SE0347

73 The Political Economy of Mercantilism
Lars Magnusson

74 Innovation and Technological Diffusion
An economic history of early steam engines
Harry Kitsikopoulos

75 Regulating Competition
Cartel registers in the twentieth-century world
Edited by Susanna Fellman and Martin Shanahan

76 European Banks and the Rise of International Finance
The Post-Bretton Woods era
Carlo Edoardo Altamura

77 The Second Bank of the United States
'Central' banker in an era of nation-building, 1816–1836
Jane Ellen Knodell

78 War, Power and the Economy
Mercantilism and state formation in 18th-century Europe
A. González Enciso

79 The Western Allies and Soviet Potential in World War II
Economy, society and military power
Martin Kahn

80 Money, Currency and Crisis
In search of trust, 2000 BC to AD 2000
Edited by R. J. van der Spek and Bas van Leeuwen

81 The Development of Modern Industries in Bengal
Reindustrialisation, 1858–1914
Indrajit Ray

The Development of Modern Industries in Bengal

Reindustrialisation, 1858–1914

Indrajit Ray

Routledge
Taylor & Francis Group
LONDON AND NEW YORK

First published 2018 by Routledge

2 Park Square, Milton Park, Abingdon, Oxfordshire OX14 4RN
52 Vanderbilt Avenue, New York, NY 10017

Routledge is an imprint of the Taylor & Francis Group, an informa business

First issued in paperback 2020

British Library Cataloguing-in-Publication Data
A catalogue record for this book is available from the British Library

Library of Congress Cataloging-in-Publication Data
A catalog record has been requested for this book

ISBN: 978-1-138-50067-9 (hbk)
ISBN: 978-0-367-66652-1 (pbk)

Typeset in Bembo
by Out of House Publishing

To
my late father and philosopher-guide,
Hirendra Nath Ray,
and
my mother and schooldays home tutor,
Srimati Minati Ray

Contents

Figures

Tables

Appendix tables

Foreword

A previous book, *Bengal Industries and the British Industrial Revolution (1757–1857)* (Routledge, 2011), established Indrajit Ray's reputation as the foremost authority on economic transition in Bengal in the early modern times. Ray reaffirms his position in the field with this second book, which follows up the story to the early twentieth century and, in the process, describes the transition from a craft-based industrial system to modern manufacturing more fully.

The origin of large-scale mining and manufacturing enterprise in India is a well-researched subject. The standard works on Indian industrialisation from the nineteenth century, by Morris David Morris, A. K. Bagchi, Rajnarayan Chandavarkar and R. K. Ray, are still widely read and remain benchmarks in the field. Within this scholarship, the story of the industrialisation in Bengal has been explored in considerable detail. Books written by A. Z. M. Iftikhar-ul-Awwal and M. Mufakharul Islam have contributed significantly to that theme. Directly or indirectly, these works have attempted to show how industrial pioneers and early entrepreneurs solved the problems of obtaining capital, technology and labour, and how that process took a distinctive trajectory in Bengal, among other reasons, because British capital dominated investment in this region. With the field being so well developed, a great deal of recent research has moved into exploring niche questions, and produced journal articles rather than books.

Ray's new book, by contrast, takes the discourse back to the bigger picture. *The Development of Modern Industries in Bengal: Reindustrialisation, 1858–1914* offers a rich narrative of the emergence of large scale modern enterprise in Bengal from the middle of the nineteenth century. More successfully than other works on industrialisation, it describes the regional economy in detail, detailing the prehistory of large-scale enterprise in this region, the origins of capital and labour, business enterprise and organisation, and the persistence and decline of traditional industry in the same fields in which mechanised work emerged. In short, it presents a more complete and coherent picture of industrialisation, in which the connecting thread is the regional economy of Bengal.

Historians of world industrialisation will find the book especially useful for two innovations it introduces. First, it incorporates the experience of handicrafts and manual labour in mining and manufacturing within the account. The mainstream historiography of industrialisation tends to treat the machine-using factories as a species of production distinct from and incompatible with the handicrafts. In recent times there has been a reaction against the tendency to see machines and crafts in sharp opposition, with a hard border separating the two spheres. Some historians have begun to recognise that craft production persisted into present times and that manual work persisted inside the mechanised factory. This book does not dispute that there were spheres of decline and obsolescence within the crafts as large-scale industry emerged; but it also shows how extensive craft production was, who these producers were, what they did to adapt to the competition, and when these adaptation strategies failed. In the process, the book pays fuller attention to labour-intensive methods in a story primarily of the rise of capital-intensive industry. Second, Ray integrates the history of Bengal with current debates and discourses in global economic history. Drawing on his well-known work on the concept of deindustrialisation, and with a diverse but rich set of case-studies, Ray sets boundaries on the concept, and suggests how it should be applied as a research tool.

A work in the best tradition of source-based research, *The Development of Modern Industries in Bengal* successfully connects its subject matter to major themes in world history as well as regional economic history – a task Ray is uniquely able to perform. It represents a major advancement in the field.

Tirthankar Roy
Professor of Economic History
London School of Economics
October 2017

Preface

The historicity of Bengal's modern industries has occupied my interest since the early 1990s. The interest has possibly been sustained so long in view of my living surroundings and the nature of my job. My home town is Barrackpore, an industrial suburb of Calcutta, where life rhythms followed the sirens of mills in my boyhood days – getting up from the bed, going to schools and colleges, and so forth. There were paper mills, jute mills, engineering firms and a host of ancillary and small-scale industries. Many of my friends work there; moreover, two of my younger brothers own export-based firms in the leather industry (Bengal is now pioneer in this line). I thus come across the stories of industrial life, their problems and prospects, whenever I stay in my home town. On the other hand, the university where I have been teaching for three decades is located in the foothills of the Himalayas, the so-called Terai region, which is dotted with tea gardens. Only a few kilometres away to the east is the Dooars, where, again, tea plantations are the mainstay of livelihood. The steep slopes of the Himalayas containing tea bushes start no later than 20 minutes' journey by road on the north. The university is thus surrounded by tea gardens, each stretching over several hectares of land, which looks like a great piece of green carpet. British culture still prevails in these gardens, as reflected in their social life (especially the club culture, manners and etiquette) and working schedules. Regular interactions take place between the university teachers and the tea gardens, with various meetings, seminars and the annual general meetings.

I started my career as a consultant in a public-sector undertaking, the West Bengal Consultancy Organisation, which provided consultancy services to industries in respect of the setting up of new ventures, revival of sick units, market surveys and so on, as also to the government for regional industrial planning. My experience in those projects has enriched my view of industrial historiography in developing countries. I also worked for a couple of years in a premier chamber of commerce in Calcutta, the Bengal National Chamber of Commerce and Industries, where, along with other assignments, I looked after three industrial associations as the secretary-in-charge: the Eastern India Glass Manufacturers' Association, Indian Tea Exporters' Association and Bengal Rice Mills' Association. My interactions with industrialists in the chamber, and various discussions at meetings of the industrial associations, have provided me analytical insights into the problems of industries. Let me add that the University of North Bengal gave me an additional assignment as the head of the Department of Tea Science for a couple of years. For the students' interest, and also for the department's sake, I had to maintain a close liaison with the tea gardens in North Bengal. Frequent interactions with tea garden management have enlightened me about various facets of tea plantation in this region. All these explain why my interest in these topics has been sustained for such a long period.

For this project I have never sought for any financial support. Nor did I take any study leave from my university to visit libraries or for drafting the manuscript. Contemporary reports and documents are scattered across various libraries in Calcutta. More important libraries that I have consulted are the National Library, Calcutta; the Commercial Library, Calcutta; the West Bengal State Archives, Calcutta; the Company Law Board Library, Calcutta; and the libraries of the Bengal National Chamber of Commerce and Industries, the Bengal Chamber of Commerce and Industries, the Indian Tea Association and the Indian Jute Mills' Association. Staying at home during my annual vacations (twice a year for more than a month each), I completed my library work in Calcutta, and prepared the manuscripts after normal assignments at the university department.

Acknowledgements

At the outset I acknowledge the late Bhabatosh Datta, a great teacher in economics, who, in the early phase of this project, advised me to study the period from 1858 to 1914 exclusively. Though initially hesitant as to the materials that could be gathered for this period, I subsequently understood the depth of Bengal's industrial historiography in the second half of the nineteenth century, and could thus fathom the weight of his advice. I here also acknowledge Professor Amiya Kumar Bagchi, who enlightened me as to the importance of industrial employment in the discussion of economic history in an erstwhile colony such as Bengal. Through his critical bent, he impressed on me the art of reading economic history in a peripheral region. I am also indebted to Professor Tirthankar Roy, who, apart from writing the foreword of this book, has painstakingly read the early drafts of some chapters and given invaluable suggestions.

I have also been enlightened by discussion in various seminars. I specifically mention the Hi-PoD (Historical Patterns of Development and Underdevelopment) conference on India and the great divergence, organised under the auspices of the Centre for Economic Policy Research (CEPR) at Fort Neemrana, Rajasthan, India, on 19–20 September 2011. I wish to thank the participants in the conference, especially Stephen Broadberry, Bishnupriya Gupta, Debin Ma, Sevket Pamuk, Rajat Datta and Tirthankar Roy.

I am indebted to the staffs of the National Library, Commercial Library and West Bengal State Archives, all in Calcutta, who untiringly supplied me books and documents in the course of my study in those libraries. I also acknowledge the secretaries of the Bengal National Chamber of Commerce and Industries, Bengal Chamber of Commerce and Industries, Indian Tea Association and Indian Jute Mills' Association, who allowed me to study books and documents in their libraries, especially the rare documents pertaining to the early years of those associations.

I am also indebted to two anonymous referees at Routledge who critically reviewed this book proposal and suggested certain issues to deal with. In the course of the review process, and subsequent to its finalisation stage, I received many suggestions, and also clarifications of my doubts, from Emily Kindleysides, senior editor in economics at Routledge and the commissioning editor of this book. I acknowledge her contribution to this project. For similar contributions, I also acknowledge Natalie Tomlinson, who became the acting editor in the absence of Emily Kindleysides. I must thank also Laura Johnson, senior editorial assistant (economics), and Lisa Lavelle, editorial assistant (economics), both at Routledge, who were my main points of contact at different stages of the publication process. I also acknowledge with thanks the prompt service and sincere cooperation of Matthew Twigg, production editor (geography, tourism and economics) at Taylor & Francis Group; Ruth-Anne Hurst, production editor at Out of House Publishing, who was the project manager for this book; and Mike Richardson, the freelance copy-editor, who completed his task to my satisfaction.

Some chapters of this book, or parts thereof, have been published in various journals/books. Most of them have been revised/enlarged for the present publication, but, without the copyright permissions from the publishers of these journals/books, this book could not have taken its present shape. In this context, I acknowledge with thanks Routledge, for giving me permission to incorporate a chapter of the book *A New Economic History of Colonial India*, edited by Latika Chaudhary et al., and Taylor & Francis, for giving permission, on behalf of the Economic History Society of Southern Africa, to incorporate an article published in the journal *Economic History of Developing Regions.* I am equally indebted to Sage Publications India Pvt. Ltd, for permissions to use the enlarged versions of my two articles in the *Indian Economic and Social History Review.* I also acknowledge Springer, for giving me licence to reproduce the material used in one of my chapters in *Encyclopaedia of the History of Science, Technology, and Medicine in Non-Western Cultures*, third edition, edited by Helaine Selin.

1 Introduction

The present chapter introduces the book in three respects: (i) the study area and the period of interest; (ii) the subject matters; and (iii) the limitations of the study. These are discussed in three subsequent sections that follow. Section I does not, however, introduce Bengal in terms of its political history, physical geography or anthropological features, as those are discussed in my previous work (Ray 2011). Rather, it defines the geographical boundaries within which the present study concentrates, since several changes occurred in this respect during my study period.

I

Modern industries started emerging in Bengal from around the middle of the nineteenth century, which motivates me to concentrate on this period. Coal mining entered into a high-growth trajectory in the 1840s, and, using the European charcoal technology for the first time, pig iron began to be manufactured at the Mohammad Bazar Iron Works in 1855. In addition, the first steam-powered jute mill was opened in 1855, commercial tea plantations were launched in 1856 and the first modern paper mill was set up in 1861. But some of these industries (in particular, iron smelting, jute processing and paper making) had ancient legacies in a cottage environment. To understand their strength and weakness in the contemporary industrial milieu, and also their contributions to Bengal's subsequent reindustrialisation, I look back to the first half of the nineteenth century, or even the second half of the eighteenth. Moreover, when a modern industry has its roots prior to the study period, I take the liberty of starting the discussion accordingly.

This study specifies 1858 as its commencing year. It is a landmark in Indian historiography since, on 2 August 1858, the British parliament promulgated the Government of India Act 1858 (21 & 22 Vict. c. 106), whereby India's governance was transferred from the East India Company to the British Crown (for the original act, see Keith 1922: 370–82). It was followed by Queen Victoria's proclamation on 1 November 1858 to the 'Princes, Chiefs, and People of India' (ibid.: 382–6), underlining that economic prosperity and social advancement in India 'can only be secured by internal peace and good government' (ibid.: 383–4). The Secretary of State was employed as a link between Britain and India; a council of 15 members was set up to assist him; an Indian Civil Service was created for the purpose of administration; and the Crown appointed a Governor General (the first viceroy) for India and governors for the presidencies (GOI 1909: 30–1). For Bengal, however, the Governor General looked after the office of governor, as Calcutta was then the capital of India, with the assistance (since 1854) of a lieutenant-governor (ibid.: 16).

Bengal's administrative jurisdiction remained largely unaltered in that transitional phase, however (ibid.). Similar to the practice in other presidencies, there was a Council in Bengal, which devised the code of 'Regulations' for its governance. Any territory, added by conquest or otherwise, came under those regulations. But when a territory was acquired, but not annexed, it was treated as a non-regulation province. There were both regulation and non-regulation provinces under the control of the lieutenant-governor of Bengal (GOB 1868: 1). The presidency then comprised eight divisions in the former (Bhaugulpore, Burdwan, Chittagong, Cuttack, Dacca, Nuddea, Patna and Rajshahi) and six divisions in the latter (Assam, Chotanagpur, Cooch Behar, Sonthal Pergunnahs, the Chittagong Hill Tracts and Cachar), with 36 and 19 districts, respectively. For 1866–7 the district-wise area and population of Bengal presidency are shown in Appendix 1.1. The appendix aggregates population to 37,535,890 over an area of 199,514 square miles, so that its population density comes to about 188 persons per square mile.

This administrative set-up was first modified in 1874 when the Assam division was separated to constitute a new entity, the North-East Frontier Non-Regulation Province (for the administrative set-up in 1880, see Figure 1.1). A large number of tea estates that had sprang up in Assam and Sylhet valleys were thus excluded from the province of Bengal. A more extensive partition followed in 1905, however, whereby a number of districts belonging to Eastern Bengal were separated. Together with the North-East Frontier Non-Regulation Province, they constituted the Eastern Bengal and Assam Province. Some important districts that Bengal had then lost were Dacca, Mymensing, Faridpore, Backergunj, Tipperah, Noakhally, Chittagong, Rajshahi, Dinajpore, Jalpaiguri, Rangpore, Bogra, Pabna, Malda and Sylhet. In addition, five Hindi-speaking districts of Chotanagpur were transferred from Bengal to the Central Provinces and six Oriya-speaking districts were annexed from the Central Provinces to Bengal.

Although the move was officially declared to be for administrative convenience, its underlying motivation came under sharp attack in view of its partitioning of Bengal along religious lines (Roy 2009; Gordon 1973; McLane 1965). Bengal's industrial economy was also dislocated, as the raw-material-cum-foodgrain zones largely belonged to Eastern Bengal, juxtaposed to the development of major industries in and around Calcutta. As people apprehended its consequences for the polity and economy of Bengal, popular agitation then broke out across the province. The *Swadeshi* movement, as it is called, also had important economic dimensions. In the belief that the partition would damage Bengal's economic prosperity, the movement called for the boycotting of foreign goods, and motivated Bengali entrepreneurs to serve the cause of development. Many indigenous (*Swadeshi*) enterprises were set up as a result (Bhattacharyya 1986).

The partition of 1905 was partially modified in 1912 by the unification of five major Bengali-speaking divisions with the province of Bengal. Two more policy decisions followed. First, Bihar and Orissa were included in a separate province, with Assam as another province. Bengal's loss in this partitioning was that a number of coal mines belonging to it were transferred to the province of Bihar and Orissa (see footnote *** of Appendix 3.1). Second, the capital of India was shifted from Calcutta to Delhi.

The study area of this book is confined largely to the post-1912 administrative jurisdiction of Bengal. Post-1858 Bengal is referred to, however, in the deliberations on some of its traditional industries (especially iron smelting and paper making) in the early nineteenth century.

The study runs through 1914. The inter-war period is deliberately avoided because of its great dissimilarity to the previous epoch in respect of the industrial environment. Contrary to the political tranquillity and economic stability from 1858 to 1914, the subsequent period witnessed booms for some industries and a dislocation of supply chains for others, with World War I, the post-war recessions, the Great Depression of 1929 and, finally, the preparations for World War II. For variations in opportunities and constraints, the industries behaved dissimilarly in this turmoil-struck phase. Confining the focus to the 1858–1914 period, the study seeks to examine on the basis of purely economic principles how Bengal was reindustrialised.

II

Bengal's traditional industries, once famous around the world, decayed to a large extent in the first half of the nineteenth century. In the second half, however, a series of new industries arose on the basis of modern technology and organisation. This volume seeks to identify the underlying reasons thereof. Situating the argument on the global movement of capital with theoretical underpinnings and empirical support, it responds to a logical curiosity: what motivated the contemporary movement of capital? To this end, this study takes up five major industries that arose in Bengal during the second half of the nineteenth century – coal mining, iron smelting and its downstream activities, jute processing, paper making and tea cultivation – and discusses various government policies and Bengal's comparative advantages in these lines of production. It analyses in detail how, on the strength of their comparative cost advantages, these industries successfully competed in contemporary markets. In jute and tea, Bengal's industries virtually monopolised the global market by the close of the nineteenth century, replacing Dundee and China, respectively. In coal, iron and paper, they became formidable competitors to British industries, which had a monopoly in India's domestic market. Furthermore, it critically examines various facets of the industries – land, labour, capital and enterprise, in addition to technology and raw materials – so that the contemporary industrial progress can be properly understood. Three of the industries – jute processing, iron smelting and paper making – had earlier been part of Bengal's traditional sector, which had been extensively developed on the strength of local technology and manpower, but which are conspicuous by their absence from historiography. This book discusses the development status of these traditional industries in the early nineteenth century; examines their technology, employment opportunities and marketing; and analyses the underlying reasons for their decay. It helps us to comprehend how traditional industries were able to surpass themselves and transform into modern enterprises in a British colony. Finally, this book reappraises the long-standing debate on India's nineteenth-century deindustrialisation by juxtaposing the demise of Bengal's traditional industries in the first half of the century with its reindustrialisation in the second half. These analyses significantly enrich the industrial historiography.

There are eight chapters that follow. Chapter 2 critically analyses the status of economic development in Bengal in the early modern age. In particular, I seek to explain why, notwithstanding its ancient economic prosperity, Bengal encountered an economic slowdown in the early modern age. This is a prelude to this study on Bengal's industrial history from 1858 to 1914, and also contributes to the literature on the 'great divergence'. It offers a critique of the existing hypotheses insofar as they fail to account for the Bengal experience sufficiently. In particular, the accent on demographic-ecological crisis as an explanation for Asian regions falling behind seems inapt for Bengal. I propose an alternative theoretical framework based on Adam Smith's understanding of the pre-modern process of economic development, and especially the role of capital inflow in the process. This alternative is tested against a detailed analysis of the monetary-fiscal trends in early modern Bengal.

Chapter 3 seeks to analyse the growth pattern of coal mining in Bengal during the nineteenth century, and also its underlying causations. It reveals that, although a first attempt was made in 1774, regular excavations of coal took off only around the middle of the next century. I argue that mining in Bengal suffered initially from a hostile attitude by the colonial government and improper institutions, and later from a lack of mineralogical knowledge, inefficient transport network and the scarcity of labour. Once the style of governance had been changed under the rule of the British Crown, the impediments disappeared. My analysis shows how these successive events domestically established comparative cost advantages in favour of Bengal coal, enabling it to successfully compete with British coal in India's domestic market in the second half of the nineteenth century. Its export ventures, especially in South and South-east Asia, are also discussed.

Chapter 4 discusses iron smelting and its downstreams in the nineteenth century. Although Bengal had a rich heritage in this field, it succumbed to market competition in the colonial era. A series of large-scale projects were started in the period from 1774 to 1879, but they could not survive. Only from 1880 onwards did the industry grow rapidly. This chapter highlights various aspects of traditional iron smelting in Bengal, and analyses the issues of deindustrialisation. This is followed by a discussion on the development process of large-scale iron smelting, with an emphasis on its comparative cost advantages vis-à-vis the United Kingdom. It argues that the failure of large-scale iron smelting in the early British rule, as also its success thereafter, may be explained by the contemporary colonial policy of store purchasing.

Chapter 5 seeks to situate Bengal's jute industry during the nineteenth century in a global perspective. It was a long-established cottage industry in Bengal that entered the global market before the advent of jute technologies in Dundee, and grew together with the Dundee mills through the mid-nineteenth century. The subsequent emergence of modern mills in Bengal further aggravated the market competition. In view of the inadequate analysis in the existing literature, I intend to investigate four important questions on the contemporary jute industry: (i) what was the development status of the traditional jute industry in Bengal around the middle of the nineteenth century; (ii) when did it enter into the phase of decline; (iii) what were the sources of comparative advantages between the Dundee and Calcutta mills; and (iv) what were the nature and consequences of the competition between them? These issues are discussed, and also quantified, wherever possible, on the basis of contemporary data and information. The welfare implications of the Bengal jute industry are also examined.

Bengal's paper-making industry is the theme of Chapter 6. It was a medieval art in Bengal, which prospered through the early nineteenth century on the basis of local raw materials, native manpower and a domestic market, but it started declining in the early 1860s. From the late eighteenth century a number of European projects also materialised, but they failed to survive in the long run. Finally, a series of successful ventures were inaugurated. This chapter analyses these different phases of paper making in nineteenth-century Bengal, highlighting the technology, raw materials, labour, capital and marketing. Finally, the colonial store purchasing policy is discussed at length, to establish that periodic amendments to it brought swings in the industry in the second half of the nineteenth century.

Chapter 7 discusses the tea plantations in Bengal, which were developed on the basis of British capital, tribal labour and what were designated as 'wastelands' in the Himalayas. In contrast to the prevailing trend in the literature to discuss plantations from the viewpoint of a colony (especially to highlight its dualistic features), the present chapter analyses the development of tea cultivation in Bengal from the global perspective. It shows that the plantations served the British interest by creating a vast, profitable outlet for British capital, and thus explains why the imperial administration promoted its development through favourable wasteland policies, efficient transport infrastructure and soft fiscal measures. Bengal also benefited thereby, as substantial employment opportunities were created, and a vast tract of wasteland was developed. Contemporary data and information are gathered to these ends from various archival sources.

I also discuss how, on the basis of its comparative advantages, Indian tea occupied the global market, where China had previously had a monopoly.

Chapter 8 summarises the findings of the chapters on the different industries, categorising them under four headings: (i) the state of major industries around 1914; (ii) capital and entrepreneurs; (iii) land and labour; and (iv) market and government policies. For topical interests, I elaborate certain general aspects of the contemporary industrial economy that have only been adumbrated in the texts – such as the managing agency system, the migration of labour and fiscal policies. The chapter concludes with a brief discussion of the basic changes in the industrial landscape of Bengal during this phase of reindustrialisation.

Finally, Chapter 9 addresses the long-standing debate on Bengal's nineteenth-century deindustrialisation. The question of India's deindustrialisation in the nineteenth century was raised by Marx, as well as by the political leaders in India's nationalist movement. But empirical support was in seriously short supply. It was much debated in the twentieth century, both theoretically and empirically. This chapter identifies the genesis of the debate, and briefly reviews its relevant theoretical and empirical underpinnings. On the basis of my previous industry-wise studies (Ray 2011), as also the present one, this chapter seeks to verify whether deindustrialisation took place in Bengal during the colonial period.

III

There are three major limitations to this study. The first one concerns the number of industries it examines. Although I discuss here only five major industries in Bengal, there were in fact many other industries, belonging to both the traditional and the modern sectors. A survey by the Department of Industries on Bengal's cottage industries in 1929 (GOB 1929) reports 95 such industries, of which four prevailed over others across the province. These were hand loom weaving, brass and bell metal manufacturing, soap making and tanning (ibid.: 5–9). The report underlines that 'hand-loom weaving is far and away the most important and valuable and widespread cottage industry of the province. From no district or centre is it absent, while in some centres such as Santipur in Nadia, Chowmohani in Noakhali, Sonamukhi, Vishnupur and others, practically the whole population is absorbed in hand-loom weaving and subsidiary occupations as their principal source of livelihood' (ibid.: 5). As to brass and bell metal, the survey reports the turnover at 'many lakhs of rupees' (ibid.: 6) and the level of employment at 36,471.

Side by side, many modern industries outside the purview of this book arose in this province. They belonged to various industrial groups such as textiles, minerals and metals, foods, drinks and tobacco, chemicals, and so on. The number of factories in these industries, and their average daily employment levels, are shown in Table 1.1.

Table 1.1 excludes jute mills (85 factories, with employment at 325,865), engineering (196 factories, with employment at 65,557), iron and steel (two factories, with employment at 9,049), and paper and printing (73 factories,

Table 1.1 Factories in Bengal outside our purview, 1920s

Industry	*Number of factories*	*Average daily employment*
Textiles (other than jute)	32	14,132
Minerals and metals (other than iron and steel)	6	742
Food, drinks and tobacco	547	29,405
Chemicals, dyes, etc.	111	14,540
Processes relating to wood, stone and glass	34	4,905
Processes relating to hides and skins	7	751
Gins and presses	680	36,680
Miscellaneous	15	2,401
Total	1,432	103,556

Source: P.P. 1930: 662–71.

Figure 1.1 Bengal Presidency in 1880

Source: Presidencies and provinces of British India. Retrieved 22 July 2017 from www.wikiwand.com/en/Presidencies_ands_provinces_of_British_India.

with employment at 10,612). This excluded list gives the number of factories at 356 and the employment level at 411,083, so that the total number of factories in Bengal comes to 1,788, with an employment level of 514,639. Industries under our study thus constitute 19.91 per cent of the total number of factories, but 79.88 per cent of their level of employment. Indeed, the inclusion of printing (along with paper mills) largely inflates the number of factories, but not the level of employment to that extent, as it was 4,393 in paper mills as against 10,612 in that group (P.P. 1930: 659). Moreover, statistics on tea plantations and coal mining are not reflected in these figures, as they were not included under the Factory Act. If joint-stock companies are considered for 1917–18 (P.P. 1920: 232), however, their number is reported at 582 for manufacturing, plantations and mining (excluding companies belonging to the banking and loans sector, insurance, navigation, railways and tramways, other trading companies, and land and building), whereas the figure is 464 for tea plantations, coal mining and jute mills. The industries under this study thus account for 79.72 per cent of joint-stock companies. Therefore, we are assured that the present volume covers a major segment of contemporary modern industries in Bengal.

The second limitation relates to the absence of any comparative study between Bengal and other provinces of India, especially Bombay and Madras. This is in a sense a compulsion for me, since the industries that I study here were developed mainly in and around Bengal on the basis of their historical legacies and/or natural endowments. It is also deliberate in the sense that this reading seeks to evaluate the competitiveness of Bengal's emerging industries in the global market environment – against British industries in particular, except for tea plantations, where China was the market leader.

Lastly, notwithstanding their topical interest amongst academia, certain issues, such as the trade union movement, labour welfare and the recruitment system of migratory workers, are not discussed. Temptations to do so are resisted in view of a rich literature on them (see, for example, Sen 1999; Bose 1986; Siddique 1995; de Haan 1995; Chakrabarty 1989; Saha 1978; Das Gupta 1976; Simmons 1976; Seth 1940). The book is instead more focused on the least discussed areas of Bengal's industrial historiography for 1858 to 1914.

Bibliography

Bhattacharyya, A. (1986) *Swadeshi Enterprise in Bengal: 1900–1920*. Calcutta: Mita Bhattacharyya.

Bose, S. K. (1986) 'A Note on Labour Movement in Bengal (1920–21)', *Social Scientist* 14 (1), 23–33.

Chakrabarty, D. (1989) *Rethinking Working-Class History: Bengal, 1890–1940*. Princeton, NJ: Princeton University Press.

Das Gupta, R. (1976) 'Factory Labour in Eastern India: Sources of Supply, 1855–1946: Some Preliminary Findings', *Indian Economic and Social History Review* 13 (3), 277–328.

De Haan, A. (1995) 'Migration in Eastern India: A Segmented Labour Market', *Indian Economic and Social History Review* 32 (1), 51–93.

Gordon, J. (1973) 'Partition, Agitation and Congress: Bengal 1904 to 1908', *Modern Asian Studies* 7 (3), 533–88.

Government of Bengal (GOB) (1868) *Annual Report on the Administration of Bengal during 1866–7*. National Library Archive, Calcutta.

Government of Bengal (GOB) (1929) *Report on the Survey of Cottage Industries in Bengal*, 2nd edn. Calcutta: Bengal Secretariat Book Depot.

Government of India (GOI) (1909) *Imperial Gazetteer of India*, vol. IV: *The Indian Empire, Administrative*. Oxford: Clarendon Press.

Keith, A. B. (ed.) (1922) *Speeches and Documents on Indian Policy, 1750–1921*, vol. I. London: Humphrey Milford, Oxford University Press.

McLane, J. R. (1965) 'The Decision to Partition Bengal in 1905', *Indian Economic and Social History Review* 2 (3), 221–37.

Parliamentary Papers (P.P.) (1920) *Statistical Abstract Relating to British India, from 1908/09 to 1917/18*. London: HMSO.

Parliamentary Papers (P.P.) (1930) *Statistical Abstract Relating to British India, from 1918/19 to 1927/8*. London: HMSO.

Ray, I. (2011) *Bengal Industries and the British Industrial Revolution (1757–1857)*. London: Routledge.

Roy, H. (2009) 'Partition of Contingency? Public Discourse in Bengal, 1946–1947', *Modern Asian Studies* 43 (6), 1355–84.

Sen, S. (1999) *Women and Labour in Late Colonial India: The Bengal Jute Industry*. Cambridge: Cambridge University Press.

Seth, B. R. (1940) *Labour in the Indian Coal Industry*. Bombay: D. B. Taraporevala Sons.

Saha, P. (1978) *History of the Working-Class Movement in Bengal*. New Delhi: People's Publishing House.

Siddique, M. A. B. (1995) 'The Labour Market and the Growth of the Tea Industry in India: 1840–1900', *South Asia* 18 (1), 83–113.

Simmons, C. P. (1976) 'Recruiting and Organizing an Industrial Labour Force in Colonial India: The Case of the Coal Mining Industry, c. 1880–1939', *Indian Economic and Social History Review* 13 (4), 455–85.

Appendix 1.1 Details of administrative divisions in Bengal, 1866–7

Division/district	*Area (sq. miles)*	*Population*	*Division/district*	*Area (sq. miles)*	*Population*
Bhaugulpore/ Bhaugulpore	4,121	1,082,650	Chumparun	3,781	750,000
Monghyr	4,200	925,040	Patna	2,242	872,000
Purneah	5,275	729,114	Saran	3,000	1,200,000
Sonthal Pergunnahs	5,375	522,000	Shahabad	4,403	1,600,000
Burdwan/ Bancoorah	4,683	74,300	Tirhoot	9,216	1,854,297
Beerbhum	2,330	827,624	**Rajshahye**/ Rungpore	4,500	1,259,362
Burdwan	2,682	1,088,813	Bogra	2,000	400,000
Hooghly	1,457	1,370,120	Dinagepore	3,829	1,000,000
Howrah	550	520,000	Malda	1,484	305,563
Midnapore	5,031	1,558,450	Moorshedabad	2,439	967,619
Chittagong/ Noakhally	3,000	544,998	Rajshahye	3,035	710,290
Chittagong	2,717	800,000	Pubna	2,044	281,366
Chittagong Hill Tracts	7,000	NA	**Assam**/Durrung	2,912	178,163
Tipperah	3,600	1,000,000	Nowgong	8,712	247,500
Cuttack/ Balasore	2,049	494,056	Seebsaugor	2,821	226,000
Cuttack	3,061	1,293,884	Kamroop	3,348	400,000
Pooree	4,082	643,536	Luckimpore	5,000	117,393
Dacca/ Backergunj	4,000	866,632	Cossyah and Jynteah Hills	5,000	118,925
Dacca	3,138	950,000	Naga Hills	NA	NA
Furreedpore	1,500	624,476	**Chota Nagpore**/ Hazareebaugh	7,028	750,000
Mymensing	6,586	947,240	Lohardunga	7,000	750,294
Sylhet	5,500	1,504,289	Maunbhoom	6,396	528,340
Cachar	5,000	200,000	Singbhoom	3,998	289,789
Nuddea/ Jessore	3,651	957,152	**Cooch Behar**/ Western Dooars	NA	NA
Nuddea	3,296	551,220	Darjeeling	800	85,000
The 24 Pergunnahs	2,523	593,079	Gowalparah	2,672	230,000
City of Calcutta	7.81	377,924	Garrow Hills	NA	NA
Patna/Gya	5,439	1,367,392	Native state of Cooch Behar	NA	NA
			Total	**199,513.81**	**37,535,890**

Notes: Sonthal Pergunnahs and Cachar are included in Bhaugulpore and Assam divisions, respectively, as those were subordinate to the commissioners of respective divisions. The city of Calcutta was not included in any division.

Source: GOB 1868: iii–v (app. A).

2 Economic slowdown in the early modern age

Alternative explanations under the 'great divergence' hypothesis

The great divergence debate reminds us that, sometime in the past, certain regions which are relatively poor today were more developed than currently wealthy countries. Later on, their relative positions changed. The debate asks two questions: when did they reverse their position; and why did the relative position change? The present chapter concentrates on the second of the two questions.

The debate concedes that, in order for regional comparisons of economic development to be meaningful, the regions should be reasonably homogeneous internally in respect of economic conditions and socio-economic and political institutions. I argue in section I that this condition held true for Bengal. What is the hypothesis being tested about Bengal in this chapter? In the divergence debate, there are two schools of thought on the relative position of regions and the causes of a change therein. One view is that, on the strength of superior institutions, Western Europe forged ahead of Asia – in particular, China and India – well before the Industrial Revolution (North and Thomas 1973; Landes 1969). The second view, sometimes called the California school, identifies the divergence as occurring towards the end of the eighteenth century or at the beginning of the nineteenth (Pomeranz 2000; Frank 1998; Wallerstein 1986; Parthasarathi 1998). This revision is also challenged in some recent studies (Roy 2010; Broadberry and Gupta 2006; Studer 2008). This study claims that Bengal encountered a lower trajectory of per capita income growth in the early modern period, and it was further depressed in the colonial era. This is consistent with all positions in the divergence debate. The originality of the study consists in the further suggestion that, in order to explain the trend, we should consider not only the exceptional traits of Europe but also the exceptional traits of Bengal itself. Many historians agree on the economic slowdown (or its continuation) in Bengal (or India) since 1757.[1] I seek to verify whether the existing hypotheses available from the divergence literature can explain the trend or not.

Originally published as "'The Great Divergence' Revisited: The Case of Bengal in Early Modern Times", in *Economic History of Developing Regions*, volume 30, issue 2, 2015, © the Economic History Society of Southern Africa, reprinted by permission of Taylor & Francis Ltd, www.tandfonline.com, on behalf of the Economic History Society of Southern Africa.

In this connection, this chapter examines the resource endowment hypothesis (as advocated by Pomeranz) and the demographic explosion hypothesis (as propounded by Brenner and Isett) in section II, and the terms-of-trade hypothesis (as proposed by Williamson) in section III. Since those hypotheses are found untenable in our specific case, section IV seeks to formulate an alternative hypothesis on the basis of a theoretical framework advocated by Adam Smith. Section V concludes. This chapter thus focuses on the historical slowdown of Bengal economy. While sections I and IV deal exclusively with Bengal, the arguments of alternative theories are discussed in sections II and III to verify their applicability in the Bengal episode only. This study does not attempt to generalise its conclusions for other countries.

There are three novel aspects of the explanation offered here for Bengal's economic decline. First, it seeks to reinterpret Adam Smith's theorisation of the process of pre-modern economic growth. Second, while the decline of Asian regions in the existing literature is often explained by an implied Malthusian-cum-ecological crisis, the present study falls back to Smith again to understand Bengal's economic turnabout. Third, this study examines the economic history of Bengal more closely than has been done in the divergence discourse, even though there have been many casual references to it.

I

While underlining the importance of the selection of regions in an analysis of world inequality in the long run, Pomeranz (2000: 7–8) argues that regions selected should have internal homogeneity in terms of institutions as well as macroeconomic indices, and, between them, there should be a parity in economic development at some historical point of time. To underpin the empirical relevance of this methodology, he points out that, although Western Europe and China began to diverge in terms of per capita income growth as early as the fourteenth century, their core regions (namely England and the Yangzi delta, respectively), possessing a good degree of inner homogeneity, stood at fairly comparable levels even in 1800.[2] A lack of inner homogeneity might thus mislead the periodisation of the event, and so also the search for its causations.

Although India is often referred to as one of the economically advanced countries in the early modern era, as a unit of study it is not ideal from this point of view. Not only was its inner diversity great at the dawn of the great divergence, but this dispersion persisted through the period from 1757 to 1857. Diversity characterised its physiography, polity, institutions and agrarian practices, which almost certainly caused inter-regional disparity in economic development as well. Politically, northern India, including Bengal, was ruled by sultanates of Turkish origin from 1206 to 1526 and by the Mughals after 1565, bringing dramatic changes in India's indigenous art and culture, including industrial arts and agrarian practices. Such was not the case in the country's southern hemisphere, which belonged to the Vijayanagara Empire of the Hindu faith from 1336 to 1565. It took about a century for India's polity to get united under the aegis of the English East India Company, however.

Regional variations were manifest in economic institutions as well, especially in the land revenue system (Embree 1969). In the greater part of the Mughal Empire, the revenue farmers (zemindars, talukdars, etc.) collected revenue on behalf of the king. In other areas, such as in parts of the Punjab and the Central Provinces, a village-level revenue system, in which the village headman was responsible for the payment of tax, was not uncommon. A further alternative involved local chieftains who collected land revenues and paid tributes to the king. Owing to such variations in the fiscal system, land, labour and commodity markets evolved differently across the country. The British rulers did not consciously try to integrate regions in these respects.

Bengal did not suffer from such heterogeneity. In particular, the province displayed physiographic similarities at large, save for the northern and eastern fringes (running through the Himalayan ranges and the coastal plain, respectively) and a small strip of land that belonged to the Chotanagpur Plateau (for a review of different historical aspects of Bengal, see Sarkar 2003: ch. 4). Its polity also remained fairly stable for centuries, resembling the greater part of India. Sometimes the provincial rulers declared their sovereignty, but this did not significantly alter the prevailing institutional milieu. In such an environment, a stable society was formed on the basis of a uniform set of socio-economic institutions. The homogeneity postulate of the great divergence debate is thus largely satisfied for the province of Bengal.

Although I do not intend to quantify here the comparative levels of development between England and Bengal, a few qualitative judgements from contemporary sources may not be out of context. When entering Murshidabad, the capital of Bengal, in 1757 Lord Clive observed that 'this city is as extensive, populous, and rich as the city of London, with the difference that there are individuals in the first possessing infinitely greater property than in the last city' (quoted in Malaviya 1918: 297). Indeed, many European travellers in the late medieval period – for example, Duarte Barbosa (1921 [1518]: 181), Ludovico de Varthema (1853 [1510]: 210) and Thomas Bowrey (1905: 131–4, 166–7) – extolled the economic prosperity of Bengal, describing it the 'paradise of nations'. Adam Smith (1937 [1776]: 20) also acknowledges the early economic development in Bengal: 'The improvement in agriculture and manufactures seem likewise to have been of very great antiquity in the provinces of Bengal in the East Indies, and in some of the eastern provinces of China.'

What is more important in the context of this debate is the way Smith explains the process of economic development through time. According to him, the division of labour represented the central force of economic prosperity in the ancient society. While theorising on the causes and consequences of the division of labour, he notes that extensive navigations on the Ganges and its tributaries extended the market reach of Bengal products, and thus ushered in the division of labour by way of enabling their producers to undertake a larger scale of production (ibid.: 3–20). Through such specialisation in work the productivity of labour was augmented, and, hence, a higher per capita income and economic prosperity were achieved. This development process in Bengal, as perceived by Smith, was initiated by the development of a transportation network, which could enhance the accessibility of local products to distant markets. This Smithian development process, as I show shortly, differs from Pomeranz's interpretation of the Smithian development process.

II

The resource endowment hypothesis begins with the proposition that England and the Yangzi delta had similar states of economic development around 1800. There were no major differences between them in respect of (i) the nature of commercial property and the rules surrounding it (Pomeranz 2000: 70–85), (ii) the nature of land, labour and commodity markets (ibid.: 17–18) and (3) overall technological knowledge (ibid.: 45, 47–8). The Smithian process of economic growth that those regions then experienced was as follows: a steady growth of population increased their population density, and thus deepened their product markets within affordable physical or cultural limits; this, in turn, led to the division of labour and rising supply through specialisation; a secular trend of moderately rising output per unit of labour thus followed, promoting overall economic prosperity (ibid.: 31–43, 170–2, 178–9).

This expansionary path had its own ceiling, defined by the extent of arable land. Once the ceiling was reached, the economy faced a Malthusian-cum-ecological crisis whereby the scarcity of land, relative to population, gave rise to shortages of food, building materials, fuel and fibres, and thus depressed the standard of living. To minimise the consequences thereof, people indulged in more labour-intensive production as well as in deforestation and soil degradation, all of which further lowered their standard of living.

Pomeranz argues that, although England and the Yangzi delta were both poised to enter into a Malthusian-cum-ecological crisis by 1800, England escaped it on the strength of two contemporary, epoch-making events that reduced the developmental pressure on land. One of them was the growing use of coal and steam power (replacing the animal source of energy) as well as chemical fertilisers (in place of organic ones). Those technological innovations enabled England to transcend itself and progress from an organic economy to an inorganic economy, reducing thereby the need for land in economic activities. Further economy followed when the New World was discovered, as it gave ecological relief to England by way of providing land-intensive products such as sugar, grains, cotton and timber. These events helped England break out of the stationary state created by the scarcity of land, and allowed it to continue on a course of Smithian prosperity.

Brenner and Isett agree with Pomeranz in respect of the initial conditions between England and the Yangzi delta as well as the periodisation of the event (Brenner and Isett 2002). Their hypothesis states that, from the dawn of the early modern age, these regions differed in social property relations, which wielded cumulative effects in various fields and ushered in the great divergence between them during 1750 to 1850. The chain of causation ran as follows.

First, during the seventeenth century, peasants of the Yangzi delta acquired customary forms of land possession with effective permanent tenancy, which gave them extra-market bargaining power on the question of rent. Since rent was thus politically determined, independent of peasants' output, landlords were not interested in investing in land, so that capital formation suffered. In contrast, British agriculture moved towards market economy from the late fifteenth century, leaving behind manorial customs whereby coercion had been the rule of rent fixation. In the wake of declining serfdom, British landlords went for large demesnes under an absolute property right, and rented out the land based on market parameters.

Second, the absence of competitive forces in Yangzi agriculture enabled its peasants to ignore efficiency in production and to prioritise their critical goals, such as social insurances against old age and illness, performances of ancestral rituals, and so on, which promoted larger families. But the English peasants sought efficiency, as they needed to survive in competitive surroundings, and did not opt for larger families lest landholdings were fragmented and became inefficient.

Third, the larger family size among the Yangzi peasantry, and the consequent high growth rate of the population, led to the subdivision and fragmentation of landholdings so that the amount of land per peasant, and also the per capita agricultural output, declined. To arrest the falling standard of consumption, the Yangzi peasants opted for greater labour intensities in production (even by replacing animal power) and for less remunerative crops. In addition, the womenfolk of peasant families took up handicrafts (especially coarse textiles) at lower returns. In consequence, the Yangzi delta economy became caught in the Malthusian-cum-ecological crisis. England was not so trapped, as larger families were absent among peasantry. There was not a similar pressure of population on the land; nor was there any secular trend of subdivision and fragmentation in land property. Instead, farm size was extended significantly in early modern England, witnessing major improvements in farm organisation and greater use of animal power, releasing labour for employment elsewhere, especially in industries. These events led, on the one hand, to rising labour productivity in agriculture and, on the other, to the growth of industries outside the peasant economy. The Smithian growth process, therefore, continued.

Both these hypotheses are constructed on the basis of an argument that a scarcity of land (that is, a low land–man ratio) generated a Malthusian-cum-ecological crisis in erstwhile developed regions in Asia, and thus retarded their economic growth. Is this view applicable to Bengal as well? In view of inadequate data on Bengal's contemporary land–man ratio, one may be tempted to settle the issue on the basis of its contemporary growth rate of population. But data constraints are present in this matter as well. If, however, India's population growth can be relied upon, a lower growth rate seems to have prevailed in Bengal. Willcox puts India's annual rate of population growth at 0.44–0.63

per cent from 1650 to 1750 (Viseria and Viseria 1983: 466). For the following half a century an international comparison indicates it at 0.1 per cent for India (including present-day Pakistan), 1 per cent for China and 0.4 per cent for Europe (ibid.). But, on account of India's great diversity, the country-level data may be misleading.

With reference to the Brenner–Isett demographic analysis, then, Bengal did not experience an explosive fertility rate in the eighteenth century. According to them, where competitive forces prevailed in agriculture (such as in early modern England), peasants' family size remained smaller and population grew very modestly; *per contra*, the absence of market forces induced a rise in the fertility rate, as in contemporary China. In Bengal agriculture, market forces were quite dominant in the eighteenth to early nineteenth century.[3] The land market grew rapidly in the province, especially after the Permanent Settlement of 1793. Since it gave property rights to zemindars, a new class of capitalist zemindars emerged in the countryside (Chaudhuri 1983a). Rent was also largely market-determined, as peasants used to migrate from high-rent to low-rent regions. Wherever market forces were significantly blurred by coercive practices, the peasants deserted. There was also a free labour market, constituted of landless labourers, tiny landholders and sharecroppers (Washbrook 1988). Although they were largely employed by zemindars in their own farming as well as in the reclamation of forest areas, relatively small landholders also employed them 'to make up the deficiencies of labourers that may be in their families' (Chaudhuri 1983a: 165). Alongside there was the credit market, which was used mainly to finance urgent expenditures by the zemindars (including the reclamation of forest lands), but also by peasants in meeting production and consumption needs. Since various purchased inputs were thus employed in agriculture (ibid.: 144), one should not expect that the efficiency aspects of production were altogether neglected in Bengal. Pulling these threads together, we should say, again with reference to Brenner–Isett, that a reasonable inference is that the family size in Bengal peasantry was small, and, hence, fertility did not rise too rapidly.

On the other hand, Bengal's mortality rate was surely on the higher side in the eighteenth century. This was partly due to tropical diseases, which often swept away whole villages. A large number of people also died in famines and flood, which were frequent in this province. As many as 11 such incidents took place in 1711–55 and 13 in 1761–93, affecting seriously the subsistence of peasants (for a detailed study on famines in Bengal in the eighteenth century, see Datta 2000: 238–84). The most serious one was indeed the famine of 1769–70, which, according to an official report, caused a death toll of 10 million people.[4] On account of that famine, as Cornwallis informed us in 1789, 'one-third of the company's territory is now a jungle inhabited only by wild beasts' (quoted in Datta 2000: 264).

This indirect evidence thus rejects the possibility of a critical land–man ratio in contemporary Bengal. For more direct evidence, however, we may seek to account for reclaimable fallow land in the province, on the one hand, and examine the conditions of its labour market, on the other. As to the former, a source reveals that, in 1793, only 30 to 35 per cent of its arable lands were put under the plough (Chaudhuri 1983a: 136). At the district level, such lands were reported at 200,000 acres in the Sunderbans in 1784, and more than 70,000 acres in the 24 Parganas in 1778. Fallow lands were also considerably available in Midnapore, Chittagong and Tippera. In fact, land reclamations were reportedly sped up only in the late eighteenth century (Chaudhuri 1983b: 302–9).

A favourable land–man ratio is also suggested by information on contemporary labour markets, especially from the evidence of the scarcity of labour in agriculture and the rising wage rate. Indeed, the former appears often in various official documents, such as in a report of the Midnapore Collectorate in 1773, which argued in favour of the permanent retention of artificers and porters to avoid labour scarcity (referred to in Chaudhuri 1983a: 170), and in the survey report of Buchanan in 1808, which noted that 'labourers or servants of any kind are difficult to procure' (ibid.). While the steady reclamation of land from the late eighteenth century onwards generated demand forces for this scarcity, the high rate of mortality, especially in the wake of famine, flood and tropical diseases, was its supply-side factor. While analysing this problem, Chaudhuri (1983a: 170) emphasises:

> A plausible inference from the nearly universal complaint about the relative scarcity of labour during the last three decades of the eighteenth century and the first two decades of the nineteenth…is the relatively high level of wages there at the time.

In Dacca, for example, the annual wages for three categories of workers increased from S.Rs. 18,[5] S.Rs. 15 and S.Rs. 12 in 1803 to S.Rs. 48, S.Rs. 36 and S.Rs. 27, respectively, in 1837 (Taylor 1840: 306), representing hikes in the range of 125 to 167 per cent.

Our direct and indirect evidence thus does not confirm the occurrence of a Malthusian-cum-ecological crisis in Bengal in the late eighteenth and early nineteenth centuries. We should further note that the story of a decline due to Malthusian-cum-ecological crisis follows from Pomeranz's interpretation of the Smithian process of development. According to this reading, the division of labour, which initiated the development process, was brought about by the growth of the market in the wake of higher population growth, subject to physical or cultural limit.[6] The higher population growth rate ultimately gave rise to a crisis in an economy in which there were no accidental factors economising the use of land (such as Pomeranz 2000: 207 identifies), or in which population growth was not favourably altered later on (as Brenner and Isett 2002: 617–18 perceive). Thus, crisis was inevitable in an economy that underwent this version of the Smithian development process. As I argue further on, demographic-ecological crisis need not be a necessary consequence of the Smithian development process. Bengal was not subject to this crisis but was potentially able to experience Smithian growth.

III

Williamson (2008) seeks to explain the great divergence by the historical movement of terms of trade between the present-day developed (core) and developing (peripheral) countries. The hypothesis is drawn on a global scale – Western Europe and its offshoots, on the one hand, and the European periphery, Latin America, Middle East, South Asia, South-east Asia and East Asia, on the other. For empirical verification of the hypothesis, estimations are mostly country-specific, as also are the references in the analysis, particularly to the United Kingdom in core countries, India in South Asia and China in East Asia. Although, for statistical analysis (especially on the terms of trade), such studies cannot be region-specific, the within-country heterogeneity issue should be seen as a qualification to the analysis.

This hypothesis does not seek to explain when the great divergence took place. Referring to the work of Maddison (and its backward extrapolation to 1775), Williamson considers that it took place sometime between 1775 and 1913, particularly before 1870. As an initial condition for the event, he surmises that, 'whether in terms of culture, geography or institution, western Europe launched modern economic growth first, carried by rising productivity growth rates, especially in manufacturing' (Williamson 2008: 357). In addition to rapid manufacturing-led growth in Western Europe, the hypothesis postulates two other initial conditions – a liberal trade policy and transport revolutions – that produced powerful and sustained forces for the great divergence. Given these initial conditions, Williamson asks why the peripheral economies staggered behind their counterparts in the core.

In this reasoning, the rapid manufacturing-led growth that Western Europe experienced in the late eighteenth and nineteenth centuries produced a sustained terms-of-trade boom for primary products. In view of the contemporary liberal trade policies and transport revolutions, the advantages of the boom could be exploited by peripheral countries, where there were comparative advantages in those product lines. In the first round, therefore, both the core and the periphery benefited. But the distribution of this gain was not symmetrical, as the core countries retained some of the productivity gains for themselves, so that an industrialisation-led great divergence began. Note that this divergence was caused by higher per capita income growth in the core, relative to that in the periphery, though the latter also grew in absolute terms. The periphery's economic setback was linked to subsequent impacts of terms-of-trade movements. In the first place, because of higher global prices for primary products, the peripheral producers transferred domestic resources from industries to agriculture, and this trend was further perpetuated when domestic industries failed to compete with imported manufacturing products. Thus, globalisation shocks brought about deindustrialisation in the periphery, leading to retardation in its per capita income growth. In contrast, the secular improvement in terms of trade reinforced better per capita growth performance in the core countries, as they specialised in manufacturing. Thus, asymmetrical dynamic impacts of secular terms-of-trade improvements further widened the development gap between them.

Second, the terms-of-trade improvements were characterised by extensive volatility, which also led to asymmetric development impacts between the core and the periphery. This asymmetry arose since the terms-of-trade volatility enhanced the risk perception in an economy. As the insurance against risk was cheaper in the core because of its developed financial institutions, higher risks could be taken there for the sake of higher returns. In peripheral countries, on the other hand, poor households took fewer risks in their saving decisions; poor firms were risk-averse in their production plans; and poor governments found it difficult to borrow at a cheap rate for financing infrastructure and education. The difference in risk-taking capacities between the core and the periphery thus led to asymmetric rates of return, and, hence, a further divergence in their growth performances.

For peripheral countries collectively, as also for certain subregions, these propositions meet empirical tests well. But they do not do so for China and India, since their terms of trade did not move in the manner predicted. For China, there was a secular slump in terms of trade before 1910. To Williamson, it was 'Chinese exceptionalism indeed' (ibid.: 364). India's evidence is also far from satisfactory: 'The boom in South Asia [India and Ceylon] up to 1861 was far weaker than the average [for the periphery] ...and this was even more true over the century to 1885–90 (no growth versus 0.7 percent per annum). [...] Like China, India was exceptional' (ibid.: 370).

In the absence of the global terms-of-trade effects, Williamson puts the burden of proof for India's great divergence on the domestic terms of trade. Recognising the process of deindustrialisation in nineteenth-century British India, he argues that it took place under the influence of domestic factors such as the increase in the frequency of droughts due to the periodic rise in the temperature of the Pacific Ocean (the El Niño hypothesis), and/or falling agricultural productivity in the wake of the gradual breakdown of the Mughal Empire (the Mughal collapse hypothesis), as identified in Clingingsmith and Williamson (2008). Because of these factors, agricultural production fell and domestic terms of trade moved against industries, so that resources were transferred from industries to agriculture, causing deindustrialisation. Williamson (2008: 375–6) notes: 'To the extent that India underwent one of the most dramatic rates of deindustrialisation in the poor periphery, that experience must be attributed to domestic forces rather than to external price shocks.' Hence, for India, the terms-of-trade hypothesis may be reconstructed like this: under domestic terms-of-trade improvements for agriculture, India suffered from strong deindustrialisation, which led to falling per capita income and, hence, its great divergence.

Such a reconstruction does not perform well for Bengal, however. My own study of five major manufacturing industries in Bengal during this period (namely cotton textiles, silk textiles, indigo dye, salt manufacturing and ship building) underlines that, far from encountering deindustrialisation, Bengal enjoyed industrial prosperity through to 1829, when the aggregate level of employment in these industries rose by about 2 million persons from a third of a century earlier (Table 9.2). Deindustrialisation started only in the early 1830s, and continued in subsequent decades through 1860, by which point about 2.15 million people had lost their livelihoods (Table 9.2). Hence, the reconstructed terms-of-trade hypothesis cannot explain Bengal's trajectory from 1757 to 1829.

IV

In this section, I suggest an explanation valid for Bengal. Bankim Chandra Chattopadhyay, the famous nineteenth-century Bengali novelist who wrote India's national song, once drew attention in a satire to how Bengal began to suffer economically with the onset of rule by the Delhi Sultanate in the early thirteenth century.[7] It is indeed true that the payment of tribute from Bengal that started under the Delhi Sultanate caused a continuous outflow of specie,[8] and might have caused a depletion of local capital stock. Trade was well developed in the region. It used to export large quantities of agricultural products such as rice, wheat, ginger, butter, opium, lac and saltpetre, as well as industrial commodities, which primarily included a wide range of cotton and silk piece goods (Krishna 1924: 26–9). These were destined for several markets in India and the Far East, or even Portuguese and other European markets. High rates of return attracted traders from far-off places, some of whom permanently settled in Bengal, while others got involved in peddlery. For the procurement of local wares, however, only bullion was exchanged, since the province was self-sufficient at large. A great inflow of bullion therefore took place. A contemporary document (GOB 1767) noted, 'Bengal…might be considered as the central point to which all riches of India were attracted. Its manufactures found their way to the remotest part of Hindustan, and specie flowed in by a thousand channels… All European companies formed their investments with money brought into the country; the Gulps poured in their treasures into this river; and across the continent, an inland trade was driven to the westward to the extremity of Gujerat.'

In view of data constraints, this study indicates a broad trend of bullion inflow from 1664 onwards and its outflow from 1582 onwards. As to the scenario in the pre-British age, the final judgement is based on the records for the early eighteenth century.

Based on data furnished by Prakash and Chaudhuri, Ray (2011) presents the time series of the inflow of silver into Bengal from 1664 to 1718 shown in Table 2.1. The total inflow of silver in this period comes to £7.8 million from Dutch sources and £5.19 million from British sources. Data on yearly imports of treasure by the English East India Company for 1708–57 (Table 2.2) show an annual growth rate of 9.65 per cent for 1708–52, however. Moreover, Bengal's share in this influx is seen to have been rising steadily at the country level – from about 17 per cent during 1708–12 to about 40 per cent during

Table 2.1 Dutch and British imports of treasure into Bengal (in £ per annum), 1664/8–1714/18

Year	*Dutch imports*	*British imports*
1664–8	119,225[1]	8,079[4]
1669–73	104,580[2]	28,404
1674–8	74,633	40,875
1679–83	111,993	111,608
1684–8	66,999	76,539
1689–93	145,473	30,394[5]
1694–8	159,353	93,980
1699–1703	212,845	187,005
1704–8	213,422	100,749
1709–13	221,079	171,660
1714–18	244,675[3]	207,934

Notes: A conversion rate of £1 = 12 florins has been adopted for the Dutch figures; 1: excluding 1666; 2: excluding 1672 and 1673; 3: excluding 1718; 4: excluding 1668; 5: excluding 1689–91.

Source: Ray 2011: 19.

Table 2.2 Annual influx of English East India Company treasure in five-year periods (in £), 1708/12–1753/7

Period	*Bengal*	*India (Bengal, Bombay and Madras)*	*Column 2 as percentage of column 3*
1708–12	49,896 (–)	299,684 (–)	16.65
1713–17	104,608 (109.65)	327,321 (9.22)	31.96
1718–22	128,415 (22.76)	456,450 (39.45)	28.13
1723–7	137,873 (7.36)	412,397 (−9.65)	33.43
1728–32	138,423[1] (0.40)	400,505 (−2.88)	34.56
1733–7	127,439[1] (−7.94)	377,749 (−5.68)	33.74
1738–42	124,052 (−2.66)	412,549 (9.21)	30.07
1743–7	195,660[1] (57.72)	502,577 (21.82)	38.93
1748–52	261,671 (33.74)	655,426 (30.41)	39.92
1753–7	131,819[1] (−49.62)	536,671[1] (−18.12)	24.56

Notes: The figures in parentheses indicate the growth rate; 1: four-year average.

Source: P.P. (1812–13).

1748–52 – signifying that this province became the most favoured destination for British silver by the middle of the eighteenth century. The figure for Dutch silver imports represents specie from Holland alone, exclusive of the company's imports from other Asian sources, especially Japan, which was quite substantial in the second half of the seventeenth century. Gaastra (1986: 104) estimates the ratio of Dutch imports of bullion from Europe and from Japan at 23:25 during the 1660s and the 1670s, so that its aggregate import was greater than what has been reported here.

Considering an annual inflow of English bullion worth £246,129 for the mid-eighteenth century, and also that the ratio of European trade from Bengal around that period was 1:0.7003 between the English and the Dutch, silver imports from Holland are estimated at £172,364 excluding the substantial flow of specie from Dutch intra-Asian trade. Harry Verelst (1772: 86), the governor of Bengal, thus observed:

> The Dutch were the greatest importers of silver, not only for purchasing home investment, but also procuring opium…and also upon account of a considerable profit arising to their servants from coining into sicca rupees, in the nabob's mint, ingots sent from Batavia.

Recognising these different sources, he estimated total Dutch imports at £300,000 per annum for around 1750. In addition, we should recognise other European sources, especially the French and the Danish, and also the Indian merchants who, by way of their business in the Red Sea and the Persian Gulf, imported silver into this province. Verelst estimated the annual inflow from these respective sources at about £200,000, £30,000 and £180,000 around the mid-eighteenth century. In aggregate, bullion inflow thus stood at S.Rs. 9.56 million per annum (at £1 = S.Rs. 10) around the middle of the eighteenth century. This was exclusive of bullion inflow from overland trade, which had flourished prior to the commencement of European sea trade with Bengal.[9] But no reliable data are available to this end. The economic development that followed in consequence of those distant trades should certainly be designated as a prototype model of Smithian development.

We should note that, in the presence of financial instruments such as bills of exchange and bonds, the trade balance in Bengal's favour was higher than what the influx of bullion suggests. Contemporary documents abound with examples indicating that European trading houses mobilised substantial funds in Bengal from the Dutch and English officials and 'free' traders (Ray 2011: 21), as well as from Indians. In the latter respect, Marshall (1976: 40) emphasises:

> Until relatively late in the [18th] century, when large British fortunes began to be made out of the conquest of Bengal, the major part of the finance for European trade was not only raised in India but actually came from Indians.

But the growth stimuli out of bullion inflows were lost to a good extent once Bengal started paying tributes to Delhi during the Sultanate period. It continued down the Mughal period, with a break of two centuries (from 1338 to 1538) when independent kings ruled Bengal. During the Mughal period, tributes were paid to Delhi out of land revenues, which were based on Todar Mal's reform in the late sixteenth century, continuing down to 1757 with certain modifications (for details, see Grant 1984 [1917]). There was initially only one type of tax under the original standard assessment (the so-called *ausil toomar jumma*), at a uniform rate of one-quarter of gross production. Accordingly, there was annual revenue of S.Rs. 6.34 million from *khalsa* lands (that is, exchequer lands) and S.Rs. 4.35 million from *jageer* lands (that is, lands on temporary tenure to support civil and military establishments), aggregating to S.Rs. 10.69 million in 1582. There was a marginal hike in land revenue in 1658, when European trading capital had just begun to flow in. The improved standard assessment (the so-called improved *toomary jumma*) was then S.Rs. 13.11 million per year in total, or S.Rs. 12 million exclusive of that from newly annexed areas. These increased revenues were partly due to higher incidences of revenue (S.Rs. 0.99 million) and partly due to a tax on recoinage (*darubzerb*) (S.Rs. 0.32 million), which was an emerging facet of Bengal finance linked to the influx of silver.

The next substantial alteration took place under Nawab Jaffier Khan in 1722. The improved *toomar jumma* of the previous period was then replaced by *jumma kumil toomary* (i.e., more perfect standard assessment), which stood at S.Rs. 14.29 million, incorporating S.Rs. 1.43 million as *wasil* (i.e., incidences from new dominions and new sources of revenue) and S.Rs. 2.15 million as *ezafa* (i.e., incidences from a higher rate of revenue). Insofar as the *ezafa* was concerned, the revision during 1658–1722 was almost double that of the period from 1582 to1658 at the average annual level. Another distinctive feature involved certain new imposts as components of *wasil*, called *sayer*, such as (i) *chunacahly* (i.e., taxes on houses, shops, bazaars, spirituous liquors, etc.) and duties on exports of silk and cloth manufactured in and around Murshidabad; (ii) *buskhsh-bunder* (i.e., the ground rents of 32 markets, chiefly dependent on European settlements in Satgaon [including Calcutta], and customs on export goods); and (iii) mint duties at Murshidabad. Still another fiscal innovation in this period was the viceregal territorial assessment (*abwab subahdary*), first introduced in 1722 and further extended afterwards, amounting to S.Rs. 2.17 million in 1739. Thus, total assessment as they stood in 1739 reached S.Rs. 16.46 million, as against S.Rs. 13.11 million in 1658 and S.Rs. 10.69 million in 1582.

The entire sum of revenue proceeds did not represent the remittance to Delhi, however. From it we should deduct the remittance through bills, the cost of revenue administration and the expenditure for the purpose of maintaining the nawab's household and court, as well as his personal savings. Although the nawab's personal savings represented leakage of specie from circulation, the others did not. In the absence of these data, however, I consider a consolidated statement of revenue and remittance on Delhi's account for the regimes of Jaffier Khan (15 years, nine months, five days) and Suja Khan (ten years, six months, 22 days) (Grant 1984 [1917]: 213–14). It shows that, on average, Bengal remitted about S.Rs. 10.56 million per annum during the first half of the eighteenth century. Suja Khan's account gives further information about the ratio of specie to bills in the remittance, namely 73:27, which helps us to quantify the outflow of specie. I am thus inclined to estimate a sum of S.Rs. 7.71 million as an annual outflow of specie to Delhi on account of remittances. To this must be added the amount of *abwab subahdary*, which the nawabs secretly exacted as their personal savings. Grant (1984 [1917]: 208–11) estimates this at S.Rs. 16 million in aggregate, or S.Rs. 1.02 million per annum, during Jaffier Khan's tenure and at S.Rs. 17 million in aggregate, or S.Rs. 1.60 million per annum, during Suja's tenure. Hence, the yearly withdrawal of specie from circulation is estimated at S.Rs. 9.02 million, assuming an annual accumulation of S.Rs. 1.31 million in the nawab's coffers. These estimates thus indicate that the annual payment of Delhi tributes (when added to the governor's hoardings) entirely exhausted the annual inflow of bullion, save for a bare 6 per cent (amounting to S.Rs. 0.54 million per year) left in circulation.

These contemporary fiscal practices adversely affected economic prosperity in the province. For a better understanding of Bengal's contemporary economic slowdown, we need to concentrate upon the relationship between bullion inflow, fiscal outcomes and economic growth, which has been intensely debated in Bengal's historiography for about a century. Writing in 1923, Moreland assesses the effects of fiscal outcomes (especially Delhi tributes) on economic growth before European trading capital began to flow in from 1650, and describes a state of monetary scarcity in Bengal (Moreland 1923: 178–82). But the scenario changed, he believes, after the infusion of European capital from 1650, which was not offset by relevant fiscal outcomes. It ushered in spiralling prices, similar to the price increases following the import of precious metal from the Spanish possessions in America into Europe in the sixteenth century (Hamilton 1929; Nef 1937; Gold 1964). Underlying this line of argument is Fisher's quantity theory of money, in which inflation is inevitable in the wake of a higher money supply provided that there is full employment in the economy, and that the velocity of money is constant.

Prakash (1976), however, argues that bullion inflow into Bengal augmented its supply of money. This was especially true in view of the contemporary monetary policies, whereby the role of the Mughal administration was confined to limited spheres – building minting infrastructure and maintaining the values of various coins corresponding to their stipulated weights (Chakrabarti 1997: 71). Another facet of Mughal monetary policy was that, with a view to combating the inflationary pressures in the wake of the bullion inflow, the government adopted a policy of yearly debasement of newly coined rupees for three consecutive years, ending what was called *sonaut*. Grant (1984 [1917]: 229) notes: 'Such was the extraordinary influx of silver into the commercial parts of the empire, from the reign of Jehangeer, that the Mogul coin of rupees…began immediately to lose something of their legal value, when thrown into circulation.' The supply of money was largely market-determined, however, as individuals could freely mint money by offering bullion at royal mints.[10] Large inflows of bullion, therefore, increased the supply of money, and could have increased the price level.

But Prakash emphasises that the quantity theory did not hold good for contemporary Bengal: the money velocity was not at all constant; nor was there full employment. The rise in savings that took place in the wake of Bengal's export surplus augmented the hoardings of bullion, thereby reducing the velocity of money (Prakash 1976: 166). Output was also increased through the reallocation of resources, such as by employing idle resources such as land in the production process (ibid.: 73–4). Theoretically, therefore, price rises were not inevitable. Moreover, empirical evidence from Dutch sources contradicts the occurrence of inflationary gap in contemporary Bengal (ibid.: 165–6; Chaudhuri 1975: 242–7).

Prakash thus analyses the relationship disregarding the question of bullion outflow from Bengal. The issue was recognised in Chaudhuri's (1975) analysis, but it only partially, since he merely accounts for individuals' remittances.[11] I have shown that if the tribute paid to Delhi is added up to individuals' remittances the sum would almost exhaust the yearly inflow of bullion into Bengal.

Although the inflow and outflow of bullion were thus balanced on a yearly basis, the question remains whether its circulation in a production year had any economic consequences. The chain of events in this case goes like this. Every year European traders injected fresh bullion into the economy. Artisans belonging to various textile concerns and other handicraft industries were the first recipients of the inflow, since agricultural products were less significant in the export list (Smith 1937 [1776]: 647). For the purchase of food and raw materials, however, they exchanged specie, so that specie then moved into the agricultural sector. Since contemporary evidence suggests low propensities to save among artisans (for a discussion on low rates of savings among Bengal artisans, see Grant 1984 [1917]: 273), this flow almost exhausted the initial inflow. The stock of specie was then skimmed off by way of agricultural taxation,[12] and sent to Delhi. Therefore, in a static framework in which there was no acceleration in bullion inflow, the question of economic growth did not arise.

In Bengal, however, there was a steady accretion in the inflow from 1650, which needs to be assessed keeping in view two sets of evidence available in the literature: (i) that there was no rise in the prices of provisions (that is, agricultural food products); and (ii) that the prices of export items increased to some extent (Prakash 1976: 167–8). In the short run, a larger inflow of specie must have increased the prices of exportables, and, hence, a rise in artisans' income. In the long run, higher prices should have induced artisans to increase their supplies by way of (i) a reallocation of resources from the domestic sector to the commercial sector (that is, growing monetisation), which was feasible as there was parallel production of those goods; and (ii) employing idle resources in production. Increased production would have depressed the price to the previous level, but, because of a time lag in the causation from the price rise to production, a steady growth in bullion inflow on a yearly basis certainly ensured that higher prices would persist in the long run, and so also guaranteed a long-run rise in artisans' income. But their additional income was taken away by way of tax (*sayers*).

Nevertheless, the increased output in the export sector should have raised the demand for agricultural raw materials, since contemporary export industries were based on agriculture. Therefore, prices of agricultural raw materials went up, inducing expanded cultivation. This could have been achieved by way of reallocating arable land and/or by bringing fallow lands under the plough. Since there was certainly a rising average cost for bringing fallow lands under cultivation (by way of clearing jungles), as well as a rising opportunity cost for the diversion of land from one crop to another, price hikes for those agricultural raw materials must have been a long-run phenomenon. Because of higher levels of production as well as higher prices, peasants' incomes must have increased on a long-run basis. But this additional income, I argue, the state squeezed away by way of higher rents. Given the contemporary custom of paying taxes and rents in terms of specie, the additional stock of precious metal that came by the route of trade was swept away from circulation. Note that there should not be any inflationary pressure outside the export-related sectors, since the disposable income (that is, income net of tax/rent) of both peasants and artisans remained largely unaltered.

Higher disposable income could have increased the level of consumption, propelling economic growth through the income–consumption multiplier. But such expansionary forces were neutralised on account of contemporary fiscal outcomes. The withdrawal of specie also generated adverse effects in the money market. Given the liquidity preference in the economy, the drain of specie left a smaller amount of money with banking houses. The supply of credit, therefore, shrank through the money–credit multiplier, leading to a higher rate of interest and, hence, a lower volume of investment. These two forces worked together to stall economic prosperity in Bengal, despite its congenial environment for the Smithian process of development.

My analysis thus suggests that the steady influx of bullion in Bengal during the late medieval and early modern period brought about higher prices and greater output only in the export-related sectors. This contradicts Moreland (who claims there was inflation across the economy) as well as Prakash (arguing for overall economic growth in the province). I also argue that the benefits of price rises and higher production for exports did not accrue to people residing in the province, as the yearly influx of specie was largely taken away by way of taxes and rents, and sent to Delhi as tribute. Bereft of any effect from the income–consumption multiplier and the money–credit multiplier, economic activities outside the export-related sectors remained unaltered.

The economic scenario in pre-British Bengal was thus characterised by brisk commercialisation, propelled by export demand, which gave rise to a great inflow of bullion. But almost the entire additional sum was skimmed off to Delhi, which meant that none in the Bengal society could enjoy the fruits of the region's buoyant economy. Disposable income per caput should thus be low in pre-British Bengal. This is, indeed, confirmed in recent studies. Roy's estimates show that, around the middle of the eighteenth century, Bengal's grain-equivalent income was only one-fifth of the income of England (Roy 2010: 187). Again, Allen estimates Bengal's welfare ratio at about unity in the 1730s (Allen 2007), as against London's welfare ratio of about 4.5 (Allen et al. 2011: 20).

The situation was further aggravated with the onset of the British rule, which stalled the inflow of bullion from 1757. The revenue burden in Bengal was not significantly increased under the early British administration (Travers 2004). But the revenue proceeds were used up for the local procurement of exportable articles so that bullion imports ceased. While the Company brought in, on average, S.Rs. 2.46 million worth of bullion per annum prior to 1757, there was not a single ounce of it on its account from 1757 to 1797 (P.P. 1812–13). Other sources also dried up as the English company marginalised rival traders. A contemporary source reveals that the bullion import on foreigners' account was barely S.Rs. 1.85 million per annum from 1766 to 1768, as against S.Rs. 9.56 million per annum prior to rule by the British, and that, with this paltry sum, they dominated trade worth S.Rs. 13.66 million per annum (Verelst 1772: 86). Thus, the comparative scenario between the pre-British and the early British periods is this: while, earlier, Delhi took away S.Rs. 10.56 million as tribute (specie and bills, taken together), merchandise worth S.Rs. 11.81 million (excluding the trade in exchange of specie) was now exported without any specie (or commodity) in exchange. Bengal thus lost an additional amount of S.Rs. 1.25 million per annum in the early British period. This process reduced per capita consumption in Bengal, and hence its welfare level. A contemporary author thus noted:

> Such manufactures, therefore, when actually consumed in Bengal, will contribute to augment the luxury of that country at the expense of its wealth, and when exported by the Company they will add to the wealth of the Company, when realized into money, at their London sales, but still at the expense of the wealth of Bengal.
>
> (Steuart 1772: 61)

Not only was the inflow of bullion curtailed, but there were reverse flows as well. Such channels of drain included (i) the wealth that the Company officials acquired by way of presents from nawabs and top officials, (ii) the financing of trade between China and England and (iii) the inter-provincial drain due to (a) the procurement of raw materials, (b) army postings at borders and (c) contributions of Bengal treasury to Bombay and Madras (ibid.: 56–61). An estimation shows that these drains amounted to S.Rs. 11.82 million per annum from 1757 to 1773 and S.Rs. 7.80 million per annum from 1774 to 1793 (Ray 2011: 31–2).

It should be noted, however, that the inflow of specie had resumed in Bengal by the late 1790s, and that the crisis of circulating money had largely abated by 1810. But the depletion of bullion stock that took place between 1757 and 1793 was not recovered for decades to come. As against the bullion outflow of S.Rs. 356.94 million during this period, the net import of silver (which was the principal medium of exchange in Bengal) amounted to S.Rs. 352.57 million between 1801 and 1829 (P.P. 1864). If we consider both silver and gold, the net import slightly exceeded its previous depletion by 1829, as it stood at S.Rs. 436.25 million from 1801 to 1829. Therefore, the conclusion is that there was a severe depletion of capital stock in Bengal through the 1790s, and the resultant crisis continued through to the late 1820s.

Since the East India Company collected revenues in its capacity as a governing body, our deliberation remains incomplete without a corresponding analysis of government expenditures. To this end, Appendices 2.1 and 2.2 present, respectively, annual revenues and annual charges[13] for the years 1811–17 (excepting 1814–15).

Appendix 2.1 shows that the government tapped many new revenue sources in this period in addition to the primitive land revenue and sayers, although the latter dominated (representing 50.73 per cent of total revenues, exclusive of its proceeds in ceded or conquered provinces). It should also be noted that two important sources in this period, salt and opium revenues, did not represent the government revenue from taxation but were, rather, the proceeds from the government monopoly on these goods. As a monopoly producer, the government earned profits constituting as much as 39.36 per cent of total revenues (exclusive of its proceeds in ceded or conquered provinces). The revenue sources suggest that the Company's government undertook a number of welfare-generating activities in this province, however, some of which yielded surplus revenue – such as postal communication and modern means of contract (through stamp papers) – while others were at the cost of the state exchequer (Appendices 2.1 and 2.2). In the latter category, I should emphasise the judiciary, including law and order, on which the government annually spent C.Rs. 6.17 million, as against an annual revenue of only C.Rs. 0.83 million during the period 1811–18. These surely underline the government's sincere efforts to maintain peace and modern justice in the contemporary society of Bengal. In aggregate, however, the net revenue from the province stood, on average, at C.Rs. 35.24 million per annum from 1811 to 1818.

To examine government expenditure more closely, Appendix 2.3 presents itemised disbursements in 1813–14 and 1817–18. Two important conclusions are suggested by this appendix. First, the net revenues were spent in these years mainly on four heads: (i) investment in Bengal[14] (including advances for chartered ships); (ii) assistances to the Company's establishments in Madras (including Hyderabad and Mysore) and Bombay; (iii) the financing of the China trade to London; and (iv) the payment of bills drawn on Mauritius, Java and the Moluccas in London. The aggregate disbursement for them is worked out at S.Rs. 41.69 million in 1813–14 and S.Rs. 41.12 million in 1817–18, as against the net revenues of S.Rs. 40.37 million and S.Rs. 31.38 million in the respective years. Indeed, from the early days of the Company's administration, these heads attracted the lion's share of government revenue (Steuart 1772: 56–61). It may be noted, however, that, for the export business, the Company annually invested about S.Rs. 9 million in export production in the 1810s, in contrast to about S.Rs. 6 million per annum from 1766 to 1769, and S.Rs. 2 million per annum from 1748 to 1756.[15] Perhaps this rising trend was related to the Company's capacity to generate revenues in Bengal.

Second, Appendix 2.3 emphasises that development projects received very little support from the exchequer. In the years under report, the government evidently took up only three such projects – town development at Calcutta, the development of a road to Juggernaut and the setting up of a college at Fort William – which altogether cost S.Rs. 323,579 in 1813–14 and S.Rs. 246,341 in 1817–18, representing only 0.80 per cent and 0.78 per cent of the net revenues in the respective years.

In sum, the expenditure pattern during the early colonial rule indicates that the government certainly adopted a host of welfare measures in Bengal, especially in the fields of law and order, modern justice and modern education, in which respect John Stuart Mill once noted that the Company administration 'has a right to take pride to itself for having accomplished so much' (P.P. 1858). But its development projects were few and far between. Moreover, the revenue proceeds were largely invested for commercial ends in the province of Bengal, and also for business and other ends outside the province, with the result that the fiscal benefits substantially leaked out under the Company's governance.

An obvious question at this stage concerns the proportion of circulating currency that leaked out during the late Mughal or the early British periods. To this end, we note that, in 1722, a 5 per cent deduction (as the rate of exchange or *batta*) on recoinage yielded S.Rs. 453,448 (Grant 1984 [1917]: 230), putting the value of total recoinage at about S.Rs. 9 million. Since contemporary law ensured that each sicca coin was restruck every three years after its minting, total circulating currency comes to S.Rs. 27 million.[16] Of this estimated amount, the outflow of specie (namely S.Rs. 9.02 million, as calculated above) constituted about 33.41 per cent. A similar estimation can also be attempted for the early British period. Grant estimates the transaction demand for money in Bengal at about S.Rs. 22 million in 1785 (apart from the liquidity demand for the payment of tax) (Grant 1984 [1917]: 277). The estimation goes like this: noting that husbandmen and manufacturers provided their family maintenance independent of each other, he reckons S.Rs. 20 million for articles of primary necessity (such as rice, wheat, fruits, oil, etc., mainly for internal consumption), S.Rs. 12 million for articles of secondary necessity (such as salt, betel leaf, tobacco, opium, saltpetre, sugar, hemp, leather, indigo, pepper, etc., again mainly for internal consumption) and S.Rs. 33 million for luxury articles (raw silk, cotton and silk manufactures, etc., mainly for export) (ibid.: 230), aggregating to S.Rs. 65 million. Under his assumption that the annual velocity of currency was three in contemporary Bengal (ibid.: 277), the amount of circulating capital comes to S.Rs.

21.67 million. Hence, the annual drainage of S.Rs. 7.80 million, as estimated for the period 1774–93, represents 36 per cent of the transaction demand for money in 1785.

Insofar as the burden of tax on the income level is concerned, the gross (or net) product of land represents a better standard in view of the disjuncture between land and trade in Mughal fiscal administration. Although land was heavily taxed, merchants were subjected to a lesser burden, so that both sea-bound and overland trade were in a flourishing condition until 1750.[17] This was why there was no shortage of currency in Mughal Bengal (the inflow of specie being ensured by the vigorous trade), though the proceeds of land tax, which was quite substantial, were taken out to Delhi. This Mughal style of tax administration largely continued through the early British rule. An estimate of Bengal's net domestic product (NDP) from land in 1791, as available in Roy (2010: 182), is S.Rs. 117 million. On the surmise that NDP from land, like the land tax, remained unchanged between the late Mughal and the early British periods (1757–73), I estimate the outflow of specie at 7.71 per cent of NDP from land in the former period, and 10.10 per cent later on.

The massive outflow of specie from Bengal led to a chain of adverse events, however. In the first place, its inevitable consequence was surely an acute crisis of circulating money. The mercantile community in Calcutta noted:

> That the scarcity of coin now felt in this capital…affects every individual to that degree, that the best houses, with magazines full of goods, are distressed for daily provisions, and that not only a general bankruptcy is to be feared, likely to involve every soul in the settlement, but a real famine in the midst of wealth and plenty.
>
> (GOB 1769)

An abrupt fall in the transaction balance directly reduced commodity prices, and raised indirectly the rate of interest by way of reducing the speculative balance. Indeed, the European mercantile community in Bengal cautioned the government that, because of the declining price level and the 'distressful tax' resulting from high interests, Bengal had come to the verge of bankruptcy (ibid.). Without disputing the gravity of these issues, I wish to suggest that, in order to understand the effects of the depletion of specie, we should reread Adam Smith.

To begin with, it is useful to contrast Bengal's experience of depleting capital with China's stationary state of large capital base, as conceived by Smith (1937 [1776]: 71–3). He argues that at a stationary level of capital, as was the case in late eighteenth-century China, the demand for labour does not increase, so there should not be any trend increase in the prevailing wage rate. But, so long as the wage rate exceeds its subsistence level, workers opt for larger family sizes, pushing the prevailing rate towards 'scanty subsistence'. Thus, the wage rate comes to a very low level in the long run, generating economic backwardness. This Smithian process thus explains the great divergence for an economy in which the stock of capital is stagnant at a high level. For such an economy, per capita income remains constant at a very low level. But, in gross terms, no falling trend is discernible in socio-economic indices. Pointing to China, Adam Smith observes:

> Its towns are no-where disserted by their inhabitants. The lands which had once been cultivated are no-where neglected. The same or very nearly the same annual labour must therefore continue to be performed, and the funds destined for maintaining it must not, consequently, be sensibly diminished.
>
> (ibid.: 73)

'But it would be otherwise in a country', Smith continues, 'where the funds destined for the maintenance were sensibly decaying' (ibid.). And, in this context, he points to late eighteenth-century Bengal. According to him, the decaying stock of capital reduced the demand for every class of workers. Unable to find employment in their respective classes, workers would opt for lower levels of work, which ultimately puts pressure on the lowest wage classes. As a result, the wage for that category of workers shrinks, bringing about want, famine and high mortality. Smith stresses, 'This perhaps is nearly the present state [i.e., in 1776] of Bengal' (ibid.). He argues:

> In a fertile country which had before been much depopulated, where subsistence, consequently, should not be very difficult, and where, notwithstanding, the three or four hundred thousand people die of hunger in one year, we may be assured that the funds destined for the maintenance of labouring poor are fast decaying.
>
> (ibid.: 73)

While thus identifying the drain of specie as responsible for the economic distress in Bengal, he observes:

> The difference between the genius of the British constitution which protects and governs North America, and that of the mercantile company which oppresses and domineers in the East Indies, cannot perhaps be better illustrated than by the different state of these countries.
>
> (ibid.)

Indeed, Allen (2007: 21) shows that Bengal's welfare ratio, which was around unity in about 1738, had dipped below unity in the early 1800.

The Smithian argument also explains the depressed state of per capita income in pre-British Bengal. Like China, Bengal also experienced a stationary but large capital base in the Mughal period. While capital was perhaps accumulated during the rule of sovereign kings in Bengal (1338–1538), when tributes were not paid to Delhi, my estimates suggest that its stock of capital remained virtually unaltered during the Mughal period, since the amount of Delhi tributes almost equalled the inflow of bullion. In such a state of affairs, as Adam Smith argues, the demand for labour remained in stasis, and the demographic expansion regulated the supply of labour to depress the wage rate at one of 'scanty subsistence'. Indeed, contemporary Bengal displayed the Smithian characteristic of showing no sign of a diminishing acreage under cultivation. This is confirmed by the trend of revenue collections by the state from the time of Todar Mal's revenue reform in 1582 through 1739 (Grant 1984 [1917]: 208–11). Available data and information thus suggest that Bengal's great divergence in the pre-British period can be explained by the Smithian argument of the stationary state of the large capital base, and its further aggravation in the early British era by the Smithian argument of decaying capital.

Two questions are pertinent at this juncture. Does this analysis belong to the genre of the drain theory, as advocated by Dadabhai Naoroji? Is there any theoretical ground suggesting that the great divergence was a monetary phenomenon? Naoroji's drain theory takes into account outflows of specie as well as commodities. When commodities were sent out against bills of exchange, it did not represent the outflow of specie. In contrast, my analysis accounts for the drain of specie alone (more particularly, the net outflow of specie), and thus gives a measure of the depletion of the capital stock, which is the crux of Smith's process of decay. This analysis is closer to Steuart's version of the drain from Bengal (Steuart 1772: 56–61). As for the second question, the short-run consequences of the reduction of specie – such as price depressions and hikes in the interest rate, as pointed out above – were surely monetary phenomena. But the depletion (or the constant level) of the stock of money capital in the real sense, which explains the great divergence in Smith's theoretical framework, is not at all a monetary phenomenon.

Let me add here that this analysis also solves an interesting riddle in Indian historiography. While analysing the case of south India in the context of the great divergence, Parthasarathi (1998: 103–5) notes that higher agricultural productivity ensured lower grain wages in the economy, which, in turn, cheapened the cost of production in textiles, making them highly competitive in the global market. This was certainly true for Bengal as well. But Broadberry and Gupta (2006) dispute this line of reasoning on the grounds that, in that case, there would have been an inflow of bullion, raising the domestic price level. They argue (ibid.: 16), 'How could such equilibrating forces have been offset for two centuries?' For Bengal, the inflow of bullion did take place, but the payments of annual tributes neutralised the 'equilibrating forces'.

V

This study questions the appropriateness of the resource constraint hypothesis and the Brenner–Isett critique for explaining Bengal's falling behind from 1757 to 1857. I argue instead that Bengal does not show strong signs of the Malthusian-cum-ecological crisis around that period, as its land–man ratio was far from the critical level. A high land–man ratio is explained based on three sets of evidence: (i) that the demographic growth in contemporary Bengal was low; (ii) that a large amount of reclaimable land was kept up even in the late eighteenth century; and (iii) that labour scarcity prevailed across the province.

I argue further in favour of a reconsideration of the Smithian development process itself. The Bengal trajectory shows that, where greater accessibility to distant markets ushered in the division of labour, a Malthusian-cum-ecological crisis was not its necessary destiny.

The study also questions Williamson's proposal on divergence. As Williamson himself acknowledges, India is not a good example of the thesis. A reconstructed terms-of-trade hypothesis, based on the shocks of domestic terms of trade, might be tenable for India, but not for Bengal, since the deindustrialisation process started in this province only around 1830.

The alternative explanation in this chapter suggests that a great inflow of bullion, which occurred on account of Bengal's export business in the early modern age, was largely matched with the outflow of specie on account of Delhi tributes. Hence, the large capital base that was created in this province under the sovereign rulers (1338–1538)[18] remained virtually stagnant during the Mughal period. There thus followed a Smithian crisis of the stationary state of the large capital stock, whereby the demand for labour remained constant but the demographic growth profile so adjusted the supply of labour that the wage rate was depressed to a level which could be characterised only as 'scanty subsistence'. The situation deteriorated further in the post-1757 period, which witnessed a large-scale outflow of specie from the province. Although the bullion inflow resumed from the late 1790s, it could not replenish the earlier depletions. The outflow of specie caused a higher rate of interest, and lower commodity prices, thus affecting the development process in the short run. In the long run, however, it depleted the economy's stock of capital, which reduced the demand for labour and thus pushed the economy into a crisis of decaying capital.

Notes

1 Raychaudhury (1983: 7) observes in this connection, however: 'Despite the Maratha raids and Alivardi's extortions, the real decline in Bengal's economy was largely a post-Plassey and even post-1813 phenomenon.'

2 Broadberry and Hindle (2011: 2) point out that 'the welfare ratio in Beijing was at about the same level as the welfare ratios in Leipzig and Milan. Pomeranz is therefore clearly correct to point to variation in the level of development within both Europe and Asia.'

3 Studer (2008: 400–18) observes that the grain markets in India were not integrated before 1850. For Bengal, however, Datta (2000: 197–8) finds an integrated provincial market in the eighteenth century.

4 In the context of that famine, Hunter (1868: 19) writes, 'The streets were blocked up with promiscuous heaps of the dying and dead. Interment could not do its work quick enough; even the dogs and jackals, the public scavengers of the East, became unable to accomplish their revolting work, and the multitude of mangled and festering corpses at length threatened the existence of the citizens.'

5 Three types of money unit have been used in this study: pound sterling, sicca rupee (S.R.) and current rupee (C.R.). The exchange rate between the pound sterling and the sicca rupee varied around S.R. 10 = £1 in this period. The current rupee (C.R.) is an imaginary currency, however. The English East India Company used it in its accounting to avoid the complexities involved in dealing with the multiple currencies that prevailed in contemporary Bengal. It had an unchanged value at '10 per cent less than dusmessa rupee' (Sinha 1965: 131). For a value of 116 for the sicca rupee, the value of the dusmessa rupee was 110, and that of the current rupee 100.

6 Pomeranz (2000: 26) notes that 'population density is not the sole determinant of Smith's "extent of the market" [...] But for elaborate specialization to be developed in many areas of economic activity – food, clothing production, building, transport, and exchange itself, there is ultimately no substitute for having many people within affordable physical or cultural distance.'

7 Through his opium-addicted character, Shree Kamalakanta, he tells us, 'From the year of 1203 I have been counting the days of my misery. I have been counting from the day when the Hindu force was eclipsed – when seventy artilleries won the battle of Bengal. Alas! How long should I count... Possibly, into the water of the Ganges the goddess of treasure drowned herself not to see her coward sons again. That event always haunts me, and I weep. I clearly see, with their swords straight towards the sky, the Muslim soldiers are entering Nawadip breaking the silence of the dead night' (Chattopadhyay 2002 [1875]: 50).

8 The words 'bullion' and 'specie' have been used interchangeably, since European traders coming with bullion immediately minted it in India (especially in Bengal).

9 Contemporary documents of the eighteenth century confirm this. Thus, a government document of 1769 (Letter from the Council to the Court of Directors, dated 5 April 1769: GOB 1769) narrates, '[T]he Bengal raw silk, cloths, & c. to a vast amount, were dispersed to the West and North, inland; as far as Guzzerat, Lahore, and even Ispahan. In proportion, therefore, to this diffusion of commerce, the quantity of specie in the country necessarily increased.' Another document (Bolts 1772: 200) describes how 'inconceivable numbers of merchants, from all parts of Asia in general, as well as from the rest of Hindostan in particular, sometimes in bodies of many thousands at a time, were used annually to resort to Bengal with little else than ready money, or bills, to purchase the produce of these provinces'. See also Chaudhuri (1975: 242–7).

10 Prakash (1988: 478) thus notes, 'The Mughal system involved monetary management by the state only in a limited way. The accretions to the supply of money were determined by the public itself subject to the availability of metals in the system and the capacity of the imperial mints.'

11 Chaudhuri (1975: 247) notes, 'It can hardly be denied that the drain from Bengal up-country during this period reached a new and great dimension. The numerous imperial officials and even big merchants, who were mostly from northern and western India, remitted huge amounts to Agra and Delhi in the form of cash. The Company's records provide a rough idea of the vast sum amassed and remitted by the *subadars* and other officials.'

12 Chandra (1966: 322) thus notes, 'The amount of surplus – particularly cash surplus at the disposal of the ruling class was another limiting factor. The major source of this surplus was the peasantry.'

13 'Charges' seem to represent the costs involved in undertaking concerned activities.

14 It primarily represents the purchases of various goods for export business.

15 The figure for 1748–56 actually represents the Company's import of bullion in Bengal (Ray 2011: 29).

16 This holds good if the proceeds of recoinage *batta* remained fairly stable over years, as it appeared in Grant's analysis (Grant 1984 [1917]: 229–30).

17 This is confirmed in the details of taxes during the Mughal period, as discussed above. See also Chaudhuri (1995: 1–9, 327–35).

18 Although there is no direct evidence to this end, it follows from the fact that Bengal paid tributes to Delhi prior to this period (that is, during sultanate rule), and also subsequently during Mughal rule, but not in the period of sovereign rulers. In the absence of any drain of specie, it must have accumulated in this period.

Bibliography

Allen, R. C. (2007) 'India in the Great Divergence'. In Hatton, T. J., O'Rourke, K. H., and Taylor, A. M. (eds.) *The New Comparative Economic History: Essays in Honor of Jeffrey G. Williamson*, 9–32. Cambridge, MA: MIT Press.

Allen, R. C., Bassino J. P., Ma, D., Moll-Murata, C., and Zanden, J. L. V. (2011) 'Wages, Prices, and Living Standards in China, 1738–1925: In Comparison with Europe, Japan, and India', *Economic History Review* 64 (S1), 8–38.

Barbosa, D. (1921 [1518]) *The Book of Duarte Barbosa: An Account of the Countries Bordering on the Indian Ocean and Their Inhabitants*, vol. II. Cambridge: Hakluyt Society.

Bolts, W. (1772) *Considerations on Indian Affairs: Particularly Respecting the Present State of Bengal and Its Dependencies*. London: J. Almon in Piccadilly etc.

Bowrey, T. (1905) *A Geographical Account of Countries round the Bay of Bengal, 1669 to 1679* (ed. R. Carnac Temple). Cambridge: Hakluyt Society.

Brenner, R., and Isett, C. (2002) 'England's Divergence from China's Yangzi Delta: Property Relations, Microeconomics and Patterns of Development', *Journal of Asian Studies* 61 (2), 609–62.

Broadberry, S., and Gupta, B. (2006) 'The Early Modern Great Divergence: Wages, Prices and Economic Development in Europe and Asia, 1500–1800', *Economic History Review* 59 (1), 2–31.

Broadberry, S., and Hindle, S. (2011) 'Editors' Introduction', *Economic History Review* 64 (S1), 1–7.

Chakrabarti, S. (1997) 'Intransigent Shroffs and the English East India Company's Currency Reforms in Bengal, 1757–1800', *Indian Economic and Social History Review* 34 (1), 69–94.

Chandra, S. (1966) 'Some Aspects of the Growth of a Money Economy in India during the Seventeenth Century', *Indian Economic and Social History Review* 3 (4), 321–31.

Chattopadhyay, B. (2002 [1875]) *Kamala Kanter Daftar* (in Bengali). Calcutta: United Publishers.

Chaudhuri, B. (1983a) 'Agrarian Relations: Eastern India'. In Kumar, D. (ed.) *The Cambridge Economic History of India*, vol. II: *c. 1751 – c. 1970*, 86–177. Hyderabad: Cambridge University Press.

Chaudhuri, B. (1983b) 'Regional Economy: Eastern India'. In Kumar, D. (ed.) *The Cambridge Economic History of India*, vol. II: *c. 1751 – c. 1970*, 295–332. Hyderabad: Cambridge University Press.

Chaudhuri, S. (1975) *Trade and Commercial Organisation in Bengal: 1650–1720*. Calcutta: Firma K. L. Mukhopadhyay.

Chaudhuri, S. (1995) *From Prosperity to Decline: Eighteenth Century Bengal*. New Delhi: Manohar.

Clingingsmith, D., and Williamson, J. G. (2008) 'Deindustrialization in 18th and 19th Century India: Mughal Decline, Climate Shocks and British Industrial Ascent', *Explorations in Economic History* 45 (3), 209–34.

Datta, R. (2000) *Society, Economy, and the Market: Commercialization in Rural Bengal, c. 1760–1800*. New Delhi: Manohar.

Embree, A.T. (1969) 'Landholding in India and British Institutions'. In Frykenberg, R. E. (ed.) *Land Control and Social Structure in Indian History*, 33–52. Madison, WI: University of Wisconsin Press.

Frank, A. G. (1998) *ReORIENT: Global Economy in the Asian Age*. Berkeley, CA: University of California Press.

Gaastra, F. S. (1986) 'The Dutch East India Company and Its Intra-Asiatic Trade in Precious Metals'. In Fischer, W. R., McInnis, M., and Schneider, J. (eds.) *The Emergence of a World Economy, 1500–1914*, 97–112. Wiesbaden: Franz Steiner Verlag.

Gold, J. D. (1964) 'The Price Revolution Reconsidered', *Economic History Review* 17 (2), 249–66.

Government of Bengal (GOB) (1767) *Fort William Consultations*, 26 September. National Library Archive, Calcutta.

Government of Bengal (GOB) (1769) *Fort William Consultations*, 20 March. National Library Archive, Calcutta.

Government of India (GOI) (1918) *Report of the Indian Industrial Commission, 1916–18*. Calcutta: Superintendent Government Printing.

Grant, J. (1984 [1917]) 'Historical and Comparative Analysis of the Finance of Bengal; Chronologically Arranged in Different Periods, from the Mogul Conquest to the Present Time'. In Firminger, W. K. (ed.) *Affairs of the East India Company (being the Fifth Report from SC of HC, July 28, 1812)*, 159–477. Delhi: Neeraj Publishing.

Hamilton, E. J. (1929) 'American Treasure and the Rise of Capitalism, 1500–1700', *Economica* (27), 338–57.

Hunter, W. W. (1868) *The Annals of Rural Bengal*. London: Smith, Elder.

Krishna, B. (1924) *Commercial Relations between India and England, 1601–1757*. London: George Routledge & Sons.

Landes, D. S. (1969) *The Unbound Prometheus: Technological Change and Industrial Development in Western Europe from 1750 to the Present*. Cambridge: Cambridge University Press.

Malaviya, M. M. (1918) 'Note [of Dissent]'. In Government of India (GOI) *Report of the Indian Industrial Commission, 1916–18*, 292–355. Calcutta: Superintendent Government Printing.

Marshall, P. J. (1976) *East India Fortunes: The British in Bengal in the Eighteenth Century*. Oxford: Clarendon Press.

Moreland, W. H. (1923) *From Akbar to Aurangzeb: A Study in Indian Economic History*. London: Macmillan.

Nef, J. U. (1937) 'Prices and Industrial Capitalism in France and England, 1540–1640', *Economic History Review* 7 (2), 155–85.

North, D. C., and Thomas, R. P. (1973) *The Rise of the Western World: A New Economic History*. Cambridge: Cambridge University Press.

Parliamentary Papers (P.P.) (1812–13) *House of Commons Paper no. 152*. London: Hansard.

Parliamentary Papers (P.P.) (1816) *Accounts, Respecting the Annual Revenues and Disbursements, Trade and Sales of the East India Company*. London: Hansard.

Parliamentary Papers (P.P.) (1820) *Accounts, Respecting the Annual Revenues and Disbursements, Trade and Sales of the East India Company*. London: Hansard.

Parliamentary Papers (P.P.) (1858) *Memorandum of the Improvements in the Administration of India during the Last Thirty Years*. London: Hansard.

Parliamentary Papers (P.P.) (1864) *House of Commons Paper no. 133*. London: Hansard.

Parthasarathi, P. (1998) 'Rethinking Wages and Competitiveness in the Eighteenth Century: Britain and South India', *Past and Present* 158 (1): 79–109.

Pomeranz, K. (2000) *The Great Divergence: China, Europe, and the Making of the Modern World Economy*. Princeton, NJ: Princeton University Press.

Prakash, O. (1976) 'Bullion for Goods: International Trade and the Economy of Early Eighteenth Century Bengal', *Indian Economic and Social History Review* 13 (2), 159–86.

Prakash, O. (1988) 'On Coinage in Mughal India', *Indian Economic and Social History Review* 25 (4), 475–91.

Prakash, O. (2001) 'Global Precious Metal Flows and India, 1500–1750'. In McGuire, J., Bertola, P. and Reeves, P. (eds.) *Evolution of the World Economy, Precious Metals and India*, 59–76. New Delhi: Oxford University Press.

Ray, I. (2011) *Bengal Industries and the British Industrial Revolution (1757–1857)*. London: Routledge.

Raychaudhury, T. (1983) 'The Mid-Eighteenth-Century Background'. In Kumar, D. (ed.) *The Cambridge Economic History of India*, vol. II: *c. 1751 – c. 1970*, 3–35. Hyderabad: Cambridge University Press.

Roy, T. (2010) 'Economic Conditions in Early Modern Bengal: A Contribution to the Divergence Debate', *Journal of Economic History* 70 (1), 179–94.

Sarkar, J. N. (ed.) (2003) *The History of Bengal*, vol. I. New Delhi: B. R. Publishing.

Sinha, N. K. (1965) *The Economic History of Bengal, 1793–1848*, vol. I. Calcutta: Firma K. L. Mukhopadhyay.

Smith, A. (1937 [1776]) *An Inquiry into the Nature and Causes of the Wealth of Nations*. New York: The Modern Library.

Steuart, J. (1772) *The Principles of Money Applied to the Present State of the Coin of Bengal*. London: D.T. Cadell & W. Davies.

Studer, R. (2008) 'India and the Great Divergence: Assessing the Efficiency of Grain Markets in Eighteenth- and Nineteenth-Century India', *Journal of Economic History* 68 (2), 393–437.

Taylor, J. (1840) *A Sketch of the Topography and Statistics of Dacca*. Calcutta: Military Orphan Press.

Travers, T. R. (2004) '"The Real Value of Lands": The Nawabs, the British and the Land Tax in Eighteenth Century Bengal', *Modern Asian Studies* 38 (3), 517–58.

Varthema, L. di (1853 [1510]) *The Travels of Varthema in Egypt, Syria, Arabia Deserta and Arabia Felix, in Persia, India, and Ethiopia, A.D. 1503 to 1508* (trans. J. W. Jones). Cambridge: Hakluyt Society.

Verelst, H. (1772) *A View of the Rise, Progress, and Present State of the English Government in Bengal: Including a Reply to the Misrepresentation of Mr. Bolts, and Other Writers*. London: J. Nourse in the Strand etc.

Viseria, L., and Viseria, P. (1983) 'Population'. In Kumar, D. (ed.) *The Cambridge Economic History of India*, vol. II: *c. 1751 – c. 1970*, 463–532. Hyderabad: Cambridge University Press.

Wallerstein, I. (1986) 'Incorporation of Indian Subcontinent into Capitalist World-Economy', *Economic and Political Weekly* 21 (4), PE28–PE39.

Washbrook, D. A. (1988) 'Progress and Problems: South Asian Economic and Social History, c. 1720–1860', *Modern Asian Studies* 22 (1), 57–96.

Williamson, J. G. (2008) 'Globalization and the Great Divergence: Terms of Trade Booms, Volatility and the Poor Periphery, 1782–1913', *European Review of Economic History* 12 (3), 355–91.

Appendix 2.1 Annual revenues in Bengal (in C.Rs.), 1811/12–1817/18

Particulars	*1811–12*	*1812–13*	*1813–14*	*1815–16*	*1816–17*	*1817–18*	*Average*
Mint duties	83,500	157,588	87,849	243,448	435,187	248,007	209,263
Post office collection	448,000	450,764	437,698	463,876	500,120	527,032	471,248
Land and *sayer* revenues	32,969,051	33,108,748	33,106,177	35,658,371	35,545,337	34,982,458	34,228,357
Customs	3,215,712	3,648,552	3,228,374	3,986,999	4,955,626	4,787,729	3,970,499
Judicial fees and fines	940,418	977,327	1,042,721	628,640	713,552	690,440	832,183
Stamp duties	529,050	532,248	557,918	1,129,014	1,214,823	1,309,790	878,807
Sale of salt	18,147,129	16,746,642	17,786,141	16,004,989	17,131,682	18,671,974	17,414,760
Sale of opium	9,246,775	7,299,401	9,640,729	10,512,601	9,416,539	8,735,983	9,142,005
Revenues in ceded/ conquered provinces	41,482,094	40,981,306	45,523,681	43,471,387	47,206,926	45,412,312	44,012,951
Miscellaneous	–	–	–	333,403	775,315	849,411	652,710
Total revenue	107,061,729	103,902,576	111,411,288	112,432,728	117,895,107	116,215,136	111,486,427[1]
Total charges	70,588,711	72,229,365	71,038,299	78,546,812	80,259,798	84,839,239	76,250,371
Net revenue	36,473,018	31,673,211	40,372,989	33,885,916	37,635,309	31,375,897	35,236,056

Notes: '–' signifies an insignificant amount; 1: row average.

Sources: 1811/12–1813/14, P.P. (1816: 6); 1815/16–1817–18, P.P. (1820: 6).

Appendix 2.2 Annual charges in Bengal (in C.Rs.), 1811/12–1817/18

Particulars of charges	*1811–12*	*1812–13*	*1813–14*	*1815–16*	*1816–17*	*1817–18*	*Average*
Mint	261,031	273,864	192,633	192,794	217,240	219,247	226,135
Post office	350,400	378,626	377,671	379,818	450,329	409,400	391,041
Collection of revenue (including stipends)	4,345,982	4,299,230	4,590,443	4,744,751	4,963,003	4,646,725	4,598,522
Collection of customs	454,603	433,493	417,732	457,930	512,860	545,404	470,337
Judicial (including police)	5,855,984	5,779,241	5,918,407	6,285,899	6,569,790	6,610,410	6,170,122
Stamp office	121,676	113,677	131,272	339,459	477,312	520,908	284,051
Salt: advances & charges	4,900,001	6,076,677	6,511,578	3,905,288	4,761,455	4,877,123	5,172,020
Opium: advances & charges	877,325	880,528	1,077,638	1,097,585	1,185,490	892,496	1,001,844
Building & fortification	777,897	1,082,785	807,442	944,079	695,534	828,493	856,038
Collection etc. in ceded/ conquered provinces	13,720,636	13,535,392	13,403,092	13,953,238	13,367,604	12,265,031	13,374,166
Marine	1,193,254	1,367,223	1,003,709	1,190,755	1,275,451	1,303,217	1,222,268
Military	29,459,872	29,343,835	29,935,287	39,779,215	40,484,599	44,295,421	35,549,705
Others	8,268,050	8,664,794	6,671,395	5,276,001	5,299,131	7,425,364	6,934,122
Total	70,588,711	72,229,365	71,038,299	78,546,812	80,259,798	84,839,239	76,250,371

Sources: 1811/12–1813/4, P.P. (1816: 7); 1815/16–1817/18, P.P. (1820: 7).

Appendix 2.3 Disbursements of the government of Bengal (in S.Rs.), 1813–14 & 1817–18

Particulars	*1813–14*	*1817–18*
Civil department: general		
Durbar charges and embassies to native courts	1,696,864	2,680,906
Temporary embassies	2,240,893	569,990
Bills to be drawn for subsidy to king of Persia and expenses to the embassy	–	20,770
Salaries of the Governor General and members of council	652,440	529,737
Public offices and establishments at the Presidency	1,655,172	2,238,127
Mint and assay offices	332,452	372,805
General post office and subordinates	325,579	352,931
Stamp office	113,166	449,059
Nizamut stipends	1,910,171	1,770,400
Pension and charitable allowances	103,558	91,494
Stationery	33,804	44,438
Others	–	1,151,367
Subtotal	9,064,099	10,272,024
Judicial		
Supreme Court of judicature and law charges	447,725	460,303
Justices of the Peace, Court of Requests and coroner	287,877	323,821
Sudder Dewanny and Nizamut Adawlat	361,623	427,639
Court of Appeal	832,549	777,822
City and Zilla Adawlat	2,140,573	2,033,586
Diet of prisoners	324,072	404,581
Provincial battalion	434,833	760,693
Provincial police	844,456	485,323
Pension to hill chiefs	19,289	20,799
Ceded and conquered provinces: charges	2,546,899	3,673,572
Stationery	7,289	–
Subtotal	8,247,185	9,368,139
Revenue		
Board of Revenue and establishments	317,653	238,932
Charges collecting land revenue and *sayer*	1,160,080	1,243,234
Poolbundy	176,822	164,469
Pensions, charitable allowances, etc.	988,962	579,841
Board of Commissioners in ceded and conquered provinces	240,730	230,948
Ceded and conquered provinces: charges for collecting revenues	6,634,152	6,214,085
Customs and duties	788,976	907,349
Stationery	21,318	15,602
Others	720,324	–
Subtotal	11,049,017	9,594,460
Salt and opium		
Salt: advances and charges	5,618,056	4,206,618
Opium: advances and charges	928,950	769,393
Subtotal	6,547,006	4,976,011

Appendix 2.3 Cont.

Particulars	*1813–14*	*1817–18*
Marine: establishment allowances and charges	890,770	1,010,015
Military department: establishment allowances and charges	26,064,043	38,735,475
Total	61,862,120	73,956,124
Extraordinary charges		
Civil department: general		
Interest on bonded and other debts, loan discharge, etc.	61,103,883	13,893,467
Bills payable	8,282,901	7,485,732
Development of the town of Calcutta	79,480	68,626
Road to Juggernaut	40,408	32,445
College at Fort William	203,691	145,270
Foreign settlements	13,978	–
Building and purchase of dead stocks	65,000	155,356
Others	535,996	3,797,645
Judicial	1,553,608	–
Advances on account, investment, ships, etc.	8,451,514	9,677,317
Supplies to Madras, Hyderabad and Mysore	18,384,094	13,227,575
Supplies to Bombay	6,406,236	10,964,652
Supplies to China	3,990,817	3,434,845
Supplies to other places	2,727,937	2,122,904
Payments of bills in London, drawn on Mauritius, Java and Moluccas	4,457,035	3,818,693
Civil department: others (excluding marine)	4,529,015	10,111,813
Marine department	244,689	113,448
Military department	1,053,531	529,905
Total	122,123,813	79,579,693
Amount remaining in different departments	20,210,399	23,257,400
Grand total	204,196,332	176,793,217

Sources: 1813–14: P.P. (1816: 41–5); 1817–18: P.P. (1820: 23–31).

3 Coal mining

Dissemination of mineralogical knowledge and railway networking

The historiography on industry ascribes special importance to coal mining in the early phase of the British Industrial Revolution. Jevons (1865: viii) observes, 'Coal, in truth, stands not beside but entirely above all other commodities. It is the material energy of the country – the universal aid – the factor in everything we do... [W]ithout it we are thrown back into the laborious poverty of early times.' To Wrigley (1961: 1–16), twin features of the industry were crucial to human civilisation. First, it helped to transform society from an organic economy – using animate sources of energy, such as wood and pack animals – to an inorganic economy based on the energy from coal, thereby augmenting economic growth elasticity in the long term.[1] Insofar as the organic sources of energy were in competition with food grains over land use, an organic economy suffered from a lower trajectory of growth. Second, the development of the coal industry led to a transport revolution based on railroads, and acted as a catalyst to the development of an array of modern industries. It was, *à la* Rostow (1960: 4–16), a lead-off industry in the take-off stage of sustained industrial growth. But the story of the development of the coal industry in Bengal was different from the British experience, as it was a latecomer on the global coal-mining map, notwithstanding its first venture in 1774 (Ray and Paul 2001: 836–8). While, in Britain, pit coal emerged to replace charcoal as a fuel, Bengal's coal industry did not start till British coal had already been in extensive use.

In this context, this chapter seeks to analyse the development of Bengal's coal industry in a way that resolves certain questions in industrial historiography. These are: (i) what was the attitude of the imperial government towards the development of this colonial industry; (ii) why was Bengal a latecomer in coal mining; (iii) where did the comparative advantage of Bengal's coal mining over the British lie; and (iv) how did Bengal coal compete with industries elsewhere, especially the British? In the process, the development implications of

Originally published in *Indian Economic and Social History Review*, volume 52, issue 4, 2015, This is an enlarged version.

this industry are also discussed. Moreover, the development story of a colonial industry such as coal is in itself a topic of interest. There is a rich body of literature on the history of the British coal industry. Among the important issues of the industry, there are analyses of early production (Nef 1932; Pollard 1980), its relationship with other industries (especially cotton textiles) (Balderston 2010; Rodgers 1960), labour (Daunton 1981; Blanchard 1972) and its productivity (Hirsch and Hausman 1983; Blanchard 1974), technological advancement (Taylor 1961; Rhodes 1945), industrial organisation (Tan 2009), and so forth. But in the Indian context, apart from textbook analyses (Gadgil 1929: 84–5, 120–1, 278–81; Roy 2011: 221–5), attention is focused mainly on land and labour (as in Chattoraj 1977; Seth 1940; Lahiri-Dutta 2001; Das Gupta 1985; Subrahmanyam 1968; and Simmons 1976a) and, to some extent, on ownership patterns (for example, Ray and Ray 1974; Bagchi 1970: 230–4; Simmons 1976b; and Palit 1999: 50–2). There is little interest in themes of trade and enterprise in the literature. This chapter seeks to deliberate on this field in detail, and also contribute to the debate on the 'great divergence'. In this debate, the California school identifies the scarcity of wood as one of the main factors behind the nineteenth-century great divergence, which Britain broke through by way of developing coal mines and steam technology (Pomeranz 2000: 19–20, 216–42, 64–7). While identifying the reasons for such asymmetric development between Europe and Asia, Parthasarathi (2011: 152, 167, 180–2) underlines the relative development pressure in these economies, and the role of the state in resolving such issues. In contrast to the state patronage in Britain, he argues, coal mining in India never received any state support, and was thus unable to develop. My reading of the development of the coal industry in Bengal, however, shows that coal mining greatly benefited from contemporary state policies, and underwent rapid development in the nineteenth century.

There are six sections in this chapter. Section I overviews, as a backdrop, the various aspects of coal-bearing rocks in India. Section II analyses the first phase of the industry's development in detail for the sake of understanding the attitude of the colonial government towards a peripheral industry. It also discusses the industry's trajectory of growth during the nineteenth century. Section III analyses why coal mining did not come up in a big way until the middle of the nineteenth century, and also how the growth-inhibiting factors were removed. Section IV discusses the industry's comparative advantages, and Section V analyses how Bengal coal successfully competed in domestic and foreign outlets, thereby reducing the import of foreign coal and augmenting the export of domestic coal. Section VI summarises the discussion by way of conclusion.

I

India's coal deposits occur exclusively in Gondwana rocks that lie beneath as many as seven of its great valleys. The dominant wisdom in academia is that these coal-bearing rocks once belonged to the Southern Hemisphere, extending from South America to Australia (Unrug 1996; Mukhopadhyay et al. 2010). This hypothesis is bolstered by the fact that all of them are characterised by a common flora, *Glossopteris.* The Gondwana continent, as it is often referred to, suffered from repeated fragmentation and drift following the Permo-Carboniferous period, giving the rocks their present shapes and sizes (Rode 1953: 9). Lithologically, various rock formations in the Gondwana system demonstrate remarkable persistence in their characteristics, motivating geologists to group them in two broad categories, the upper Gondwana and the lower Gondwana, which were crystallised during the Mesozoic and the Palaeozoic ages, respectively, with an average thickness of 11,000 feet and 13,000 feet. Their further classifications in India are the Jabalpur series, Rajmahal series and Mahadeva series for the former, and the Panchet series, Ranigunj series, Karharbari series, Barakar series and Talchir series for the latter.

The story of genesis that runs through the literature summarised above suggests that there should be certain semblances among Gondwana rocks across continents. Indeed, on the basis of fossil plants, a palaeontologist of the Geological Survey of India (GSI) drew similarities between lower oolite and the Jabalpur series, lias and the Rajmahal series in the upper Gondwana, Keuper and the Panchet series and Buntsandstein and the Damodar and Talchir series in the lower Gondwana (referred to in Ball 1881: 59). Therefore, the coal seams of these Indian rocks should be fairly comparable with those elsewhere. In addition, a GSI record reveals that the area of Gondwana rocks in India is greater than that in Britain – namely 35,000 square miles as against 18,000 square miles – as well as Spain (8,000 square miles), Japan (6,000 square miles) and Germany (3,000 square miles) (Hughes 1873: 65). Although the United States has the highest occurrences of this rock, Bengal dominates from the viewpoint of the thickness of seams. A GSI document thus remarks:

> Even that land of monstrosities and natural wonders, the United States of America, can exhibit nothing to compare with the gigantic seams of the Hengir and Damuda coal fields, some of which are one hundred and sixty, one hundred and twenty, and a hundred feet thick.
>
> (ibid.: 64)

From the viewpoint of coal deposits, the upper Gondwana formations are of little importance, since the coal occurs exclusively in the lower Gondwanas. Even across the latter, deposits in Bengal vary widely, with the Barakar and the Ranigunj at the top of the scale. Between them, however, the former surely bequeaths a greater variety – indeed, as many as are available in the Indian subcontinent – but the latter dominates in terms of quality, as well as compositional uniformity. Even in considering the thickness of the deposits the Ranigunj series is superior, its benchmark coming in at 5,000 to 6,000 feet, as against its neighbour's maximum thickness at 3,800 feet in the Jheria field and 2,000 feet in the Ranigunj. The Talchir series does not contain any coal deposit but forms the base of all coal-bearing rocks. It mainly consists of sandstones, fine shally silts and boulder beds.

Geographically, however, coal deposits occur extensively in two places: Rajmahal and Ranigunj. The former refers to the region along the western side of the detached group of low hills, the so-called Rajmahal Hills, stretching from Suri in the Birbhum district northwards to the neighbourhood of the Ganges. By the middle of the nineteenth century coal deposits were discovered here along the Brahmani basin, as also in the valleys of the Bansloi and the Goomani, and towards the north-western end of the hilly range near Boorah (for details of this coalfield, see Oldham 1867: 4–5). The coal measure in this field was exposed over 70 square miles, and got a market nomenclature of Birbhum coal, or Adji coal, as it was transhipped to Calcutta on the river Adji (or the Ajoy, as it is now called). Although the output was by and large inferior, its occurrence near the surface soil made the field a forerunner in India's coal-mining history. It was mainly used for sundry purposes, such as lime burning and brick making, as required for the construction of the railways. A small proportion could be used for generating steam, however. Thus, for example, the Dhoba Sugar Works worked with captive Adji coal (10,000 to 15,000 maunds per annum) (P.P. 1841: 23) in its boiler from the 1830s. We also have evidence confirming good-quality coal from Erskine's mines, located in this field: '[S]mall sample [of Erskine's coal] sent for trial consisted of large blocks from 50 to 60 pounds each kept up steam well' (Smith 1841: 19).[2]

India's largest coal reserve, however, was found in Ranigunj. From the east of the town of Ranigunj, the coal-bearing bed extended several miles through the west of Barakar, running for about 30 miles in length and about 18 miles in breadth, so that its area comes to about 500 square miles. It had a general dip from the northern boundary to the south, at angles varying between 5° and 20°. Towards the southern boundary the bed gradually thinned, and it was finally cut off by a great fault. Taking into account the inconsistencies and irregularities of the bed, a mid-nineteenth-century source estimates its reserve at about 18.60 billion ton (Oldham 1867: 5–6).

Two major rivers traversed through these fields, the Ajoy in the Rajmahal and the Damodar in the Ranigunj, both flowing into the Ganges, and thus connecting them with Calcutta, an one end, and north India, at the other. The former joined the Ganges 70 miles above Calcutta, and the latter 25 miles below it. From the transit points, these confluences were 110 miles and 160 miles away, respectively, so that these river routes were almost equal (P.P. 1841: 21). As coal mines in the Rajmahal field were located farther from the transit points on the river, however, they incurred higher expenses.

Among other coal-bearing fields in the neighbourhood, I should mention the Jheria, which ran for 200 square miles 16 miles west of the Ranigunj field, and also the Bokaro, lying over 220 square miles two miles west of the Jheria field, both on the valley of the Damodar (Ball 1881: 73–4). According to the mid-nineteenth-century estimate, their reserves stood at some 465 million tons and 1.5 billion tons, respectively.

II

These mineralogical details were known to Calcutta's coal circle around the middle of the nineteenth century, but not two decades earlier. Thus, while commenting on a report of the Coal Committee (1838), a contemporary source (Blanford 1865: 5) observes, 'So little was the value of the [Ranigunj] field known and appreciated at this time…that it was considered as second in importance to the Sylhet field. It appears strange that a tract so near Calcutta should have been so little investigated.' Of course, local people, and also some British adventurers, had known about it for a long time – but its commercial exploitation waited for several decades to overcome early hurdles. Contemporary events suggest, as we will see shortly, that coal mining was delayed by about seven decades for the want of a congenial industrial environment, which was only exacerbated by the indifferent attitude of the state from 1774 to 1808, and by poor institutional support up to the early 1840s.

The genesis of coal mining in this province dates back to 1774, when Messrs Sumner, Heatly and Redfearne was set up. It took leasehold land from the government, bordering Panchet and Birbhum districts, at a 20 per cent rent, promising to sell 10,000 maunds of pit coal annually to the government at 2¾ Arcot rupees per maund (of 80 *sicca* weight per *ser*) for the initial five years, and at the market price thereafter (for details of the lease, see the letter addressed to Warren Hastings by George Vansittart et al. dated 15 August 1774, and the resolution on the Burdwan report, in Heatly 1842: 816–18). Although as many as six mines were excavated by 1775, and 2,500 maunds of coal were shipped to Calcutta, the project failed because of an adverse government report on its quality. The report (available in Heatly 1842: 821) stated: 'It is plain from this trial between the two sorts of coals, that with one maund of the British, the same work may be performed that can be done with two maunds of the country, in much less time, and with not near so great a waste of iron.' The project was then discontinued as the government refused to buy its output. It should be noted that the Bengal government was the only bulk buyer in the contemporary coal market.

Though unsuccessfully launched, the firm left certain legacies that characterised the future course of development in Bengal's coal mining. First, the site that the firm had chosen came up again and again for investigation until its commercial success took hold. Moreover, its leasehold area[3] became the hot spot for coal-mining projects in the following century. Second, since mining technology was unknown among the local populace, the adventurers envisaged the need for experienced European miners. Indeed, miners were engaged from Europe, though they could not survive. S. G. T. Heatly, the descendent of one of the promoters, writes, 'Tradition current in our family, that he [S. G. Heatly] brought out regularly-bred miners from Europe, and local tradition, according to Mr. Jones, confirmed the fact of Europeans having been engaged in the work, but carried off by a destructive fever' (Heatly 1842: 822). This was also an important legacy for the future development of the industry, in which Europeans were dominant not only in British-owned mines but in the mines owned by Indians as well. In the initial years coal companies used to employ both European supervisors and miners. As the local people gradually learnt the art of deep mining, people from abroad were retained only for supervision tasks. Third, as the coal industry was a highly labour-intensive one, the firm envisaged that the question of labour should be suitably addressed for its long-term success. In the lease appeal for land, they sought some uncultivated lands, contiguous to mines, so that 'we may be able to entice the labourers in future to settle on the spot' (Sumner, 'Proposal for Working Coal Mines and Selling Coal in Bengal', in Heatly 1842: 814–15); they also sought some cultivable lands for their subsistence farming. The government's sanction of the lease incorporated these provisions. In fact, this model of labour procurement prevailed over the following centuries. In the initial phase, when local workers were available, mining companies acquired the proprietorship from zamindars over several villages together so that they could have control over labour supply. Once the local sources were exhausted they recruited tribal people, especially Santhals, from the neighbouring state to settle on the leasehold, uncultivated lands near the collieries.

There are two alternative hypotheses explaining the failure of this pioneer project. The primitive one is related to the quality of coal seams. We have seen above that, on the weight of an adverse report from a government expert, the commercial viability of the project was lost. But the adverse report of the trial did not necessarily reflect the poor quality of seams deposited in the field, but that of what is called the surface coal, as the specimens were drawn from the surface of the soil, not by way of deep mining. In fact, surface coal mining was found equally inefficient in England. Thus, the Board of Revenue put on record in 1778 ('The Government Order in Consequence of the Report', in Heatly 1842: 821–2) that 'they have no doubt from this trial of their meeting with good coal, if they will be at the trouble of searching deeper for it, as this appears to have been gathered only from the surface of the mines'. The Marquis of Hastings (Lord Moira), Governor General of India, also gave a similar judgement: '[T]here is coal here [in Ranigunj] well calculated for military purposes; that surface coal may be expected to fail here as in England, where some of the excavations reach a depth of 205 yards before proper coal is met with' (Heatly 1842: 834). This leads us to a second set of questions: even though the government knew in 1778 that the experiment was ill designed, why did it not ignore the report and conduct further investigations for coal specimens? Is this an indication of the government's apathy towards this vital energy source in Bengal? Indeed, the promoters of the pioneer project believed it so. They were on record expressing the view that 'they were unfairly dealt with, owing to the strong interest made by the coal contractors at home [in England]' (ibid.: 815). This surmise is corroborated by the fact that, when the Court of Directors sought the government's opinion on the substitutability of Bengal coal for the British (often referred to as sea coal), the Military Board noted that 'an ample supply of sea-coal is actually a saving of expenses' (quoted in Heatly 1842: 825), since charcoal was locally inadequate, and underlined the importance of its regular import from England in view of the uncertainty in local mining. Together with such blatant conflicts of interest, remarks made by S. G. T. Heatly point us to an anti-colonial sentiment that was dominant in British governance in the wake of the American War of Freedom. Heatly (1842: 823) notes, 'Lord Cornwallis brought out a disposition systematically opposed to anything like colonial independence. Smarting under the humiliation inflicted on him by the Americans, he undeviatingly discouraged colonization.' He continues, 'No plan which tended to make India a self dependent state met his approbation, and at no period of the empire here do the records exhibit such a bareness of projects for developing the resources of the country.' This explains, according to him, why neither the original promoters, nor anybody else, sought to resuscitate the project.[4]

The government attitude changed when the mounting coal imports strained the exchequer, and the Court of Directors decided in 1808 to relocate the ordinance works from Bengal to England in case local coal could not be obtained. The change in government attitude is evident in that a further trial was made of Bengal coal, and, when it also confirmed the earlier findings,[5] the government commissioned a detailed investigation by a mechanical engineer, William Jones, at the behest of Mathew Smith – a prominent shipwright in Calcutta who had been using Panchet coal for some years past. Jones first chose Jheria, where a good seam was manifest only at a depth of nine feet, but discarded it for the want of transportation.[6] Finally, he selected Mudgeah (Mejia, as it is now called), which had a good conveyance link with Calcutta. Furthermore, a bed of good coal (about 20 feet thick) was available at 39 feet beneath the soil. He records:

> I am of the opinion it is the cleanest coal I ever saw, and must be of great value for culinary and other purposes, as well as for Smiths' use...and I am certain that the coal of this mine when taken up clean will answer every purpose, and is superior to most English coal.
>
> ('Letter from W. Jones to the Secretary to the Government of Bengal, dated 22 May 1816', in P.P. 1831: 779)

His findings heralded the age of coal mining in India.[7]

In addition to sponsoring the prospecting project, the government also promoted Jones to pioneer mining projects in 1816. A loan of Rs. 40,000 was provided to him under the security of Alexander & Co., an agency firm in Calcutta. Jones successfully excavated several mines with what were state-of-the-art facilities, including captive arrangements for river transportation (for details, see Ghosh 1997: 143–9). But he died in 1821, and, in spite of his successful efforts, the project passed on to its guarantor firm, Alexander & Co.

Although the government's attitude had thus changed, the industrial environment remained unfavourable for the want of proper institutions, especially law and order. Quite in line with Schumpeter's discourse on imitating entrepreneurship (Schumpeter 1964 [1939]: 75), the success of the pioneer firm attracted a plethora of projects from businessmen in Calcutta. But, by fair means or foul, Alexander & Co. resisted them to retain a monopoly in the market.[8] For smooth functioning at Ranigunj, a contemporary colliery required (i) a lease of land where coal seams occurred;[9] (ii) a shipping place on the river for conveyance to Calcutta; (iii) a road between mines and the place of shipment; and (iv) a lease of several villages from the zemindar to gain control over the labour supply. On one or other of these issues, Alexander & Co. challenged the authorities of the aspiring firms, causing them trouble. Very often the matter was brought to the court of law; and, more often than not, private musclemen were deployed to settle the score. A contemporary author notes:

> When endless law suits were the prices at which alone it was possible for any one to commence mines in the Ranigunj district, it is not surprising that the greater number of speculators would be discouraged, and the longest purse would, in the end, have all the advantage.
>
> (Blanford 1865: 157)

Indeed, the resistance from Alexander & Co. explains why only one firm could be set up in the 1820s – Bell's mine at Chinakuri in 1823. Jessop & Co. also excavated a mine in 1824, but closed it down in the following year at the behest of Alexander & Co.

After 1830, however, a few mines started emerging – three by Jessop & Co., one each at Narayankuri, Chanchi and Nuchibad; and two by Rogers & Co., at Chankidanga and Mahmudpur, respectively – adding up to six for the 1820–34 period. As Alexander & Co. gradually lost its monopoly control, the law and order disturbances gradually waned, though they continued at a moderate level for some more years to come. Thus, in 1859, Thomas Oldham, the first superintendent of the Geological Survey of India, reported:

> I can not conclude this report without urging the most serious attention to the terrific drawback to the full development of this most valuable field which exists in the very lawless and disgraceful manner in which some of the larger proprietors in the field, and more especially one firm, obtain or seek to obtain their objects by force. If a boundary be disputed, if a roadway be required, the first appeal with these parties is in no case to the Court of Law for a calm and unbiased investigation of facts. The ground in dispute is forcibly taken possession of, often with loss of life, and the loser is then permitted to seek his remedy by a process of law.
>
> (Oldham 1859: 30–1)

He calculated that annual payments to the *lattials* (traditional musclemen, fighting with long sticks) were almost equal to the payments for general superintendence.

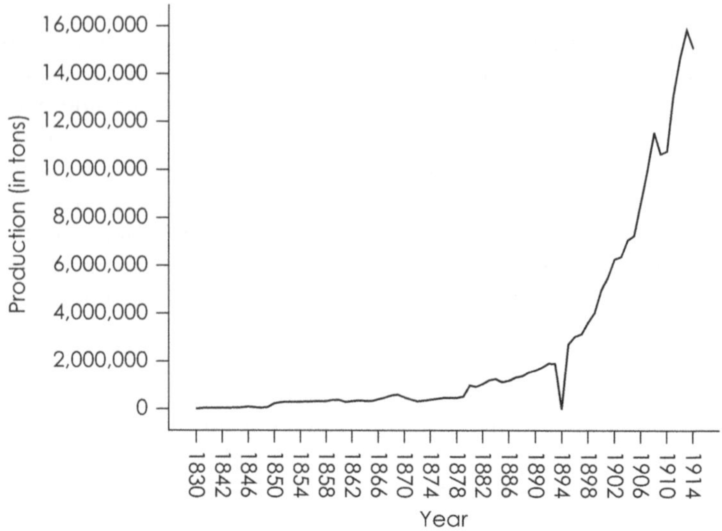

Figure 3.1 Coal production in Bengal, 1830–1914

In the 1830s Bengal was hit with economic depression, leading to the collapse of several agency firms, including Alexander & Co. Taking advantage of the crisis, Carr, Tagore & Co.[10] purchased Alexander & Co. in 1835 and Bell's Chinakuri mine in 1837, while Gilmore, Homfray & Co. took over Jessop's Chanchi and Nuchibad mines in 1835. A duopoly competition was thus set in Bengal's coal market, which was further accentuated after Carr–Tagore excavated several new mines in 1840. To restrain the cut-throat price competition that followed, these two companies unified as one firm, the Bengal Coal Company, in 1843, which survived through the third quarter of the twentieth century. With the abating of unfair competition, the industry was poised for steady development. Many new firms were established, escalating the level of output. The output evidently rose from 42,846 tons in 1842 to 235,589 tons in 1850, and further to 325,000 tons in 1858 (see Appendix 3.1). Figure 3.1 shows that this was the first phase of its steady development. In this respect, Oldham wrote in 1859:

> I paid a hurried visit to this field in 1851–52, soon after my first arrival in the country. At that time there were scarcely half a dozen pits at work in the whole field. Nothing struck me in greater surprize than the almost total neglect of so valuable and important a district. But the scene has totally changed now. Every known locality where coal is, or has been seen, has been worked into. Quarries are seen in full work, where formerly nothing but barrenness existed.
>
> (Oldham 1859: 24)

In another publication, he reported that there were more than 115 collieries/ pits in Ranigunj in 1866 operating under 55 firms, of which five had been set up between 1834 and 1844, 15 between 1845 and 1855 and 29 between 1856 and 1866 (Oldham 1867: xxxiv).

To understand the industry's growth pattern, in Appendix 3.1 I have constructed a time series of its production, employment and export, as well as the import of coal into Bengal. In view of data constraints, some estimations are involved in this series: (i) the compound rate method is employed to estimate missing figures; the rates are worked out on the basis of available data for their corresponding preceding and succeeding years; (ii) where only yearly average figures are available, they are converted into annual data on the basis of the compound rate of change; (iii) in the production series, estimates are made for 1851–7 on the basis of new mines excavated in respective years and their corresponding levels of output in 1858; in view of a general trend of rising output in new mines, an upward bias is suspected in them; and (iv) in the employment series, data are estimated for missing years using average labour productivity for preceding and succeeding years. I have not estimated employment figures for 1830–81 on the basis of the productivity norm as labour productivity does not remain constant in the long run. Indeed, in mining, there are great oscillations even when advanced technology is used (for the underlying reasons thereof, see Taylor 1961: 49–51; and Hirsch and Hausman 1983: 145–6). Nor do I estimate an export series for 1876–9, in view of its erratic movements around that period. Note also that miners' productivity is calculated only when both output and employment data are available. Appendix 3.1 is presented in an abridged form in Table 3.1, however. The production series and export–import series are plotted in Figures 3.1 and 3.2, respectively.

Figure 3.1 demonstrates that Bengal's coal output remained virtually stagnant between 1856 and 1866. The stagnation occurred in spite of the large-scale entry of firms in this period, as noted above. Perhaps the time lag between the setting up of a firm and the winning of coal explains this stagnation. Production picked up after 1866, however, but it was again aborted shortly afterwards, and plummeted in the early 1870s. From 1880 there was a high trajectory of growth, continuing through 1914. The annual rate of growth is worked out at 26 per cent for 1875–9 and 1880–4, and 16 per cent for 1890–4 and 1895–9. For 1875–9 and 1910–14 as a whole, the annual growth rate is approximately 82 per cent (see Table 3.1).

The industry's progress is also learnt from the growth statistics of firms and their investment level. The number of working mines in this province evidently grew from 45 in 1882 to 305 in 1910 (GOI 1910: 32), exhibiting a growth rate of 20.63 per cent per annum. They were heterogeneous in size, ranging from tiny pits under domestic enterprises to big mines, where joint-stock companies dominated. The growth of joint-stock companies and their nominal capital are shown in Table 3.2.

Table 3.2 shows that nominal capital in India's coal-mining companies increased from Rs. 28.95 million in 1905 to Rs. 97.10 million in 1916, and,

Table 3.1 Coal statistics for Bengal (per annum), 1840–1914

Period	*Production(tons)*	*Employment*	*Productivity (tons/worker) (col. 2/col. 3)*	*Import(tons)*	*Export(tons)*
1840–4	42,960	NA	–	NA	0
1845–9	69,022	NA	–	NA	0
1850–4	281,463	NA	–	50,986[2]	Ins.
1855–9	326,954	NA	–	59,074	Ins.
1860–4	336,227	NA	–	39,661	Ins.
1865–9	475,147	NA	–	53,033	Ins.
1870–4	385,733	NA	–	65,389	1,182
1875–9	465,712	NA	–	73,645	4,376[4]
1880–4	1,083,198	21,324[1]	50.80	90,804	106
1885–9	1,310,308	23,857	54.92	46,837	11,356
1890–4	1,846,443	28,013	65.91	10,761	50,632
1895–9	3,310,785	43,128	76.77	64[3]	350,202
1900–4	6,034,410	77,048	78.32	Ins.	743,172
1905–9	9,613,236	92,771	103.62	Ins.	742,171
1910–14	13,905,318	120,900	115.01	Ins.	832,685

Notes: 'Ins.' signifies an insignificant amount; 1: 3-year average (1882–84); 2: 2-year average (1853–54); 3: only for 1895; 4: only for 1875.

Source: Appendix 3.1.

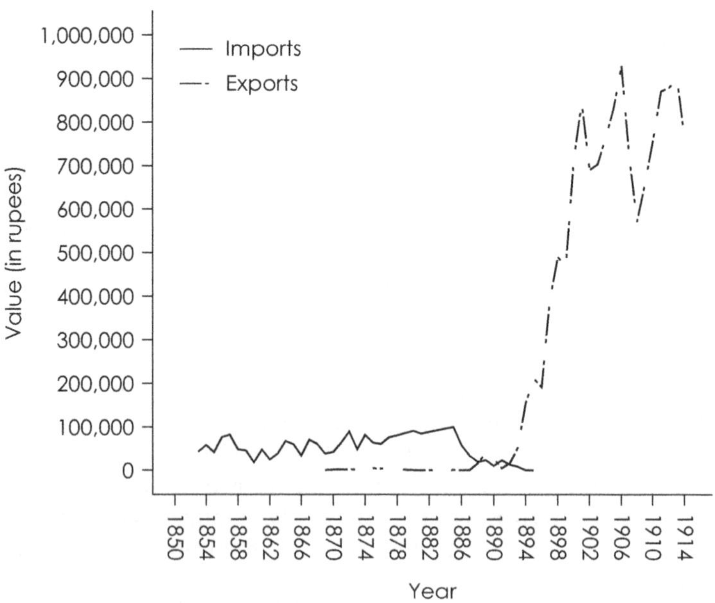

Figure 3.2 Bengal's imports and exports of coal, 1850–1914

Table 3.2 Growth of joint-stock companies in coal mining and their capital, 1905–16

Year	*Number of joint-stock companies*		*Nominal capital (million Rs.)*		*Capital/company (million Rs.)*
	Bengal	*India*	*Ranigunj*	*India*	*India*
1905	48	49	28.70	28.95	0.5908
1906	64	66	40.08	40.89	0.6195
1907	121	125	73.92	85.10	0.6808
1908	119	128	74.20	88.73	0.6932
1909	119	129	72.61	86.88	0.6735
1910	119	129	72.61	86.89	0.6736
1911	124	139	70.23	88.17	0.6343
1912	129	143	71.05	88.62	0.6197
1916	151	159	83.36	97.10	0.6107

Source: GOI, Director General of Commercial Intelligence, *Note on the Production of Coal in India*, various issues during 1906–17.

Table 3.3 Average dividend paid by seven large coal companies in Bengal (in %), 1901/5–1911/15

Company	*1901–5*	*1906–10*	*1911–15*
A	37 ½	96	91
B	17 ½	53	48
C	17	36 ½	10 ½
D	16 ½	25	16 ⅖
E	8	40 ½	36 ½
F	12	52	28 ½
G	8 ½	32	42 8/9

Source: GOI (1919: 9).

in Ranigunj alone, from Rs. 28.70 million to Rs. 83.36 million in the same period. These represent annual growth rates of 21.40 per cent and 17.31 per cent, respectively. The average size of those companies comes to Rs. 0.59–0.69 million for India as a whole, however, suggesting that they operated on large scales. This rapid flow of investment might be explained by the high dividends that mining companies used to provide. A source indicates that, for large companies in Bengal, the average dividend rate stood at 8 to 38 per cent from 1901 to 1905, which grew to 25 to 96 per cent from 1906 to 1910, then 10 to 91 per cent from 1911 to 1915 (Table 3.3). For most of these companies, dividend payments scaled up substantially in this period.

Although British capitalists occupied the lion's share in this industry, the presence of Bengali entrepreneurs was by no means insignificant. We have already noticed that Dwarkanath Tagore was one of the pioneer entrepreneurs who set up the Bengal Coal Company, the largest firm in the industry. The second largest concern, located at Searsole, was also owned by a Bengali entrepreneur, Gobin Pundit. In fact, out of 37 collieries in 1859, ten were held indigenously (Oldham 1859: 18–22). The number increased to 40 in 1897 (Sen 1966: 69). Two points should be noted in this context. First, indigenously held mines were tiny in size, yielding on the average (save for the Searsole mine) only 78,000 maunds in 1859, as against the industry's average output of 243,000 maunds per annum. An official document ('Letter from the Secretary to the Revenue and Agriculture Department, Government of India, dated 28 April 1886', in GOB 1886) corroborates this: 'The smaller coal mines are mostly worked by natives.... and are on a very petty scale and more like badly made tanks than anything else.' Second, indigenous enterprises in this coal belt ran largely on promoters' capital; joint-stock companies constituted only about 10 per cent of them (Sen 1966: 69; and Lokanathan 1935: 153f.).

Along with the spurt in mining, employment opportunities grew steadily. The number of workers was 21,324 per annum in the 1880–4 period, but 77,048 in 1900–04 and 120,900 in 1910–14 (see Table 3.1), exhibiting annual growth rates of 13.07 per cent and 5.69 per cent, respectively. According to the Labour Enquiry Commission (1896), 60.77 per cent of total workers worked underground (with 41 per cent working as hewers), and 39.23 per cent on the surface (GOB 1896: 9). The proportion of male, female and child workers was 73:23:4 underground, and 56:35:9 on the surface.

III

A pertinent question at this stage is: why was Bengal's coal mining so limited until the middle of the nineteenth century? The question is more relevant in view of our finding that it underwent explosive growth afterwards. Three factors are identified to this end: (i) inadequate mineralogical knowledge; (ii) inefficient transportation; and (iii) the shortage of labour. There was little contemporary knowledge about the mineralogy of Ranigunj, since its coalfield was surveyed only as late as 1845–6 (Gee 1940: 313), and, prior to this, the development of the industry was reliant on memory – that is, the memory of the 'old man' residing in the locality (Oldham 1867: 2). Indeed, the question of coal mining cropped up time and again from 1774. But it was referred to administrative officials, who were not specialists on the subject. On one occasion a Burdwan district official confessed:

> In making this tender of my service, I cannot avoid remarking, that my knowledge as a mineralogist is very confined, and that it appears a business requiring a person well versed in the nature of coal, of which it would be uncandid not to declare my ignorance.
>
> (Letter of T. Marriott, dated 6 April 1809, in Heatly 1842: 829)

The information he ultimately furnished was based on the knowledge of 'an aged Bramin [an upper caste Hindu]' (ibid.: 828).

With the establishment of the Geological Survey of India in 1851, many experiments were carried out, and it went a long way to disseminate various data and information about the coalfield. There was a great debate among contemporary mineralogists about the marketability of Bengal coal vis-à-vis the English. Oldham undertook a chemical test for 55 Bengal specimens at the International Exhibition in London (1862), and found 52.2 per cent fixed carbon, 31.9 per cent volatile matter and 15.5 per cent ash, on average (Oldham 1867:19). In contrast, similar tests for English coal, as available in Calcutta, revealed the respective matters at 68.1 per cent, 29.2 per cent and 2.7 per cent. Since the effective power of coal varies directly with the availability of fixed carbon, Bengal coal should be about 30 per cent less efficient than its counterpart. Moreover, a higher ash content left substantial deposits of slag after burning, so that the furnace bars were blocked, and their ventilation was obstructed. These also involved higher costs, as (i) additional firemen and coal trimmers were to be deployed to handle a greater volume of coal, and (ii) a larger volume of useless matters (about 12.8 per cent more of ash) had to be carried. To Oldham, therefore, Bengal coal had little prospect beyond the local market (ibid.: 23).

David Smith, government coal and iron viewer, and Theodore Hughes of the GSI would contradict this conclusion. While acknowledging Oldham's findings of assays, they underline the market potential of Bengal coal on the basis of two arguments: (i) that the technical snags arising from the higher ash content could be addressed by suitably designing the blast furnace; indeed, those complications were involved in conventional British-made appliances, which were meant for the use of English coal; and (ii) that the lower efficiency of Bengal coal was more than compensated for by its low pit-bank price, as we will shortly discuss. Smith thus remarks, 'After mature consideration, I am led to the conclusion, which I feel I can state with much confidence, that this coal would be found very manageable in the blast furnace under considerations I have already stated…' (Smith 1856: ii). In addition, Hughes emphasises:

> The quality of Indian coal is usually denoted by the adjective bad, but I believe this word has been too freely used… [I]t is justifiable to entertain the idea that if our fields had been more extensively opened out and worked to a great depth, coal would have been met with of a quality sufficiently good to make us cautious in regard to the indiscriminate use of the word bad.
>
> (Hughes 1873: 16)

Repeated explorations of these fields by the GSI ultimately removed the misunderstandings.

For the existing mines, however, the conveyance of coal posed a serious threat. Before the advent of railways, the Ranigunj coalfield had irregular transport links with Calcutta, where coal was consumed in bulk. It was served only by waterways on the Damodar, a mountain torrent that was navigable only for ten weeks a year during the rainy season. Once the season was over, the market supply became perfectly inelastic. Thus, for instance, the Coal Committee noted in 1836, 'This difficulty actually occurred in the past season and great disappointment was accordingly experienced in the upper stations of the Ganges in particular, which did not receive the supplies for their depots till long after they were required' ('Report of a Committee for the Investigation of Coal and Mineral Resources of India, General Proceedings, Resolutions, 28 December 1836', in P.P. 1841: 89). Boats were also frequently lost in transit, rendering transhipment an expensive task. While deliberating on these issues, the Coal Committee concluded that, 'so long, therefore, as the Damooda is the only means of delivery, the degree of enterprise directed towards the Burdwan mines must be comparatively limited' (ibid.: 155).

The industry was also saddled with labour problems. Most of the miners hailed from a local tribe, the Bauris, who never adopted industrial disciplines. Many contemporaries alleged that they were, by profession, cultivators first and miners thereafter, and, in spirit, least ambitious and enterprising. In a good monsoon season the majority of them were exclusively involved in agriculture, and turned to mines only when there were floods or drought. A field survey by the Geological Survey of India recorded: 'During the two seasons in which the survey was curried on, viz. 1858–59 and 1859–60, the partial failure of the crops in the Ranigunj or adjoining districts, and the high price of food, compelled a much larger number of men than usual to have recourse to the mines for subsistence' (Blanford 1865: 171–2). The common complaint was that 'they worked when they liked, retired when they liked, were always ready with an excuse to stop work, and refused to work until some imaginary grievances were rectified' (P.P. 1899: 85). But these were the traits of labour in early mining for every society, including the British.[11] A contemporary statesman, W. R. Dunstan, observes:

> In some respects, the Bauri Collier's characteristics are amusing, like those of his western prototype. He is very fond of getting drunk, especially at the week ends, and very disinclined to go to work on Mondays. … [In the working days, taking his daily wage, he] goes cheerfully home, and remains up half the night drinking and singing with his companies (he is very social in his habits), incomprehensively happy with his tuneless tom-tom.
>
> ('Report on the Coal Supply of India', in P.P. 1899: 85)

A high incidence of absenteeism was another allegation against the miners. Such incidents also took place in late nineteenth-century Britain,[12] which was reflected in an inverse relationship between the wage rate and the supply of labour (Hirsch and Hausman 1983: 147).

These apart, what concerned the industry was the shortage of labour that loomed large during the 1840s and the 1850s, when the number of mines mushroomed. Workers were drawn exclusively from the vicinities of the mines, where population density was low. Moreover, inadequate transport facilities eliminated the scope of immigration in those places. The problem was further compounded by a limited number of working days among the local populace – only four days a week (P.P. 1899: 83) – whereby the effective supply of labour was further reduced.

These barriers to growth disappeared, however, with the onset of the railway age. The East Indian Railway started its service between Ranigunj and Calcutta in 1855, and was extended in every direction in subsequent years. The Jamuna Bridge was opened up in 1865, connecting the field initially with Allahabad, and then with Cawnpore, Agra, Ghaziabad, Delhi, Amritsar and Lahore in northern and north-western provinces. A direct connection was laid with western India in 1869 when the East Indian Railway was adjunct with the Great Indian Peninsula Railway. An additional link was obtained when the Bengal Nagpur Railway was formed incorporating the Nagpur Chhattisgarh Railway in 1886–7. In the south, the East Indian Railway provided Ranigunj links jointly with the Great Indian Peninsula Railway and the Madras Railway (for details, see 'History of Railways', in P.P. 1902). Thus, by the 1880s, Ranigunj's rail network incorporated major coal markets in the country.

Railways contributed to coal mining in two ways: (i) as a bulk consumer, it directly augmented its demand; and (ii) it did so indirectly by providing easy access to distant markets. The industry's early growth in the 1840s and the 1850s was largely due to railway constructions, especially those of the East Indian Railway, when inferior coals, as available from the mines along the river Ajoy, were used. By the time the construction had been completed, and such demands subsided in 1860, the company started using indigenous coal for generating steam. In that year it took about 12.50 per cent of local output, which steadily rose to 46.88 per cent in 1866 (Oldham 1867: 27–8). This rising share certainly suggests that, in the absence of adequate support from industrial consumers, the railways directly promoted coal mining in Bengal.[13]

Once the East Indian Railway was consuming local coal profitably, other railway companies followed suit. This included Eastern Bengal Railway (consuming 28,932 tons in 1886–7), Oudh and Rohilkhand Railway (40,661 tons), Tirhoot Railway (7,191 tons), Cawnpore–Achnera Railway (3,631 tons), Dacca Railway (1,712 tons) and Nalhati Railway (360 tons), all of which exclusively used Bengal coal by the mid-1880s (P.P. 1887b: 42). Some companies – such as the Rajputana–Malwa Railway, North Western Railway and North Bengal Railway – used both domestic and imported coals. The practice became increasingly popular, and by the early twentieth century it was a rule of business among railway companies. In 1877 domestic coal accounted for 71.87 per cent of total coal consumption by railways, which went up to 97.15 per cent in 1900 and 99.29 per cent in 1904 (see Table 3.4). 'In other words,' an official publication of 1905 tells us, 'twenty years ago foreign coal was a serious item in the fuel supplies of the railways: it is now imported in mere samples' (Holland 1905: 21).

Table 3.4 Coal consumption by Indian railway companies (in tons), 1884–1904

Year	*Imported coal*	*Indian coal*	*Total*
1884	197,342 (17.40)	936,804 (82.60)	1,134,146 (100)
1889	224,776 (27.86)	582,147 (72.14)	806,923 (100)
1894	127,520 (10.75)	1,059,159 (89.25)	1,186,679 (100)
1899	82,446 (5.03)	1,557,000 (94.97)	1,639,446 (100)
1900	54,339 (2.85)	1,855,610 (97.15)	1,909,949 (100)
1901	13,248 (0.67)	1,956,601 (99.33)	1,969,849 (100)
1902	21,469 (1.02)	2,091,992 (98.98)	2,113,461 (100)
1903	17,696 (0.80)	2,203,889 (99.20)	2,221,585 (100)
1904	17,432 (0.71)	2,447,341 (99.29)	2,464,773 (100)

Note: The terms in parentheses represent the percentage of the total.

Sources: 1884: P.P. (1887b: 42); 1889: P.P. (1891: 124); 1894: P.P. (1895a: 174); 1899–1903: Holland (1906: 20); 1904: Holland and Fermor (1910: 34).

As a carrier of Bengal coal to distant markets, however, railways initially played a conservative role. The collieries were not provided with the rolling stock they needed. 'Neither engines nor trucks can be given for this coal trade in sufficient quantity, and the consequent uncertainty of obtaining carriage for coal, prevents proprietors from sending it to the stations' (Oldham 1859: 24). In addition, the railway sidings were few and far away from all mines, save for a few big ones, as their construction costs were debited to collieries' accounts. Big companies such as Bengal Coal could afford such sidings while others sought to avail themselves of them. Smaller collieries brought their output by road to the sidings of big mines, but were always treated as rivals.

> [E]ven the collieries in the immediate vicinity of the terminus [located at the premises of the Bengal Coal Company] have a difficulty in obtaining a means of access to it. How much greater, therefore, must be this difficulty for those whose locality is further removed.
>
> (ibid.)

The most critical issue, however, was the question of freight. The contemporary coal circle repeatedly complained about high railway freight charges, which, they believed, checked traffic, restricted their trade and thus discouraged the extension of mining in Bengal. Echoing such allegations, Juland Danvers, government director of railways, observed in the mid-1870s, 'This has been too much the case hitherto; and therefore railways have not yet conferred upon the country the full benefits, nor yielded the profits, which they might have done' (P.P. 1876b: 11). Because of the high railway freight costs, water transportation largely mopped up the coal traffic, especially during the rainy season. In 1858, for example, railways carried out only 122,824 tons of coal, constituting 40 per cent of total coal traffic (Oldham 1859: 24).

When these initial shortcomings, including the question of freight, were addressed, railways became a popular mode in the mining belt. Prima facie, it appears that water transport was the cheapest mode, conveying coal at Rs. 2.73 a ton in the Ranigunj–Calcutta sector, as against Rs. 4.75 a ton by rail. But it involved many incidental costs – for storage (on riversides[14]), wastage and the loss of boats – amounting to as much as Rs. 2.73 per ton ('Report of a Committee for the Investigation of the Coal and Mineral Resources of India', in P.P. 1841: 137). Hence, actual costs on the waterways come to Rs. 5.46 a ton – that is, Rs. 0.71 higher than the railway freight. Moreover, the railways provided a perennial service, which certainly promoted market confidence in the supply chain.

Rail transportation also eased the scarcity of labour by stimulating immigration (for migration, see Das Gupta 1985; Simmons 1976a; and Seth 1940). Migratory workers consisted mainly of the Santhals, an aboriginal tribe, hailing from Chota Nagpur, and the Santhal Parganas of Bihar. They were strongly built, courageous and hard-working, so highly suited for mining. Thanks to their emotional attachment to landholdings, they could be easily tempted into mining by a piece of leasehold land. As they migrated with their families, and claimed lower wages for other family members – females and children – the industry also thereby gained. In addition, there were Muslim immigrations from the Manbhum district of Bihar, as also from within the province – who worked in masonry, boring and coal cutting – as well as up-country workers, the Beldars, working in quarries. These apart, there were the Bhuiyas, Kurmis, Dosadhs, Goalahs, Kols and Gouds, who came and settled around collieries looking for miscellaneous jobs. These inward migrations enhanced the supply of labour so much that, for a couple of years to come, the industry never complained of the paucity of labour. Indeed, scarcity did not crop up again until the 1890s, and fresh excavations at Jheria, but further immigration took care of it (Foley 1906: 34).

This analysis thus suggests that the potential for coal mining that had remained dormant in Bengal for seven decades was unleashed in the wake of two government policies that had been adopted under the Company's rule but were not vigorously pursued until the rule of the British Crown from 1858 onwards. One was the prospecting of coal on behalf of a government organisation, the GSI. The knowledge thus gathered gave confidence to investors on the viability of coal mining in Bengal, and helped them shape their business strategies. An equally important policy decision was the construction of railways in India. Although, in the context of alternative investments between railways and irrigation, this policy was severely criticised by contemporary Indian statesmen, including Gopal Krishna Gokhale (Gadgil 1929: 144), my analysis emphasises that, but for the railways, coal mining would have been delayed further, and India would have missed out on a cheap source of vital energy for economic development.[15]

IV

Along with the industry's steady growth, its technology also advanced (for technological aspects, see Ball 1881: 71–2; Seth 1940: 3–5, 9; Blanford 1865: 163–71; and Jha 1982). Initially, coal was largely won through open workings and quarries, as the seams lay near the surface, and no more than picks and shovels were used, relying entirely on muscle power. But, as the surface seams were exhausted, deep mining became necessary, involving scientific methods. In contemporary mining, two methods were broadly followed: the longwall method and the bord and pillar method. The preparatory works, called the development of mining, were the same in both cases. To start with, two shafts (one downcast [A] and one upcast [B]) were sunk (Figure 3.3), and connected to each other for the sake of ventilation of air in the mine (Greenwell 1889: 192–3). Then there commenced the driving of drifts 'Ab', 'Ac', 'Bg' and 'Bi' to ensure there was a pillar effect around the shafts, so that they would not collapse. Once these were completed, coal was won out of the face as follows: from the points b and c, the drifts 'be' and 'cf' were driven in a water-level direction, and they were accompanied by consort drifts 'gh' and 'ik' at a distance of about 40 yards. This ensured the necessary circulation of air within the mine. These drifts continued for about 150 yards in each direction. Similar drifts, such as 'lm' and 'no', were also sunk to win coal out of a face. These completed the preparatory works.

In the longwall method, the working of the mine took place along the wall faces, say 'lm' and 'no', which were divided into suitable 'stints'. The miners were distributed along the face of the work to win the coal at a same pace. In

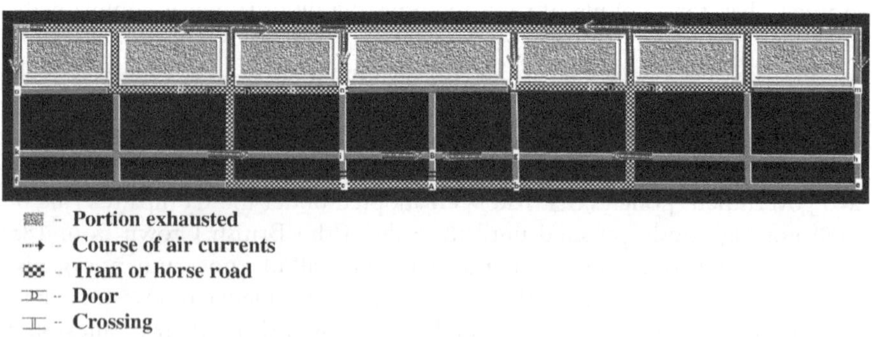

Figure 3.3 The longwall method
Source: Sketch by the author from Greenwell 1889: plate 56, fig. 1.

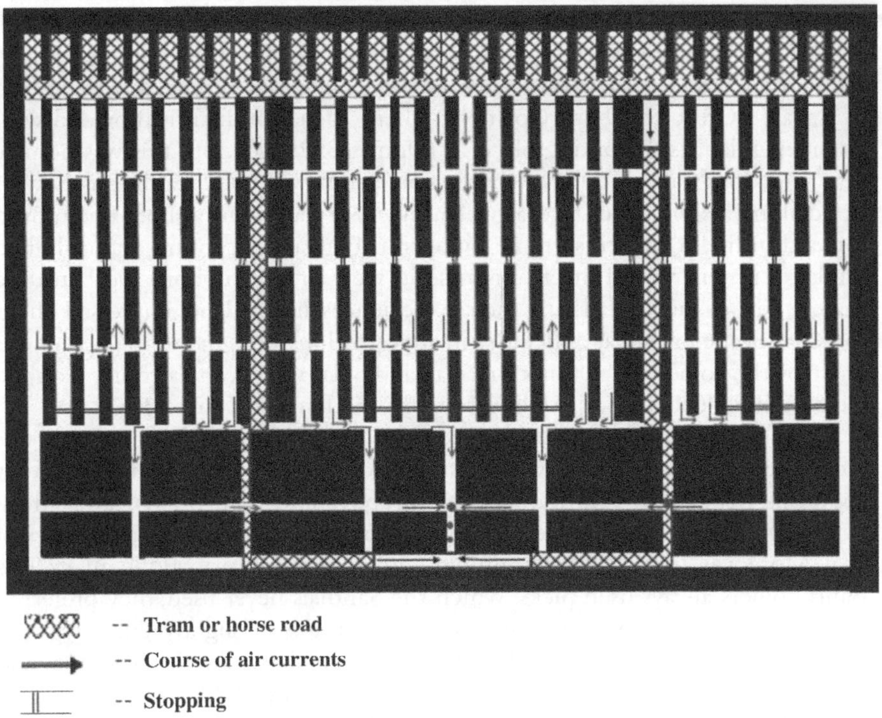

Figure 3.4 The bord and pillar method
Source: Sketch by the author from Greenwell 1889: plate 56, fig. 3.

the bord and pillar method, however, an entire wall was not worked together (Figure 3.4). Instead, bords were made by excavating 4–5 yards in width at a distance of 2 yards or more from each other, and the rubbish was piled up by the side of the bord as it advanced. When these bords were driven up to a limit, they were further worked laterally, leaving 'walls' between them. Those walls acted as pillars, which were worked away afterwards.

Bengal universally followed the pillar-and-post method of deep mining. Although it was a variant of the bord and pillar system, it contained certain principles of the longwall method, which became popular in the South Wales mines from the early nineteenth century. Once one bord was completed, the pillars that held the roof up were removed. This was in contrast to the bord and pillar system, in which the 'broken' workings began only after all bords were completed (Daunton 1981: 580–4). The longwall method certainly involved less wastage, but it was suitable where coalfields were liable to 'squeeze', and coals were friable. But, in Bengal, the seams were hard, so that any road (bord) through them stood intact. Holland (1905: 44) thus notes, 'Owing to the thickness of most of the Indian seams, it is not easy to devise any more suitable plan of working.' In addition to this geological underpinning, the local custom among miners was also in favour of the pillar and post system. Bengal miners always enjoyed a good amount of freedom ('or rather licence': Ball 1881: 71) in the stall, working with other family members. Without any supervision, they decided their own pace of work. This was similar to the custom in Britain's Great Northern Coalfield, where 'each workman is provided with an independant [*sic*] working place…' (Dunn 1852: 135). But this was not the case with longwall workings, where supervision was both feasible, as hewers stood along a continuous face, as well as necessary, as the face should be moved forward in line. The British mine owners in Bengal were aware that a shift to the latter system would meet resistance in view of the stubborn local attitude against any change.[16] Perhaps their experiences in England impressed them so: 'One of the principal difficulties in adopting longwork lies in the objections made by the colliers: they think that stall and pillar is safer, and a collier likes the seeming independence of a stall to himself' (Bedlington 1861: 130).

But Bengal's method of hewing seemed imperfect. In England the coal was 'holed below' – that is, cut away at the bottom, and then wedged down from above; in Bengal, though, it was cut out above and then broken away from below by crowbars and wedges, involving greater wastage and irregular sizes of coal. Moreover, until 1880 the mining equipment was very rudimentary. The Bauri colliers always used picks, which the Santhals never used; they preferred crowbars. The picks were single-headed, consisting of slightly curved pieces of iron tipped with steel, badly balanced. The crowbars, like the hammers and wedges, were also made of poor materials, mostly forged old iron.

Things began to change from about 1880, when trained managers were recruited from England with long experience in British mining. There were four main operations in coal mining: (i) the hewing of coal; (ii) bringing it to roadways; (iii) carrying the coal to the shaft bottom; and (iv) raising it to the pit bank. Following technological advances in British collieries, gunpowder was first used in Bengal in 1879, which subsequently spread across the industry. It substantially increased the productivity in hewing. Artificial ventilation was introduced through ventilating furnaces. Better technology was also introduced in the field of carrying coal to the shaft bottom, and raising it to the pit bank – a field of technological advancement that explained Britain's major productivity gains during the third quarter of the nineteenth century (Taylor 1961: 57). Tubs were provided to carry coal from the coalface to roads; underground tramlines were laid up to the pit bottom; and cages were fitted to raise coal to the pit bank. The pulley was installed with steam pumps, winding engines and Lancashire broilers. Small locomotives were also deployed for the conveyance of coal to railway sidings. All these innovations undoubtedly led to productivity gains. In addition, old implements were replaced; for example, single-headed iron picks by double-headed steel picks, and iron wedges and hammers by steel ones. Pump sets were used to replace expensive hand bailing, and tin lamps took the place of earthen lamps and primitive torches. Bengal collieries thus got a new technological makeover in the last quarter of the nineteenth century.

There is no doubt that cheap labour underpinned the development of coal mining in Bengal. But what concerned the contemporary collieries was the low productivity of miners in Bengal, compared to those in other coal-producing countries. In 1902, for example, it was only 75 ton per worker in Bengal, as against 464 in South Wales, 280 in the United Kingdom overall and 285 for the British Empire as a whole (excluding India) (Holland 1905: 40). British productivity thus exceeded that of Bengal by 3.73 times. This productivity difference was more striking in hewing. For hewers, the productivity was 137 tons per annum in Bengal (calculated on the basis of 22,098 hewers in 1896: GOB 1896: 8–9), but 589 tons in Britain,[17] suggesting a 4.30 times productivity difference. For underground workers as a whole, the productivity was 93 tons per annum in Bengal (calculated on the basis of 32,334 underground workers: GOB 1896: 8–9) and 291 tons in Britain (Taylor 1961: 69), which is a 3.13 times difference. Britain achieved a higher productivity at the face, however, by replacing the pillar and stall by the longwall method after 1850 (which avoided the 25–60 per cent wastage of available coal in pillars: Holland 1905: 44), and also by introducing shot firing in the place of gunpowder (Taylor 1961: 57). Two points should be noted in this context, however. First, it is seen in Appendix 3.1 that as many as 24,415 new workers were recruited in Bengal mines between 1899 and 1902, and 38,147 between 1905 and 1908; in other words, in three years, new recruits were one in slightly above three (3.38) of the total workforce in the former period, and one in less than three (2.94) in the latter. Such a large incidence of raw recruits must have reduced the average labour productivity in an industry in which hands-on experience was crucial. Let me cite in this context that, in British coal mining, the number of new recruits was 79,000 from 1899 to 1901 – that is, one in six of the total workforce – which significantly curtailed Britain's labour productivity (ibid.: 54). As they gradually became experienced, however, there should have been a rising trend. Second, there was indeed a rising trend in miners' productivity in Bengal. Appendix 3.1 shows that it grew steadily from 47.87 tons per miner in 1886 to 87.56 tons in 1896, 103.97 tons in 1906 and further to 120.61 tons in 1913. A source confirms this rising trend for the beginning of the twentieth century; according to it, productivity increased from 68 tons in 1899 to 70 tons in 1901, and further to 84 tons in 1904 (Holland 1905: 40).

What is more striking in the context of the industry's competitiveness was that, notwithstanding the lower productivity, the wage component in the average cost was comparatively low in Bengal. In the first half of the twentieth century the share of wage in the pit bank value was only 39 per cent in Bengal, as against 63 per cent in Britain, 53 per cent in the Netherland and 48 per cent in France. The wage cost per ton was also lowest in Bengal (see Table 3.5).

This comparative advantage was explained by two factors. First, hewers' wages were paid in Bengal in terms of bucket-loads (Foley 1906: 37) carrying about six maunds (i.e., about 222 kg), so that their low productivity could not inflate the cost of production. Second, the wage rate per bucket was very low in this province, and it remained fairly stable through to 1894. On the

Table 3.5 Comparative labour costs of coal extraction in Bengal vis-à-vis that in other countries, early 1930s

Country	*Wage cost(Rs. per ton)*	*Share of wage in pit-mouth value (%)*
Britain	5.63	63.3
Germany	5.14	46.7
Netherland	4.51	53.4
Belgium	2.75	48.1
Poland	2.66	46.2
France	2.47	48.3
Bengal	1.13	39.0

Source: All-India Mineworkers' Federation, Memorandum to the Indian Coalfields Committee, in Coal Mining Committee (1937: 321).

assumptions of 23 working days in a month and the winning of three buckets of coal per hewer per day, their monthly wage rate is estimated at Rs. 5.52 in 1859 (Blanford 1865: 172), Rs. 7.00 in 1882, Rs. 5.62 in 1885, Rs. 7.38 in 1890, Rs. 8.33 in 1892 and Rs. 6.00 in 1894 (GOB 1896: 8). It rose steeply only after the opening of the Jheria coalfield in 1895. It reached Rs. 16.56 in 1895 (Seth 1940: 93), Rs. 15.18 in 1896 (Foley 1906: 43), Rs. 10.35 in 1900 (Seth 1940: 93) and Rs. 18.69 in 1906 (Foley 1906: 31).

For contextual interest, let me discuss here in a nutshell the welfare aspect of employment in this industry. Though certainly low by international standards, the colliery wage rates in Bengal must have been higher than those prevailing in Bihar and the United Provinces; otherwise, large-scale immigration would not have taken place. Indeed, those regions provided Rs. 3 to 5 per month for agricultural labour in the 1880–4 period (GOB 1896: 7), as against an opportunity of earning Rs. 6 to 8 per month in mines. Contemporary writers, therefore, remarked that '[t]he miner's pay is high' (Blanford 1865: 172). A comparatively higher wage for mining labourers can also be deduced from the temporary nature of immigration in this coalfield.

> The best class of workers worked for about three years... [T]heir object being to buy so many bighas of land they wanted worth a few hundred rupees. Once they had made this sum they would suddenly disappear, when they thought they had settled for good.
>
> (Foley 1906: 44)

Indeed, compared to the prevailing wages for unskilled labour in Calcutta, and even for agricultural labour in the Burdwan district, the wages for mining were lower (GOB 1896: 7). But a miner earned higher income in mines working with other family members. Along with his wife and two children, he could earn more than Rs. 9 a month in 1860 (Seth 1940: 92–3), which was 'double the amount for an ordinary peasant or day-labourers' (Hunter 1876: 115) even in 1874.

The comparative cost advantages that low labour costs generated were counterbalanced, however, by high conveyance costs and a limited span of transportation in a year. Prior to the age of railways, the price of domestic coal in Calcutta was around Rs. 5.73 per ton, consisting of Rs. 3 as the pithead price and Rs. 2.73 as carrying costs. Imported coals, on the other hand, were sold on average at Rs. 13.75 per ton. Since transportation by boat involved an incidental cost of Rs. 2.73 a ton, as noted above, the price comes to Rs. 8.46, which, given a 30 per cent inefficiency of Bengal coal vis-à-vis the English, gives the former's efficiency-adjusted price at Rs. 11 a ton. Thus, the effective price of Bengal coal was lower only by Rs. 2.75 a ton than that of English coal. Now, if coal was purchased in the rainy season for consumption throughout the year, the cost of storage would have been much higher than this. Hence, Bengal coal was competitive in Calcutta only around the rainy season, while, in the rest of the year, English coal dominated.

From 1855 onwards, however, the price of imported coal climbed. From Rs. 15.35 per ton in 1854, it rose to Rs. 15.79 in 1855, Rs. 18.35 in 1858 and Rs. 20.77 in 1860.[18] The average price was Rs. 18.11 a ton from 1858 to 1860. In contrast, the tonnage price of domestic coal was Rs. 7. 75 (at a pithead price of Rs. 3 and a railway freight cost of Rs. 4.75), which gives it an efficiency-adjusted price of Rs. 10.08 throughout the year. By implication, then, it got a price advantage of Rs. 8.03 per ton over English coal throughout the year. The opening of the Suez Canal in 1869 substantially reduced the conveyance costs of British coal, however, and thus promoted its market edge. This was why, as I have already noted, Bengal's coal production plummeted in the early 1870s. Subsequently, though, the effect was counterbalanced by a steep rise in the domestic price of English coal, enabling Bengal mining to revive again. It was reinforced in the mid-1870s when the East Indian Railway reduced freight to win over competition from water transport (P.P. 1876b: 12 n).

Although Ranigunj coal thus got a stronghold in Bengal, as well as in North India (P.P. 1872: 213), by the 1880s, it was unable to venture as successfully into Bombay. Imported coals dominated among its bulk consumers, railways and cotton mills. Twin factors might have acted behind this failure. One was higher railway freights in this sector, compared to what was charged for coal traffic between London and Bombay. The Great Indian Peninsula Railway purchased coal in England at about 8s. 1d in 1879, which, along with a freight cost of £1 4s. 10d, implies its landed price in Bombay at £1 12s. 11d (P.P. 1880: 12), or about Rs. 16, per ton. This was similar to the experiences of the Bombay Railways, Baroda Railways and Central Indian Railways. *Per contra*, the East Indian Railway charged Rs. 25 a ton in the Ranigunj–Bombay sector (GOB 1896: 3), which was only 1,147 miles in distance. Hence, at a pithead price of Rs. 3 a ton, the Ranigunj coal could not be sold at less than Rs. 28 per ton – that is, Rs. 12 a ton higher than the price of the English coal. A source tells us, however, that the railway freight charge for the Singareni coal was one-sixteenth pie per maund per mile (ibid.), which gives a freight cost of Rs. 7.70

per ton in the Ranigunj–Bombay sector. At this rate, the price of Ranigunj coal comes to Rs. 10.70 a ton for Bombay, which was surely very competitive. While pointing to this freight discrimination, the Labour Enquiry Commission (1896) notes:

> At present, Bengal coal is shut out of the [Bombay] market...because... Singareni coal has...special concessions, not only against English, but against Bengal coal. We are not aware why these special concessions have been granted, but may undoubtedly fall hard on Bengal coal.
>
> (ibid.)

The other factor was a large degree of ignorance on the part of consumers. Bombay coal users seemed indifferent to Bengal because of the poor quality of its initial consignments in the early 1880s. They were unaware of the superior-grade coal that many collieries in Bengal delivered. They were also unaware of the fact that the furnaces they had been working with using English coal must involve technical complexities if Bengal coal was used. They therefore 'hastily conclude[d] it a failure' (ibid.: 4). This ignorance subsequently dissipated as the usage of Bengal coal spread.

Three favourable events from the mid-1880s onwards established the comparative advantages of Ranigunj coal at Bombay. First, in 1886–7, the Bengal Nagpur Railway provided a 120-mile shorter network between Ranigunj and Bombay, reducing freight costs by Rs. 5 a ton. It was also the first Bombay-based company that consumed indigenous coal in 1889–90. Second, the cost price of English coal rose steeply upwards in Bombay during the late 1880s. As against Rs. 16.86 a ton in 1884–5 and Rs. 16.25 in 1885–6, it became Rs. 17.06 in 1886–7, Rs. 19.43 in 1887–8 and Rs. 22.74 in 1888–9 (P.P. 1890a: 30–1). Finally, there was a sharp reduction in railway freights in 1894–5, from 0.62d per ton-mile (or Rs. 22.80 a ton between Ranigunj and Bombay) in 1879 to 0.30d per ton-mile (Ball 1881: 122) (or Rs. 11.24 per ton for the route) in 1894–5. These ensured the competitiveness of the domestic industry at Bombay, as it could sell there at Rs. 14.74 per ton (for a pithead price of Rs. 3.50), suggesting an efficiency-adjusted price of Rs. 19.16. The cost of conveyance was lower still if a modal mix of railways and waterways was attempted. In this case, the cost was Rs. 8.31 to 11.56 a ton (Ball and Simpson 1913: 121–3[19]), which attracted many a shipper. In 1893, for example, around 46,000 tons of coal was shipped using this modal mix (P.P. 1895a: 174).

V

Once the comparative advantages were in favour of the Bengal coal industry, it could replace imported coals from the domestic market, which had been steadily expanding from about the middle of the nineteenth century in the wake of booming manufacturing activities and public works. Among the industries that sprang up in this period, there were jute mills and presses, iron and steel manufacture, engineering, paper manufacturing, flour mills, rice mills, sugar mills and chemical manufacturing, which extensively consumed coal (for the growth of factories in Bengal, see GOI 1930: 662–4). In addition, there was rapid growth of tea plantations, where charcoal was initially used for processing, but was later substituted by pit coal. Notwithstanding an impressive growth in industries, however, the railways retained their market prominence by the strength of their service network (running over 29,307 miles in 1913–14: Gadgil 1929: 142). The Indian Industrial Commission (1916–18) informs us that, in 1916, railways consumed 33.6 per cent of domestic output, as against 16.7 per cent for bunkers, 5.6 per cent for jute mills, 5.5 per cent for cotton mills, 5.1 per cent for iron and brass foundries and engineering workshops, and 3.6 per cent for inland steamers (GOI 1918: 18).

Bengal's growing coal market had initially survived on large-scale importation. Appendix 3.1 shows that its imports were 45,877 tons in 1859, which rose to 89,775 tons in 1872 and further to 100,000 tons in 1885. After that, however, as Figure 3.2 demonstrates, imports nosedived, and became grossly insignificant by 1895. For India as a whole, though, imports continued even thereafter, as Bengal coal remained less competitive in west India, especially Bombay. In Table 3.6, India's imports are seen growing annually at 39.32 per cent from 1853–7 to 1883–7. But they turned downwards thereafter, and declined at 3.39 per cent per annum from 1883–7 to 1903–07.

These shortfalls in Bombay were met from Bengal. It supplied 440,806 tons in 1898 and 881,806 tons in 1903 (Holland and Fermor 1910: 26), and thus became a dominant seller there. Bengal coal became predominant in south India as well, mainly in Madras, where its intake was 193,102 tons in 1898 (ibid.: 26), rising up to 221,035 tons in 1904 (ibid.: 40). From Madras it catered

Table 3.6 Annual imports of coal into India (in tons), 1853/7–1903/7

Period	*Quantity*
1853–7	60,549
1858–62[1]	110,452
1863–7	203,057
1868–72	346,328
1873–7	398,101
1878–82	656,334
1883–7	774,842
1888–92	768,593
1893–7	634,894
1898–1902	315,620
1903–7	250,195

Note: 1: 1861 excluded.

Sources: 1853–78: Hughes (1879: 84); 1879 & 1880: P.P. (1886a: 225); 1881–1904: Ball and Simpson (1913: 116–17); 1905–7: Holland and Fermor (1910: 34).

to other south Indian ports, such as Mandapam, Marmagoa, Negapatam and Pondicherry. Karachi (now in Pakistan) was also supplied, with 245,918 tons in 1904. I here emphasise that India's coal imports came mainly from Britain: 88.84 per cent in 1897–8, as against just 5.93 per cent from Australia and 5.14 per cent from Japan (ibid.: 23). Therefore, in this realignment of the Indian coal market, British interests suffered.

Bengal coal could also successfully venture into the global market. In the early 1870s, when it began, the push was irregular and insignificant, as the export market was wrongly targeted. Initial consignments that were sent to Britain could not compete with its domestic coal on account of their inferior quality and higher cost, insurance and freight (CIF) prices. These ventures were, therefore, aborted. Only from the mid-1880s did regular exports take hold. Two factors underpinned this success. One of them was certainly its comparative cost advantages around 1900. At Ranigunj, production cost per ton was only 3s. 8d (i.e., Rs. 2.76) in 1902, but as high as 8s. 2¾d in the United Kingdom, 8s. 10¼d in Germany, 5s. 8¼d in the United States, 7s. 9d in Australia, 10s. in New Zealand and 9s. 3d in Canada (ibid.: 18). The other was the introduction of a rebate of railway freights towards coal exports. In the early 1890s a rebate of 10 per cent was provided to this end, which was further enhanced to 20 per cent in 1902. As a consequence, exportable coals became cheaper by Rs. 2 a ton. A contemporary estimate is that these freight rebates increased exports by about 14 per cent in 1903 (Ball and Simpson 1913: 122). Appendix 3.1 shows that Bengal exports grew very rapidly from 1888. From 15,796 tons in 1888, they increased to 711,874 tons in 1900, undergoing an annual growth rate of 367.22 per cent. Exports stood at 928,400 tons in 1906. The import–export graphs in Figure 3.2 suggest, however, that Bengal became a net exporter of coal before the mid-1890s. Country-wise exports of Bengal coal are shown in Table 3.7.

Three broad conclusions follow from Table 3.7. One, Bengal exported coal mainly to Asian countries, such as Ceylon, Burma, the Straits Settlements, Sumatra and Aden, and, to a lesser extent, to some African countries, such as Mauritius and British East Africa. Of these countries, Ceylon in South Asia and Burma and the Straits Settlements in South-east Asia constituted the major outlets. These three countries were provided with 257,251 tons, 264,344 tons and 142,256 tons, respectively, in 1903. Two, Aden in South-west Asia was also coming up in a significant way in the early twentieth century. Three, from 1897 to 1904, the market of Sumatra in South-east Asia appeared steady but not very significant, whereas the outlets in Mauritius and British East Africa were irregular as well as insignificant.

In Burma, Bengal coal met competition mainly from Britain, which had long been dominant there. But, in the face of competition from Bengal, British exports to Burma fell from 78,000 tons in 1888–9 to 47,800 tons in 1889–90 (P.P. 1891: 149). Bengal gained thereby, strengthening its exports from only 70 tons in 1887–8 to 53,000 tons in 1889–90. They rose further to 287,397 tons in 1904. Japan, on the other hand, emerged as the main competitor in Ceylon and

Table 3.7 Major export destinations of Indian coal (in tons), 1897–1904

Country	*1897*	*1898*	*1899*	*1900*	*1901*	*1902*	*1903*	*1904*
Ceylon	104,524	214,986	180,909	368,031	335,651	274,010	257,251	374,754
Burma	203,232	169,979	188,619	200,469	242,777	261,213	264,344	287,397
Straits	85,280	93,462	86,951	65,715	89,592	89,567	142,256	143,729
Sumatra	–	–	3,531	10,863	10,690	14,655	13,975	30,802
Mauritius	7,317	2,708	18,128	5,759	18,745	14,690	8,802	13,431
Aden	8,094	14,416	4,000	53,305	47,194	21,214	43,410	14,598
British East Africa	3,619	150	–	20,569	16,922	11,562	13,612	7,162

Note: 1897–8 is taken as 1897, etc.

Sources: Holland (1905: 24); for Burma 1897: GOI (1899: viii).

the Straits Settlements. To Ceylon, it exported 32,380 tons in 1904, as against only 6,300 tons in 1901. But still it lagged far behind Bengal, which supplied about 374,754 tons in 1904, as against 6,993 tons in 1888. Japan had a clear lead in the Straits Settlements, however, where the volume of exports in 1904 was 400,628 tons from Japan and 143,729 tons from Bengal. Japan was also very competitive in Mauritius and Sumatra.

VI

Let me now summarise. This study generates some important conclusions on coal mining in Bengal. First, coal-bearing rocks in this province resembled those in the major coal-producing countries of the world, so their yield should not be qualitatively very inferior to them. Second, the Company's governance was largely responsible for the initial delays in this economic activity. For a couple of years the state was indifferent towards it, and then, later, the law and order situation impeded its growth. Third, three factors have been identified for the underdevelopment of coal mining in the first half of the nineteenth century: (i) the dearth of mineralogical knowledge; (ii) inefficient transport facilities; and (iii) shortages of labour. In this respect, my conclusion is that governance under the British Crown from 1858 expedited the accumulation of mineralogical knowledge and the construction of the railways, whereby these bottlenecks were removed. Fourth, comparative cost advantages came to favour Bengal in the second half of the nineteenth century, so that it successfully competed in domestic markets and abroad. In view of these factors, coal mining grew rapidly in this province. In 1914 Bengal produced about 15,100,000 tons of coal and employed as many as 132,500 miners.

This study confirms that, although it was a late starter in the global context, the coal-mining industry in Bengal was central to the economic development of the subcontinent in the nineteenth century and afterwards. Its cheap output was very useful to the railways, both for their construction and for the generation of steam. The railways, in turn, promoted modern industries by providing them with this vital fuel, and also enabling their easy access to distant input and output markets. These largely explain why the development of coal mining in the first half of the nineteenth century was followed by the advent of the railway age around the middle of the century and, subsequently, the rise of many modern industries in the second half of the century. My analysis also reinforces the conclusion that it was not a case of a one-way linear relationship but, rather, of overlapping circular causations. Without the railways, coal mining could not have secured its competitive edge in the market; in addition, the industrial demand for coal was crucial for the development of the mining industry. Indeed, contemporary state policies, including the promotion of railways, were integral factors in this development.

Notes

1 Wrigley (1961: 4) notes, 'The decisive technological change which freed so many industries from dependence upon organic raw materials was the discovery of a way of using coal where once wood had been essential.'
2 In fact, this coal (4,000 maunds) was once delivered to the steamers, who used it by mistake as Burdwan coal, but no complaint was made (Smith 1841: 16).
3 It was surrounded by the Ajoy and the Damodar to the north and the south, respectively, and by Burdwan and Panchet in the east and the west, in order.
4 He laments, '[A]ccordingly in a short time the "young forgot it, and the old had died". Round its history grew "A daily darkening pall: It sank subdued,/ In cold and unrepining quietude"' (Heatly 1842: 823).
5 That was so because the sample was again drawn from the same heaps from where Messrs Sumner, Heatly and Redfearne had supplied some 30 years back (Heatly 1842: 830).
6 Jones writes, 'From Chinnacoory Ghaut upwards [to Jheria], the navigation becomes progressively bad, and is totally obstructed at a place called Bandycoul, situated seven miles above the Beorucur [Barakar]. The river is here completely studded with close grained granite, quarry and sparry stones' ('Copy of a letter from W. Jones to William Butterworth, Esq., Chief Secretary to the Government of Bengal, dated 12 September, 1815', in P.P. 1831: 778). He abandoned the site on the conviction that 'it being the first attempt at regular mining in this country...one partial failure might throw the business back for years [again]' ('Copy of a letter from W. Jones to Thomas Fortescue, Esq., Secretary to the Government of Bengal, in the Territorial Department, dated 22 May, 1816', in P.P. 1831: 779).
7 Jones also sank three shafts for prospecting coal in Birbhum. He observed, 'The coal of all these three beds, is of an excellent quality; its cleanliness renders it peculiarly adapted for culinary purposes; it resembles the *Sunderland* coal in every respect, but leaves more cinders and ashes' (Jones 1833: 166, emphasis in original).
8 Monopoly (alongside its tyranny and oppression) was also noticed in the early history of British coal industry at Newcastle (Turner 1921: 7–12).

9 As the right to the mineral wealth was not vested in the government, a prospective miner acquired the lease of land on a royalty-based lease agreement from landowners (Gee 1940: 314).

10 The main promoter of the company was Dwarkanath Tagore. For details, see Kripalani (1981: 82–91).

11 For early British miners, Blanchard (1972: 100) thus describes, 'Each year with spring ploughing and lambing past, he [the farmer-cum-miner] would pick up his basket of tools, don his lather "bradder" and set off each day from about the middle of April to the hills overlooking his farm to grab for ore.' See also Blanchard (1974: 3).

12 Taylor (1961: 53) thus notes, 'Wage rates moved upwards in each year from 1898 to 1900 and the workman was in a position to increase both his earnings and his leisure. With this rise in wages, therefore, there came a parallel growth in absenteeism.'

13 Oldham (1867: 28) shows that the consumption of coal, other than that by railways, remained fairly stagnant in that period.

14 The prevailing practice was to store coals by the side of the river shipment point so that, in the rainy season, those could be quickly loaded for shipment ('Report of a Committee for the Investigation of the Coal and Mineral Resources of India', in P.P. 1841: 80).

15 In fact, the Chinese coal industry grew rapidly only after 1903–15, when railways linked its major cities (Wright 1981: 328–31).

16 Local miners even resisted the better picks, hammer, lamps and weighing machines (Seth 1940: 9). In this regard, a document of 1865 (Blanford 1865: 165 fn) notes, 'It is a remarkable circumstance that, although, forty-five years ago, coal mining was unknown in India, the miners have now become so attached to a particular method, and to the employment of particular tools, that they resist the attempt to introduce any alternation as severely as if the innovation interfered with their religious ceremonies.'

17 For British coal mining, Taylor (1961: 70) estimates 3.57 ton per hewers' shift worked, 9.37 shifts per fortnight (i.e., 0.65 shifts per day), 5.27 working days per week (i.e., 274 days a year) and 7.33 per cent absenteeism (i.e., 92.67 per cent presence at work). Hence, the productivity comes to $3.57 \times 0.65 \times 274 \times 0.9267 = 589$ tons a year.

18 Calculated from the value and volume of import as available in P.P. (1867: 46–7) and Hughes (1879: 84).

19 Freight by sea between Calcutta and Bombay cost Rs. 4 to 6.50 per ton; freight by railway between Ranigunj and Calcutta cost Rs. 2.56 per ton less a shipment rebate of Rs. 2; and the selling price at mines was Rs. 3.75 to 4.50.

Bibliography

Bagchi, A. K. (1970) 'European and Indian Entrepreneurship in India, 1900–39'. In Leach, E., and Mukherjee, S. N. (eds.) *Elites in South Asia*, 223–56. Cambridge: Cambridge University Press.

Balderston, T. (2010) 'The Economics of Abundance: Coal and Cotton in Lancashire and the World', *Economic History Review* (new series) 63 (3), 569–90.

Ball, V. (1881) *The Diamond, Coal and Gold of India: Their Mode of Occurrence and Distribution*. London: Trübner.

Ball, V., and Simpson, R. R. (1913) 'The Coal Fields of India', *Memoirs of the Geological Survey of India* 41 (1), 1–147.

Bedlington, R. (1861) 'The Longwork System'. In *Proceedings of the South Wales Institute of Engineers*, vol. II, 225–31. Merthyr Tydfil: South Wales Institute of Engineers.

Blanchard, I. (1972) 'The Miner and the Agricultural Community in Late Medieval England', *Agricultural History Review* 20 (2), 93–106.

Blanchard, I. (1974) 'Labour Productivity and Work Psychology in the English Mining Industry, 1400–1600', *Economic History Review* (new series) 29 (1), 1–23.

Blanford, W. T. (1865) 'On the Geological Structure and Relations of the Raniganj Coal Field, Bengal', *Memoirs of the Geological Survey of India* 3 (1), 1–195.

Chattoraj, R. N. (1977) *The Story of Coal*. Dhanbad: Dhanbad Publications.

Coal Mining Committee (1937) *Report of the Coal Mining Committee*, vol. II. Delhi: Manager of Publications (Government of India).

Das Gupta, R. (1985) 'Migrants in Coal Mines: Peasants or Proletariats, 1850s–1947', *Social Scientist* 16 (13), 18–43.

Daunton, M. J. (1981) 'Down the Pit: Work in the Great Northern and South Wales Coalfields, 1870–1914', *Economic History Review* (new series) 34 (4), 578–97.

Dunn, M. (1852) *A Treatise on the Winning and Working of Collieries*, 2nd edn. London: Simpkins & Marshall.

Dunstan, W. R. (1905) 'Report on the Coal Supply of India', Records of the Geological Survey of India no. 32, part 1. Calcutta: Geological Survey of India.

Foley, B. (1906) *Report on Labour in Bengal*. Calcutta: Bengal Secretariat Book Depot.

Gadgil, D. R. (1929) *Industrial Evolution of India*, 2nd edn. Oxford: Oxford University Press.

Gee, E. R. (1940) 'History of Coal Mining in India', *Indian National Science Academy* 6 (3), 313–18.

Ghosh, A. (1997) 'Guru Jones: A Private Engineer in the Colonial Trap', *Indian Journal of History of Science* 32 (2), 139–59.

Government of Bengal (GOB) (1872) *Annual Statement of Trade and Navigation for Bengal Presidency, 1870–71*. National Library Archive, Calcutta.

Government of Bengal (GOB) (1886) *Proceedings of the Revenue and Agriculture Department*, no. 1, April. West Bengal State Archives, Calcutta.

Government of Bengal (GOB) (1896) *Report of the Labour Enquiry Commission*. Calcutta: Bengal Secretariat Press.

Government of Bengal (GOB) (1897) *Annual Report on the Administration of Bengal Presidency during 1895–6*. National Library Archive, Calcutta.

Government of Bengal (GOB) (1901) *Annual Report on the Administration of Bengal Presidency during 1899–1900*. National Library Archive, Calcutta.

Government of Bengal (GOB) (1908) *Annual Report on the Administration of Bengal during 1906–7*. National Library Archive, Calcutta.

Government of Bengal (GOB) (1909) *Annual Report on the Administration of Bengal during 1907–8*. National Library Archive, Calcutta.

Government of Bengal (GOB) (1910) *Annual Report on the Administration of Bengal during 1908–9*. National Library Archive, Calcutta.

Government of Bengal (GOB) (1914) *Annual Report on the Administration of Bengal during 1912–13*. National Library Archive, Calcutta.

Government of Bengal (GOB) (1916) *Annual Report on the Administration of Bengal during 1914–15*. National Library Archive, Calcutta.

Government of Bengal (GOB) (1917) *Annual Report on the Administration of Bengal during 1915–16.* National Library Archive, Calcutta.

Government of India (GOI) (1899) *Financial and Commercial Statistics of British India.* National Library Archive, Calcutta.

Government of India (GOI) (1910) *Note on the Production of Coal in India.* National Library Archive, Calcutta.

Government of India (GOI) (1916) *Note on the Production of Coal in India.* National Library Archive, Calcutta.

Government of India (GOI) (1918) *Report of the Indian Industrial Commission, 1916–18.* Calcutta: Superintendent Government Printing.

Government of India (GOI) (1919) *Report on the Production and of Consumption of Coal in India.* National Library Archive, Calcutta.

Government of India (GOI) (1930) *Statistical Abstract for British India.* National Library Archive, Calcutta.

Greenwell, G. C. (1889) *A Practical Treatises on Mine Engineering*, 3rd edn. London: E. & F. N. Spon.

Heatly, S. G. T. (1842) 'Contributions towards a History of the Development of the Mineral Resources of India', *Journal of the Asiatic Society of Bengal* 11 (2), 811–35.

Hirsch, B. T., and Hausman, W. J. (1983) 'Labour Productivity in the British and South Wales Coal Industry', *Economica* (new series) 50 (198), 145–57.

Holland, T. H. (1905) 'Review of the Mineral Production of India during the Years 1898 to 1903', Records of the Geological Survey of India no. 32, part 1. Calcutta: Geological Survey of India.

Holland, T. H. (1906) 'The Mineral Production of India during the Years 1898 to 1903', Records of the Geological Survey of India no. 33, part 1. Calcutta: Geological Survey of India.

Holland, T. H., and Fermor L. L. (1910) 'Quinquennial Review of the Mineral Production of India during the Years 1904 to 1908', Records of the Geological Survey of India no. 39, part 1. Calcutta: Geological Survey of India.

Hughes, T. W. H. (1873) 'Coal in India', Records of the Geological Survey of India no. 6, part 3. Calcutta: Geological Survey of India.

Hughes, T. W. H. (1879) 'Statistics of Coal Importation into India', Records of the Geological Survey of India no. 12, part 1. Calcutta: Geological Survey of India.

Hunter, W. W. (1876) *Statistical Account of Bengal*, vol. IV. London: Trübner.

Jevons, W. S. (1865) *The Coal Question.* London: Macmillan.

Jha, D. P. (1982) 'Science and Technology (Coal Mining) in India in Eighteenth–Nineteenth Century', *Indian Journal of History of Science* 17 (2), 377–91.

Jones, W. (1833) 'Description of the North West Coal District', *Asiatic Researches* 18 (1), 163–70.

Kripalani, K. (1981) *Dwarkanath Tagore, a Forgotten Pioneer: A Life.* New Delhi: National Book Trust, India.

Lahiri-Dutta, K. (2001) 'From Gin Girls to Scavengers: Women in Raniganj Collieries', *Economic and Political Economy* 36 (44), 4213–21.

Lokanathan, P. S. (1935) *Industrial Organisation in India.* London: G. Allen & Unwin.

McLead, H. H. (1907) 'Speech' (chairman, Indian Mining Association), in *Transactions of the Mining and Geological Institute of India*, vol. I, 56–8. Calcutta: Mining and Geological Institute of India.

Mukhopadhyay, G., Mukhopadhyay, S. K., Roychowdhury, M., and Parui, P. K. (2010) 'Stratigraphic Correlation between Different Gondwana Basins of India', *Journal of the Geological Society of India* 76 (3), 251–66.

Nef, J. U. (1932) *The Rise of the British Coal Industry*, 2 vols. London: George Routledge & Sons.

Oldham, T. (1859) *Report of the Raneegunge Coal Field, with Special Reference to the Proposed Extension of the Existing Line of Railway*. Calcutta: Geological Survey of India.

Oldham, T. (1867) *Coal Resources and Production of India, House of Commons Paper no. 69*. London: Hansard.

Palit, C. (1999) *Growth of Commerce and Industry in Bengal*. Calcutta: Bengal National Chambers of Commerce and Industries.

Parliamentary Papers (P.P.) (1831) *Select Committee on the Affairs of the East India Company, Minutes of Evidence*, vol. III. London: Hansard.

Parliamentary Papers (P.P.) (1841) *Dr M. Clelland's Report on the Coal Fields of India*. London: Hansard.

Parliamentary Papers (P.P.) (1867) *Statistical Abstract Relating to British India, from 1840 to 1865*. London: HMSO.

Parliamentary Papers (P.P.) (1870) *Moral and Material Progress and Conditions of India for 1868–69*, vol. 53. London: Hansard.

Parliamentary Papers (P.P.) (1872) *Maps and Statistical Information with Reference to India for 1870–1*, vol. 44. London: Hansard.

Parliamentary Papers (P.P.) (1874) *Maps and Statistical Information with Reference to India for 1872–3*, vol. 49. London: Hansard.

Parliamentary Papers (P.P.) (1876a) *Statement of the Trade of British India with British Possession and Foreign Countries for 1870–1 to 1874–5*, vol. 57. London: Hansard.

Parliamentary Papers (P.P.) (1876b) *Administrative Report on the Railways in India for 1875–6*, vol. 56. London: Hansard.

Parliamentary Papers (P.P.) (1880) *Administrative Report on the Railways in India for 1879–80*, vol. 52. London: Hansard.

Parliamentary Papers (P.P.) (1883) *Review of Trade and Navigation of British India with Foreign Countries*, vol. 70. London: Hansard.

Parliamentary Papers (P.P.) (1886a) *Maps and Statistical Information with Reference to India, 1884–5*, vol. 60. London: Hansard.

Parliamentary Papers (P.P.) (1886b) *Review of the Trade of British India with Foreign Countries, 1884–5*, vol. 58. London: Hansard.

Parliamentary Papers (P.P.) (1887a) *Moral and Material Progress and Conditions of India for 1885–86*, vol. 62. London: Hansard.

Parliamentary Papers (P.P.) (1887b) *Administrative Report on the Railways in India for 1886–87*, vol. 62, London: Hansard.

Parliamentary Papers (P.P.) (1888) *Moral and Material Progress and Conditions of India for 1886–87*, vol. 76. London: Hansard.

Parliamentary Papers (P.P.) (1890a) *Statement of the Trade of British India with British Possession and Foreign Countries for the Years 1884–85 to 1888–89*, vol. 57. London: Hansard.

Parliamentary Papers (P.P.) (1890b) *Administrative Report on the Railways in India for 1889–90*, vol. 58. London: Hansard.

Parliamentary Papers (P.P.) (1891) *Review of the Trade of British India with Foreign Countries, 1890–1*, vol. 58. London: Hansard.

Parliamentary Papers (P.P.) (1895a) *Administrative Report on the Railways in India for 1894–5*, vol. 73. London: Hansard.

Parliamentary Papers (P.P.) (1895b) *Statement of the Trade of British India with British Possession and Foreign Countries for the Years 1889–90 to 1893–94*, vol. 73. London: Hansard.

Parliamentary Papers (P.P.) (1899) *Extracts from the Annual Reports, Imperial Institute, Indian Section, for the Years 1896–97, 1897–98 and 1998–99*, vol. 65. London: Hansard.

Parliamentary Papers (P.P.) (1902) *Administrative Report on the Railways in India for 1901*, vol. 73. London: Hansard.

Parthasarathi, P. (2011) *Why Europe Grew Rich and Asia Did Not: Global Economic Divergence, 1600–1850*. Cambridge: Cambridge University Press.

Pollard, S. (1980) 'A New Estimate of British Coal Production', *Economic History Review* (new series) 32 (2), 212–35.

Pomeranz, K. (2000) *The Great Divergence: China, Europe, and the Making of the Modern World Economy*. Princeton, NJ: Princeton University Press.

Ray, I., and Paul, K. (2001) 'Beginnings of Coal Industry in Bengal'. In Indian History Congress (ed.) *Proceedings of the Indian History Congress I, Millennium (61st) Session, 2000–2001*, 836–47. Kolkata: Indian History Congress.

Ray, R., and Ray, R. (1974) 'European Monopoly Corporations and Indian Entrepreneurships, 1913–1922: Early Politics of Coal in Eastern India', *Economic and Political Economy* 9 (21), M53–M55.

Rhodes, E. C. (1945) 'Output, Labour and Machines in the Coal Mining Industry in Great Britain', *Economica* (new series) 12 (46), 101–10.

Rode, K. P. (1953) 'The Gondwana Formations of India and the Nature of Gondwana Land', Memoir of the Rajputana University Department of Geology no. 2. Udaipur: Rajputana University, Department of Geology.

Rodgers, H. B. (1960) 'The Lancashire Cotton Industry in 1840', *Transactions and Papers (Institute of British Geographers)* 28, 135–53.

Rostow, W. W. (1960) *The Stages of Economic Growth: A Non-Communist Manifesto*. Cambridge: Cambridge University Press.

Roy, T. (2011) *The Economic History of India, 1857–1947*, 3rd edn. New Delhi: Oxford University Press.

Schumpeter, J. A. (1964 [1939]) *Business Cycles: A Theoretical, Historical and Statistical Analysis of the Capitalist Process*, abridged edn. New York: McGraw-Hill.

Sen, S. K. (1966) *Studies in Economic Policy and Development of India, 1848–1925*. Calcutta: Progressive Publishers.

Seth, B. R. (1940) *Labour in the Indian Coal Industry*. Bombay: D. B. Taraporevala Sons.

Simmons, C. P. (1976a) 'Recruiting and Organizing an Industrial Labour Force in Colonial India: The Case of the Coal Mining Industry, c. 1880–1939', *Indian Economic and Social History Review* 13 (4), 455–85.

Simmons, C. P. (1976b) 'Indigenous Enterprise in the Indian Coal Mining Industry, c. 1835–1939', *Indian Economic and Social History Review* 13 (2), 189–218.

Smith, C. W. (1841) *Reports of a Committee for the Investigation of the Coal and Mineral Resources of India*. Calcutta: Military Orphan Press.

Smith, D. (1856) *Report of the Coal and Iron Districts of Bengal*. National Library Archive, Calcutta.

Subrahmanyam, K. V. (1968) 'Shades of Darkness: The Annals of the Coal Industry', *Economic and Political Economy* 3 (40), 1515–26.

Tan, E. S. (2009) 'Market Structure and the Coal Cartel in Early Nineteenth-Century England', *Economic History Review* (new series) 62 (2), 350–65.

Taylor, A. J. (1961) 'Labour Productivity and Technological Innovation in the British Coal Industry, 1850–1914', *Economic History Review* (new series) 14 (1), 48–70.

Turner, R. (1921) 'English Coal Industry in the Seventeenth and Eighteenth Centuries', *American Historical Review* 7 (1), 1–23.

Unrug, R. (1996) *The Assembly of Gondwana Supercontinent: Contrasting Histories of East and West Gondwana*. Oxford: Oxford & IBH Publishing.

Wright, T. (1981) 'Growth of Modern Chinese Coal Industry: An Analysis of Supply and Demand, 1896–1936', *Modern China* 7 (3), 317–50.

Wrigley, E. A. (1961) 'The Supply of Raw Materials in the Industrial Revolution', *Economic History Review* (new series) 15 (1), 1–16.

Appendix 3.1 Growth of coal mining in Bengal, 1830–1914

Year	*Production (in tons)*	*Employment*	*Output/miner (in tons)*	*Import (in tons)*	*Export (in tons)*
1830	6,213[1]	–	–	–	–
1839	36,697[2]	–	–	–	–
1840	38,641[2]	–	–	–	–
1841	40,690[2]	–	–	–	–
1842	42,846[2]	–	–	–	–
1843	45,117[2]	–	–	–	–
1844	47,508[2]	–	–	–	–
1845	62,385[2]	–	–	–	–
1846	91,743[2]	–	–	–	–
1847	64,500*	–	–	–	–
1848	45,000[3]	–	–	–	–
1849	81,481[4]	–	–	–	–
1850	235,589[1]	–	–	–	–
1851	288,804*	–	–	–	–
1852	288,804*	–	–	–	–
1853	297,060*	–	–	43,562[28]	–
1854	297,060*	–	–	58,410[28]	–
1855	306,234*	–	–	41,987[28]	–
1856	313,940*	–	–	76,712[28]	–
1857	314,982*	–	–	82,078[28]	–
1858	325,000[5]	–	–	48,714[29]	–
1859	371,821[6]	–	–	45,877[6]	–
1860	376,531[6]	–	–	18,535[6]	–
1861	290,572[6]	–	–	47,969[6]	–
1862	322,139[6]	–	–	25,257[6]	–
1863	354,766[6]	–	–	38,683[6]	–
1864	337,127[6]	–	–	67,860[6]	–
1865	328,842[6]	–	–	60,321[6]	–
1866	402,729[6]	–	–	34,130[6]	–
1867	479,233[7]	–	–	70,627[30]	–
1868	564,933[8]	–	–	61,367[30]	–
1869	600,000[9]	–	–	38,720[30]	282[36]
1870	488,400*	–	–	42,433[31]	1,180[36]
1871	397,558*	–	–	63,929[31]	1,205[37]
1872	322,443[8]	–	–	89,775[31]	2,062[37]
1873	346,949*	–	–	48,688[31]	1,465[37]
1874	373,317*	–	–	82,120[31]	0[37]
1875	401,689*	–	–	63,821[31]	4,376[37]
1876	432,409[8]	–	–	61,091[31]	–
1877	467,002[8]	–	–	76,278[31]	–
1878	504,362[8]	–	–	81,007*	–
1879	523,097[8]	–	–	86,030*	–
1880	988,565[10]	–	–	91,270[32]	410[38]
1881	930,203[10]	–	–	85,044[32]	9[38]
1882	1,038,872[10]	18,030[21]	57.62	88,700*	0[38]
1883	1,200,957[10]	22,443*	–	92,515*	10[38]
1884	1,257,392[10]	23,498*	–	96,493*	101[38]

(continued)

Appendix 3.1 Cont.

Year	*Production (in tons)*	*Employment*	*Output/miner (in tons)*	*Import (in tons)*	*Export (in tons)*
1885	1,123,700[10]	22,745[22]	49.40	100,000[33]	500[11]
1886	1,186,802[10]	24,794[22]	47.87	58,000*	199[11]
1887	1,319,090[10]	22,316*	–	33,640*	315[11]
1888	1,380,594[10]	23,356*	–	19,376[34]	15,796[11]
1889	1,541,356[10]	26,076*	–	23,170[34]	39,972[11]
1890	1,626,245[10]	27,512*	–	10,047[34]	26,336[11]
1891	1,747,122[10]	24,834[23]	70.35	22,812[34]	4,515[11]
1892	1,920,050[10]	29,495[23]	65.18	12,831[34]	15,725[11]
1893	1,902,866[11]	27,453[23]	69.31	8,113[34]	52,302[11]
1894	2, 035,934[11]	30,773[24]	66.16	0[35]	154,282[11]
1895	2,716,155[11]	35,339*	–	64[35]	211,407[11]
1896	3,037,920[11]	34,697[25]	87.56	–	191,030[11]
1897	3,142,497[11]	38,801*	–	–	390,979[11]
1898	3,622,090[12]	48,673[26]	74.42	–	490,290[11]
1899	4,035,265[12]	58,130[26]	69.42	–	467,306[11]
1900	4,978,492[12]	72,790[26]	68.40	–	711,874[11]
1901	5,509,431[12]	79,620[26]	69.20	–	845,953[11]
1902	6,259,236[12]	82,545[26]	75.83	–	690,208[39]
1903	6,361,212[12]	74,538[26]	85.34	–	703,319[39]
1904	7,063,680[13]	75,749[24]	93.25	–	764,508*
1905	7,234,103[14]	74,072[27]	97.66	–	831,400[14]
1906	8,617,820[14]	82,885[27]	103.97	–	928,400[14]
1907	9,993,348[15]	96,301[27]	103.77	–	722,451[15]
1908	11,559,911[16]	112,219[27]	103.01	–	571,310[16]
1909	10,661,000[17]	98,376*	–	–	657,292*
1910	10,779,000[17]	99,465*	–	–	756,215*
1911	13,150,020[18]	115,637[18]	113.72	–	870,210[18]
1912	14,675,288[18]	125,510[18]	116.93	–	879,000[18]
1913	15,846,695[19]	131,389[19]	120.61	–	899,000[40]
1914	15,075,587[20]	132,500[19]	113.79	–	759,000[40]

Notes: * Estimated; ** for 1841–4, an annual average figure is given; *** the administrative jurisdiction of Bengal was reconstituted on 1 April 1912, and a number of coalfields were included in the province of Bihar. Hence, the figures for Bengal in the sources are very low. For 1914 both low and high figures are available in sources (see source no. 20 of this table). Taking the proportion of both high and low figures in 1914 (i.e., 15,075,587/4,424,540 = 3.408) as a multiplicative factor, these figures are estimated.

Sources: 1: P.P. (1841: 137) (it is an average for the four years 1828–31); 2: Blanford (1865: 158–9**); 3: McLead (1907: 56–8); 4: Oldham (1859: 25); 5: Oldham (1859: 24); 6: Oldham (1867; 26); 7: P.P. (1870: 12); 8: Ball (1881: 72) (for the three years 1876–8 the average value is given at 467,907); 9: P.P. (1872: 19); 10: P.P. (1895a: 72); 11: P.P. (1902: 8); 12: Holland (1905: 29); 13: Holland (1906: 5); 14: GOB (1908: 73–4, 81); 15: GOB (1909: 73–4, 80); 16: GOB (1910: 74, 81); 17: GOB (1909: 73); 18: GOB (1914: 60, 68***); 19: GOB (1916: 67***); 20: GOB (1917: 74); 21: P.P. (1886a: 211) (Ranigunj's output and employment have been considered); 22: P.P. (1888: 105); 23: GOB (1896: 2); 24: Foley (1906: 29); 25: Foley (1906: vii); 26: Holland (1905: 39); 27: Holland (1905: 41); 28: Hughes (1879: 83); 29: P.P. (1874: 103); 30: GOB (1872: 16); 31: Hughes (1879: 86); 32: P.P. (1883: 34) (for 1879, the proportion of Bengal in India's total import, and India's total import have been considered); 33: P.P. (1887a: 75); 34: P.P. (1895b: 19); 35: GOB (1897: 175); 36: GOB (1872: 16); 37: P.P. (1876a: 93); 38: P.P. (1886b: 34); 39: Holland (1905: 17–18); 40: GOI (1916: 25).

4 Iron smelting and its downstreams

Conflicts in the core–periphery relationship

Bengal has a rich heritage in iron and steel manufacturing. Evidence for it in ancient times is available in contemporary rock-cut temples – such as in the Udayagiri Hills (BCE 150), the Buddha Gaya (BCE 100 – CE 100) and the Amravati Tope (CE 300–400) – where there are many sculptures of swords, daggers, spears, bows, arrows, battleaxes, shields, etc., made of iron or steel. Similar evidence is available in the temples of later ages – for example, in the temples of Bhubaneswar (CE 650) and Kanarak (CE 1237) (Fergusson 1864; Mitter 1880). Referring to these sculptures, a government monograph remarks, 'That the weapons depicted [in those temples] are those which were used in Bengal at this period we may safely conclude from the fact that the temples are built in Bengal, and that the weapons were chiefly if not entirely made of iron or steel…' (Watson 1907: 2). Apart from sculptures, some temples were constructed using iron and steel extensively. In the Kanarak temple, for example, there is a bar of iron, 23 feet in length and 11½ inches in breadth and thickness; a line of iron beams as a support to the roof; and 'wrought' iron beams as a false ceiling. An architectural historian thus remarks that these pieces of evidence bespeak 'a knowledge of the properties and strength of the material that is remarkable in a people who are now [1874] so utterly incapable of forging such materials' (Fergusson 1874: 428). One piece of direct evidence for steel, the most ancient, is a spear (or lance), called the Peshro Bullum, that the Nawab of Murshidabad carried at the head of procession. Made of highly tempered steel with gold embossing, it certainly belonged originally to a king of the Hindu faith prior to the Common Era. It is so believed in view of the fact that (i) the image of god Vishnu and his carrier, the Gorror, are borne on the blades and (ii) its ornamentation resembles those on the Orissan temples (Watson 1907: 3).[1] In addition, there is a large iron gun, the Bachawali Tope, now standing on the debris of the palace at Murshidabad. Possibly made sometime in the twelfth to fourteenth centuries, it has two parts: a chamber of about 3½ feet long with a girth of 4 feet; and a barrel some 11½ feet long with a girth of 7¾ feet, at the muzzle (ibid.: 119).

This ancient Hindu craftsmanship greatly changed, however, once it had come under the cultural influence of Persia, Arabia and the Punjab during Mughal rule. Its unique evidence is the Johan Kosha, a large cannon lying at

Murshidabad, which was built at Dacca in 1637, chiefly using wrought iron. For the eighteenth century, many such pieces of evidence are available in the royal arsenals at Burdwan and Murshidabad (ibid.: 7–8). The former's weaponry, enriched with various types of swords, spears and matchlock guns, was mostly manufactured at a smiths' village, Kamarpara, six miles away from the town of Burdwan. Many workers migrated thence to Murshidabad to work on armaments for the Nawab. The industry was evidently developed also in Birbhum (mainly at Suri and Bishnupur), Gaya and Pratapnagar (in Khulna) to supply weapons to local kings and chieftains. Murshidabad was also supplied from Patna, Munghyr and Bhagalpur.

While this evidence makes it clear that, for iron smelting and its downstreams, skilled manpower was indigenously available, this study also confirms local endowment of iron ores, and a rising domestic demand, especially in the second half of the nineteenth century. Therefore, a natural question in historiography is: why did iron smelting not arise here in a big way? Three alternative hypotheses are available to this end: (i) that there was inadequate demand to support any large-scale project (Oldham 1852: 14); (ii) that colonial policies impaired the viability of the domestic industry (Headrick 1990: 295–6; Parthasarathi 2008); and (iii) that high prices prevailed for its inputs – especially, charcoal, iron ore and transportation (Roy 2010: 4). As a central thesis, this chapter takes up the second argument.

The iron and steel industry attracts many studies in historiography. In the British context, it discusses the industry's overall development in the pre-modern (Hammersley 1973; Flinn 1958; Johnson 1951; Raistrick and Allen 1938) and modern (Harris 1988; Hyde 1977; Birch 1967; Aston 1963) periods, as also certain specific questions on labour (Shiells 1990; Holt 1977), organisation (Evens, Jackson and Ryden 2002; Awty 1957; Burn 1947) and trade (Childs 1981; Allen 1979; McCloskey 1974). Indian historiography is also quite rich. At the country level, there are scholastic studies on the industry's historical status – for example, Parthasarathi (2008), Biswas (1994), Bhattacharyya (1970), Rao (1963) and Pillai (1923) – on its technology – such as Roy (2010), Roy (2008), Ramachandran (1984), Bhardwaj (1982), and Hedge (1973) – and on mineralogy – for example, Murty (1982) and Karan (1957). But regional discussions are conspicuously lacking, save for a few, such as Sanyal (1968). In addition to enriching the literature by means of a regional focus, this study unveils three new dimensions. First, the industry is never discussed in the context of India's nineteenth-century deindustrialisation. I discuss this issue, focusing on the downfall of the traditional industry, as well as the loss of employment it suffered. Second, this study analyses the comparative cost advantages of iron smelting between Britain and its colony, which has not yet been discussed in the literature. Third, it narrates the transition of the industry from the traditional sector to a modern set-up, and explains the underlying delay on the basis of the colonial environment.

The plan of this chapter is this. Section I reviews the availability of iron ore in Bengal to ascertain whether the industry's prosperity suffered for the want of minerals. Section II discusses the status of traditional iron smelting around the middle of the nineteenth century. The deindustrialisation issue is also deliberated here. Section III brings out the development process of large-scale iron smelting in Bengal, highlighting its comparative cost advantages vis-à-vis Britain. Finally, I analyse in Section IV how the government's store purchase policy promoted imports from England, against the interests of the domestic industry. Section V concludes.

I

Iron ores were deposited in two adjacent regions in Bengal, the Damuda (Damodar) Valley and the Rajmahal Hills. Lying 120 miles north-west of Calcutta, the former runs for about 39 miles from east to west, and 18 miles from north to south. Four types of rocks are found in this valley: Mahadeva (500 feet), Panchet (1,500 feet), Damuda (8,400 feet) and Talchir (800 feet), in descending order (Medlicott and Blanford 1879: 179). In the Damuda bed, there are three groups of rocks: in descending order, the Ranigunj (5,000 feet), ironstone shales (1,400 feet) and the Barakar (2,000 feet).

Iron ores are mainly available in ironstone shales, which appear as a distinct ridge of elevated ground over the Barakar bed. Running in the east–west direction along the Barakar, they thin out in the south-west corner, where the Ranigunj group overlaps them. These ironstones consist of black carbonaceous shales (called the black band), and break into small angular fragments containing seams of argillaceous iron ore. They occur at 6 to 10 feet intervals showing thickness at 2 to 12 inches (Blanford 1865: 76). Their upper layers provide greater yields, and also better quality, than lower layers. There are two other sources of ironstone. One is the upper segment of the Ranigunj rock, where the nodules of ironstone scatter over surface soils. Those nodules also contain iron. In view of its abundance 'over a large area' (Medlicott and Blanford 1879: 182), traditional iron smelting thrived on them. Ironstones also occur at a depth of 700 to 900 feet in the Ranigunj bed. These occurrences are dominant in the western and southern segments of the valley. Although they are completely overlapped by the Panchet bed in the west of Asansol town, they reappear again further east, where they are even exposed in some places, especially in streams. Sometimes carbonaceous shales are seen with intercalated seams of clay iron ore.

To assess the iron ore availability in this valley, a series of investigations were conducted in the second half of the nineteenth century. One such study (Blanford 1865: 76) reveals that, for a bed of 150 feet depth, the mineral constitutes one part in 17 of the bed. This estimate is exclusive of ironstone nodules, as available on the surface soil, which vary in thickness from 6 inches to 3 feet. Another study (Smith 1856) reports that, for a depth of 52 feet, four seams occur: one clay ironstone bed (18 inch thickness), two good-quality black band beds (26 inches each, on average), and one inferior black band bed (18 inches). Thus, clay iron constitutes one part in 34 of the entire bed, and the black band one part in nine. Because of a lower yield, however, the black band provides only a slightly greater amount of iron ore than the corresponding yield from clay iron. These ironstone beds are not continuous, however, but when one seam thins out another comes in, so that 'in quarrying, or in mining by large excavations, a tolerably uniform produce might, on the whole, be expected' (Blanford 1865: 76).

Contemporary assays also suggest encouraging results. For 29 samples, an assay shows the iron content at more than 50 per cent for four samples, 45 to 50 per cent for seven samples and 40 to 45 per cent for eight samples. Taking them together, the average iron content comes to 38.92 per cent, 'a fair and productive percentage' (ibid.: 194).

The other iron-bearing field, the Rajmahal Hills, is located at about 20 miles north of the Damuda Valley, extending from Suri in Birbhum to Kahalgaon in Bhagalpur. These hills are almost flat on the top, with their plateaus dipping towards the east. Rock groups in this region are the alluvium, the laterite and the Gondwana. The Gondwana is composed of the Rajmahal group, the Mahadeva group, the Barakar group and the Talchir group.

Iron ores are available here in three geological formations: (i) sandstones, (ii) trappean clay-stones and (iii) laterite. Sandstones, belonging to the Barakar and the Mahadeva ages, occur in conjunction with the conglomerates and shales containing veins and nests of brown hæmatite (a mineral consisting of ferric oxide, an important ore of iron). The bed runs south to north over the entire range, save for a few interruptions, covering mainly the western side (Oldham 1865: 267–9). These stones are generally greyish white in colour, but often stained in deep red as the peroxide of iron percolates on them. Iron ores, as available in these formations, are of good quality, occurring mainly in nodular masses in dark shales. These were the main sources of iron ores, which tribal smelters, the *kol*, used (Ball 1877: 87).

These beds of conglomerates, sandstones and shales are covered with extensive sheets of basaltic and other trappean rocks, which contain tolerably pure brown hæmatite. In some places, layers of pisolitic iron are met with while, in some others, iron oxide (partly earthy and partly magnetic) occurs. An interesting feature in this geology is that sandstones and trappean rocks occur in succession three to four times – a feature that geologists explain by the conjecture of periodic volcanic eruptions. '[T]hese forces were exerted at successive intervals after periods of repose, throwing out immense flows of molten lavas; while during these periods of repose, the deposition of clays, gravels and sands, arising from ordinary causes continued to proceed' (Oldham 1865: 272). This is why plentiful supplies of iron ores are available here.

Another source of iron ore is the laterite, which forms the highest bed throughout the Rajmahal Hills. It is considerably thick, sometimes as much as 200 feet, and slopes gradually from the western part of the region to the Gangetic plain. It is a porous argillaceous rock, impregnated with iron peroxide, which contains 25 to 35 per cent of metallic iron (Medlicott and Blanford 1879: 349). Iron is found either in a state of entirely hydrated peroxide (limonite), or partly hydrated and partly anhydratous peroxide. A nineteenth-century geologist has described it as 'highly ferruginous, and in many places so charged with peroxide of iron that it can be used as an ore of iron' (Oldham 1865: 274). In most cases, iron is deposited at the base of the bed, possibly coming from the underlying basaltic trap. Even where laterite occurs independent of the trap, it 'is sometimes sufficiently rich to be worked as an ore' (Ball 1877: 88).

Assays of nine laterite samples, however, indicate the percentage of metallic iron at 15.0 to 35.6 and that of iron peroxide at 21.4 to 50.8 per cent (Medlicott and Blanford 1879: 350). Although ores thus obtained could be worked out, its average yield is less than what is obtained elsewhere in this region – namely about 43.01 per cent, as found in an assay of 29 samples drawn randomly from this region (Ball 1877: 94). The viability of iron smelting was, therefore, assured. A GSI geologist thus confirmed in 1875, 'There is in my own mind no doubt as to an abundant supply of iron-stone within a moderate distance of Mullarpore [near Suri]' (ibid.: 90). For an average capacity of 500 tons of pig iron per month, ores would be available from the Damra field alone for 30 years, though the geologist stressed that, 'by increasing the mining radius by 2 or 3 miles, ample ore could be raised to furnish very much larger works' (ibid.).

For the manufacture of iron, two more materials are required, one for flux and the other for fuel. Limestone is not adequately available here. But *kunkur* might be used for the purpose, and this abounds in the Rajmahal Hills. Its large deposits are found along the edges of hills, especially their western flanks, as also on the banks of the Ganges, especially at Sukri-gully, where it occurs in regular beds. Oldham notices that 'in some places thick and extensive deposits of nodular kunkur cover the low broken ground at the base of the hills' (Oldham 1865: 275). Such deposits occur in the Damuda Valley as well. 'A large quantity [of flux material] might however be derived from the kunkur deposit on the banks of the Barakar, in the neighbourhood of Ramnagar and Boldi, on the left bank, and east of Dumarkhunda, on the right bank' (Blanford 1865: 195).

For the purpose of fuel, both charcoal and pit coal were available in and around these regions. In view of the steady depletion of the forests, the Ranigunj coal was perhaps the best choice for local iron smelting in the second half of the nineteenth century. There were some initial objections in this regard, however, especially in view of its high proportion of ash, which caused technical problems in the furnace, as did its higher proportion of phosphorus, which rendered the iron 'cold short' (i.e., it became cold quickly). These reservations subsequently subsided, as the former could be resolved by suitably designing the furnace, and the latter by utilising better coals (Ray 2015a: 477–8).

II

Traditional iron smelting was confined to the Rajmahal Hills region. It spread across its plains (belonging to the district of Birbhum) as well as the hills, with a division of labour into mining/quarrying, smelting and refining. Mining was organised on very small scales, with rudimentary implements being used. From the survey of Buchanan Hamilton (1809–13) we come across several such mines

(Martin 1838: 190–3). Because of the deposition of ores in different geological formations, the method of mining varied. The dominant practice was, indeed, the 'bell pit' method (Ball 1877: 90), especially where the mineral was available near the surface soil. In this method, a shaft (a sloping passage) of about 18 to 21 inches in diameter was dug up to the bed of ore, and then the gallery was formed. Mining was carried out till the outbreak of rains, or till the gallery collapsed. Even when mining was put on hold for the rains, the roof would collapse under the weight of water. Therefore, a new pit had to be excavated. Iron-bearing fields were thus dotted with bell-shaped pits. In some trappean veins, however, iron ores were mixed with earth, clay, quartz, pebbles, etc. In such cases, further processing was required. Ores were dried up, and winnowed, so that some impurities, such as earth and clay, were removed. Hard materials, such as pebbles or quartz, that were retained in them were removed by repeated hammering and winnowing.

Contemporary mining had two shortcomings, however. First, pillars were never maintained in mines, even though this would have maximised output, and also minimised roof collapse accidents. Martin (1838: 169) thus notes, 'The leaving pillars to support the roof, is a mystery far beyond their present attainments in the art of mining; and, when mentioned, was received with numerous frivolous objections.' Second, Bengal miners laid more emphasis on the convenience of work than the productivity of a field. Often they would neglect hard lumps, which required strenuous labour to mine (ibid.: 193). Many promising deposits were also deserted halfway through: 'Below this depth [about 1½ foot at Dumka] the mine becomes compact, and the natives neglected it, as too troublesome…' (ibid.). Perhaps the easy availability of ores in alternative sources explains such apathy. Otherwise, Bengal's iron smelting might have started to decline when those mines were deserted.

A more convenient source was the river bed, where hill torrents brought iron ores in the monsoon. They were impregnated in small pebbles. The pebbles were first winnowed to remove siliceous matter, and then crushed to extract the ore. Further winnowing followed to cleanse out rubbish materials. Many such river beds are noticed by Martin, especially to the east of Jathaurnath, Paharidihi and Bhungri Simar.

In smelting, a unique technology prevailed across the province. Its mechanical device was built on two major components, a furnace and a pair of bellows (see Figure 4.1). The furnace was mud-built and contained a hollow inner surface, which gradually widened towards the bottom ('c' in the figure). This inner cavity ('b'–'c') was joined with a pair of bellows at d through a pipe of baked clay ('e'). At d, where there was a semicircular hole, the pipe was placed on a brick, and the openings round the pipe were covered by moist sandy clay. There were five components in a bellow: a muzzle, a cylinder of wood, a hide of goat (or deer), a string and a bamboo. The cylinder of wood was hollowed, and a muzzle of bamboo was inserted into it. At the top of the hollowed wood, a goat's skin was fastened tightly to contain air in it. At the centre of the skin, there was a small hole serving two purposes: (i) it

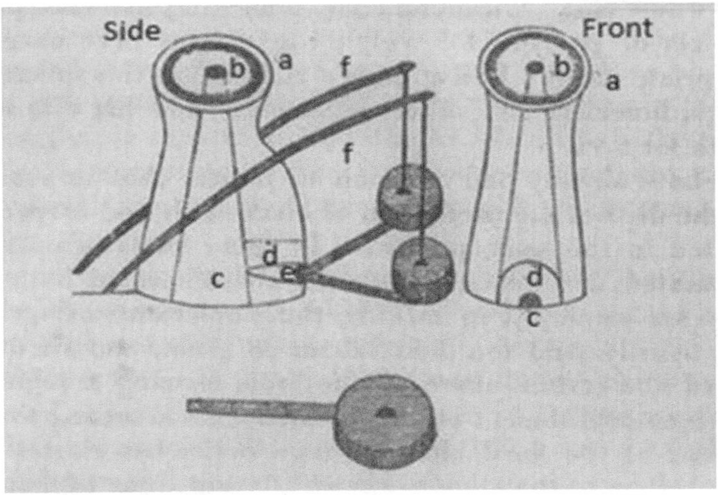

Figure 4.1 Iron-smelting apparatus
Source: Martin (1838: 262).

Figure 4.2 Iron smelting in the Rajmahal Hills using the apparatus shown in Figure 4.1
Source: Watson (1907: plate VI, fig. 1).

Figure 4.3 Iron smelting in Birbhum, showing three men bellowing using the Figure 4.1 apparatus, one man organising molten iron, his two helpers standing by his side

Source: Ball (1877: 86, plate V).

contained a wooden button to hold a string that was tied with a bamboo; the bamboo acted like the spring of a turner's lathe (as 'f' in the figure); and (ii) it allowed air to enter into the skin. Two such bellows were placed side by side. When a bellow was at rest, the string upheld the skin and air entered into it. To provide a blast of air in the furnace, the bellower put his heel on the hole of one skin, and then depressed it. The air passed on from the skin to the furnace through the muzzle. He then repeated the process on the other bellow. The blast was thus continuously supplied. Furnaces all over the province were built on this principle, though the measurements of furnace and bellows differed (Figures 4.3 and 4.4).[2]

Pure iron ores were used in smelting since the traditional furnace could not vitrify their stony particles (Martin 1838: 261). Such ores and charcoal were kept ready at hand in a given proportion, usually at 20 *sers* to 1 maund. To start with, charcoal was placed into the furnace and lit up, the blast was blown and ores were poured in. Once the charcoal was burnt, fresh charcoal and ores were added. This was repeated till their entire stocks at hand were exhausted through a continuum of blast. Once every half an hour a stick was pierced through the clay wall around 'd', whence a small quantity of slag came out and solidified, removing impurities from the molten matter. The entire process took no more than three to four hours, however. The pipe was then removed, its

Figure 4.4 Iron refining (bellowing) in Birbhum using the Figure 4.1 apparatus
Source: Ball (1877: 87, plate VI).

surrounding clay was dismantled and the charcoal was raked out and quenched. Finally, the smelter gathered semi-fused iron from the furnace using tongs with long wooden handles. One such smelting provided about 6–7 *sers* of crude *(kutcha)* iron.

Crude iron was forged by application of heat and hammer. In Birbhum, there was a division of labour between smelting and refining, but it was not exclusively so in the hills. Both smelters and blacksmiths were often found refining crudes alongside their respective jobs. Exclusive forgers were also not uncommon. For a group of five to six persons at each forge, the job demanded that crude iron be heated to a high temperature, and then repeatedly hammered while it remained hot (Figures 4.4 and 4.5). The entire process was repeated at least three to four times so that impurities were reduced to a tolerable level.[3] About one-fourth of its weight was lost in this process. Finally, the refined iron was formed into wedges, bars or plates for sale in markets.

As to the industry's production level in the early British period, direct evidence is not exhaustive. From various contemporary field surveys, however, we gather the following iron-smelting hamlets in Bengal: Ganpur, Dhudiakanda and Banskta (Ball 1877: 88); Deocha, Damra, Ganpur and Bellia Narainpore (Oldham 1852: 8–9); Bharcata, Deocha, Damra, Ganpur and Sibperbaree (as also its neighbourhoods in the Mullarpore Pargana: Jackson 1845: 755);

Figure 4.5 Iron refining (heating and hammering) in Birbhum, showing one man (on the top) bellowing using the Figure 4.1 apparatus, one man holding unrefined iron and two men hammering

Source: Ball (1877: 87, plate VI).

Gautcole and beneath that range of hills, towards Soosnah on the south-west side, and beneath the Birbhum Hills on the north-east (Homfray 1842: 738); Virkati, Kalidaspur and Ramkamal (Buchannan 1831: 8); and Kuji, Osla, Belhar, Beldiha, Mongrar, Asnahatari, Rangga, Paharidihi, Sejuya, Bhungri Simar, Nuni, Pokhariya, Chanda Bathan, Gamra and Dumka (Martin 1838: 190–3). Production figures are available only in Oldham and Martin.

Oldham estimates annual production for four smelting clusters in Birbhum. It runs as follows: given the production of 20 to 25 maunds (or 22.5 maunds, on average) of crude iron per week at each furnace, the annual production at the furnace level comes to 1,100 maunds (leaving two weeks for religious festivals) – that is, 41 tons (at 1 ton = 26.79 maunds); since there were 30 furnaces each at Deocha and Balia Narainpore, six at Damra and four at Ganpur (i.e., 70 in total), annual production of crude iron is estimated at 2,870 tons. Since one-fourth of crude iron was lost in refining, the amount of refined iron is 2,152 tons per annum (TPA).

Compared to the scale in Birbhum, smelting units were tiny where the *kol* was involved (Ball 1877: 88). In the Bhagalpur district, Martin notes that each furnace produced, on average, 30 maunds of crude iron per annum. As there were 320 such furnaces, the aggregate output is estimated at 9,600 maunds, or

358 tons, of crude iron and 268 tons of forged iron per annum. Taking Oldham and Martin together, Bengal's annual outturn comes to 3,228 tons of crude iron and 2,420 tons of refined iron around the mid-1800.[4]

Was it the level of production prior to the Company's rule? Traditionally, the local industry catered mainly to four markets: arms and ammunition, agricultural implements (such as ploughs, spades, crowbars, pickaxes, blades, etc.), transport appliances (especially iron tyres for bullock carts, iron shoes for bullocks and horses, as also in boat making) and household articles. The British rule surely put an end to the industry's defence market, as arms and ammunition were procured from abroad. Additionally, the first arms and ammunition manufacturing unit was set up at Ichapore in 1787, and its requisite iron was imported from England. But other market segments survived. Similar to the practices in other civilisations, Bengal also extensively used iron in agriculture, in transportation and in various household utensils (Watson 1907: 36–42). For manufacturing these articles, a large number of blacksmiths must have been employed in the countryside. The 1901 census of Bengal reveals as many as 82,443 blacksmiths across the province.

Watson estimates that per capita iron requirement for village blacksmiths was about 450 kg per annum in the early twentieth century, however. Taking this as a norm (along with the population of blacksmiths), the estimate for Bengal's demand for iron at the blacksmiths' end comes to about 37,000 TPA. On the assumption that local demand for traditional iron products did not increase between 1750 and 1900, I argue that the domestic smelting industry should have been able to cater to this market. This estimate suffers from an upward bias to the extent that local demand for traditional iron products rose in that period. The upward bias is largely counterbalanced, however, since the estimate does not account for the fall in the traditional arms and ammunition market during British rule.[5]

The crucial question, then, is whether the supply sources were altered in the colonial period. We here note that, from the debut of the colonial era, British iron became an important import article. The East India Company evidently imported it into Bengal to the tune of 100 tons on 21 November 1764 (Srinivasachari 1962: 62), 150 tons on 13 December 1765 (ibid.: 106) and 300 tons on 21 November 1766 (ibid.: 203). Simultaneously there was vast clandestine trade, in which the officers of Company ships were involved. We thus come across a confession of two captains of Company ships in 1766 stating that 'they had taken at Madeira… large quantity of lead, iron, cannon, shot and copper' (ibid.: 142). This was in February; three months later we are again informed that 200 tons of iron were imported through clandestine routes (ibid.: 181). Along with iron, illegal trading took place in arms and ammunition as well (Sinha 1959: 76, 113), at which Bengal artisans had once excelled. These pieces of evidence confirm the popularity of imported iron in contemporary Bengal.

If Bengal's iron market is assumed to have been static in the early British period, the inevitable conclusion from rising imports is that Bengal's iron smelting should have declined in this period. The fall is then quite substantial, from 37,000 TPA to 2,420 TPA. Indeed, Homfray and Buchanan indicate such a state of affairs. According to Homfray in 1842, 'The iron…is smelted now in but a very few locations; but the whole country has in different places been subjected to the workers of iron. Scarcely a spot of five miles square within this field but the scoriæ of iron are found in great quantities…' (Homfray 1842: 737). Similarly, according to Buchanan in 1810, 'The richest mines of Virbhum [Birbhum] are close adjacent to its S.E. side, and probably are connected with it in mineral affinity, for mines were formerly wrought at Virkati in Sultangunj, and at Kalidaspur, in Ambar, both on the eastern side of this division; but these have been abandoned, and are now entirely choked, so as to be inaccessible' (Buchanan 1831: 8). There was no evidence of the exhaustion of ores in these places.

Bengal's historiography suggests, however, that iron smelters in the province continuously moved from one place to another, so that smelting concentrations shifted. This judgement is based on the evidence of the scatter of iron slag in many places where no furnace was found. Oldham thus notes that 'the great heaps of refuse adjoining many of the villages, where no furnaces now exist, and where they have not existed within the memory of any of the inhabitants, indicate that this very exhausting process has taken place; that the ore in the vicinity has been worked out, and the occupation therefore abandoned [in those place, and shifted to new sites]' (Oldham 1852: 10; see also Sanyal 1968: 104–5). He emphasises that this was the only viable route to profitability for them.[6]

But an abandoned site does not necessarily suggest the industry's migratory nature. For one thing, there is no evidence to justify the view that smelters in Birbhum or the *kol* in the hills were nomadic tribes. Rather, they belonged to settled civilisation. This is confirmed in Martin, where we find that, in some villages, iron smelting provided a livelihood only for five months, and 'that they wrought in their farms, and in collecting Mahuya flowers for the remaining, except during the two months of marriage feasts, when very little work is done in that part of the country' (Martin 1838: 263–4). Second, so long as there was a division of labour between mining and smelting, as mentioned above, and a developed iron ore market prevailed (Sanyal 1968: 104), there was no compulsion for smelters to abandon a site once local ores had been exhausted. Moreover, even in the second half of the nineteenth century, large deposits of iron ores were noticed in the places where iron smelting had been abandoned – for example, in the vicinity of Mallarpur in Birbhum, where contemporary geologists such as Hughes and Ball proposed large-scale iron smelting in the 1870s (Ball 1877: 89–92); or at Dumka, where 'compact' deposits of ores were noticed after the smelters had deserted (Martin 1838: 193). I argue instead that these abandoned sites signify the industry's decline in the late eighteenth century and early nineteenth.

This reasoning begs a question, however: why was Bengal's iron smelting unable to face competition from Britain? Two factors might be responsible here: inferior quality and/or higher cost prices. On the quality question, several contemporary sources admired Bengal iron. Indeed, charcoal iron was not suitable for certain purposes, such as those used in railways, where toughness was the only desired property. But, where malleability was the primary criterion, charcoal iron was aptly recognised (Oldham 1852: 9).[7] Bengal's technology gave it a further edge as no flux was used in smelting. Oldham (1865: 281) thus remarks that 'the excellent quality of the iron obtained [in Bengal], and its admirable adaptation for many purposes are unquestionable'. Similarly, Jackson (1845: 755) argues, '[N]o flux is used in smelting it, which is done entirely with wood charcoal; a manner of working which may have a good effect on the produce, which is said to be of good quality.' In fact, Bengal's crude iron contained a thick outer crust of brittle material, entirely slag, and an inner mass of tough, malleable iron. 'The inner portion, however, was worked with great ease at the forge and welded perfectly, behaving as charcoal iron of the best quality' (Watson 1907: 24).

Comparative cost disadvantages were, then, responsible for the industry's decline. Contemporary sources inform us that the cost of smelting in Bengal was Re 0.68 per maund (Jackson 1845: 755), and, together with the cost of refining, Rs. 1.50 per maund (or £4 8d. a ton) at the work site (Martin 1838: 265). Moreover, further refinement was made at the blacksmiths' end, involving wastage of 33 to 50 per cent (ibid.). Finally, therefore, the cost price of Bengal iron comes to £6 7s. a ton at the work site. At this cost price, it could not compete with English bar iron, available at Calcutta at £6 to £8 per ton, especially in view of its substantial cost of conveyance from interior places (for transportation in the Rajmahal Hills, see Martin 1838: 285–8). Only in the event of a high import price did domestic iron get a good market. Thus, a government document of 1873 reveals that iron 'is produced in moderate quantities in the native method... [i]n these days of dear iron...' (GOB 1873: 136). My analysis therefore agrees with what Warth wrote in 1881: 'In many places in India iron is made from pure ore, but before cheaper iron was imported from England much more iron and steel used to be made than is made at the present time' (Warth 1881: 1).[8]

The decline of traditional iron smelting had catastrophic effects on employment. To estimate the loss of employment, I assume after Martin (1838: 264) that a family of five members smelted 30 maunds (i.e., 1.12 tons) per annum and that a six-person forge refined 2.80 tons per year. In that case, for 49,333 tons of crude iron,[9] 220,237 persons were employed, and, for 37,000 tons of refined iron, 79,285 persons, giving total employment at 299,522 around the middle of the eighteenth century. In the middle of the nineteenth century it had fallen to just 19,596 (14,410 in crude iron and 5,186 in refined iron), so that the loss of employment comes to 279,926.

III

The genesis of large-scale iron smelting in Bengal dates back to 1774, when Indra Narain Sarma, a feudal aristocrat, sought land to lease in Birbhum. But he never turned up, even though the government sanctioned the lease at an annual rent of Rs. 5,000. Three years later the project was again floated by two British entrepreneurs, John Farquhar and Thomas Motte. They first chose Jheria ('Memorial of M/s Motte and Farquhar, December 1877', in Heatly 1842: 822), which belonged to the Damuda Valley, but later shifted to the Loha Mahal, in the Rajmahal Hills. Exclusive privileges were obtained, free of duty, in lieu of an annual rent, as well as a sale contract with the government for cannons, shots and shells at a discount rate (20 per cent less than the CIF prices of imported articles). The government even advanced Rs. 15,000 for the erection of a furnace, which helped them to commence production in 1779.

Although it had been launched very successfully – offering its output at Rs. 5 a maund at Calcutta, as against Rs. 10 to Rs. 11 for the English (O'Malley 1910: 69) – the project survived only for ten years. Institutional shortcomings were evidently responsible for its failure. In the absence of any custom or law regarding the ownership of minerals in the early British period, the local zemindar claimed for royalties on production despite the government's exemption thereof. The disputes and litigations that consequently followed seriously hampered its activities. A district document thus notes, 'The records are full of accounts of disputes and contests with the natives, who actually claimed that the revenue from the *Loha Mahals* belonged to them…' (O'Malley 1910: 69). Under the sanction of a sudder court (the supreme court of revenue) the local landlord imposed royalty at Re 1 for each smelting (giving about 25 maunds), and 6 pies (i.e., 2 paisa) for each maund of refining, amounting to Rs. 1.96 per ton in aggregate. Interestingly, such authority was nowhere specified in contemporary laws (Jackson 1845: 755–6), but it seriously hampered the financial viability of the project. Moreover, skilled manpower was not locally available, necessitating Europeans to engage; but, in view of the frequent 'disease and death' (Heatly 1842: 822) among them, overhead expenses escalated.

Then a lull followed over the next six decades. Two schemes were floated meantime in the Damuda Valley, using coke as a fuel – one by Jessop & Co. in 1839 (Srinivasan 1983: 14) and the other by Bengal Coal Company around that time (Smith 1856: 21). But they were ultimately abandoned, and the Rajmahal Hills remained the site of choice. In 1855, however, Mackay & Co. set up Mohammad Bazar Iron Works (near Suri in Birbhum) using European charcoal technology. Because of its large capacity (2½ tons of pig iron per day: McFarlane 1907: 151), it took a lease over seven square miles of forest land, and thus generated severe backwash effects for native iron smelting. It took the iron ore and charcoal that would otherwise have gone to native smelting, as also local workers who had earlier been self-employed. Alien technology was no barrier to local recruits, as they could 'quickly acquire the skill, necessary for all the operations in the manufacture of iron from blast furnace…' (Smith 1856: 13).

A new horizon was thus heralded in Bengal's iron smelting. In contrast to the semi-fused iron obtained in traditional smelting, it now turned out pig iron, and very competitively too, at only Rs. 2 a maund in 1860–1. It also excelled qualitatively. According to a contemporary report, 'The quality…of the pig iron is stated by the professional officers of Government who examined the works, to surpass English pig iron, and if more of it were obtained and sold at the price of imported English pig iron, a considerable profit would be realised' (GOB 1862: 125). But it concentrated on a single product, pig iron. The production of cast iron was aborted for 'the want of experienced moulders' (ibid.); and the recasting of iron was never tried. The firm ran successfully from 1856–7 to 1860–1, but its profitability was lost thereafter, and could never be revived in spite of two changes in ownership – once in 1860–1, when a native entrepreneur ensured 'the strictest economy' (ibid.), and then in 1872, when the landlord, to whom the lease of land had lapsed, prohibited native smelting in his jurisdiction.[10] Finally, Burn & Co. acquired it in 1873. The installed capacity was augmented to 500 tons a month to ensure scale economies; in addition, coke was substituted for charcoal, heralding the age of coke iron in India. But the financial outcomes of those strategies were too weak to retain Burn & Co. in business. And there ended the story of Birbhum, which had lasted from 1774 to 1873. Ball (1881: 362) remarks, 'It fully supports the truth of the old adage that history repeats itself. The same sanguine hopes, the same attempts to carry on work in spite of discouraging circumstances, the same failures and the final loss of expended capital, are recorded in the accounts of each attempt.'

At this point, the obvious question is: why did these ventures fail? On the supply side, the adverse factor was surely the scarcity of charcoal. As early as 1852 Oldham (1852: 9) noticed that '[t]he forests and jungles are disappearing before the axe of the charcoal-burner, and the plough is steadily taking possession of lands very recently covered with impenetrable wood'. It was further aggravated in the next decade, when the production of charcoal iron was 'closed [in many places] owing to the gradual diminution of the jungles and the consequently increased prices of charcoal' (GOB 1862: 125; see also P.P. 1874: 103). It is true that the seven square miles of forest land that Mackay & Co. took on lease were sufficient for an outturn of 900 tons of charcoal iron per year (that is, 2½ tons per day). Given that one ton of iron required 1½ tons of charcoal and the yield of charcoal per square mile (taking the renewal of trees at 15 years) was 211 TPA (Ball 1877: 92–3), the stretch of forest land should be 6.4 square miles. But it required scientific plantation, which should begin at least seven to eight years prior to the production schedule. That was conspicuously absent. Ball (1877: 92) additionally points out: 'Even with the most scientific treatment, the soil in the laterite areas is too poor to admit of the free or rapid growth of timber.'

In addition, there must have been problems elsewhere; otherwise, Burn & Co.'s use of coke as a fuel would have worked better. The critical issue in this case was the market domain, which I shall discuss shortly. Let me just add that this nascent industry never received any pecuniary support from the government. Its policy statement was that '[t]he production of good iron in India is a matter of great importance, but the manifestation of Government interest in such enterprise is necessarily limited to the employment of the metal on public work, if the quality and price be such that it can be used with advantage' (GOB 1862: 125).

Table 4.1 Comparative costs of iron smelting in the Damuda Valley and south Wales (20,000 tons per annum), 1850

Particulars	*South Wales*		*Damuda Valley*	
	Rates (per ton)	*Amount (in £)*	*Rates (per ton)*	*Amount (in £)*
Iron stone (93,000 tons)	9s. 3d	43,290	3s.	14,040
Coal (130,000 tons)	4s. 6d	29,250	2s.	13,000
Limestone (18,500 tons)	3s.	2,770	27s.	23,356
Total		75,310		50,396

Source: Williams (1850: 125–30).

From the early 1870s, however, the Damuda Valley came into prominence. David Hiram Williams, geological surveyor to the Company, had first brought it into the limelight when he underlined its comparative advantages vis-à-vis south Wales in 1850 (Table 4.1). He worked out that, for a capacity of 20,000 TPA, a project in Bengal had a comparative cost advantage of £24,914.

Oldham puts the cost figure for the Damuda Valley at £57,676, however, giving a margin of advantage of £17,634 (Oldham 1852: 11). Of course, a project in Bengal involved additional costs of freight and insurance for importing machinery from abroad. But those were more than compensated by the freight charges (20s. a ton), insurance (2 per cent) and duty (5 per cent) which English iron had to bear at Calcutta. A favourable judgement was also given by a government expert from England (P.P. 1874: 103). His estimate is that the unit cost of pig iron was Rs. 24 a ton at Ranigunj, as against Rs. 37.66 in south Wales (Table 4.1). This estimate is based on the price of coal at Rs. 3 a ton, that of iron ore at Re 1 a ton and that of *kunkur* at Rs. 1.80 a ton.

The first venture in this valley was the Bengal Iron Works, which James Erskine formed in 1870 with a project cost of Rs. 500,000. At Kulti it had two blast furnaces (20 tons per day each), where coke was used as a fuel, and well-equipped foundries of 3,800 TPA were launched. Starting production in 1875, it produced 12,700 tons of pig iron through 1879 in aggregate. It certainly created high hopes in society. A local daily (*The Statesman*, Calcutta, 8 March 1876) reported, 'We regard this experiment with equal interest and anxiety. Every attempt to make iron in India by European process had failed; success will now inaugurate an economic revolution in the country. India will, at no distant date, supply herself with her own iron.' But it could never earn a profit, and, therefore, finally wound up in 1879. For a few months Messrs Marillier and Edward worked its foundries, but the continuing financial losses aborted their efforts too.

A host of factors contributed to its failure. On the production side, I may identify three such factors: (i) a higher ash content in the coke, which drove up the costs of production, as a larger amount of flux was required in smelting, and there was also more ash to be cleared manually; (ii) a high rate of interest, especially for an initial loan taken from the British government (Bhardwaj 1982: 231); and (iii) a long distance (about 1¾ miles) from the nearest water source, the Barakar, which required expensive pumping arrangements. A high production cost was thus involved. Its costs of production in 1875 stood at Rs. 65 a ton, as against Rs. 60 for English iron at Calcutta (von Schwarz 1882: 3–4). By 1878 it had been able to reduce the cost to Rs. 40, but by then the latter had become Rs. 29 a ton. In 1879, when the firm was closed, the English pig iron was being sold at Rs. 35 a ton, still Rs. 5 less than the price of the domestic iron. On the demand side, however, the difficulty arose from its single line of production, pig iron, for which the domestic market was yet to develop in the absence of foundries. As a bulk buyer, the government mainly purchased castings, rather than pig iron (Srinivasan 1983: 32). The colonial store purchase policy, to be discussed shortly, further narrowed its outlets.

In 1880–1, however, the government took over the concern, bearing in mind the extensive use of pig iron in public works and railways. The surplus output was sold on the open market. Available evidence suggests that, as Barakar Iron Works, it ran successfully for about 8½ years, earning a profit, albeit a small one (GOB 1890: 197), in certain years. The pig iron market was growing very rapidly then. In 1884–5, for example, strong demand prevailed, and pig iron production rose to 6,630 tons – 2,000 tons for open market sales and 4,630 tons for captive uses (GOB 1886: 197). But the market was very oscillatory. In 1886–7, for example, the demand was so low that the inventory accumulated from 677 tons to 3,683 tons.[11] But it survived with the support of strong government demand.

State ownership was relinquished in 1889–90, however. Possibly this was due to the Secretary of State, who disliked government participation in business (Srinivasan 1983: 33).[12] The ownership then went to a London-based company – Bengal Iron and Steel – which was formed in 1890 with paid-up capital of £50,000. A thorough modernisation followed (for details, see McFarlane 1907). Moreover, the installed capacity was enhanced, by stages, to 520,000 TPA for pig iron and 25,000 to 30,000 TPA for castings in 1907. Steel plants (20,000 TPA) were also installed in 1904. With these extensions and modernisations, its investment totalled Rs. 7,000,000 in 1907.

Available evidence confirms that the company performed well. According to a government report dated 1901, 'In the Barakar iron-works in the Burdwan district, the outturn increased considerably, the value estimated during the year being about sixteen lakhs [Rs. 1,600,000] as compared with nine lakhs [Rs. 900,000] in 1895–96' (GOB 1901: 147). It increased further to Rs. 2,409,798 in 1901–2 and Rs. 2,440,035 in 1902–3 (GOB 1904: 68). Table 4.2 shows that, from 1898 to 1913, production steadily increased from 19,719 tons to 59,187 tons for pig iron, and from 7,833 tons to 17,536 tons for castings, exhibiting annual growth rates of 13.34 per cent and 8.26 per cent, on average, respectively.

This development was inspired by buoyant engineering activities in and around this province. Four market segments were important to this end: iron

Table 4.2 Production and use of iron ore at Bengal Iron & Steel Company (in tons), 1898–1913

Year	*Production*		*Use of iron ore*
	Pig iron	*Castings*	
1898	19,719[1]	7,833[1]	NA
1899	19,631[5]	NA	NA
1900	22,583[4]	8,177[4]	57,000[6]
1902	33,180[1]	11,499[1]	NA
1903	28,318[1]	9,644[1]	NA
1904	40,932[2]	14,882[2]	89,333[2]
1905	44,764[2]	18,802[2]	91,697[2]
1906	46,890[2]	11,764[2]	90,840[2]
1907	39,312[2]	12,304[2]	78,140[2]
1908	37,692[2]	11,595[2]	73,027[2]
1909	38,634[3]	12,216[3]	71,970[3]
1910	35,933[3]	7,930[3]	42,033[3]
1911	49,183[3]	14,500[3]	39,931[3]
1912	58,883[3]	13,857[3]	93,881[3]
1913	59,187[3]	17,536[3]	108,078[3]

Sources: 1: Watson (1907: 14); 2: Holland and Fermor (1910: 104); 3: Holland and Fermor (1915: 101); 4: P.P. (1901: 132); 5: P.P. (1900: 119); 6: P.P. (1902: 183).

foundries, arms and ammunitions, workshops (mainly railways) and dockyards. We noted earlier that, in the absence of foundries, the pig iron market was limited even in the late 1870s. But the number of iron and brass foundries evidently increased from four in 1881 to 15 in 1891, 25 in 1901 and further to 38 in 1903 (GOI 1908a: 270). Table 4.3 shows that, in 1911, there were 12 large foundries, employing at least 200 persons each, and 15 more with smaller set-ups.

Pig iron was also used extensively in the arms and ammunition industry, which expanded in a big way in the 1870s.[13] Aggregate employment in this industry was 7,552 in 1911. The gun and shell factories at Cossipore and Ichapore also rolled special steel using two 10 ton acid open hearth furnaces, where 40 to 60 tons of steel were produced per diem. Although the output was primarily intended for captive use, open market sales were frequent. Steel was also produced at the East Indian Railway workshop at Jamalpur, where a steel foundry (with a capacity of 300 tons per month) and rolling mills (400 tons per month) were installed. There were altogether 13 large workshops in 1911, out of which six belonged to railways, and another one (Shalimar Loco Engineering) worked for them. Most of these workshops had foundry facilities. Total employment in this branch was 27,136. Last but not least, dockyards became a major consumer of iron, as iron ships increasingly replaced wooden ones in the second half of the nineteenth century (MacGregor 1984). In view of the many ships calling at the Port of Calcutta,[14] the industry concentrated

Table 4.3 Major engineering firms in Bengal, 1911

Industry/firm	*Number of workers*	*Industry/firm*	*Number of workers*
Foundries		Dockyards	
Howrah Iron Works	4,402	Royal Indian Marine	1,550
Bengal Iron & Steel	3,582	River Steam Navigation Company	1,271
Howrah Foundry	1,490	India General Steam Navigation	1,331
British India Engineering	1,252	Port Commissioners	1,213
Jessop & Co.	591	British India	628
Victoria Iron Works	499	Hoogly Docking & Engineering Works	225
Mackintosh Burn's Iron Foundry	480	Others	100
Vulcan Iron Works	442	**Subtotal**	6,318
Shalimar Workshops	440	Workshops	
Saxeby Farmer & Co.	260	B. N. Railway Workshop, Kharagpur	6,450
Ganges Engineering Works	250	E. I. Railway Workshop, Jamalpur,[1] Lilua, Rampurhat, Nalhati	15,111
W. Leslie & Co.	214	Locomotive & Carriage, Kanchrapara	2,158
15 smaller foundries (fewer than 200 workers)	1,447	Electrical Tramways, Calcutta & Howrah	1,395
Subtotal	15,349	Calcutta Electric Supply	246
Arms and ammunition		Telegraph Workshop	639
Ammunition Factory, Dumdum	2,681	Calcutta Municipal Workshop	330
Rifle Factory, Ichapore	2,050	Interlocking Workshop, Calcutta	200
Gun & Shell Factory, Ichapore	1,550	Shalimar Loco Engineering, Howrah	200
Foundry & Shell Factory, Cossipore	1,271	3 smaller workshops (fewer than 200 workers)	407
Subtotal	7,552	**Subtotal**	27,136
		Total	56,355

Sources. GOI (1911: 1–9, 52, 54, 56–8); 1: Watson (1907: 46).

in and around Howrah. There were six dockyards in 1911, giving employment to 6,318 persons in aggregate. Table 4.3 works out total employment in these industries at 56,355 in 1911.

Another source, however, provides a comparative status of engineering industries between Bengal and India in 1906; the data are presented in Table 4.4. There are some discrepancies between Tables 4.3 and 4.4, as the former lists only larger concerns, as against the totals enumerated in the latter. Table 4.4 demonstrates that Bengal had a major cluster of engineering industries, however, accounting for 41.27 per cent of total employment. Save for railway

Table 4.4 Employment in engineering industries in Bengal and India, 1906

Industry	*Employment*	
	Bengal	*India*
Foundries	16,629	26,123
Arms and ammunition	9,201	15,957
Dockyards	7,230	12,632
Workshops	26,656	89,970
Total	59,716	144,682

Source: GOI (1908b: 78–9).

workshops (for which the rest of India accounted for 70.37 per cent), Bengal dominated in foundries (63.66 per cent), arms and ammunition (57.66 per cent) and dockyards (57.23 per cent).

Arms manufacturing strictly belonged to the government sector, and the works relating to rolling stock largely to various railway companies. Those apart, almost all large-scale enterprises ran under British capital and belonged to joint-stock companies. Among such organisations, more important ones included Howrah Docking Company (Rs. 400,000 as paid-up capital for 1905), Hooghly Docking & Engineering Company (Rs. 500,000), Jessop & Co. (Rs. 900,000), John King & Co. (Rs. 300,000), Burn & Co. (Rs. 4,900,000), Shalimer Works (Rs. 325,000), Vulcan Iron Works (Rs. 220,000), Bengal Engineering Company (Rs. 100,000) and Calcutta Conveyance Company (Rs. 2,100,000) (GOI 1907). These aggregate to about Rs. 9.75 million, and, together with the investment of Bengal Iron and Steel, Rs. 16.75 million.

Bengali entrepreneurs also participated in this development process, but were confined to smaller undertakings. Among prominent entrepreneurs in this business, let me cite Kishorilal Mukherjee (Sibpur Iron Works) (O'Malley 1909: 109), Radha Mohan Poramanik (Commercial Dock), Tarak Nath Poramanik (Caledonia Dock), Joy Gopal Mullick (Hoogly Dock Yards), Ramkonoo Sircar (East India Dock), Issur Chunder Manjee (Indian Iron Foundry), Heero Lall Seal (Taragon Iron Works and Building Yard) and Pitambur Mookerjee (Iron Foundry) (Banerjee 1872: 81–4). Another source tells us that, in 1901, there were 16 small engineering firms in Howrah, indigenously held, with output valued at Rs. 139,000 (Owens and Nandy 1978: 61). They mainly produced weights for scales, sugarcane presses, rollers, bolts, machinery for oil and jute mills, building and carriage materials, railings and iron safes. The presence of indigenous entrepreneurs is also noticed in Watson (1907: 46): 'There are a large number of smaller firms…under native management in and near Calcutta.' Referring to a contemporary directory, he informs us that about 149 such firms belonged to the engineering industry in 1907 (ibid.).

This study thus suggests that, with the decline of traditional iron smelting, Bengal's employment had fallen by about 280,000 by the middle of the nineteenth century; but the modern smelting industry (along with its downstreams) generated employment for about 60,000 persons. The net loss was then 220,000. But this should be qualified by the quality of employment – especially the perenniality of jobs, as well as the wage rate. While the traditional industry could not provide employment round the year (Martin 1838: 263–4), workers were not laid off seasonally in modern set-ups (Foley 1906: 22–3). Again, Martin calculates that the earnings in the former were Rs. 2.75 per month for smelting and Rs. 3.87 per month for refining (Martin 1838: 264–5), giving an average monthly income of Rs. 3.31. In contrast, an unskilled labourer at Bengal Iron and Steel Works got Rs. 8.12 per month (Foley 1906: xxxiv). The wage rate was higher still for skilled labour. In 1905 it was Rs. 17.22 for a fitter, Rs. 19.32 for a carpenter, Rs. 19.37 for a moulder, Rs. 15.45 for a case maker, Rs. 15.16 for an engineer and Rs. 15.17 for a blacksmith. Taking all the categories together, the average monthly wage comes to Rs. 15.69, which is 4.74 times greater than that in the traditional industry. This gain was at the cost of the loss of employment, which I have estimated at 4.67 times the gain in employment in this modern industry. Only a value judgement can resolve whether society was worse off in the modern state of affairs.

IV

I have adumbrated that Bengal's engineering market was poised for take-off around the middle of the nineteenth century on the basis of public works and railroad construction. It enabled Mohammad Bazar Iron Works to run profitably through 1860–1. But the scenario changed abruptly in 1862. The domestic market shrank so much thereafter that its profitability could not be ensured even with the use of state-of-the-art technology. I here argue that this turnaround was largely due to the government's store purchase policy, introduced in 1862.

According to this policy, all government stores (including those for the railways) were to be procured through the Stores Department in London, where testing appliances, and technical manpower, were available. Prima facie, the quality question dominated the decision. But contemporary documents tell us that the underlying objective was to preserve the Indian market for British industries. Thus, in 1862, the Secretary of State communicated, '[A]ll articles manufactured in England should be procured only through the Stores Department of the India Office' ('History of the Rules for the Supply of Articles for the Public Service in India, 1862–1918', in GOI 1920: 163). The interests of Indian industries were totally ignored. 'There is no trace in this resolution of any policy of encouragement of local industries, nor was the question of local purchase referred to' (ibid.). Only in 1876 was the issue discussed at length by the Stores Purchase Committee, which the Secretary of State set up. The committee was sympathetic to 'the development of a local system of supply in India' (ibid.: 164), but denied any relief to the engineering industry. Its recommendation was that 'all special machinery and appliances, such as engineering, railway and telegraph plant and material, would almost necessarily be obtained through the Store Department' (ibid.). Thus, the stores purchase rules of 1871 and 1878 (as also the directives of the Secretary of State in 1862) explain why large-scale iron works could not run profitably in the 1860s and 1870s.

The Secretary of State pursued the matter further, however. He went on record in 1878 saying that 'the special attention of local Government should be drawn to the importance of substituting local manufactures for European articles even at some temporary increase in cost…' (ibid.: 165). A great debate followed. There were three points of opposition from the British engineering interests: (i) that the paucity of test appliances in India would impede inspection, causing quality to suffer; (ii) that the few Indian firms then in existence were not conducive to any of the economic advantages that free competition bred; and (iii) that cost advantages in local procurement would also be absent, since their raw materials were imported from England. The Indian administration favoured the guideline for the sake of the economy, however, and also because the supply chain would not be dislocated even in wartime. On the weight of the latter arguments, the policy framework tilted towards domestic industries through a resolution of the Finance Department in 1883. The prologue reads, 'The Governor-General in Council…desires again to invite the special attention of local government to the expediency of supplying the wants of Government by the purchase in the local market of articles of bona fide local manufacture' (ibid.). It clarifies that 'there is no reason why articles manufactured in India should not be obtained locally, even though the raw material necessary for their manufacture may have been imported from Europe' (ibid.: 167–8). Because of this policy reform, the value of government stores, manufactured in India, rose from Rs. 3,942,000 in 1882–3 to Rs. 7,071,000 in 1884–5, implying a growth of about 80 per cent.

Two points should be stressed in this context. First, the directives for local purchase were often flouted at lower levels, so that imports continued. Stores imported through the India Office, together with those on private accounts, rose from Rs. 18,476,000 in 1882–3 to Rs. 25,597,000 in 1884–5 (ibid.: 168). Second, at the behest of the British iron interests (ibid.: 165, 171), the government of India classified iron bars and plates as finished products, rather than raw materials, so that 'objections to local purchase [were] applied in the highest degree' (ibid.: 174). Therefore, domestically produced iron bars lost market share in public works and the railways. Alarmed by its cascading effects, Indian houses sought its repeal, both individually – such as through a memorandum submitted by 35 firms – and collectively, through the chambers of commerce at Madras and Karachi. In forwarding those representations, the government of India wrote to the Secretary of State in 1890, '[T]here was a very widespread feeling among iron manufacturers in India that their operations were unduly hampered by the prohibition of orders on behalf of the Government. That there was some force in the argument' (ibid.: 172). The question of inadequate competition, as noted above, was also turned down: 'We are of opinion that the scheme should not be allowed to drop on account of this fear… [since] there are undoubtedly administrative and economic advantages in procuring them in India' (ibid.: 172–3). This attitude of the Indian administration paved the way for further relaxation of the store purchase rules in 1891, however. The amendments contained a detailed list of indigenously produced goods that could be purchased in India. The list was further extended in 1898 and again in 1909.

I should emphasise here that, although they were certainly catalytic to the development of engineering industries in Bengal, those reforms never provided protection to domestic industries. Local purchases were made strictly on the basis of 'quality and price' (GOB 1862: 125). That was, indeed, the blatant philosophy of the Secretary of State. He noted, 'Care was, however, to be taken to guard against any supposition that these measures were adopted in any other interests than those of economy and against any claim for the protection of local industry…' (ibid.: 173). The merits of the policy should be understood in terms of the extent to which it provided a level playground to domestic industries vis-à-vis the British. Even that was not acceptable to the British iron interests, insofar as it adversely affected them. To the British administration in India, though, good governance was evidently a priority. Its communication to the Secretary of State emphasises, 'The Government of India could not take into account the probable effect on English manufactures of any action on their part which might tend to develop local efforts. They had repeatedly pledged themselves to encourage the purchase of the products of local industries and to foster local enterprises and their pledge had been endorsed by successive Secretaries of State' (ibid.: 185). This was the ethical underpinning of the policy reforms in store purchases.

Liberalisation of the store purchase policy bolstered the demand side for Bengal's engineering industries. This is evident in Table 4.5. In government's stores (excluding paper and paste board), the share of Indian manufactures are seen to have risen from 19.45 per cent in 1908–9 to 30.52 per cent in 1909–10, and further to 38.83 per cent in 1911–12. The share averaged 41 per cent from 1910 to

Table 4.5 Purchases of government stores (excluding paper and paste board) (in thousand Rs.), 1907/8–1911/12

Type of stores	*1907–8*	*1908–9*	*1909–10*	*1910–11*	*1911–12*
Indian goods	1,610 (25.71)	1,268 (19.45)	1,292 (30.52)	1,302 (30.39)	1,818 (38.83)
Foreign goods bought in India	1,380 (22.04)	1,203 (18.46)	165 (3.90)	1,001 (23.36)	176 (3.76)
Foreign goods bought abroad	3,272 (52.25)	4,047 (62.09)	2,776 (65.58)	1,982 (46.25)	2,688 (57.41)
Total	6,262 (100)	6,518 (100)	4,233 (100)	4,285 (100)	4,682 (100)

Note: The terms in parentheses represent the percentage of the total.

Source: GOI (1920: 236).

1914 and 52 per cent from 1914 to 1919 (GOI 1920: 10). These statistics confirm that domestic engineering industries must have gained a firm base by 1919.

Appendix 4.1 displays the source-wise store purchases of various government departments (including the railways) in 1910/11 to 1913/14. The overall share of Indian manufactures works out at 40.78 per cent. The railways took a smaller share than this (35 per cent), but local products dominated in government purchases, both central (51.71 per cent) and local (45.33 per cent). These figures speak to the significance of domestic engineering industries in the contemporary market.

V

There are four major findings in this study. First, prior to British rule in India, iron smelting developed in Bengal, along with a host of downstream industries based on locally available iron ore. But deindustrialisation took place in iron smelting thereafter. I argue that, notwithstanding its excellence in quality, the industry declined because of its comparative cost disadvantages against British iron. Second, a series of large-scale ventures took place in Bengal between 1774 and 1879, but none could survive. Only from 1880 onwards did the sustained development of iron smelting, and its downstreams, take place in the province. Third, the industry's initial failures and its subsequent development are explained by the contemporary store purchase policy of the government, though it does not explain Bengal's deindustrialisation in iron smelting. The store purchases created a totally new demand connected with public goods and a civil engineering drive. Even if the policy initially favoured domestic producers, it could not possibly arrest the decline of the indigenous handicrafts industry, because this industry did not operate on a scale sufficient to supply the demands. Fourth, there was an employment loss of 280,000 in the traditional industry, but a gain of about 60,000 in the modern industry. The net loss was, therefore, 220,000. I argue that this loss of employment should be qualified by the difference between them in terms of the quality of the jobs.

Notes

1 He notes that temple sculptures also suggest that 'this spear was made in Bengal' (ibid.).
2 The description of furnaces here is based on that by Martin (1838: 261–3) for Bhagalpur district. A similar description is available in Watson (1907: 21–2) for Dumka (see Figure 4.2) and Anon. (1831) for Amdeah, near Sambhalpur. In the Kasya Hills, however, furnaces were accommodated in large grass huts, and the bellows were operated for blast both by hand and by leg (Anon. 1832).
3 This process was also followed in the United Kingdom and the United States before the innovation of the puddling method (Temin 1964: 456).
4 This is based on the surmise that the industry was developed only in Birbhum and its adjoining areas in the Rajmahal Hills. In this connection, Sanyal (1968: 105) notes: 'A considerable portion of the demand for iron must have been met by

the products of Birbhum since the iron manufacturing industry of Bankura and Manbhum is never known to have assumed a significant proportion of the total.'

5 Traditional demand for iron might increase due to population growth. But its growth rate was low in Bengal during the eighteenth and nineteenth centuries, on account of various tropical diseases and frequent floods (Ray 2015b: 131). Moreover, as Roy (2008: 383) points out, the consumption of iron products increased between 1815 and 1914, but imported iron was largely used: 'For example, cutlery, which had been a semi-specialized urban branch of smithy, quickly switched over to Swedish and Sheffield steels, strengthening its own craft skills and yet cutting off ties with indigenous smelting.' In addition, many household appliances that village blacksmiths had earlier manufactured were imported around 1900. In 1900–1, for example, Bengal imported hardware and cutlery valued at Rs. 905,681 (Watson 1907: 15).

6 'Where the profit is so small, the addition of a few miles to the distance from which either the raw ore, or the charcoal for its fusion, has to be brought, will be quite sufficient to turn the balance' (Oldham 1852: 10).

7 The production of charcoal iron initially declined in Britain, but later revived to some extent (Inwood 1985: 297–8) using modern charcoal technology (Temin 1964: chaps. 3, 7).

8 Indeed, Roy (2008: 383) also offers a similar conclusion: 'That a manufacturing tradition such as this survived so long points to the economic power of consumers who were prepared to pay the high prices for its output. When these markets disappeared, new markets firmly shut their doors to indigenous iron.'

9 Since one-fourth of crude iron was wasted on refining, 37,000 tons of refined iron is obtained from 49,333 tons of crude iron.

10 It led to the closure of the lone native concern at Deocha, comparatively large in size though it was. Although the literature claims that the traditional industry was totally ruined thereby (see, for example, Ball 1877: 88), a government document of 1874–5 reveals that there were six such concerns smelting 200 maunds of iron each, on average (i.e., about 45 tons in aggregate) per year (P.P. 1876: 47).

11 A government report for 1886–7 (GOB 1888: 182–3) thus underlines, 'The year under review was an unfavourable one at the Burrakur Iron Works owing to the public demand for pig-iron being much less than during the previous year... The foundry work was comparatively slack... The orders for miscellaneous casting, however, steadily increased, but...it does not consume sufficient iron to cause any very sensible diminution in the stock.'

12 Note that its market prospect was not bleak around that time. This is evident in that, in 1888–9, a proposal was submitted for a new blowing engine and to place both of its furnaces in blast (GOB 1890: 197).

13 Ammunition Factory, Dumdum and Foundry & Shell Factory, Cossipore, were set up in this period (GOB 1873: 126).

14 In 1868–9, for example, 875 ships arrived at this port with a total load of 804,986 tons (GOB 1870: xli).

Bibliography

Allen, R. C. (1979) 'International Competition in Iron and Steel, 1850–1913', *Journal of Economic History* 39 (4), 911–37.

Anon. (1831) 'Account of the Process of Making Iron at Amdeah, near Sambhalpur', *Gleanings in Science* 3 (34), 330.

Anon. (1832) 'Smelting of Iron in the Kasya Hills', *Journal of the Asiatic Society of Bengal* 1 (4), 150–1.

Aston, T. S. (1963) *Iron and Steel in the Industrial Revolution*, 3rd edn. Manchester: Manchester University Press.

Awty, B. G. (1957) 'Charcoal Ironmasters of Cheshire and Lancashire 1600–1785', *Transactions of the Historical Society of Lancashire and Cheshire* 109, 71–124.

Ball, V. (1877) 'Geology of the Rajmahal Hills', *Memoirs of the Geological Survey of India* 13 (2), 1–87.

Ball, V. (1881) *A Manual of the Geology of India: Economic Geology*. Calcutta: Geological Survey of India.

Banerjee, C. N. (1872) *An Account of Howrah: Past and Present*. Calcutta (no pub.).

Bhardwaj, H. C. (1982) 'Development of Iron and Steel Technology in India during 18th and 19th Centuries', *Indian Journal of History of Science* 17 (2), 223–33.

Bhattacharyya, S. (1970) 'Iron Smelters and the Indigenous Iron and Steel Industry of India: From Stagnation to Atrophy', *Journal of Indian Anthropological Society* 5 (1/2), 133–51.

Birch, A. (1967) *Economic History of the British Iron and Steel Industry 1784–1879: Essays in Industrial and Economic History with Special Reference to the Development of Technology*. London: Frank Cass.

Biswas, A. K. (1994) 'Iron and Steel in Pre-Modern India: A Critical Review', *Indian Journal of History of Science* 29 (4), 579–610.

Blanford, W. T. (1865) 'On the Geological Structure and Relations of the Raniganj Coal Field, Bengal', *Memoirs of the Geological Survey of India* 3 (1), 1–195.

Buchanan, F. (1831) 'On the Minerals of the Rajmahal Cluster of Hills', *Gleanings in Science* 3 (25), 1–8.

Burn, D. L. (1947) 'Recent Trends in the History of the Steel Industry', *Economic History Review* (first series) 17 (2), 95–102.

Childs, W. R. (1981) 'England's Iron Trade in the Fifteenth Century', *Economic History Review* (new series) 34 (1), 25–47.

Evens, C., Jackson, O., and Ryden, G. (2002) 'Baltic Iron and the British Iron Industry in the Eighteenth Century', *Economic History Review* (new series) 55 (1), 642–65.

Fergusson, J. (1864) *The Rock-Cut Temples of India*. London: John Murray.

Fergusson, J. (1874) *A History of Architecture in All Countries: From the Earliest Times to the Present Day*. London: John Murray.

Flinn, M. W. (1958) 'Revision in Economic History XVII: The Growth of the English Iron Industry 1660–1760', *Economic History Review* (new series) 11 (1), 144–53.

Foley, B. (1906) *Report on Labour in Bengal*. Calcutta: Bengal Secretariat Book Depot.

Government of Bengal (GOB) (1862) *Annual Report on the Administration of Bengal, 1860–1*. National Library Archive, Calcutta.

Government of Bengal (GOB) (1870) *Annual Report on the Administration of Bengal, 1868–9*. National Library Archive, Calcutta.

Government of Bengal (GOB) (1873) *Annual Report on the Administration of Bengal, 1871–2*. National Library Archive, Calcutta.

Government of Bengal (GOB) (1886) *Annual Report on the Administration of Bengal, 1884–5*. National Library Archive, Calcutta.

Government of Bengal (GOB) (1888) *Annual Report on the Administration of Bengal, 1886–7*. National Library Archive, Calcutta.

Government of Bengal (GOB) (1890) *Annual Report on the Administration of Bengal, 1888–9.* National Library Archive, Calcutta.

Government of Bengal (GOB) (1901) *Annual Report on the Administration of Bengal, 1899–1900.* National Library Archive, Calcutta.

Government of Bengal (GOB) (1904) *Annual Report on the Administration of Bengal, 1902–3.* National Library Archive, Calcutta.

Government of India (GOI) (1907) *Joint Stock Companies in India, 1905–06.* National Library Archive, Calcutta.

Government of India (GOI) (1908a) *The Imperial Gazetteers of India*, vol. VII. Oxford: Clarendon Press.

Government of India (GOI) (1908b) *Statistics of British India for 1906–07 and Preceding Years*, part I: *Industrial.* National Library Archive, Calcutta.

Government of India (GOI) (1911) *List of Factories and Other Large Industries in India.* National Library Archive, Calcutta.

Government of India (GOI) (1920) *Report of the Stores Purchase Committee.* Simla: Government Central Press.

Hammersley, G. (1973) 'The Charcoal Iron Industry and Its Fuel, 1540–1750', *Economic History Review* (new series) 26 (4), 593–613.

Harris, J. R. (1988) *The British Iron Industry, 1700–1850.* Basingstoke, UK: Macmillan Education.

Headrick, D. (1990) *The Tentacles of Progress: Technology Transfer in the Age of Imperialism, 1850–1940.* New York: Oxford University Press.

Heatly, S. G. T. (1842) 'Contributions towards a History of the Development of the Mineral Resources of India', *Journal of the Asiatic Society of Bengal* 11 (2), 811–35.

Hedge, K. T. M. (1973) 'A Model for Understanding Ancient Indian Iron Metallurgy', *Man* 8 (3), 416–21.

Holland, T. H., and Fermor, L. L. H. (1910) 'Quinquennial Review of the Mineral Production of India during the Years 1904 to 1908', Records of the Geological Survey of India no. 39, part 1. Calcutta: Geological Survey of India.

Holland, T. H., and Fermor, L. L. H. (1915) 'Quinquennial Review of the Mineral Production of India, Revised for the Years 1909 to 1913 by H. H. Hayden and L. L. Fermor', Records of the Geological Survey of India no. 46, part 1. Calcutta: Geological Survey of India.

Holt, J. (1977) 'Trade Unionism in the British and US Steel Industries', *Labour History* 18 (1), 5–35.

Homfray, J. (1842) 'A Description of the Coal Field of the Damoodah Valley, and the Adjacent Countries of Beerbhoom and Poorooleah, as Applicable to the Present Date 1842', *Journal of the Asiatic Society of Bengal* 11 (2), 723–39.

Hyde, C. K. (1977) *Technological Change and the British Iron Industry, 1700–1870.* Princeton, NJ: Princeton University Press.

Inwood, K. (1985) 'Productivity Growth in Obsolescence: Charcoal Iron Revisited', *Journal of Economic History* 45 (2), 293–8.

Jackson, W. (1845) 'Memorandum on the Iron Works of Beerbhoom', *Journal of the Asiatic Society of Bengal* 14 (2), 754–6.

Johnson, B. L. C. (1951) 'The Charcoal Iron Industry in the Early Eighteenth Century', *Geographical Journal* 117 (2), 167–77.

Karan, P. P. (1957) 'Iron Mining Industry in Singhbhum–Mayurbhanj Region of India', *Economic Geography* 33 (4), 349–61.

MacGregor, D. R. (1984) *Merchant Sailing Ships, 1850–1875: Heyday of Sails*. London: Conway Maritime Press.

Martin, M. (1838) *The History, Antiquities, Topography, and Statistics of Eastern India*, vol. II. London: W. H. Allen.

McCloskey, D. N. (1974) *Economic Maturity and Entrepreneurial Decline: British Iron and Steel, 1870–1913*. Cambridge, MA: Harvard University Press.

McFarlane, W. (1907) 'Barakar Iron Works', *Transactions of the Mining and Geological Institute of India* 1, 147–53.

Medlicott, H. B., and Blanford, W. T. (1879) *A Manual of the Geology of India*, part I: *Peninsular India*. Calcutta: Geological Survey of India.

Mitter, R. (1880) *The Antiquities of Orissa, Illustrated with Photographic Plates*, 2 vols. Calcutta: W. Newman.

Murty, K. S. (1982) 'Geological Science in India in the 18th–19th Century', *Indian Journal of History of Science* 17 (1), 164–78.

Oldham, T. (1852) 'Report of the Examination of the Districts in the Damoodah Valley and Beerbhoom, Producing Iron Ore'. In *Selection from the Records of the Bengal Government*, vol. VIII, 2–24. Calcutta: Geological Survey of India.

Oldham, T. (1865) 'Notes upon the Geology of the Rajmahal Hills', *Memoirs of the Geological Survey of India* 3 (1), 263–82.

O'Malley, L. S. S. (1909) *Bengal District Gazetteers, Howrah*. Calcutta: Bengal Secretariat Book Depot.

O'Malley, L. S. S. (1910) *Bengal District Gazetteers, Birbhum*. Calcutta: Bengal Secretariat Book Depot.

Owens, R. L., and Nandy, A. (1978) *The New Vaisyas: Entrepreneurial Opportunity and Response in an Indian City*. Durham, NC: Carolina Academic Press.

Parliamentary Papers (P.P.) (1874) *Moral and Material Progress of India for 1872–3*, vol. 49. London: Hansard.

Parliamentary Papers (P.P.) (1876) *Moral and Material Progress of India for 1874–5*, vol. 56. London: Hansard.

Parliamentary Papers (P.P.) (1900) *Statement of the Trade of British India with British Possessions and Foreign Countries for 1898–99*, vol. 57. London: Hansard.

Parliamentary Papers (P.P.) (1901) *Statement of the Trade of British India with British Possessions and Foreign Countries for 1899–1900*, vol. 49. London: Hansard.

Parliamentary Papers (P.P.) (1902) *Statement of the Trade of British India with British Possessions and Foreign Countries for 1900–01*, vol. 73. London: Hansard.

Parthasarathi, P. (2008) 'Iron Smelting in the Indian Subcontinent c. 1800'. Paper presented at the S. R. Epstein memorial conference, London School of Economics and Political Science. Retrieved from www.lse.ac.uk/economicHistory/seminars/Epstein%20Memorial%20Conference/PAPER-Parthasarathi.pdf on 25 July 2015.

Pillai, P. P. (1923) 'Iron and Steel Production in India', *Economica* 7, 55–66.

Raistrick, A., and Allen, E. (1938) 'The South Yorkshire Iron Industry 1690–1750', *Economic History Review* (first series) 9 (2), 168–85.

Ramachandran, S. (1984) 'Iron and Steel Technology: Options for India', *Sādhnā* 7 (3), 181–202.

Rao, K. N. P. (1963) 'A Brief History of the Indian Iron and Steel industry'. Paper presented at International symposium on recent developments in iron- and steel-making with special reference to Indian conditions, National Metallurgical Laboratory, Jamshedpur, India. Retrieved from http://eprint.nmlindia.org/5558 on 25 July 2015.

Ray, I. (2015a) 'Dynamics of Bengal Coal Mining in the Nineteenth Century: Dissemination of Mineralogical Knowledge and Railway Networking', *Indian Economic and Social History Review* 52 (4), 463–99.

Ray, I. (2015b) '"The Great Divergence" Revisited: The Case of Bengal in Early Modern Times', *Economic History of Developing Regions* 30 (2), 125–56.

Roy, T. (2008) 'Knowledge and Divergence from the Perspective of Early Modern India', *Journal of Global History* 3 (3), 361–87.

Roy, T. (2010) 'Did Globalization Aid Industrial Development in Colonial India? A Study of Knowledge Transfer in the Iron Industry', *Indian Economic and Social History Review* 46 (4), 579–613. Also available at http://eprint.lse.ac.uk/27396/1.

Sanyal, H. (1968) 'The Indigenous Iron Industry of Birbhum', *Indian Economic and Social History Review* 5 (1), 101–8.

Shiells, M. E. (1990) 'Collective Choice of Working Conditions: Hours in British and US Iron and Steel, 1890–1923', *Journal of Economic History* 50 (2), 379–92.

Sinha, N. K. (ed.) (1959) *Fort William–India House Correspondence*, vol. V: *1767–1769*. Delhi: National Archives of India.

Smith, D. (1856) *Report to the Government of India on the Coal and Iron Districts of Bengal*. National Library Archive, Calcutta.

Srinivasachari, C. S. (ed.) (1962) *Fort William–India House Correspondence*, vol. IV: *1764–1766*. Delhi: National Archives of India.

Srinivasan, N. R. (1983) *The History of the Indian Iron and Steel Company*. Burnpur: Steel Authority of India.

Temin, P. (1964) *Iron and Steel in Nineteenth Century America: An Economic Inquiry*. Cambridge, MA: MIT Press.

Von Schwarz, C. (1882) *Report on Iron Works in the Ranigunj Subdivision of the District of Burdwan in Bengal*. National Library Archives, Calcutta.

Warth, H. (1881) *Manufacture of Iron and the Future of the Charcoal Iron Industry in India*. Simla: Government Central Press.

Watson, E. R. (1907) *A Monograph on Iron and Steel Work in the Province of Bengal*. Calcutta: Bengal Secretariat Book Depot.

Williams, D. H. (1850) *A Geological Report on the Damodah Valley*. London: J. H. Cox (by order of the Court of Directors).

Appendix 4.1 Average value of stores purchased by the government and railways (in thousand Rs.), 1910/11–1913/14

Department	*Imported stores purchased in India*	*Produce of India*		*Purchased through Home Board*	*Purchased outside India*	*Total*
		Govt. factories	*Private dealers*			
Govt. of India						
Mints	25	15	150	122	–	312
Printing and stationery	167	3	3,072	765	–	4,007
Post and telegraph	276	40	331	1,898	–	2,545
Survey of India	15	1	62	162	–	240
Secretariat Department	131	16	171	28	17	363
Subtotal	**614**	**75**	**3,786**	**2,975**	**17**	**7,467**
Local govt. and administration						
Bengal	472	45	571	216	11	1,315
Others	4,533	725	5,651	2,767	435	14,111
Subtotal	**5,005**	**770**	**6,222**	**2,983**	**446**	**15,426**
State-owned railways						
Eastern Bengal	187	–	419	8,401	–	9,007
Others	1,781	72	15,764	26,800	–	44,417
Subtotal	**1,968**	**72**	**16,183**	**35,201**	**-**	**53,424**
Private railways						
East Indian	2,889	5,366	6,077	12,301	–	26,633
Others	617	–	3,794	5,511		9,922
Subtotal	**3,506**	**5,366**	**9,871**	**17,812**	**-**	**36,555**
Army Dept.	659	6,227	5,355	7,118	–	19,359
Total	**11,752**	**12,510**	**41,417**	**66,089**	**463**	**132,231**

Source: GOI (1920: 202–3).

5 Jute processing

Triumph against Dundee

Jute is a crop of early human civilisation. A nineteenth-century source (Watt 1972 [1889–93]: 410) refers to Pliny (79 CE) while identifying an Egyptian pot herb as melochia, which was the native vocabulary for edible jute. The plant was subsequently documented in various literatures down to the end of the Middle Ages. We thus have a fifteenth-century source (Simon Januensis, as cited in Watt 1972 [1889–93]: 410) narrating the peddlery of this vegetable alongside the streets of Babylon; and a sixteenth-century document (Ray 1738: 49–50) telling us that it was a regular crop along the Euphrates that the Jews at Aleppo were very fond of. Only in 1588 was it included in the scientific literature as a species from Africa (Watt 1972 [1889–93]: 407). The crop is far more antique in the Indian subcontinent, however. Historians believe that Kautilya's *Arthasastra* (written in about BCE 300) refers to this plant under a broad nomenclature of hemp (Kangle 1972: 125,147), as was the practice down to the early modern age. This is confirmed by Milburn (1813: 283), who classifies Indian hemp as 'sunn, ghore-sunn and paut', the last being the Bengali nomenclature for jute. While commenting on this classification, Watt (1972 [1889–93]: 409) notes that 'the plant in question [*paut*] was in all probability C. olitorius'. Abul Fazl's reference (1948: 123) to sackcloth in *Ain-i-Akbari* as a dress material in eastern and northern Bengal seems also to be a variety of jute. The translator of *Ain-i-Akbari*, H. S. Jarrett, in particular believes it so in view of the concentration of the industry at Rangpore, the heartland of jute in Bengal (ibid.: 123).[1] As a distinct fibre, however, as *jhut*, an Oriya word for 'jute' in India, the product was referred to for the first time in the logbook of a ship in 1746, as pointed out by Sir Richard Temple in 1901 (quoted in Watt 1972 [1889–93]: 410). The English vocabulary evidently acquired the term in 1791. A Company letter from Bengal in that year reads:

> We are continuing our searches for a new Article for Export to Great Britain...We sent a Number in the Packet, Samples of clean Hemp of this country, one of rough Hemp, and one of Jute (we know no English name for this) the material of which Gunnies and the Ropes used in cording Bales is made.
>
> (cited in Gauldie 1987: 115)

Such a distinction was further noticed two years later in a government document, which reports exports under the heading 'hemp other than jute' (GOB 1793).

Notwithstanding these repeated references to Bengal's traditional culture of jute, industrial historiography pays little attention to its cottage jute industry. Indeed, a vast literature does exist on the modern jute industry, focusing on Dundee (see, for example, Stewart 1998; and Lenman, Lythe and Gauldie 1969) and Bengal (Wallace 1928; and Palit and Kayaria 2007), the two locations where the industry was concentrated from about the middle of the nineteenth century. But the absence of references to the traditional industry causes serious gaps in the story. For one thing, Dundee's industrial development would have been starved of raw materials had the industry not been developed beforehand in Bengal, motivating the large-scale cultivation of jute, though Bengal's rigid cropping pattern in the contemporary society surely did not permit jute cultivation to expand so rapidly as to feed the development at Dundee. The emerging Dundee mills also inherited a global jute packaging market that this traditional industry had nurtured over years. In spite of these significant contributions of Bengal's traditional jute industry, some authors – such as Bagchi (1980: 262–90) and Iftikhar-ul-Awwal (1982: 157–93) –ignore its existence altogether, while others – for example, Buchanan (1934: 241–2),[2] Morris (1994: 556–72), Chaudhuri (1994: 851–3) and Sethia (1996) – make only passing reference to it. But none seeks to correlate it to Dundee's development.[3] The literature further lacks an in-depth study of the comparative advantages between Dundee and Bengal in this line of production, which perhaps explains the industry's locational shift during the second half of the nineteenth century. Indeed, all the studies on Bengal's modern jute industry refer to the Dundee mills as its predecessor (Bagchi 1980: 262–90; Sethia 1996), but, in view of the latter's failure, they identify only certain factors (such as cheap labour and the local availability of raw materials) without making any attempt to quantify the underlying comparative cost advantages. Keeping these lacunae in view, the present chapter seeks to situate the development of the modern jute industry in Bengal during the nineteenth century. In particular, I focus on the contemporary market dynamics that led to the decline of Bengal's traditional industry and put in place the modern jute industry. For topical interest, the latter's welfare implications in the contemporary society are also discussed.

The plan of this chapter is this. Section I narrates the status of the traditional jute industry in Bengal around the mid-nineteenth century. Section II discusses the triangular competition that emerged after the development of modern jute mills in Dundee and Bengal, and shows how Bengal jute mills came to occupy the monopoly position in the global market. In Section III, I analyse various sources of comparative advantage that enabled Bengal mills to successfully compete with their counterparts in Dundee, and also their welfare implications. The last section concludes my argument.

I

Jute was cultivated on diverse land formations in Bengal, from the high land (called *suna*) to the low land (called *sali*), from the dry riverbed (called *chur*) to dry land, and even in the humid land of recently formed alluvium (Kerr 1874: 22–4). Great variation was also noticed in the soil texture where it was sown, though this led to varying productivity. Higher productivity was obtained in loamy and clay soils, rich in sand, but it deteriorated as the laterite component and the salinity of the soil increased. These features also caused great variations in the seasonality of the plant, which commenced between February and June (for jute cultivation, see Banerjee 1955: 152–62). The earliest variety, the *bilan*, was planted during February and available in the market during July and August. For the late variety, the *uttariya*, these seasons were around June and November, respectively. This seasonal variation ensured a prolonged availability of raw jute in the market, providing a great advantage to this cottage industry for which warehousing facilities were virtually absent.

Table 5.1 displays the district-wise cultivation of jute in Bengal and the availability of its fibre in 1872. These statistics emphasise that erstwhile East Bengal (that is, present-day Bangladesh) outstripped its western counterpart in several respects. First, in respect of land under jute, 15 districts in eastern Bengal (including Dinajpore) totalled 589,250 acres of land, as against 178,500 acres in 11 districts of West Bengal. Relative to total agricultural land, jute acreage constituted 3.35 per cent in the former, but 1.53 per cent in the latter. Second, their yield rates per acre were in the order of about 15 maunds and 13 maunds, on average. Third, quality-wise the excellence of the former was reflected in its product varieties, such as the *uttariya*, *deswal*, *karimganji*, *barkrabadi* and *narrainganji*, which the market greatly preferred over the *desi* variety, the predominant species in West Bengal. The *desi* was always used locally, and never sold in distant markets till 1868 (Lefranc 1873: 14).

Traditional jute technology* involved three distinct processing stages: (i) retting and stripping, (ii) spinning and (iii) weaving. The cultivators in Bengal (called *ryots*) initially processed jute using a very simple technology. The central task in this case was to remove, by the application of water, the natural gum that sticks to fibres on the stem. To this end, the *ryot* used to submerge on average ten to 15 bundles of jute plants, each containing 50 to 100 plants, into

*This part is based on my article 'Jute in Bengal', originally published in H. Selin (ed.) *Encyclopaedia of the History of Science, Technology, and Medicine in Non-European Cultures*, 3rd edition, 2415–19, 2016, © Springer Science+Business Media, Dordrecht. Reproduced with permission by Springer.

Table 5.1 District-wise area and production of jute in Bengal, 1872

District	*Agri. land (million acres)*	*Jute land (thousand acres)*	*Jute production (thousand maunds)*	*District*	*Agri. land (million acres)*	*Jute land (thousand acres)*	*Jute production (thousand maunds)*
Pubna	0.88	122.88	1,873.20	Malda	0.67	3.50	52.50
Dinajpur	1.65	117.63	1,764.43	Murshidabad	1.11	3.67	54.99
Rangpore	1.60	100.00	1,500.00	24 Parganas	2.92	47.16	707.45
Mymensing	1.34	84.00	1,260.00	Hoogly	0.64	32.00	160.00
Bogra	0.41	48.60	698.98	Midnapore	2.30	8.00	120.00
Dacca	1.68	40.00	600.00	Burdwan	1.80	4.00	60.00
Faridpur	0.86	16.67	249.99	Howrah	0.22	2.67	39.99
Goalpara	2.77	15.00	225.00	Nadia	NA	1.00	15.00
Rajshahi	1.28	14.33	214.99	Tippera	2.00	78.39	1,175.83
Backergunj	0.20	11.67	174.99	Purnea	2.40	75.00	1,125.00
Jessore	2.52	12.60	189.07	Cuttak	1.27	4.23	63.42
Noakhally	0.60	3.64	54.54	Puri	NA	1.00	15.00
Nowgong	0.82	1.46	21.85	Balasore	0.54	1.00	15.00
Chittagong	0.98	0.10	1.50	Kamrup	NA	0.31	4.65
Sylhet	NA	0.67	9.99	Durrung	1.68	0.19	2.79
Darjeeling	0.16	1.50	22.50	Cachar	1.53	0.05	0.82
Jalpaiguri	1.26	50.00	750.00	**Total**	**38.69**	**927.92**	**13,598.47**
Cooch Behar	0.60	25.00	375.00				

Source: Kerr (1874: 65).

roadside ponds where water was stagnant. They avoided running water, as it delayed the fermentation process and also damaged the quality of the fibres. To keep them properly sunk, a raft-like wooden structure, filled up with turf and clods of earth, was put on them so that the plants were not directly exposed to the sun; otherwise, they became specky. Sods were always avoided to maintain the colour of the fibres. The disintegration of the fibres involved bacterial action, however, whereby the gas emerging from decomposing plants caused bubbles in the water. The frequency of the bubbles indicated the status of the retting, which had matured by eight to 20 days depending upon the quality of the plants as well as the water. Under-retting caused problems when stripping, while over-retting damaged the strength and colour of the fibres. Once barks had been loosened and their fibres had become soft, stripping was carried out in four stages within a couple of days. In knee-deep water, a dresser took up five to six stalks together in the left hand and, using a mallet in his/her right hand, beat them flat at the bottom (Figure 5.1). After every beating, the bundle was turned skilfully. In the second stage, he/she broke the stalks off about two feet from the bottom, so that the fibre ends could be held tightly by hand. In the third stage, the stems were jerked to and fro in the water, stripping off the fibres. Finally, impurities were removed in the pond, and the fibres were rinsed

Figure 5.1 Jute retting and stripping in the nineteenth century
Source: Carter (1921: 10).

and dried in the sun. For marketing purposes, however, those fibres were again bundled in parcels of one to two maunds each. About 70 lb. of dry fibre could be obtained in ten hours.

A simple technology was thus followed in the retting and stripping of jute. Despite several institutional supports for mechanisation, it still survives. The low family income of the peasantry partly explains the lack of interest in mechanisation. But no less important is the question of quality, in which the traditional technology dominates over its mechanical alternative. In this context, expert testimonies make the point that, compared to the latter, the former yields softer fibres and ensures better colour, lustre and strength (Carter 1921: 11).

The spinning of jute used to be a key support to rural livelihoods in Bengal, engaging the whole family in labour. It was customary for artisans to keep hanging bundles of jute fibres together from their thatched roofs so that every family member could spin in his/her leisure hours. For the sake of yarn variety, however, three alternative implements were used – the d'hera, t'ảkku and ghurghuria – involving different technological processes.

The first process involving d'hera span yarns for coarser cloths, such as gunnies and sail cloths (called *gun*). The instrument was of cylindrical design with a number of bamboo (or wooden) spokes on the body and an iron handle on the right-hand side. The process involved four stages. In the first stage, the spinner drew a given number of strands from the hanging bundles, noted above, tied their upper ends to a post (or to one of the bamboos in the thatched roof of his/her cottage) and dressed the other ends to tie up with the instrument. In the second stage, he/she held the instrument on his/her left hand and twisted the strands using its handle in his/her right hand. In the third stage, when sufficiently twisted, the thread was wound up on the body of the d'hera, and the first stage was reverted to. In the final stage, threads were taken off from the d'hera and arranged in a ball, which was locally called *loti*.

The second process involving t'ȧkku was used to spin finer yarns, for sack cloths (locally called *tat*), which poor people wore as apparel and used as sleeping mats. The t'ȧkku was a conical wooden implement, 12 to 15 inches long and with a 1½ inch diameter at the base tapering to ½ inch at the top. Three stages were involved in this process. In the first stage, spinners squatted on the floor and pulled out several strands from the hanging bundles to group them into a thin tissue or ribbon (somewhat similar to rope without any twist). One end of the ribbon was held in the left hand, and the other end was attached to the spindle of the t'ȧkku. In the second stage, the instrument was stroked against the thigh (or the sole of the feet), causing it to rotate and thereby imparting twists to the fibre. The degree of twisting depended on the distance the t'ȧkku had to traverse in spinning the yarn round it. Generally, 15 to 18 inches of yarn could be spun in one operation. In the third stage, yarns were collected in the roller of the t'ȧkku (locally called *fetia*). When a sufficient amount of thread was spun, it was separated from the *fetia*.

The third process, involving the ghurghuria, was meant for spinning rope-making yarn. It was a very rudimentary device, made up of two pieces of wood (about 20 inches in length, five to six inches in breadth, and two to three inches in thickness), fixed crosswise at the centre by an elongated nail (Figure 5.2). The top of the nail served as a hinge where the lower ends of ten to 20 jute strands were tied. With the upper ends hinged on a post, the spinner rotated the instrument with a full blow so that it continued rotating for some time, imparting twist to the strands. A spinner could operate with three to four ghurghurias at a time drawing jute from the attached bundle on the post. When the fibres were adequately twisted on a particular instrument, they were wound up in its body, and their upper ends were joined by manually twisting them with another set of strands. The spinning process was then repeated. When about 200 metres of yarn had thus been spun, they were brought to an open field, where bamboos were dug in two rows about 200 metres apart. The yarns were tied to the bamboos. When an adequate number of yarns were thus arranged, two spinners took up two yarns at their respective ends and twisted them manually together. When they were adequately twisted, they took up another yarn to twist it with the previous one to add thickness and strength. The process continued until the requisite thickness was obtained.

Weaving was traditionally done on a contraption that consisted of five bamboos (or wooden spars), 36 to 40 inches in length. One of them was hung from a post, another was horizontally secured to two posts at their top and three others were placed in between them one after another, in such a way that two

Figure 5.2 A ghurghuria
Source: Photograph by the author from a Cottage Jute Unit in Birbhum, West Bengal.

of them could be used for warping and one for weft. Warping was done by two central bamboos, which acted as lease rods, on the one hand, and as cams, on the other, to provide the necessary shedding motions during weaving. It should be mentioned that warp yarns, which spinners provided in the form of a ball, were not treated with any dressing or stiffening materials at the weaving stage. The central-most bamboo was used for weft, however. Weft was arranged on a split bamboo, measuring 18 to 22 inches in length and 1½ inches in breadth. It performed a similar task to that of a shuttle in the power loom.

Despite the fact that this traditional contraption was very tedious, causing interruptions and delays in the production process, jute weavers in Bengal could ensure a high standard of quality for their end products. Even compared to the late nineteenth-century mill products, their quality dominated in two important aspects – evenness and purities. Expert opinions are on record as saying that traditional technology ensured even spacing both in warp and in weft, and also that its finished products contained few sticks, gaws (narrow depressions) or snarls, which often characterised the mill products (ICJC 1952: 8).

Table 5.2 brings out the salient features of the traditional jute industry in Bengal. It indicates in the first place that the industry spread over as many as 23

Table 5.2 District-wise development status of the cottage jute industry in Bengal, 1872

District	*Type of fibre*	*Industrial use(maunds)*	*Product mix*	*Market destination*	*District*	*Type of fibre*	*Industrial use(maunds)*	*Product mix*	*Market destination*
Jalpaiguri	Jute	187,500	Gunny bags	¾ for export	Rangpore	Both good and inferior jute	50,187	Paper, gunny bags etc.	Local use and export
Hoogly	*Desi* jute	120,000	Ropes, gunny cloth, bags	Export	Mymensing	More of inferior jute	12,000	Gunny bags, paper	Local use
Cooch Behar	Jute	41,250*	Various gunny cloths, *mekhli*	Local use	Faridpur	*Desi*, *bogi*, *belun*, *mesta*	1,700	Gunny sail, twine, cord	NA
Murshidabad	Jute	38,000	Gunny bags, rope, sack cloth, nets etc.	Local use	Pubna	Baboon, *hemtal*, *shoynee*, *mesta*, *desi*	1,350	Gunny and sack cloth	Local use and export
Malda	*Mesta*, *kosta* for paper, inferior jute	25,000	Gunny cloth, paper, thread	Local use	Chittagong	Jute	1,200	Rope, gunny	Local use
Midnapore	*Kosta*, *naskarkani*, *kangra* jute, etc.	13,200*	Gunny, ropes, strong cord	Gunny bags for export	Jessore	Both good and inferior jute	780	Gunny bags, sails, twine, ropes	Local use and export
Burdwan	Both good and inferior jute	6,100	Gunny cloth and bags, twine, ropes	Local use and export to Calcutta	Backergunj	*Mesta*, *kosta* for paper, inferior jute	600	Gunny bags, paper	Local use and export

Darjeeling	Red, white and *marah*, *emleah*, *chera-mara*	2,475*	Gunny cloth, fishing nets, ropes	Local use	Sylhet	*Mesta*, *kosta* for paper, inferior jute	405	Gunny bags, cloth	Local use and export
24 Parganas	*Desi* jute	640	Gunny, twine	Export	Noakhally	Inferior jute, *mesta* for paper	105	Ropes, paper	Local use
Birbhum	*Desi*, *doolaganji*, *narrainganji* jute	600	Gunny bags	Export	Tripura	*Mesta*, *kosta* for paper, inferior jute	2,125	Gunny bags	Local use and export
Dinajpur	Jute	233,514	Gunny, twine	Local use and export	Cuttak	Jute	500	Gunny bags, rope, paper	Local use
Dacca	*Mesta*, *kosta* for paper, inferior jute	90,000	Rope, bags, paper, sails, twine, gunny cloth	¼ for local use, ¾ for export	**Total**		829,231		

Note: '*' = estimated.

Source: Kerr (1874: 82).

districts of lower Bengal, out of which 11 districts belonged to eastern Bengal, ten to West Bengal and two outside Bengal proper. Such a wide spatial dispersal, which was a common feature for contemporary traditional industries, was lost in the later course of the industry's development with modern technologies. Second, from the viewpoint of the district-level raw jute consumption, the table emphasises that the industry's development was fairly balanced between eastern and western Bengal. Because of the absence of data for Midnapore, Cooch Behar and Darjeeling in the source, I estimate them using the average proportion of the industrial use of raw jute in different districts of West Bengal, which is about 11 per cent, and the output of raw jute in those districts, as given in Table 5.1. The estimates are 13,200 maunds for Midnapore, 41,250 maunds for Cooch Behar and 2,475 maunds for Darjeeling. Thus, the industrial use of raw jute comes to 434,765 maunds for West Bengal, as against 391,841 maunds in eastern Bengal, giving a ratio of 1: 0.90, which confirms the regionally balanced development of the industry. Third, notwithstanding the spread of the industry across the province, a good amount of concentration is noticed at the regional level. Thus, about 96 per cent of raw jute consumption in eastern Bengal was accounted for by three of its districts, namely Dinajpur, Dacca and Rangpore, and about 89 per cent of that in West Bengal by its constituent districts of Jalpaiguri, Hoogly, Cooch Behar and Murshidabad.

Fourth, various grades of raw jute, as available in this province (see column 2 of Table 5.2), must have encouraged the industry to diversify its product mix. The table reveals that, barring a few districts such as Jalpaiguri, none was specialised in a single line of production, so that different fibres found commercial outlets locally. While gunny bags and cloth were certainly a dominant product line in the majority of the districts, ropes and twine were no less important in some of them. Certain districts concentrated in specialised product lines, however, such as handmade paper, sails and dress cloth, which modern jute mills never ventured into later on. Thus, handmade paper was manufactured extensively in Dacca, Malda and Mymensing, sail cloth in Dacca and Jessore, while Cooch Behar specialised in a typical dress material called the *mekhli*, which local people wore frequently.

Fifth, although both domestic and export[4] markets lent support to the contemporary development of the industry, the latter dominated. While a few districts manufactured exclusively for either of them, the majority catered to both. The exclusive export-processing zones were located near the Port of Calcutta – for example, Hoogly, the 24 Parganas and Birbhum – and the domestic market was catered to from relatively remote districts, such as Malda, Cooch Behar, Darjeeling and Murshidabad in the northern part of West Bengal, and Mymensing, Chittagong and Noakhally in eastern Bengal. Dacca in the east and Jalpaiguri in the west supplied both extensively, however. Out of 829,231 maunds of Bengal's aggregate industrial use of raw jute in Table 5.2, the source identifies market destinations for 532,470 maunds. The latter disaggregates to 342,565 maunds for export and 189,905 maunds for local markets, giving a ratio of 1.80:1 between them. This surely underlines the importance of distant markets for the industry. It should be noted here that both local and export markets consisted of a multi-tier network of intermediaries. Big merchants often maintained agency houses at major marts, and transacted through *paikars* and *baparis* (for details, Buchanan 1934: 241–2). Those latter intermediaries used to announce by beating drums in villages what amounts of different products they intended to buy in the forthcoming season. While such announcements were made around the end of June, the actual transactions took place between August and February. The merchants, in turn, sold them to domestic end users and exporters.

Several sources corroborate that, prior to the spread of modern technologies in Dundee, Bengal's handmade jute articles were packaged for global trading, and slowly created their own market (Sethia 1996: 73; Kundu 1956: 222–3). From Table 5.3 we gather that such ventures began in 1828, when more than 15,000 bags were exported at about Rs. 28,000. The total rose to 78,260 pieces in 1833 and further to 233,246 pieces in 1836, their values being in the order of Rs. 143,509 and Rs. 441,592, respectively. A further insight from a different source (P.P. 1840: 1) is that many of those consignments were destined for the United Kingdom, though North America had been in the market almost from the beginning. The UK intake was 14,565 pieces in 1828–9, 9,688 pieces in 1829–30 and 30,867 pieces in 1831–2. In the last two years North America imported 1,326 and 1,981 pieces, respectively.

Available statistics also confirm that, against the steady diffusion of modern jute technologies in Dundee, the industry not only resisted an immediate collapse but, rather, grew apace in terms of global trade for about two decades after that. Table 5.4 reports that as many as 12 countries bought such products from Bengal in 1850–1 though some of them had only insignificant shares. The bulk of them were despatched to North America, hitherto an insignificant destination, which purchased as many as 2.29 million pieces in 1850–1 – that is, more than a quarter of Bengal's aggregate exports. Additionally, Penang and

Table 5.3 Annual exports of jute products from Calcutta, 1828–37

Year	*Quantity (in pieces)*	*Value (in Rs.)*
1828	15,392	27,712
1829	7,840	12,436
1830	11,162	23,498
1831	34,171	70,701
1832	35,500	67,682
1833	78,260	143,509
1834	32,824	55,771
1835	17,747	36,345
1836	233,246	441,592
1837	124,303	181,066

Source: P.P. (1840: 1).

Table 5.4 Exports of gunny cloths and bags from Calcutta, 1850–1

Destination	*Bags and cloths(in pieces)*	*Percentage of total exports*
United Kingdom	69,636	0.77
Hamburg	2,180	0.02
North America	2,290,427	25.35
Coast of Coromandel	1,955,150	21.64
Malabar	2,054,075	22.73
Penang and Singapore	1,043,600	11.55
Ceylon	357,290	3.95
New South Wales	32,125	0.36
Java	242,550	2.68
Pegu	672,950	7.45
Mauritius	213,980	2.37
Cape of Good Hope	82,750	0.92
Guam	15,000	0.17
Arabian and Persian Gulf	4,000	0.04
Total pieces	9,035,713	100.00
Total value (in Rs.)	2,159,782	

Source: Wallace (1928: 1).

Singapore imported together 1.04 million pieces. Domestically, support came from Malabar and Madras, which purchased 2.05 million and 1.96 million pieces, respectively. The only disquieting feature was the decline of the United Kingdom's share, from a height of more than 95 per cent in the early 1830s to less than 1 per cent in 1850–1. It is not unexpected, however, in view of the fast pace of development among the Dundee mills.

To assess the industry's global marketability in the nineteenth century, Appendix 5.1 presents time series of its export from 1828 to 1894 and their three-yearly moving averages. Three adjustments are made in the series. First, in view of data constraints, the series is estimated for 1838–49, 1851 and 1873–5 on the basis of the compound rate of change in their respective intervals. Second, data for 1876 to 1880 are available in terms of quantity (particularly jute bags), which are converted into values at Rs. 0.18 per bag, as prevailed in 1885–6 (for an export of 7,240,928 pieces of gunny bags, the value was Rs. 1,238,886: GOB 1891: 33). Third, the sterling values of export for 1852 to 1859 are converted into rupees at £1=Rs. 10. Figure 5.3 represents the series and Table 5.5 reports its five-yearly average values.

The table points to an annual growth rate of 45.23 per cent for the period from 1835/9 to 1845/9, and thus supports the hypothesis that the industry had strong resistance against the development at Dundee. Further prosperity is evident in the fact that the series crossed the Rs. 2 million mark in 1850–4 and Rs. 3 million in 1855–9.[5] Export values for this decade, though oscillatory in actual series, are fairly stable in their moving averages. Figure 5.3 emphasises that the rising trend of the series since 1835 was suddenly aborted in 1860, however,

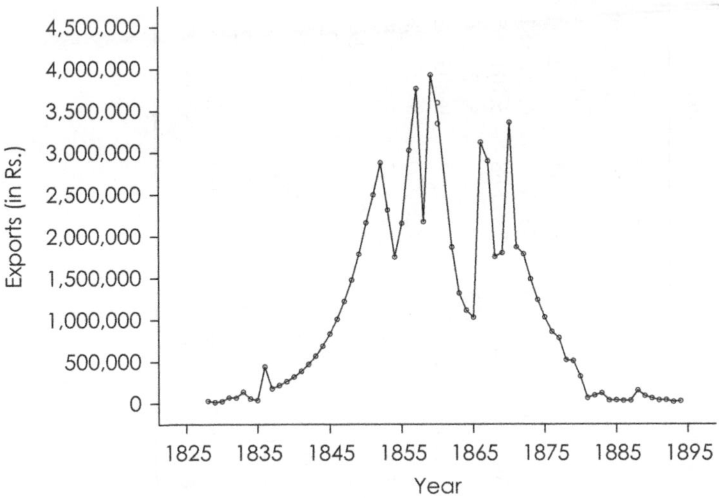

Figure 5.3 Exports of handmade jute articles from Bengal, 1828–94

Table 5.5 Exports of jute articles from Bengal, 1828/9–1890/4

Year	*Annual exports (in Rs.)*
1828–9	20,069
1830–4	71,832
1835–9	228,638
1840–4	486,880
1845–9	1,262,841
1850–4	2,316,938
1855–9	3,007,086
1860–4	2,246,000
1865–9	2,118,080
1870–4	1,945,488
1875–9	729,743
1880–4	128,119
1885–9	68,077
1890–4	35,659

Source: Appendix 5.1.

and a declining phase followed. This issue will be taken up in the next section. I note here simply that this finding goes against the hypothesis in the existing literature that the decline of this industry started in 1830.[6]

Table 5.6 reports time series of handmade jute articles that entered into Calcutta from various interior districts of the province between 1877/8 and

Table 5.6 Imports of handmade jute bags into Calcutta from different districts (in pieces), 1877/8–1898/9

Year	*Hoogly*	*24 Parganas*	*Dinajpore*	*Rangpore*	*Jalpaiguri*	*Purnea*	*Darjeeling*	*Burdwan*	*Others*	*Total*
1877–8	393,586	303,543	3,789,704	117,285	380,650	494,230	–	–	142,700	5,621,698
1878–9	262,360	138,273	8,641,095	511,732	484,342	549,910	–	–	310,679	10,898,391
1880–1	1,089,434	1,414,715	2,753,347	593,741	612,941	–	–	–	705,053	7,169,231
1881–2	977,141	681,526	4,859,278	2,526,158	1,484,198	–	–	–	873,903	11,402,204
1884–5	78,598	298,844	991,955	1,537,200	2,492,210	94,145	420	169,425	553,784	6,216,581
1885–6	639,428	409,427	479,840	933,070	892,535	292,200	560,630	149,067	744,868	5,101,065
1886–7	965,896	628,789	255,300	1,222,410	2,333,660	62,510	898,520	155,125	–	6,522,210
1887–8	2,911,087	1,018,369	474,500	1,008,980	2,952,390	193,140	1,052,660	194,766	–	9,805,892
1888–9	3,341,410	849,284	1,425,315	374,080	1,349,880	113,680	694,960	148,609	426,310	8,723,528
1889–90	1,230,993	321,439	1,406,555	330,505	1,500,450	26,075	588,385	144,450	342,847	5,891,699
1890–1	521,316	193,696	1,877,575	886,206	3,171,735	48,260	1,201,935	149,953	506,602	8,557,278
1892–3	1,775,401	116,063	1,539,932	536,095	1,513,820	41,530	734,965	317,583	619,632	7,195,021
1893–4	1,558,664	391,309	985,835	346,226	1,487,010	55,606	524,860	173,107	930,671	6,453,288
1894–5	1,135,116	790,216	2,290,155	333,725	881,415	226,480	502,670	180,423	1,062,292	7,402,492
1897–8	1,746,927	666,186	1,427,160	124,705	1,355,655	177,495	697,900	254,444	1,194,752	7,645,224
1898–9	3,361,854	4817,829	1,109,265	40,045	1,208,165	41,340	515,305	230,087	1,054,349	12,378,239
Average	1,374,326	814,969	2,144,176	713,885	1,506,316	172,614	664,434	188,920	676,317	8,255,957[1]

Notes: '–' indicates an insignificant amount; 1: row total.

Source: GOB, *Annual Report on the Administration of Bengal*, various issues.

1898/9. Since Calcutta was the only seaport in this region, we learn from this table where the industry was developed for the export market. According to the table, this segment of the industry was localised at Dinajpore, Jalpaiguri, Hoogly, the 24 Parganas and Rangpore, which together accounted for about 80 per cent of the aggregate intakes at Calcutta. Individually, they shared on average 25.97 per cent, 18.25 per cent, 16.65 per cent, 9.87 per cent and 8.65 per cent, respectively. Almost all these districts belong to the previous list of major jute manufacturing districts in Bengal.

A comparison between Tables 5.5 and 5.6, however, reveals an important feature of the industry. While, in Table 5.6, no sign of decline is evident for 1877–99, with the intakes of Calcutta at 8.27 million pieces per annum in 1890/1–1898/9 (that is, Rs. 1.49 million at Rs. 0.18 per bag), Table 5.5 suggests a steady decline in their exports from 1860 onwards, reaching about Rs. 36,000 per annum in 1890–4. In the early 1890s, therefore, the export constituted less than 2.50 per cent of what flowed into the city. In fact, Calcutta received 7,645,224 pieces in 1897–8 and 12,378,239 pieces in 1898–9, but exported only 1,505,500 and 1,612,845 pieces, respectively, outside Bengal (GOB 1900: 158). These are surely suggestive of an extensive local market for those traditional articles even at the end of the nineteenth century (Carter 1921: 5; ICJC 1952: 4–9). Indeed, the industry's footprints in later years are also traced in contemporary census statistics. According to the census of 1901, 43,820 workers were employed in the manufacturing of fibre mats, bags, ropes, nets and sackcloth while their trades engaged another 9,675 persons (GOI 1903: 453), giving an aggregate of 53,495. The source does not clarify whether these data accounted for fibres other than jute as well, however.

Jute artisans usually hailed from different Hindu sects, such as the Kapalis in east Bengal and the Palias in north Bengal (Buchanan 1934: 242). Depending on the level of skill, their income level varied. An early twentieth-century source reveals that an average female worker wove a jute mat of 72 × 45 square inches in 12 hours, and earned about Rs. 1.50 (ICJC 1952: 8). At this rate, the wage comes to two annas per hour – that is, Rs. 26 per month (for eight working hours per day and 26 working days per month). A source, however, indicates the industry's average monthly wage rate at Rs. 13 to 15 for four-hour working days (ibid.) (that is, Rs. 26 to 30 for eight-hour working days).

To estimate the industry's employment opportunities in its heyday, we note that the census of 1881 clearly indicates that 12,808 persons were engaged in the manufacturing of jute ropes and cords (GOI 1883: tab. 29). For other jute articles, however, the figure is given at 35,833, which surely include workers at modern mills as well. Since the investment level in such mills is estimated at Rs. 15 million in 1880 and the capital–labour ratio at Rs. 698 per labourer for 1880–4 (Table 5.14), the mill employment level comes to 21,490. Hence, for the traditional industry, the employment in 'other' jute articles should be 14,343, and, together with those employed in rope and cord making, about 27,151. On this basis, I estimate the industry's employment level at 638,473 for the middle of the nineteenth century, given its average export level of Rs.

3.01 million in 1855–9 and Rs. 128,000 in 1880–4. The underlying assumption, however, is that the ratio of exports to local consumption remained fairly stable between those periods. An upward bias might be involved in the estimate if the ratio had declined. Nevertheless, these large employment opportunities, as estimated here, belie the prevailing hypothesis in the literature: 'Since all the manufacturing methods there [in Bengal], for a considerable time were manual ones, the industry – if such it could be called – moved along slowly, providing employment only for the needs of a small section of the community on the Eastern shores' (Woodhouse and Kilgour 1921:1).

II

The modern jute industry had a chequered growth pattern in Dundee after a technological breakthrough in 1836, and the same applies to Bengal after 1855, when Dundee technologies were largely adopted. Although, for a couple of decades, Dundee's development could not tarnish the prospects of Bengal's traditional jute industry, later it was suffocated owing to triangular competition in the late nineteenth century. The nature of the competition was like this: in the early years Bengal's modern jute mills targeted India's domestic market for their outlets, compelling its traditional industry to look for sales abroad; but there it encountered stiff competition from the Dundee mills, so that both of its channels were increasingly sealed up. This is not to claim, however, that there was no competition from the Dundee mills in India, or from Calcutta mills abroad. We will see that the competition was largely triangular everywhere; only the intensity of the competition differed from market to market.

In India's domestic market (outside Bengal) the sale of Bengal jute goods was virtually in stasis from 1863 to 1872, moving mostly around the range of Rs. 2 to 4 million (Kerr 1874: appendix L). The lion's share of these consignments, about 75 to 93 per cent, was sent to Bombay, with Madras emerging steadily. Other domestic markets were irregular, and also insignificant, never absorbing more than Rs. 100,000 in aggregate per year. To assess the share of Calcutta mills in this market, I assume: (i) that those mills ran under full loom utilisation; (ii) that each loom produced 12,470 bags per year;[7] and (iii) that the entire mill output was sold outside the province. While the domestic sales of Calcutta mills may be derived from Table 5.14 (column 4) on the basis of these assumptions, a similar series for the traditional industry is obtained by deducting these from the aggregate sale of such goods in domestic markets.[8] On this methodology I estimate that, in 1865–6, modern mills domestically sold 13.59 million bags, and traditional units 18.21 million, thus sharing the market by a ratio of 43:57. This ratio increased to 50.42:49.58 in 1870–1, and further to 58:42 in 1872–3. Thus, whereas the hand loom products dominated India's domestic market even in 1865–6, the Calcutta mills had seized the position by 1870–1. This upswing continued, as is evident in Table 5.7, with the market share ratio increasing to 70:30 in 1875–6 and about 95:5 from 1885–6 onwards.

Table 5.7 Exports of Bengal jute products to domestic and foreign markets (in million pieces), 1875/6–1890/1

Year	*Domestic market*			*Foreign market*			*Grand total*		
	Power loom	*Hand loom*	*Total*	*Power loom*	*Hand loom*	*Total*	*Power loom*	*Hand loom*	*Total*
1875–6	21.64[1]	9.24[1]	30.88	17.55	1.14	18.69	39.19	10.38	49.57
1876–7	NA	NA	27.64[2]	29.00	3.56	32.56	–	–	60.20
1877–8	28.45	4.32	32.77	24.42	0.68	25.10	52.87	5.00	57.87
1878–9	17.01	2.85	19.86	42.07	1.83	43.90	59.08	4.68	63.76
1884–5	37.10	2.66	39.76	76.71	4.92	81.63	113.81	7.58	121.39
1885–6	39.57	1.93	41.50	61.69	0.50	62.19	101.26	2.43	103.69
1886–7	34.39	2.33	36.72	63.50	0.40	63.90	97.89	2.73	100.62
1887–8	44.29	1.92	46.21	72.57	0.41	72.98	116.86	2.33	119.19
1888–9	35.86	1.72	37.58	95.86	1.04	96.90	131.72	2.76	134.48
1889–90	36.05	1.83	37.88	94.68	0.63	95.31	130.73	2.46	133.19
1890–1	49.84	5.20	55.04	95.51	1.10	96.61	145.35	6.30	151.65

Notes: '–' indicates an insignificant amount; 1: in the absence of any distinction between power loom and hand loom bags for 1875–6, the estimation is made based on the ratio between them for exports to Bombay in 1875–6 – namely 4,954,940 hand loom bags and 11,651,430 power loom bags; 2: the available figure is for six months; it has been converted into an annual figure.

Source: GOB, *Annual Report on the Administration of Bengal*, various issues.

As to the foreign competition that the traditional industry faced, we note that Dundee's jute market grew up largely replacing other packaging materials, such as hemp and flax, as is evident in the reduced amount of their imports into Dundee (Chapman 1938: 46). It must have seized Bengal's traditional market as well, which was quite extensive. But any conclusion to that effect is to some extent blurred by the triangular competition in the market that I have already referred to. Since Bengal mills did not venture outside India's domestic market before 1864–5 (Playne 1917: 643), however, any diminution of foreign exports from Bengal before that year represented Dundee's penetration into Bengal's traditional market; moreover, as Bengal mills enjoyed comparative advantages over their rivals at Dundee (as discussed later), such a conclusion follows whenever and wherever (domestic or foreign markets) Bengal's aggregate exports declined.

Based on the above surmise, I conclude from the last column of Table 5.8 that Bengal's traditional industry began to shrink in the foreign market from 1867–8, and that by 1872–3 the market had declined by Rs. 1.74 million. Certain export destinations, such as Penang and Singapore, as also Java, that are reported in 1850–1 (Table 5.4) are altogether absent in Table 5.8, signifying that those countries had been reduced to insignificance by 1863–4. If their intakes for 1850–1, namely Rs. 307,390 at the prevailing price of Rs. 0.239 per bag (Table 5.4), are accounted for, the market loss comes to Rs. 2.05 million. Moreover, in certain Far East countries, such as China, the Strait

Table 5.8 Exports of gunnies, cloth, twine and rope from Calcutta to foreign ports (in Rs.), 1863/4–1872/3

Year	*United Kingdom*	*North America*[1]	*Aden*	*France*	*West Indies*	*Java*	*China*	*Australia*[2]	*Cape of Good Hope*	*Strait Settlement*	*Ceylon*	*Others*	*Total*
1863–4	20,876	572,453	5,536	–	9,990	33,950	22,722	60,785	21,895	271,175	72,718	17,399	1,109,499
1864–5	40,552	461,780[3]	5,707	549	22,300	12,125	47,256	73,182	12,575	131,708	108,150	182,866	1,098,750
1865–6	241,779	2,106,758	11,156	34,525	9,600	89,265	2,230	107,589	18,744	179,374	129,844	63,839	2,994,703
1866–7	227,170	2,785,872	7,842	3,766	5,170	–	30,335	220,146	23,540	197,822	107,415	3,819	3,612,897
1867–8	268,248	2,148,401	19,982	600	5,640	54,294	28,181	68,839	26,286	214,421	56,202	3,499	2,894,593
1868–9	1,875	690,589	13,460	–	–	31,205	83,646	177,321	26,948	596,735	130,127	1,835	1,753,741
1869–70	16,310	747,604	8,597	–	–	25,347	9,535	124,503	12,540	645,308	207,441	8,503	1,805,688
1870–1	1,474	2,799,716	6,789	–	2,283	20,275	16,325	139,717	25,100	269,342	74,014	11,397	3,366,432
1871–2	55,517	1,068,689	8,599	12,525	–	32,516	37,160	188,075	14,320	336,144	114,056	9,156	1,876,757
1872–3	8,072	544,836	13,330	–	–	9,000	54,868	380,567	50,288	547,226	175,125	88,137	1,871,449

Notes: '–' indicates an insignificant amount; 1, 2: imports of San Francisco and New South Wales, available separately, are included in the series of North America and Australia, respectively; 3: this figure also includes an export amount of Rs. 8,187 to South America.

Source: Kerr (1874: appendix L).

Settlements and Ceylon, and also the Cape of Good Hope, the series initially fell but later rebounded. Perhaps the former movement was due to the failures of the traditional industry while the latter might be better explained by a steady penetration of Bengal jute mills therein. Such movements also took place in Australia and its surrounding ports. If all these declines are accounted for, it comes to more than 20 per cent of Dundee's total exports in 1875. The export destinations that shrank significantly after 1867–8, however, were the United Kingdom and North America. For the United Kingdom there was a decline from Rs. 268,248 in 1867–8 to Rs. 8,072 in 1872–3, and for North America from Rs. 2.79 million in 1866–7 to about Rs. 545,000 in 1872–3. Presumably, all these markets opted for Dundee products.[9]

Not only did the Dundee mills capture a significant segment of Bengal's traditional overseas market, but they encroached into the domestic market of Bengal as well. Available evidence shows that, by 1871, they shared this market by 3.45 million cwt, which gradually increased to 4.27 million cwt in 1874, 5.94 million cwt in 1882 and further to 7.39 million cwt in 1883 (P.P. 1887: 373). Three-way competition was thus evident in India's domestic market. Similar competition came to prevail in Bengal's traditional foreign outlets also, as its modern mills became increasingly dominant there. In this context, I refer to Table 5.7 (columns 5 and 6), where Bengal's hand loom products are seen to have an ever-decreasing share, juxtaposed against the steady inroads made by its power loom output. The table reveals that the former decreased, albeit with oscillations, from 3.56 million pieces in 1876–7 to 1.10 million pieces in 1890–1, whereas Bengal mills increased their sales from 29 million pieces to 95.51 million pieces in this period. Consequently, the traditional sector was confined to a narrow segment of about 1 per cent of the foreign market by 1890–1.

Several factors account for the downfall of the traditional industry. In the first place, Bengal's traditional technology did not condition the fibre before spinning; even the application of water was restricted only to the moistening of roots (ICJC 1952: 7). In contrast, the question of softening jute by moisturisation received the greatest attention from the dawn of modern jute technology. In particular, raw jute was initially treated by oil or emulsion, and then by water, in the batching process, so that the end products became much softer, as well as stronger, than hand-spun ones. Second, because of its mechanical devices for drawing fibre strands, and also for spinning, weaving and calendaring, modern technology yielded precise uniformity, which was totally absent from hand loom products. Third, traditional technology also failed to turn out the product sizes that the emerging market sought for. For hessian products, for example, the modal size of width was 46 to 52.5 inches; for this range, about 75 per cent of Calcutta looms were designed in 1949 (ibid.: 26). But the width of hand looms varied from 28 to 32 inches (ibid.: 8), leaving the emerging market largely beyond its reach. Possibly the traditional industry could not go for upgrading and modernisation in line with market dynamics, since inflows of investment were inadequate, compared with the modern mills at Dundee and Calcutta.

Poor artisans worked only with rudimentary equipment that was manufactured and maintained at village-quality levels. Even 'hand spinning wheels do not find favour because of their high cost to purchase' (ibid.: 7).

These several factors explain why Bengal's traditional industry virtually disappeared from the jute packaging market by the early 1890s. With this axis of the triangular competition thus subdued, head-on competition arose between the Dundee and Calcutta mills. In fact, from about 1865–6 the Calcutta mills began to invade the markets lying in the Far East,[10] where, as the following discussion shows, they enjoyed comparative advantages over the Dundee mills similar to those in India's domestic market. In five such countries, namely British Burma, Java, China, the Strait Settlements and Ceylon, Bengal's aggregate exports of jute products (hand loom and power loom together) stood at Rs. 1.44 million in 1864–5 (Table 5.8 and Kerr 1874: appendix L). It increased to Rs. 2.47 million in 1868–9, and further to Rs. 4.21 million in 1872–3. The underlying growth rate works out at 24.05 per cent per annum. Since it was a decaying phase for Bengal's hand loom products, this rapid market expansion must have reflected the market presence of its modern jute mills. Further progress in two of these markets, namely China and the Strait Settlements, is evident in Table 5.9. The former is seen to have grown from 0.41 million pieces per annum in 1873–5 to 9.72 million pieces per annum in 1885–9, and the latter from 2.98 million pieces per annum to 10.29 million pieces per annum during the same period.

Bengal mills then gradually took on Australia, New Zealand and North America. A common rhythm in the export series for those countries in Table 5.8 is that, although a falling trend appeared there in the late 1860s, it was checked afterwards and an upward trend dominated. For Australia and its

Table 5.9 Annual exports of bags from Bengal to different foreign ports (in million pieces), 1873/5–1910/14

Year	*United Kingdom*	*United States*	*Egypt*	*China*	*Australia and New Zealand*	*Strait Settlement*	*Cape of Good Hope*	*Others*	*Total*
1873–5[1]	0.06	1.12	0.10	0.41	1.51	2.98	0.07	0.83	7.08
1875–9[2]	2.98	8.35	1.55	5.86	8.42	6.13	0.28	1.49	35.06
1880–4[3]	2.86	15.40	1.12	10.69	15.76	9.46	0.85	3.63	59.77
1885–9[4]	10.67	13.94	1.94	9.72	18.03	10.29	1.91	11.75	78.25
1905–9[5]	72.87	699.55	23.82	24.75	57.35	31.07	14.94	15.43	939.78
1910–14[6]	86.24	896.24	25.85	35.13	82.30	37.26	21.45	15.96	1,200.43

Notes: The figures for Egypt include the Levant from 1905 onwards; the figures for the Cape of Good Hope include Mauritius from 1905 onwards.

Sources: 1: P.P. (1876b: tab. 24); 2: GOB (1881: xxvi); 3: GOB (1886: tab. 12); 4: GOB (1891: 33); 5: P.P. (1908: tab. 156) and GOI (1913: tab. 10); 6: GOI (1913a: tab. 10) and GOI (1918: tab. 14).

neighbouring ports, the series declined from Rs. 0.22 million in 1866–7 to Rs. 0.07 million in 1867–8 but then gradually recovered to Rs. 0.38 million in 1872–3 (Table 5.8). Similarly, from Rs. 2.79 million in 1866–7, the series for North America fell to Rs. 0.69 million in 1868–9 but bounced back to Rs. 2.80 million in 1870–1. Given the competitive aspects of Bengal's hand loom and power loom products against the products of Dundee, I consider, as before, that to a large extent the falls in earlier years reflected the competitive failure of hand loom products, whereas the subsequent revivals of the market should be attributed to the modern mills in Bengal. I therefore conclude that the Bengal mills began to successfully compete with the Dundee mills in those markets from the early 1870s. A government report of 1876–7, indeed, confirms this conclusion:

> The Indian mills now command a practical monopoly of the Asiatic and a large portion of the American and Australian markets and have in the past years largely extended their exports to China. This has deprived the Dundee manufacturers of some of the main outlets for their trade, and their demand for raw jute has consequently fallen.
>
> (GOB 1878: 165)

To show that those emerging trends continued in the long run, I refer to Table 5.9, where the series for Australia and New Zealand are seen to increase from 1.51 million bags per annum in 1873–5 to 18.03 million per annum in 1885–90, and those for the United States from 1.12 million per annum to 13.94 million per annum in the respective periods. In addition, Egypt increased its annual intake from 0.10 million pieces to 1.94 million pieces, and the Cape of Good Hope from 0.07 million to 1.91 million, in the same time frame. With these advances into different markets, Bengal's overseas consignments of jute bags rose to 78.25 million pieces per annum – that is, Rs. 17.22 million at Rs. 0.22 per bag – in the late 1880s, as against Rs. 1.87 million in 1872–3 (Table 5.8).

Not only did the Bengal mills defeat their counterparts in Dundee in foreign markets, but they could successfully compete with them in the British domestic market as well. The first onslaught in this respect befell its domestic yarn market. Although it represented the decline of an important segment of British industry, its weaving branch got an advantage as a result, since yarns became available at lower prices. Imports of yarn into Britain rose in volume from 1.62 million lbs to 8.09 million lbs, and in value from £55,000 to £297,000, from 1875 to 1885 (Tariff Commission 1905: 3733). A falling trend, however, came to prevail thereafter, especially in the value series, which slid down from £142,000 per annum in 1885–90 to £85,000 per annum in 1900–4, leading to a fall in its average price from £3.28 to £1.46 per 100 lbs. In the face of such a drastic price cut, the downward drift in the volume of yarn imports – evident in the source – surely signalled the decline of jute weaving as well. Indeed, the intra-industry trade between Bengal and the United Kingdom in this line confirms the competitive failure of the Dundee mills.[11] Table 5.10 shows that,

Table 5.10 Intra-industry trade of jute goods between Bengal and the United Kingdom (in Rs.), 1885/6–1889/90

Year	*Bags*		*Cloths*		*Others*		*Total*		*Trade surplus of Bengal*
	Bengal–UK	*UK–Bengal*	*Bengal–UK*	*UK–Bengal*	*Bengal–UK*	*UK–Bengal*	*Bengal–UK*	*UK–Bengal*	
1885–6	1,240,390	14,800	401,190	120,520	3,230	25,150	1,644,810	160,470	1,484,340
1886–7	1,431,890	3,240	156,940	67,650	1,620	17,270	1,590,450	88,160	1,502,290
1887–8	558,050	75,750	77,530	124,990	11,950	17,260	647,530	218,000	429,530
1888–9	3,524,400	20	425,240	89,790	28,820	21,090	3,978,460	110,900	3,867,560
1889–90	5,073,410	0	1,073,120	92,300	239,480	21,790	6,386,010	114,090	6,271,920

Source: P.P. (1892: 200).

Table 5.11 Growth of the Dundee jute industry, 1874–1905

Year	*Number of factories*				*Number of spindles*	*Number of power looms*
	Spinning	*Weaving*	*Spinning and weaving*	*Total*		
1874	26	20	63	109	229,000	9,599
1878	26	39	50	115	219,000	11,288
1885	30	37	51	118	264,000	12,083
1890	25	37	51	113	279,000	14,107
1905	25	44	38	107	277,000	13,704

Source: Tariff Commission (1905: 3788).

between 1885 and 1890, Bengal increased its exports of jute products to the British market steeply, from Rs. 1.64 million to Rs. 6.39 million, while at the same time curtailing similar imports from Dundee from Rs. 0.16 million to Rs. 0.11 million. Its surplus in this exchange thus rose by about Rs. 4.79 million in this period.

The moribund state of affairs at Dundee is evident in Table 5.11. The table indicates a state of stagnation among Dundee's spinning mills between 1874 and 1905, though four such mills sprang up in 1878–85; and a further dismal picture for those who spun and wove simultaneously. The number of mills belonging to the latter category steadily fell from 63 in 1874 to 38 in 1905. Possibly some of them were subsequently converted into exclusive weaving concerns, so that a rising trend prevailed in their number from 1874 to 1904. Insofar as the spindle and loom capacities were concerned, however, the industry definitely witnessed a setback after 1890. Between 1890 and 1905 the former declined from 279,000 to 277,000, and the latter from 14,107 to 13,704.

I seek to assess the state of affairs at Dundee from the demand side as well, taking into account Britain's import and re-export of jute goods. In 1897 imports stood at £1.63 million, out of which £374,000 were absorbed domestically, and £1.26 million were re-exported (Tariff Commission 1905: 3740). While the level of domestic absorption varied in the range of £270,000 to £480,000 between 1897 and 1904, the level of re-exports increased steadily, from £1.26 million to about £2 million during that period, thus spoiling the export market of the Dundee manufacturers. If we deduct the re-exports from the export series as available in the report of the Tariff Commission (1905: 3765), the United Kingdom's exports of domestically manufactured jute goods come to £847,000 in 1897, £569,000 in 1898, £202,000 in 1900, £2,000 in 1903 and £33,000 in 1904. These confirm a total eclipse of Dundee's global market.

The sequence of events from 1855 to 1892 thus suggests that the emerging jute mills in Bengal won the three-way competition that besieged the contemporary packaging market, and moved towards a global monopoly. In conceding this in 1894, a government document remarks:

> Though the claim occasionally heard, that Dundee has been transported to the banks of the Hughli, may not be more than a hyperbole licensed by the poetry of commerce, still there is little reason why it should not ultimately become a fact in the jute trade that the fibre is worked up within easy distance of the place of production into the form in which it is to be used.
>
> (P.P. 1894: 312)

In these competitive struggles, however, the modern jute industry in Bengal never encountered any discriminatory policies, such as those from which many of its industries had suffered during the Company raj (1757–1857) (Ray 2011: 251–3). Indeed, at the insistence of Dundee interests, a committee was constituted in 1919 to safeguard their future. But it concluded:

> The Committee was unable to recommend artificial means to enable the United Kingdom to compete with another portion of the Empire, and are of the opinion…that it rests with the manufacturers to take the necessary steps to economize working expenses to the utmost…
>
> (quoted in Carter 1921: 175)

In this connection, Bagchi (1980: 262) notes that 'Dundee did not give up its earlier supremacy without a struggle, which found its expression in the use not only of the usual economic weapons but also of political pressure'. But, owing to its other interests (especially the supply of jute machinery), he emphasises, 'the hostility did not break out into open warfare'.

Once the Calcutta mills had won against the competition from Dundee, there was no question of their defeat elsewhere. The floodgates of global demand had, therefore, been unveiled to the industry, accelerating its pace of development. This was echoed in the speech by the president of the Indian Jute Mills Association (IJMA) in 1907: '[I]t appears perfectly certain that we can get an outlet for all we can produce at present prices… I have no anxiety as regards our consuming markets developing to such an extent that everything we can make will find a market' (IJMA 1908: ii). While only about 7 million gunny bags had annually been exported outside the country in 1873–5, the figure climbed to 78 million in 1885–9, and further to 1.20 billion in 1910–14 (Table 5.9). Although it was an unrelenting upswing, there were temporal variations in the rate of growth. In particular, a high growth rate prevailed between 1885–9 and 1905–9 – as high as 55 per cent per annum – in contrast to the 6 per cent and 14 per cent growth in the previous two quinquennia, respectively. This was indeed the phase when Dundee's jute industry entered into oblivion.

The US market was the prime catalyst to this development, however. Although, in 1873–5, this market took less than 16 per cent of Bengal's exports of gunny bags, it shared about three-quarters in 1910–14 (Table 5.9). Much of this progress occurred between 1885/9 and 1905/9, when the market expanded from about 14 million to 700 million pieces annually. The United Kingdom came to occupy the second largest position, though it had earlier been of lesser

Table 5.12 Annual exports of hessian cloth from Bengal to different foreign ports (in Rs.), 1875/9–1905/6

Year	*United Kingdom*	*United States*	*Argentina*	*Others*	*Total*
1875–9[1]	140,291	251,668	–	706,746	1,098,705
1880–4[2]	107,500	337,093	–	195,540	640,133
1885–9[3]	432,638	1,010,863	–	350,059	1,793,560
1896–9[4]	1,482,053	9,643,573	2,378,218	1,226,845	14,730,689
1900–4[4]	2,228,572	17,618,182	5,316,584	3,535,460	28,698,798
1905–6[4]	2,857,890	25,193,630	9,675,790	4,306,090	42,033,400

Notes: '–' indicates either an insignificant amount or included in 'Others'; the '1896–9' figure is a four-year average.

Sources: 1: GOB (1881: xxvi); 2: P.P. (1885: tab. 12); 3: GOB (1891: 33); d. P.P. (1907: tab. 150).

importance as Dundee manufacturers had been dominant. From 1910 to 1914 it annually imported 86 million pieces, as against 0.06 million pieces from 1873 to 1875. Australia and New Zealand were also bulk buyers for these articles, together purchasing more than 82 million pieces per annum between 1910 and 1914. Other regular buyers included China, the Strait Settlements and the Cape of Good Hope.

The Calcutta mills also had extensive foreign outlets for hessian cloth, though it was, comparatively, a later development. Annual exports of this product amounted only to Rs. 1.10 million in 1875–9, and that was further depressed to Rs. 0.64 million in 1880–4 (Table 5.12). The growth set in only thereafter, escalating its annual proceeds sharply to Rs. 1.79 million in 1885–9, Rs. 14.73 million in 1896–9 and further to Rs. 42.03 million in 1905–6. The table reveals that the United States was again the bulk purchaser in this market, however, sharing about 60 per cent in 1905–6, followed by Argentina and the United Kingdom, with their respective intakes at Rs. 9.68 million and Rs. 2.86 million.

The rapid expansion of global demand made the industry highly export-oriented. Its export share, which had already been on the high side at about 45 per cent by 1875–6 (columns 2 and 5 in Table 5.7), rose further to about 84 per cent in 1904 and culminated at 91.93 per cent in 1914 (Table 5.13). In contrast, India's domestic markets (outside Bengal) took about 7 per cent in 1914 and the local market less than 1 per cent. Two alternative arguments might be put forward to explain the lower sales on the domestic side. The first is the inadequate demand for jute packaging materials in the domestic market. But this proposition does not seem tenable, in view of the fact that India's domestic market (outside Bengal) absorbed more than Rs. 3 million worth of those products in 1872–3 (Kerr 1874: appendix L). The alternative explanation is that, in view of the higher returns in the global market, the Calcutta mills avoided domestic outlets and opted for sales abroad. In this case, the traditional industry should have dominated the domestic market, particularly the local outlets in and around the province, where the Calcutta mills used to supply very

Table 5.13 Market shares of various jute products from Bengal (in %), 1904–14

Year	*Foreign ports*	*Indian ports*	*Local consumption*
1904	83.55	13.81	2.64
1905	86.40	11.85	1.75
1906	88.95	10.20	0.85
1907	88.33	10.92	0.75
1908	89.07	10.49	0.44
1909	89.93	9.22	0.85
1910	89.21	9.77	1.02
1911	88.58	9.84	1.58
1912	88.37	10.02	1.61
1913	90.59	8.54	0.87
1914	91.93	7.33	0.74

Sources: IJMA *Annual Report*, various years.

little. This proposition is in agreement with our previous finding that a large proportion of the hand loom goods that came to Calcutta from the interior of the province were sold locally. In addition, the contemporary census data, presented above, corroborate this.

III

The skyrocketing demand in the global market accelerated the industry's growth, especially when the local supply of raw jute was very elastic. Gathering data from different sources, Table 5.14 presents the industry's growth pattern from 1855 to 1915. The industry's nominal capital for 1855–89 is estimated based on a norm of Rs. 3,500 per loom, which includes the construction costs of mill buildings, warehouses, managers' quarters and overseers' barracks, as well as the cost of looms with all accessories, including spinning and engine power (Carter 1921: 177). The table points out that, while only 27 jute mills had been operating in Bengal from 1885 to 1889, as many as ten new mills sprang up between 1890 and 1904, and another 30 between 1904 and 1915, giving an aggregate of 67 jute mills by the end of our study period. Their spindle and loom capacities increased likewise, and became 789,236 and 37,541, respectively. A sum of Rs. 85.73 million was sunk as the nominal capital. For 1908–9, their aggregate production is reported at Rs. 183.50 million (IJMA 1909: 60).

A number of countries in Europe and North America also started jute manufacturing during the second half of the nineteenth century. But prohibitive tariffs and bounties often explained their development (Tariff Commission 1905: 3656–66). Thus, in 1879, Germany imposed a tariff of about 12 per cent on jute yarn and 24 per cent on jute goods in addition to a 5 per cent subsidy on freight on steamers. France likewise sanctioned a £4 15s. duty on foreign jute articles in 1892, generating a 24 per cent price advantage to its domestic

Table 5.14 Growth of modern jute mills in Bengal, 1855/9–1914/15

Year	*Number of mills*	*Number of spindles*	*Number of looms*	*Nominal capital (million Rs.)*	*Average daily employment*
1855–9	2	NA	620	2.17	NA
1860–4	4	NA	1,090	3.82	NA
1865–9	4	NA	1,090	4.27	NA
1870–4	15	NA	3,456	14.25	NA
1875–9	19	NA	4,313	14.96	NA
1880–4	27	88,000	5,361	18.76	38,800
1885–9	27	88,000	5,361	18.76	38,800
1890–4	28	182,696	9,103	33.70	68,140
1895–9	32	264,255	12,874	46.35	92,876
1900–4	37	357,366	17,409	43.07	120,406
1905–9	49	561,769	26,489	59.90	180,866
1910–14	61	713,229	34,088	77.88	218,596
1914–15	67	789,236	37,541	85.73	236,294

Sources: 1855–79, Wallace (1928: 56–7); 1880–1904, GOB: *Statistical Abstract for British India*, various issues; 1905–14, IJMA: *Annual Report*, various issues.

manufacturers. A similar price advantage, of 29 per cent, was generated in Austria. But India never extended any state patronage to this industry.[12] Therefore, a pertinent question is: on what grounds did the Bengal jute mills compete with their counterparts in Dundee?

I argue here that Bengal won the global competition in view of its strong comparative advantages in jute manufacturing. To explain this, I delve mainly into three aspects of the industry: (i) raw material costs; (ii) transportation costs; and (iii) labour costs. I also argue that the organisational structure of the industry and its pattern of growth also generated significant cost advantages.

In respect of (i), we note that the export price of raw jute at Calcutta, although as low as Rs. 1.81 per maund in 1833–7 and Rs. 1.50 per maund in 1838–42, steadily increased to Rs. 4.56 per maund during 1868–72 (for a time series of raw jute prices from 1828 to 1898, see Kundu, Basak and Sarkar 1959: 316). In contrast, a source indicates that, in 1872, its average price was Rs. 1.65 per maund in the districts of eastern Bengal, and Rs. 2.19 per maund in the districts of West Bengal, giving an average of Rs. 1.92 per maund (Kerr 1874: 36). In view of the three-tier network in the jute trade (ibid.: 62–4), I add to this a 30 per cent profitability at each of two stages of transaction (assuming that the interior prices referred to those prevailing in village markets). This gives a price of Rs. 3.24 per maund at which the Calcutta mills possibly purchased raw jute. Thus, exclusive of freight implications, they enjoyed a price advantage of Rs. 1.32 a maund for raw materials over their rivals in Dundee. This estimate is a close approximation of what the contemporary jute mills at Dundee frequently pointed out. According to them, the Calcutta mills enjoyed a cost advantage of £3 per ton (that is, Rs. 1.11 per maund) because of their proximity to raw material sources ('Evidence of W. Longair', in Tariff Commission 1905: 3926).

For lower transportation costs as well, Bengal enjoyed comparative advantages in India's domestic markets, and also in the markets of Far Eastern countries such as Burma, China, Java, Ceylon and the Strait Settlements, where jute packaging was extensively used for the conveyance of grain, flour, seeds, coffee, sugar, etc. The contemporary freight rate between Calcutta and London is reported at 80s. a ton (that is, Rs. 1.48 per maund) (ibid.: 3927). Taking raw jute from Bengal and sending jute products back here thus involved about Rs. 2.96 a maund (since raw jute does not significantly reduce in weight after processing). At least at this level the prices of Bengal jute products should be less than those of Dundee goods in India's domestic market, as well as in the markets of the Far East.[13] Even in the British market, Calcutta mills could dominate because of the high freight costs between London and Dundee, namely 26s. 6d. a ton (that is, about Rs. 0.49 a maund) ('Evidence of J. B. Don', in Tariff Commission 1905: 3900). The cost price of Bengal jute goods involved a transport cost of Rs. 1.48 per maund in London, whereas the cost of Dundee products included a one-way freight charge from Calcutta to London (at Rs. 1.48 a maund) and the to-and-fro freight between London and Dundee (at Rs. 0.98 a maund), aggregating to Rs. 2.46 per maund. The Calcutta mills then surely enjoyed a cost advantage over the Dundee mills in the British domestic as well as overseas markets, which were supplied from London. Indeed, several witnesses before the British Tariff Commission in 1905 lamented this issue. The Commission's report notes,

> Some firms state that the freight rates they have to pay are a greater drawback to their trade in yarns than foreign tariffs. This opinion is by no means general, but there is practical unanimity as to the severe burden under existing conditions both of the railway and shipping rates on all branches of the industry.
>
> (Tariff Commission 1905: 3695)

The low cost of labour was yet another source of comparative advantage for Bengal. Since the modern mills had arisen in and around Calcutta, where artisans had long been exposed to the culture of jute, they got a reserve army of such workers owing to the depressed state of the traditional industry. In fact, the first jute mill was set up in Serampore in view of the fact that 'it was not only close to and easy access to Calcutta, but was also one of the chief centres for the jute hand loom manufacture (Dhaniakhali, Sheoraphuli, Baidyabati and Bhadreswar)' (Sen 1999: 23). In addition, Rungta (1985: 116) tells us that '[t]he supply of labour came mainly from the population living within walking distance of the Mills (say, about five miles) attracted to work for the wages offered by the Mills. Even though wages were low and labourers worked from dawn to dusk, the supply seems to have been sufficient, except during the monsoons' (see also Das Gupta 1976: 280–9). For similar reasons, workers also flocked to those mills from the neighbouring districts, such as Burdwan, Birbhum and Murshidabad, which were the erstwhile seats of jute processing. Indeed, available documents confirm that, till about 1885, jute mills mobilised their workers largely from within the province (Foley 1906: 14). For the excess supply of labour, however, the mill owners enjoyed privileges in the labour market. They evidently enforced 90 hours of work per week, as against 55 hours in the United Kingdom, 63 hours in Germany and France, 66 hours in Austria and 69 hours in Belgium (Tariff Commission 1905: 3697). Such an extended working schedule was possible only in the presence of buyers' control over the labour market. According to a source, 'The working hours of Calcutta are 90 per week. It has been proved that the real advantage to the producer is in having the larger output and longer working period. They justify it on the ground that they have great control of labour' (ibid.: 3931). In addition to economising the wage rate, this state of affairs also ensured lower overhead costs, generating another source of comparative advantages. Victor Fraenkl, a Dundee jute exporter (Tariff Commission 1905: 3943), thus emphasises, 'That continuous running [of machinery 'day and night'] may mean a low 12 per cent advantage in cost of production, for Calcutta is manufacturing about 33 per cent cheaper than Dundee.' But they believed it to be 'unfair' (ibid.) competition, as it arose out of India's less stringent factory regulations, and expected that 'this great disparity between the Factory Acts of India and Great Britain may be gradually lessened' ('Evidence of W. Longair', in Tariff Commission 1905: 3927). But it continued, and certainly gave a great stimulus to the development of the modern jute industry in Bengal (for arguments against stringent factory regulations in India, see IJMA 1908: iii–vi; and IJMA 1909: 1–4).

For a comparative study, let me calculate the wage rates for different countries, standardising the duration of work at 55 hours per week. For spinners, the standardised wage rate is found at Rs. 4.50 for Dundee, Rs. 3.50 for Austria, Rs. 4 for Belgium and Rs. 4.25 for France. For Calcutta, a source (Foley 1906: x) reveals the weekly wage at Rs. 2 annas 10 for ordinary spinners and Rs. 3 annas 7 for skilled spinners, giving an average of Rs. 3.02. At 90 hours a week, this gives a rate of Rs. 1.85 per 55-hour week. Even if a shorter working period of 72 hours per week is considered, the standardised rate comes to Rs. 2.31 per week, which is 48.67 per cent cheaper than that for Dundee. I emphasise here that a lower labour cost in spinning generated significant comparative advantages, since wages constituted two-thirds of the weekly expenses in this activity, the other third consisting of expenditures on coal, oil, furnishings, railway carriages, taxes, etc., leaving raw material costs out of account ('Evidence of A. Proctor', in Tariff Commission 1905: 3917). In the weaving branch also, similar wage variations are noticed between Dundee and Calcutta. From the British Tariff Commission (1905) we learn that, exclusive of factory overhead costs, the average wage rate was 15s. 6d per week, or about Rs. 7.50, in Dundee (Tariff Commission 1905: 3908). In Foley's report, however, the wage rate at Calcutta is reported at Rs. 4 per week for an ordinary weaver and Rs. 6.50 per week for a skilled weaver (Foley 1906: 9), giving an average rate of Rs. 5.25 per week. Even if we consider the working hours of 72 per week in Calcutta, it comes to Rs. 4.01 per 55-hour week. A wage difference of 46.53 per cent is thus implied. My estimation thus suggests that, compared to the Dundee mills, the wage rate in Calcutta was cheaper at least by 48 per cent in spinning and 46 per cent in weaving.

The jute mills in Bengal also enjoyed comparative advantages in three other respects. One was surely related to the question of land. There is ample evidence in the literature describing the Dundee mills as struggling in multi-storeyed buildings with acute shortages of space as well as water (Turner 1952: 107–12). But both land and water were in plentiful supply in contemporary Bengal, so that the Calcutta mills could afford spacious office accommodation and comfortable factory sheds (Carter 1921: 165–70), often stretching over several acres of land.[14] These were quite astonishing to managers and foremen hailing from Dundee. Whatley (2005: 6) thus describes it,

> Unlike in Dundee, where access to water and space were at a premium and mills and factories and much housing had to be built several storeys high, and in which conditions were cramped and airless, most Indian mills were well built, single-storey structures, spacious and well lit – something that often came as a surprise to those who had grown accustomed to life and work in the densely packed town of Dundee, its mills and chimneys crammed alongside the deteriorating housing stock.[15]

Second, Calcutta mills enjoyed a cost-effective transportation network thanks to their location on the bank of the Hooghly, a branch of the river Ganges, since its other branch, the Padma, flew across the rich jute-growing belt of the present-day Bangladesh, with its numerous tributaries, through which the mills obtained raw jute from the hinterland. It also provided easy accessibilities to up-country markets in the north and the Port of Calcutta in the south. In addition, the railways could provide services at their doorstep, as they were clustered within narrow geographical limits. The Budge–Budge Mill was located 12 miles below Calcutta and the Goureepore Mill about 28 miles above it, with all the other mills dispersed in between. Most of them were situated on the left bank of the river, however, with their sidings connected with the Eastern Bengal State Railways (Carter 1921: 166). The mills on the right bank similarly enjoyed the service of the East Indian Railway. Through the Jubilee Bridge over the Hooghly at Naihati, close to Goureepore and just above Chandernagore, these two railways were interconnected to run across the heartland of Bengal's jute districts.

Third, the industry met its energy requirements from the large deposits of coal in the neighbourhood of Calcutta, the Ranigunj coalfield. Many European collieries had sprung up there from the 1840s, and they could despatch their output with lower freight costs (Rs. 4.75 a ton: Ray 2015: 481) once the rail service between Calcutta and Asansol commenced in the late 1850s. By way of minimising energy costs, these twin developments in the mid-nineteenth century generated locational advantages for the Calcutta jute mills.

Another important source of its comparative advantage was the managing agency system (Basu 1958; Tyson 1961), under which the industry flourished. It was an organisational innovation in nineteenth-century Bengal, whereby the agents floated joint-stock companies to provide them with managerial services, charging fees thereof, and got rid of their ownership stakes once the production commenced (or at some other opportune moment). In several cases, they also took over sick and closed firms with similar objectives in view. As many as 14 such managing houses nurtured the development of the modern jute industry in Bengal during the second half of the nineteenth century.

Thanks to this organisational structure the industry gained operational efficiency on various grounds. In the first place, it achieved a high level of efficiency in the mobilisation of funds, both from within the country and abroad. While the majority of the contemporary mills mopped up investment from within the province on the strength of their managing agents' goodwill in the market, a few of them successfully accessed the global capital market, particularly in cases in which their managing agents had roots in Britain. Although the fortunes from Dundee mills were mainly invested in North America (Gilbert 1939), the contribution of Scotland towards this industry was not insignificant. In this context, I may cite the examples of Finlay, Muir & Co., George Henderson & Co., McKinnon, McKenzie & Co., Schoene, Kilburn & Co., Andrew Yule & Co., Gladstone, Wyllie & Co., Thomas Duff & Co. and McNeil & Co. There is evidence that they often persuaded international industrial houses to invest in this industry – such as George Henderson & Co. did with the Borneo Company Ltd[16] – and, sometimes, they went for financial innovations, as in the case of the Kamarhatty Jute Mill, which James Jardine, Skinner & Co. floated with a high debt–equity ratio, Rs. 707,000 (estimated): Rs. 400,000, which gave rise to 'large dividends on very small earnings' (Playne 1917: 131). A government report (P.P. 1915: 63) notes that, in 1913–14, the industry's paid-up capital (including debenture) stood at £9,972,000, 'of which about 3 millions represent sterling capital'. In terms of the Indian currency, these represent Rs. 149,580,000 and Rs. 45,000,000, respectively. These figures suggest that more than 30 per cent of jute investment in Bengal came from Britain. The industry's development did not, therefore, suffer from the want of investment at its nascent stage.

Moreover, as the managing agents simultaneously managed a host of companies in diverse industries – such as Bird & Co. which was involved in more than 20 lines of business; Jardine, Skinner & Co., with eight lines of business; and Gillanders, Arbuthnot & Co., with six lines of business (for details, see ibid.: 85, 128, 204) – the average fixed costs should have been low for individual establishments in view of scope economies that arise out of technical sub-additivities in management (Baumol and Blinder 2009: 274). In addition, the industry had the cost advantages of vertical integration, since agents such as Jardine, Skinner & Co., Bird & Co. and Gillanders, Arbuthnot & Co. carried out business concurrently in jute manufacturing, coal mining, water and railway transportation, banking and insurance, as well as in electricity in later days. The jute mills under their agencies must have obtained those goods and services from their sister concerns on soft terms. Again, when a particular agent managed a number of jute mills together – such as Thomas Duff & Co. managing the Samnugar Jute Mill, the Titaghur Jute Mill and the Victoria Jute Mill, employing more than 100 European and 31,000 native workers together (Playne 1917: 109) – there must have been enormous scale economies. Such scope and scale economies gave definite cost advantages to the Calcutta jute mills operating under the managing agency system.

The industry's pattern of growth also generated certain cost advantages. It appears from Table 5.14 that, from 1885/9 to 1914/15, there was a 148 per cent growth in the number of mills, a 797 per cent growth in their spindle capacity and a 600 per cent growth in their loom capacity. These differing growth rates suggest that the industry must have undergone a massive expansion of scale at the firm level. To verify the changes in scale, we note that, while, in 1885–9, each mill had on average a capacity of 199 looms and 3,259 spindles, this level had expanded to 560 looms and 11,780 spindles by 1914–15. Therefore, the inference is that the industry grew in Bengal through the entry of new firms as well as through the expansion of existing ones. The former gave rise to external economies, and the latter the economies of scale, both of which underpinned the industry's competitive edge and higher profitability in the long run.

The question of tariffs also generated market advantages for the Calcutta mills in many countries. Since most of the jute-manufacturing countries imported raw materials from Bengal, they did not dare to impose prohibitive tariffs on Calcutta's manufactured jute lest Bengal retaliated. But in none of these countries were articles from Dundee spared. Thus, for instance, since 1892 there had been a £4 15s. duty on foreign jute articles in France, which had previously imported substantially from Dundee. According to a Dundee firm, 'We were sending a quarter of our products to France till the duty in 1892 made our trade dwindle away' (Tariff Commission 1905: 3656). A jute good sent directly from Calcutta to any port in France was admitted duty-free. If, however, it was sent via England, 'it pays a surtax' even if it was not landed there. This must have been a boon to Calcutta's mills in the competition.

Turning to the question of the industry's welfare implication in society, we note that it hinged primarily on the question of employment opportunities, since the benefits arising out of investment in the industry did not accrue to the local populace as European entrepreneurs were in charge of the management of its affairs. The question of employment generation should be studied in the present context, however, taking into account both its quantitative and qualitative dimensions (for jute workers and their trade union movements, see Ghosh 2000; Ghosh 1990; Chakraborty 1981; and Sen 1999). Looking at its quantitative aspect, we find that the industry was carried out in Bengal on the basis of a highly labour-intensive technology. Indeed, one of the primary reasons for its emergence was the reserve pool of workers, as already noted. Since these workers could be employed at lower wages, the emerging mills should have opted for more of a labour roundabout method of production. This argument is corroborated by the evidence that Bengal mills employed six to seven persons per loom, as against only two persons per loom in Dundee (Wallace 1928: 62). In spinning as well, as Sethia (1996: 84) notes, 1 ton of manufactured yarn in Bengal required four times as many person-hours as were required in Dundee. Second, the modern jute technology per se was highly labour-intensive, requiring both a skilled and an unskilled workforce. A jute expert thus makes it clear: 'Regarding labour, jute is an essentially labour-oriented industry. The manufacturing processes are mostly mechanical and the labour complement is largely tied to the number of machines worked' (G. Sivaraman, 'Cost Reduction in the Jute Industry', in IJMA 1968: 91–7). Of the two distinct branches of the industry, presses and mills, the former employed skilled hands for sorting and baling, and unskilled ones for carrying materials over different places (ICJC 1952: 192–6). Labour intensity was certainly high in the case of manual baling, but it fell significantly when hydraulic machines were employed. In the latter branch, however, bales of jute coming from the presses were first inspected thoroughly for classification between hessian and sacking materials (ibid.). This was done manually. The bales were then passed through six different stages, namely batching, preparing, spinning, winding, weaving and finishing, involving various degrees of mechanisation. Since quite a large number of machines were deployed in these processes without any significant level of automation for carrying materials from one machine to another, a good number of semi-skilled and unskilled workers were called for. To work at machines some amount of skill was certainly required, but it could be obtained through on-the-job training for shorter durations (Foley 1906: x).

Because of its high labour intensity, the industry created substantial job opportunities. From a level of 38,800 in 1880–4 the industry's average level of daily employment increased to 68,140 in 1890–4, 120,406 in 1900–04 and further to 236,294 in 1914–15 (Table 5.14). The firm-level data are also quite impressive. A contemporary survey reveals that job opportunities at individual mills ranged from 2,300 to 7,000, with as many as ten mills (out of 29 mills under survey) providing jobs to more than 5,000 workers each. Substantial jobs were also created at jute presses. The census of 1901 enumerated their aggregate employment at 13,729 (GOI 1903: tab. XV).

The rapid growth of the industry also attracted migratory labour from the mid-1880s, which changed its labour composition in the subsequent period. Sen (1999: 26–7) points out three contemporary circuits of migration in contemporary Bengal: (i) to eastern districts of Bengal, from Muzaffarpur, Saran, Gaya, Patna and Bhagalpur in Bihar and Bengal's western districts, such as Midnapore, Bankura and Birbhum; (ii) to plantations in British and foreign colonies from the United Provinces, Bihar and the Central Provinces; and (iii) from Bihar to tea plantations in north Bengal, Assam and the Surmah Valley. Because of their location, the jute mills drew workers from all these circuits. A survey among 70,000 jute workers in 1895 noticed 35,000 to 40,000 migratory workers from north-western provinces and Bihar (cited in GOI 1896: 10). There was migration from Andhra Pradesh and Orissa as well (de Haan 1997: 925–6). These migrations were largely underpinned by the scarcity of land, low rural wages and social repression in their places of origin. On the other hand, the relatively high wage rates offered by the jute industry acted as the pull factor. In 1911 a coolie earned between annas 2 and annas 3 and paises 3 per diem in Saran, as against annas 5 in the Bengal jute mills (Yang 1989: 197).

For the evaluation of welfare gains, we should recognise, apart from the direct employment, the number of persons financially dependent on the jute mill workers, and also various types of indirect employment. According to the census of 1911 (GOI 1913: 342–3), the industry generated employment for 200,446 persons in spinning and weaving and 13,842 persons in baling, giving an aggregate employment of 214,288. Since the census further reports 111,941 persons as being financially dependent on these workers, I consider that the industry directly provided livelihood to 326,229 persons in 1911. A great deal of indirect employment was also created in the industry's forward and backward streams. One of its important linkage effects took place in the tertiary sector, in which the census of 1901 (GOI 1903: tab. XV) reckoned employment opportunities for 10,594 persons in the raw jute trade. Since a large segment in this category represented self-employed people, the return thereof should have been remunerative. Additional employment was also created in agriculture, as the acreage under jute was extended significantly. From the available sources we gather that the area under jute cultivation in Bengal increased from about 768,000 acres in 1872 (Table 5.1, only Bengal proper) to 2.93 million acres in 1912 (IJMA 1913: statement 15), and the yield of jute fibre from 0.41 million tons (Table 5.1, converted at 1 ton = 27 maunds) to 1.53 million tons in the same period. Extensive employment must have been generated as a result. To estimate it, we note that, in the cultivation of jute, about 39,600 persons were employed in Backergunj and 69,167 persons in Jessore (Kerr 1874: 35). Given their production levels of jute as in Table 5.1, the output per person comes to 0.13245 tons, on average. At this rate, the level of employment for additional jute production from 1872 to 1912 (namely 1.12 million tons) works out at 8,456,022. This confirms Chaudhuri's conclusion that '[i]n spite of this potential source of instability there is little doubt that the export of jute brought a substantial degree of prosperity to the peasants of Bengal' (Chaudhuri 1994: 853). The industry thus generated welfare gains through the creation of livelihood directly for 326,229 persons and indirectly for 8,466,616 persons.

Turning to the question of labour income, we notice in Table 5.15 a great variation in the wage rate across workers' gender, age and the level of training. It varied from Rs. 1.12 per week for ordinary child labour to Rs. 11 per week for a mechanic. At jute presses, however, the wage rate varied mainly with the nature of job. The average wage rate was paises 42 per *pucca* bale for importing porters, annas 12 per day for exporting porters and annas 12 to Re 1 per day for press porters. A sorter earned on average annas 12 per day, and a press worker Rs. 1.72 to Rs. 2 per bale (Foley 1906: xxxvi–xlii).

Table 5.15 Weekly wages in Bengal jute mills (in Rs.), 1906

Department	*Ordinary worker*	*Trained worker*
Porting: Adult male	2.25–2.36 (i.e., 2.30)	2.50–2.72 (i.e., 2.61)
Adult female	1.84–2.84 (i.e., 2.34)	2.06
Children	1.00–1.25 (i.e., 1.12)	1.36
Average	1.92	2.01
Winding: adult male	3.00	4.00
Sewing: both adult male and female	2.50	3.00
Spinning: children	2.60	3.42
Weaving: adult male	4.00	6.50
Mechanic: adult male	NA	10.00–12.00 (i.e., 11.00)

Source: Foley (1906: x).

These wages were rated high in the contemporary standard. A Factory Act document of 1895–6 (GOB 1897: 135) reports that the monthly wage rate was Rs. 8 to 10 for male operatives, Rs. 4.50 to 6.00 for female operatives and Rs. 4 to 5 for child operatives (that is, Rs. 9, Rs. 5.25 and Rs. 4.50 on average, respectively). In contrast, according to Table 5.15, a male worker in jute mills earned on average Rs. 14 per month in winding, Rs. 21 in weaving and Rs. 11 in sewing, giving an average of Rs. 15.33 per month; a female worker earned Rs. 11 per month in sewing and a child Rs. 12.04 per month in spinning. Compared to the average factory wages, therefore, the jute industry offered a 70 per cent higher wage to adult male workers, a 110 per cent higher wage to female workers and a 168 per cent higher wage to child spinners. A further benefit was generated as the jute mills usually employed all family members together, so that workers' family income was augmented. It was also beneficial to the management, getting thereby a larger supply of labour with more regular attendance. In the contemporary society, however, a worker's family usually consisted of five members. For such a family, with two sons and one daughter, Foley estimates the family income at Rs. 17 per week (Foley 1906: x) – that is, Rs. 68 per month. A family income at this level was very attractive, and 'eagerly sought for by the agricultural and fisher-men class, not only in the neighbourhood, but for a distance' (GOI 1913: 529). While the demand gap in the labour market was certainly the main driving force behind these wage phenomena, a contemporary source adds another explanation, namely high wages at alternative job opportunities, though 'probably on a somewhat lower scale of comfort' (ibid.): 'These two main causes – the independence of Indian labour owing to the fact that he possesses other and congenial means of livelihood and the deficient labour supply – govern the whole situation' (ibid.).

The industry's strong linkage with agriculture also generated a series of welfare gains in addition to the creation of jobs, which I have discussed above (for the effect of the industry on the *ryots*, see P.P. 1874: 111). In many districts, jute cultivation was undertaken in fallow land, so that welfare gains followed from a greater proportion of land being under the plough ('Reports of the Collectors from Purnea, Jalpaiguri and Darjeeling', in Kerr 1874: 53); in addition, the cultivation of jute could be suitably accommodated in the prevailing cropping pattern, leaving the outputs of other crops largely unaffected. In the latter respect, a contemporary district report notes that 'it can be grown with advantage upon land which, after it [jute] has been reaped, can be sown with mustard, and in some cases with rice, & c.' (Kerr 1874: 53).[17] Moreover, as a cash crop, jute infused a good amount of liquidity into the agrarian society, and thus heralded a monetised economy in the countryside. According to the collector of Dacca, since 'his jute crop is so much cash in his pocket...a very great deal of the prosperity of the cultivating class [followed] here [due] to the influx of hard cash in return for jute' (ibid.). Let me also emphasise that jute was by far the most profitable crop in the contemporary agriculture. For the years 1904 to 1913 the market value per acre works out at Rs. 128.79 for jute, as against Rs. 54.62 for rice, Rs. 31.33 for wheat and Rs. 25.04 for cotton (Imperial Institute 1921: 3). These factors explain why jute was substituted for other crops (especially rice) in later years. While summing up these impacts of the industry, however, a report from Mymensing observes, 'In an economic point of view, jute has been an immense boon to the inhabitants... It has enabled them to utilise lands which were previously of little value, and it has poured silver into the district till the great bulk of the people are decidedly raised above a condition of poverty' (Kerr 1874: 53).[18]

IV

This study thus clarifies certain important issues relating to the nineteenth-century jute industry in Bengal. Basically, it was a traditional industry of the province that had been developed over the past centuries on the basis of locally available raw materials, as well as the domestic market. Explorations in the foreign market began in 1828 and, within a couple of years, success followed. My evidence points out that the industry created a global market before the advent of new technologies in Dundee in the late 1830s, and penetrated further subsequently – something the emerging Dundee mills could not arrest. Rather, they grew together through the middle of the nineteenth century. As the higher-technology mills took root in Bengal as well, however, the market was besieged with a triangular rivalry, whereby the traditional industry encountered insurmountable competition from the Calcutta mills in the domestic market (outside Bengal) and from the Dundee mills in foreign outlets, and ultimately succumbed to them. It was virtually extinguished from the latter by 1875–6 and from the former by 1885–6. Further conclusions about the traditional industry are: (i) that it generated employment opportunities for about 638,000 artisans in the middle of the century; (ii) that it survived through the early twentieth century, though at a low ebb, mainly by catering to local markets; and (iii) that, because of its prior development, the emerging mills, both in Dundee and Calcutta, got a ready supply of raw materials from Bengal, and also a ready jute-packaging market.

The eclipse of the traditional industry, however, led to head-on competition between the long-standing mills at Dundee and the new ones in Bengal. Although their technologies were similar, the latter enjoyed enormous comparative advantages on account of their proximity to the raw material zone, cheap labour and low-cost transport, as also various scale and scope economies associated with the managing agency system under which they flourished. The Calcutta mills first captured the domestic market, then intruded into the markets of the Far East, before finally proceeding to other continents. This study has shown that, by the close of the nineteenth century, they had come to dominate the global packaging market, including the domestic market in Britain, ushering in a phase of decline for the Dundee mills. With their rivals thus defeated in the competition, the Bengal mills grew at a fast rate from the early 1890s, and by 1914–15 as many as 67 large-scale mills had emerged in the province, involving an investment of Rs. 85.73 million. The study concludes that this development contributed significantly to economic welfare in the contemporary society, by way of creating livelihoods directly for more than 326,000 persons and indirectly for about 8.46 million persons. Further gains followed as the industry infused silver currency, the medium of exchange, into the rural society. The uniqueness of these stories lies in that, while almost all the traditional industries waned in the colonial hinterland in the wake of the Western Industrial Revolution, this industry exemplifies a case of Western development generating a strong linkage effect in a colonial economy. Moreover, it was one of only a few industries in the colony that were able to graduate from a cottage milieu to the factory system of production – a development paradigm that reprised the historical course of the industrialised countries, such as the United Kingdom, but involved a low level of transitional pain.

Notes

1 In fact, Abul-Fazl (1948: 92) writes, 'Of the bark of the plant [the San (hemp)] strong ropes are made. One kind of this plant bears a flower like the cotton tree, and is called Pat-san. It makes a very soft rope.'

2 Buchanan (1934: 242) observes, 'The British Isles had thus taken over another Indian textile industry and placed it under power machinery and the factory system.'

3 Morris (1994: 567) has hinted, however, that it was the traditional jute industry that motivated the development of modern jute mills in Bengal. Noting the substantial growth of the handicraft sector and the expansion of its market, both in India and abroad, he observes: 'These developments attracted the attention of George Auckland...to import spinning equipment and mechanics from Dundee.'

4 The source identifies any sale outside the district as an export. The same practice is followed here.

5 For this period Tyson (1953: 6) observes that 'Indian hand-made jute cloth enjoyed a market in three continents'.

6 Gadgil (1929: 61) notes, 'Thus the years following 1830 saw a rapid decline in the jute handloom industry of Bengal.'

7 In 1872–3, 16,000 tons of raw jute produced 9.5 million bags at the Baranagore Mill (GOB 1874: 226). That is, each ton produced 593.75 bags. Again, at the Calcutta Jute Mill, 260 looms consumed 109,294 cwt of raw jute in 1878–9 (GOB 1880: 206) – i.e., each loom consumed 420.36 cwt, or 21 tons. Hence the number of bags each loom produced comes to 12,469 per year.

8 Export values of jute goods to Indian ports, as available in Kerr (1874: appendix L), are divided by the bag price of Rs. 0.22 to estimate the quantity series of bag equivalents. The series is 31.80 million for 1865–6, 30.17 million for 1870–1 and 31.81 million for 1872–3.

9 A government report (P.P. 1876a: lxxii) notes, 'The exports to the United States, which formerly were important, have gradually dwindled away to comparative insignificance, America being supplied more cheaply with bags and cloths from Dundee, and locally manufactured.'

10 A government report (P.P. 1887: 237) thus notes, 'Jute manufactures [of mills] first appear in the returns for 1866–7, where they were exported to the value of 366,755 *l*.'

11 Krugman (1980) argues that such intra-industry trades arise out of the economies of scale. See also Krugman and Obstfeld (1991: 131–4). I will discuss later that Bengal mills enjoyed various comparative advantages over Dundee mills, including the economies of scale.

12 In 1869 a tariff of 7.5 per cent was imposed on the import of jute goods into India, but it was soon repealed after complaints by Dundee manufacturers. See Masrani (2007: 112).

13 A government document (P.P. 1876a: lxxii) thus observes, 'Exports to Ceylon, Persia, and other countries whose shores lie on the Indian Ocean, also show an increase. Bengal will probably always be able to do a flourishing trade in gunny bags and cloth with those countries, and defy competition from other quarters.'

14 Buchanan (1934: 244) thus notes, 'A single mill with all its buildings occupies a considerable area, often up to 100 or more acres.'

15 While describing the buildings of Bengal jute mills, Buchanan (1934: 245) notes, 'Generally, there are tennis courts, spacious lawns which, for a few rupees per month, the gardener keeps in luxuriant grass and beds of blossoming flowers. With tropical shrubbery and tropical touches in the architecture these places are most inviting.'

16 The Borneo Company invested in Bengal in spite of its original interest in mining, and that too 'in the island of Borneo or in some part or parts thereof'. In fact, the *Hong Kong Daily News* remarked in 1858: 'This Borneo Company...is also embarking large sums in the erection of machinery in Bengal... Such an enterprise is, of course, highly laudable, but what in the name of all that is consistent, has the Borneo Company to do with it?' Cited in Cox and Metcalfe (1998: 60, 64).

17 A government report (P.P. 1874: 40) also observes, 'Twenty years ago the *ryot* who happened to have a spare bit of land, would grow it [jute] for his own use. Now, next to paddy, it is the principal product of Bengal.'

18 In addition, a contemporary government document (P.P. 1876b: xx) notes, 'On the whole, notwithstanding occasional disappointment, the jute trade has brought a wide and steady stream of wealth to the Bengal cultivation.'

Bibliography

Abul-Fazl A. (1948) *Ain-i-Akbari* (trans. H. S. Jarrett), vol. II. Calcutta: Baptist Mission Press.

Bagchi, A. K. (1980) *Private Investment in India, 1900–1939*. New Delhi: Orient Longman.

Banerjee, B. (1955) 'Jute: Especially as Produced in West Bengal', *Economic Botany* 9 (2), 151–74.

Basu, S. K. (1958) *The Managing Agency System in Prospect and Retrospect*. Calcutta: World Press.

Baumol, W. J., and Blinder, A. S. (2009) *Economics: Principles and Policies*, 11th edn. Mason, OH: South-Western Cengage Learning.

Buchanan, D. H. (1934) *The Development of Capitalist Enterprise in India*. New York: Macmillan.

Butt, J., and Ponting, K. (eds.) (1987) *Scottish Textile History*. Aberdeen: Aberdeen University Press.

Carter, H. R. (1921) *Jute and Its Manufacture*. New York: Macmillan.

Chakraborty, D. (1981) 'Communal Riots and Labour: Bengal's Jute Mill Hands in the 1890s', *Past and Present* 91, 140–69.

Chapman, D. (1938) 'The Establishment of the Jute Industry: A Problem of Location Theory', *Review of Economic Studies* 6 (1), 33–55.

Chaudhuri, K. N. (1994) 'Foreign Trade and Balance of Payments'. in Kumar, D. (ed.) *The Cambridge Economic History of India*, vol. II: *c. 1751 – c. 1970*, 878–904. Hyderabad: Cambridge University Press.

Cox, H., and Metcalfe, S. (1998) 'The Borneo Company Limited: Origins of a Nineteenth Century Networked Multinational', *Asia Pacific Business Review* 4 (4), 53–69.

Das Gupta, R. (1976) 'Factory Labour in Eastern India: Sources of Supply, 1855–1946: Some Preliminary Findings', *Indian Economic and Social History Review* 13 (3), 277–328.

De Haan, A. (1997) 'Unsettled Settlers: Migrant Workers and Industrial Capitalism in Calcutta', *Modern Asian Review* 31 (4), 919–49.

Foley, B. (1906) *Report on Labour in Bengal*. Calcutta: Bengal Secretariat Book Depot.

Gadgil, D. R. (1929) *Industrial Evolution of India*, 2nd edn. Oxford: Oxford University Press.

Gauldie, E. (1987) 'The Dundee Jute Industry'. In Butt, J., and Ponting, K. (eds.) *Scottish Textile History*, 112–25. Aberdeen: Aberdeen University Press.

Ghosh, P. (1990) 'Communalism and Colonial Labour: Experience of Calcutta Jute Mill Workers, 1880–1930', *Economic and Political Weekly* 25 (30), PE61–PE72.

Ghosh, P. (2000) *Colonialism, Class and a History of the Calcutta Jute Mill Hands, 1880–1930*. Hyderabad: Sangam Books.

Gilbert, J. (1939) *A History of Investment Trusts in Dundee*. London: P. S. King & Son.

Government of Bengal (GOB) (1793) *Board of Trade, Consultations, 14 January*. West Bengal State Archives, Calcutta.

Government of Bengal (GOB) (1874) *Annual Report on the Administration of Bengal during 1872–73*. National Library Archive, Calcutta.

Government of Bengal (GOB) (1878) *Annual Report on the Administration of Bengal during 1876–77*. National Library Archive, Calcutta.

Government of Bengal (GOB) (1880) *Annual Report on the Administration of Bengal during 1878–79*. National Library Archive, Calcutta.

Government of Bengal (GOB) (1881) *Annual Statement of the Sea-borne Trade and Navigation of Bengal Presidency with Foreign Countries and Indian Ports, India, 1879–80*, vol. 1. National Library Archive, Calcutta.

Government of Bengal (GOB) (1882) *Annual Statement of the Sea-borne Trade and Navigation of Bengal Presidency with Foreign Countries and Indian Ports, India, 1880–81*, vol. 1. National Library Archive, Calcutta.

Government of Bengal (GOB) (1886) *Annual Statement of the Sea-borne Trade and Navigation of Bengal Presidency with Foreign Countries and Indian Ports, India, 1884–85*, vol. 2. National Library Archive, Calcutta.

Government of Bengal (GOB) (1891) *Annual Statement of the Sea-borne Trade and Navigation of Bengal Presidency with Foreign Countries and Indian Ports, India, 1889–90*, vol. 1. National Library Archive, Calcutta.

Government of Bengal (GOB) (1896) *Annual Statement of the Sea-borne Trade and Navigation of Bengal Presidency with Foreign Countries and Indian Ports, India, 1894–95*, vol. 2. National Library Archive, Calcutta.

Government of Bengal (GOB) (1897) *Annual Report on the Administration of Bengal during 1895–96*. National Library Archive, Calcutta.

Government of Bengal (GOB) (1900) *Annual Report on the Administration of Bengal during 1898–99*. National Library Archive, Calcutta.

Government of India (GOI) (1883) *Report on the Census of India, 1881*. Calcutta: Bengal Secretariat Press.

Government of India (GOI) (1896) *The Report of the Labour Enquiry Committee*. Calcutta: Bengal Secretariat Press.

Government of India (GOI) (1903) *Report on the Census of India, 1901*, vol. VI(A), part II. Calcutta: Superintendent Government Printing.

Government of India (GOI) (1913) *Report on the Census of India, 1911*, vol. V, part II. Calcutta: Superintendent Government Printing.

Government of India (GOI) (1913a) *Annual Statement of the Sea-borne Trade of British India with the British Empire and Foreign Countries, 1907–08 to 1911–12*. National Library Archive, Calcutta.

Government of India (GOI) (1918) *Annual Statement of the Sea-borne Trade of British India with the British Empire and Foreign Countries, 1917*. National Library Archive, Calcutta.

Iftikhar-ul-Awwal, A. Z. M. (1982) *The Industrial Development of Bengal, 1900–1939*. New Delhi: Vikas Publishing House.

Imperial Institute (1921) *Indian Trade Enquiry: Reports on Jute and Silk*. London: John Murray.

Indian Central Jute Committee (ICJC) (1952) *Report on the Marketing of Jute and Jute Products*. Calcutta: Indian Central Jute Committee.

Indian Jute Mills Association (IJMA) (1906) *Annual Report*. Calcutta: IJMA.

Indian Jute Mills Association (IJMA) (1908) *Annual Report*. Calcutta: IJMA.

Indian Jute Mills Association (IJMA) (1909) *Annual Report*. Calcutta: IJMA.

Indian Jute Mills Association (IJMA) (1913) *Annual Report*. Calcutta: IJMA.

Indian Jute Mills Association (IJMA) (1968) *Symposium on the Jute Industry*. Calcutta: IJMA.

Kangle, R. P. (1972) *The Kautilīya* Arthaśāstra, part II. Delhi: Motilal Banarsidass.

Kerr, H. C. (1874) *Report on the Cultivation of, and Trade in, Jute in Bengal*. Calcutta: Bengal Secretariat Press.

Krugman, P. (1980) 'Scale Economics, Product Differentiation, and the Pattern of Trade', *American Economic Review* 70 (5), 950–9.

Krugman, P., and Obstfeld, M. (1991) *International Economics: Theory and Policy*, 2nd edn. New York: HarperCollins.

Kundu, B. C. (1956) 'Jute – World's Foremost Best Fibre II: Technology, Marketing, Production and Utilisation', *Economic Botany* 10 (3), 203–40.

Kundu, B. C., Basak, K. C., and Sarkar, B. (1959) *Jute in India*. Calcutta: ICJC.

Lefranc, E. (1873) *Culture and Manufacture of Ramie and Jute in the United States*. Washington, DC: Government Printing Office.

Lenman, B., Lythe, C., and Gauldie, E. (1969) *Dundee and Its Textile Industry*. Dundee: Abertay Historical Society.

Masrani, S. (2007) 'International Competition and Strategic Response in the Dundee Jute Industry During the Inter-war (1919–39) and Post-war (1945–1960) Period: The Case of Jute Industries, Buist Spinning, Craiks and Scott & Fyfe' (unpublished PhD dissertation, University of St Andrews). Retrieved from http://hdl.handle.net/10023/415 on 30 May 2011.

Milburn, W. (1813) *Oriental Commerce: Containing a Geographical Description of the Principal Places in the East Indies, China, and Japan, with Their Produce, Manufactures, and Trade*. London: Black, Parry.

Morris, M. D. (1994) 'The Growth of Large-Scale Industry'. In Kumar, D. (ed.) *The Cambridge Economic History of India*, vol. II: *c. 1751 – c. 1970*, 553–676. Hyderabad: Cambridge University Press.

Palit, S., and Kayaria, S. (2007) *Jute Industry: A Historical Perspective*. Calcutta: Firma K. L. Mukhopadhyay.

Parliamentary Papers (P.P.) (1840) *Select Committee on East India Produce*. London: Hansard.

Parliamentary Papers (P.P.) (1869) *Statistical Abstract Relating to British India, from 1867/8 to 1876/7*. London: HMSO.

Parliamentary Papers (P.P.) (1874) *Moral and Material Progress and Condition of India During the Year 1872–73*. London: Hansard.

Parliamentary Papers (P.P.) (1876a) *Moral and Material Progress and Condition of India for the Years 1870–71 to 1874–75*. London: Hansard.

Parliamentary Papers (P.P.) (1876b) *Trade of British India with British Possessions and Foreign Countries, 1870–71 to 1874–75*. London: Hansard.

Parliamentary Papers (P.P.) (1885) *Moral and Material Progress of India during the Years 1882–83 and 1883–84*. London: Hansard.

Parliamentary Papers (P.P.) (1887) *Statistical Abstract Relating to British India, from 1876/7 to 1885/6*. London: HMSO.

Parliamentary Papers (P.P.) (1892) *Moral and Material Progress and Condition of India, 1890–1*. London: Hansard.

Parliamentary Papers (P.P.) (1894) *Moral and Material Progress and Condition of India during the Year 1891–92 and Nine Preceding Years*. London: Hansard.

Parliamentary Papers (P.P.) (1907) *Statistical Abstract Relating to British India, from 1896/7 to 1905/06*. London: HMSO.

Parliamentary Papers (P.P.) (1908) *Statistical Abstract Relating to British India, from 1897/8 to 1906/07*. London: HMSO.

Parliamentary Papers (P.P.) (1915) *Moral and Material Progress and Condition of India, 1913–14*. London: Hansard..

Playne, S. (ed.) (1917) *Bengal and Assam, Bihar and Orissa: Their History, People, Commerce, and Industrial Resources*. London: Foreign and Colonial Compiling and Publishing.

Ray, I. (2011) *Bengal Industries and the British Industrial Revolution (1757–1857)*. London: Routledge.

Ray, I. (2015) 'Dynamics of Bengal Coal Mining in the Nineteenth Century: Dissemination of Mineralogical Knowledge and Railway Networking', *Indian Economic and Social History Review* 52 (4), 463–99.

Ray, J. (1738) *A Collection of Curious Travels and Voyages, Containing Dr Leonhart Rauwolf's Journey into the Eastern Countries* (trans. J. Ray), vol. II. London: S. Smith & B. Walford.

Rungta, S. (1985) 'Bowreah Cotton and Fort Gloster Jute Mills, 1872–1900', *Indian Economic and Social History Review* 22 (2), 109–37.

Sen, S. (1999) *Women and Labour in Late Colonial India: The Bengal Jute Industry*. Cambridge: Cambridge University Press.

Sethia, T. (1996) 'The Rise of Jute Manufacturing Industry in Colonial India: A Global Perspective', *Journal of World History* 7 (1), 71–99.

Stewart, G. (1998) *Jute and Empire*. Manchester: Manchester University Press.

Tariff Commission (1905) *Report of the Tariff Commission*, vol. II: *The Textile Trades*, part VII: *Evidence on the Flax, Hemp and Jute Industries*. London: P. S. King & Sons.

Turner, W. H. K. (1952) 'The Evolution of the Textile Industry within Dundee', *Transactions and Papers (Institute of British Geographers)* 18, 107–19.

Tyson, G. (1961) *Managing Agency: A System of Business Organisations*. Calcutta: Hooghly Printing.

Tyson, G. (1953) *The Bengal Chamber of Commerce and Industry, 1853–1953: A Centenary Survey*. Calcutta: Bengal Chamber of Commerce.

Wallace, D. R. (1928) *Romance of Jute: A Short History of the Calcutta Jute Mill Industry 1855–1927*, 2nd edn. London: W. Thacker.

Watt, G. (1972 [1889–93]) *Dictionary of the Economic Products of India*, 6 vols. Delhi: Cosmo Publications.

Whatley, C. (2005) 'Dundee and India: Roots, Rivalry and Interdependence', lecture given at India Exhibition, University of Dundee, 22 February. Retrieved from https://web.archive.org/web/20120422235721/http://www.dundee.ac.uk/archives/indiaexhib/indiaexhibitionwhatley.htm on 11 February 2018.

Woodhouse, T., and Kilgour, P. (1921) *The Jute Industry, from Seed to Finished Cloth*. London: Pitman.

Yang, A. (1989) *The Limited Raj: Agrarian Relations in Colonial India, Saran District, 1793–1920*. New Delhi: Oxford University Press.

Appendix 5.1 Exports of handmade jute articles from Bengal (in Rs.), 1828–94

Year	*Exports*	*3-year moving average*	*Year*	*Exports*	*3-year moving average*	*Year*	*Exports*	*3-year moving average*
1828	27,712[1]		1851	2,491,309[2]	2,508,400	1874	1,236,529[2]	1,250,383
1829	12,426[1]	21,215	1852	2,874,110[3]	2,599,003	1875	1,029,658[2]	1,041,204
1830	23,498[1]	35,545	1853	2,311,590[3]	2,311,200	1876	857,424[5]	656,874
1831	70,701[1]	53,961	1854	1,747,900[3]	2,070,947	1877	783,540[5]	720,806
1832	67,682[1]	93,297	1855	2,153,350[3]	2,308,210	1878	521,454[5]	605,172
1833	141,509[1]	88,321	1856	3,023,380[3]	2,979,750	1879	510,523[5]	452,389
1834	55,771[1]	77,875	1857	3,762,520[3]	2,985,948	1880	325,191[5]	299,838
1835	36,345[1]	177,903	1858	2,171,940[3]	3,286,233	1881	63,800[6]	161,206
1836	441,592[1]	219,668	1859	3,924,240[3]	3,145,317	1882	94,628[6]	93,257
1837	181,066[1]	280,583	1860	3,339,770[3]	3,619,147	1883	121,343[6]	83,869
1838	219,090[2]	221,752	1861	3,593,430[3]	2,933,883	1884	35,635[6]	64,642
1839	265,099[2]	268,319	1862	1,868,450[3]	2,259,387	1885	36,950[7]	34,212
1840	320,769[2]	324,666	1863	1,316,280[3]	1,432,266	1886	30,051[7]	33,025
1841	388,131[2]	392,846	1864	1,112,070[3]	1,152,310	1887	32,074[7]	71,835
1842	469,639[2]	475,344	1865	1,028,580[3]	1,752,927	1888	153,381[7]	91,128
1843	568,263[2]	575,167	1866	3,118,130[3]	2,347,103	1889	87,930[7]	100,232
1844	687,598[2]	695,951	1867	2,894,599[4]	2,588,212	1890	59,384[8]	61,184
1845	831,993[2]	842,101	1868	1,751,906[4]	2,147,897	1891	36,239[8]	44,969
1846	1,006,712[2]	1,013,942	1869	1,797,185[4]	1,768,042	1892	39,283[8]	30,837
1847	1,218,122[2]	1,232,920	1870	3,355,035[4]	2,339,940	1893	16,987[8]	27,557
1848	1,473,927[2]	1,491,834	1871	1,867,601[4]	2,333,649	1894	26,402[8]	
1849	1,783,452[2]	1,805,720	1872	1,783,312[4]	1,711,959			
1850	2,159,782[9]	2,144,848	1873	1,484,963[2]	1,501,601			

Sources: 1: P.P. (1840: 1); 2: estimated; 3: P.P. (1869: 46–7); 4: Kerr (1874: appendix L); 5: GOB (1882: 32); 6: GOB (1886: 34); 7: GOB (1891: 33); 8: GOB (1896: 24); 9: Wallace (1928: 1).

6 Paper making

The changing attitude of colonial governance

Paper making is a medieval craft in Bengal. Its antiquity, unknown as yet,[1] may be speculated on from the debate over the invention of paper in ancient civilisations. The majority wisdom in the debate is that, in CE 105, the eunuch Tsh'ai Lun of China invented paper from plant fibres,[2] which the Arabs learnt from a Chinese captive at the Battle of Samarqand (CE 751) (Hannawi 2012). Al-Beruni writes, 'It was in China that paper was first manufactured. Chinese prisoners introduced the fabrication of paper into Samarkand, and thereupon it was made in various places, so as to meet the existing want' (for the English version of Al-Beruni's work, see Sachau 1910: 171). From Samarqand and Khurasan, paper gradually made inroads into India, giving rise to its paper-making craft. That paper was manufactured in India on the eve of the last millennium is confirmed by Abu Hamid al-Gharnati (1080–1169). He puts on record, 'The paper made at Balkh favourably compared to that of Iraq, Khurasan and India' (Al-Gharnati 1979 [c. 1135]: 202). The industry developed rapidly in India during the reign of Mohamed bin Tughlak (1325–51), however, and in Kashmir during the reign of Sultan Zainu'l-'Abdin (1417–67) (Ramaseshan 1989: 106; see also MacFarlane 1987; and Raitt 1930). In both these places Arabian technology prevailed. Gosavi (2011: 21) contests the Chinese origin of paper technology, however, and advocates that 'Indians knew the art of papermaking by beating cotton since [BCE] 327' (see also Gosavi 1987; and Gosavi 1983). His logic is that, out of ten specimen of Chinese paper that are kept in the British Library at London, five papers containing the Sogadian script (with many Sanskrit words) are made of cotton fibre. Since ancient Chinese technology did not use cotton as a raw material, China cannot claim the innovation. He argues that the Sogadians translated the Buddhist scriptures in Chinese. 'Some of these translators took bundles of paper with them from India' (Gosavi 2011: 21). Gosavi's view is contradicted in Losty (1983: 108–10).

In the medieval period, however, a large number of people belonging to the Muslim faith undertook paper making in Bengal, possibly carrying out the north Indian tradition. The Hindus might have acquired the technology from them. But quite a different technology prevailed in manufacturing what was called 'Nepali paper', which predominated on the northern frontier adjacent to Bhutan and Tibet. Regarding that technology, a British Resident at Nepal wrote in 1831, 'I conjecture that the art of paper making was got by the Cis-Himalayan Bhoteahs, via Shassa, from China. A paper of the very same sort being manufactured at Shassa; and most of the useful arts of these regions having flowed upon them, through Tibet, from China; and not from Hindustan' (Hodgson 1832: 11). In a Chinese travelogue of 1406, however, there is a reference to paper manufacturing in Bengal from the bark of tree (as followed in making Nepali paper, discussed in Section II), which 'is smooth and glossy like a deer's skin' (Gode 1969: 8). Gode stresses, 'This reference to the manufacture of paper in Bengal made by a Chinaman is very important as it has a direct bearing on the history of Indian paper industry' (ibid.).

Contemporary documents indicate that Bengal's paper industry was quite developed in the early nineteenth century (Mookerji 1908; Kerr 1874: 83–96). Many scholastic studies also corroborate it. But the existing literature focuses mainly on technology and raw materials – for example, MacFarlane (1993), Ramaseshan (1989), Bag (1982), Ghori and Rahman (1966) and Hunter (1939). Textbooks on India's economic history – such as Roy (2011), Bagchi (1972) and Gadgil (1933) – also discuss the industry's history, but briefly along with other industries, and dealing predominantly with mechanical manufacturing. The present chapter analyses it in detail for the nineteenth century as a whole, however, so that the traditional industry and its modern counterpart are both focused on together. It helps us to understand how a traditional craft rose to the height of a modern industry in an erstwhile British colony. This study also gives a new dimension to the nineteenth-century deindustrialisation debate, since this industry is nowhere discussed in this context. It shows how the British imperial policy, especially the store purchase rules, eroded the marketability of Bengal's cottage industry and delayed the emergence of mechanical paper making.

There are five sections in what follows. Section I analyses the industry's cottage environment, which prevailed through the first half of the nineteenth century. Section II deliberates on early European ventures in this industry, which could not survive in the long run. Section III discusses various facets of mechanical paper making in Bengal that successfully emerged during the second half of the nineteenth century. Finally, Section IV delves into the contemporary store purchasing policy, and discusses its impacts on the domestic industry. Section V concludes.

I

Paper making flourished in Bengal during the medieval epoch. It was then carried out extensively in Murshidabad, Malda, Hooghly, Patna and Arwal (Ghori and Rahman 1966: 137–8), which subsequently diffused to other districts – such as Burdwan (especially Niala, Satgong, Manad, Shahabazar and Moynone), Balasore, Bankepur, Shahar, Hurihar Gunge, and also in Calcutta, Dinajpore and Dacca (Sen 1836: 89). The paper-making technology that prevailed in many of these places is available in Carey (1836: 87–8), Sen (1836: 88–93), Martin (1838: I, 33–4, 334, 544), Kerr (1874: 84–9) and Watt (1908: 865).

According to Sen, the type of raw materials that were used in the industry varied from place to place, presumably in consideration of their local availability and prices. They included fresh fibres such as flax, hemp and jute, as well as old and worn-out gunny bags, sails, paper, cotton, rope and cables. Lime and *sajee-matee* (carbonate of soda) were used in processing, and starch gruel in sizing. Very rudimentary implements were employed for the purpose. In Sen's description, these were: (i) three big earthen vessels (called *gumla*); (ii) two squared boards; (iii) one large, smooth board; (iv) a heavy stone (or a log of wood); (v) one wooden stick; (vi) a square wooden frame (called a *chowka*); (vii) two sticks (called a *chapa* and a *hachka*); (viii) one levered foot paddle (called a *dhenki*), made of (a) a piece of solid timber (10–16 feet long, 12–25 inches broad, and proportionately thick), (b) a pestle of iron (or iron-covered wood) and (c) a mortar of stone (or iron-lined wood); (ix) a sieve (called a *chatree*), made of fine split bamboo, woven with horses' hair; and (x) a beating machine (called a *pitna*), consisting of (a) a piece of concave, smooth wood with its lower part buried in the ground and (b) a mallet.

Native paper making involved seven processes. The first process was cleansing, whereby raw materials were cut into pieces and immersed in a *gumla*, full of water, for one to two days to remove their dirt. They were often agitated, and fresh water was supplied till the dirt was removed. The fibres were then taken out of the water and dried in the sun. They were again put into another *gumla*, containing water with solutions of *sajee-matee* and lime, so that they were softened within a few days. The second process involved pounding of those fibres by *dhenki*, whereby raw pulp was formed. It was again cleansed in a third *gumla*, in which the water was frequently changed without agitating the pulp. Once it had been cleansed, fresh water was poured in, along with lime and *sajee-matee* solutions, and agitated repeatedly by the wooden stick to win a final pulp. At the floor of this pulp in the *gumla*, the artisan placed the *chowka*, and the third process began. He agitated the water soup vigorously, immersed the *chatree* in it with the help of the *chapa* and *hachka*, and placed it on the *chowka*. The *chowka* was then lifted up, and shaken gently so that the thin layer of pulp that was collected on the *chatree* became plain. It was then kept on the square board. Some 200 to 250 sheets were thus collected on the board one upon another. Over those sheets, however, another square board was placed with the weight of a heavy stone (or a log of wood), so that water was expunged therefrom overnight. Next morning the sheets were taken up, and spread over matted walls (or on clean grass) to dry. This was the fourth process.

The fifth and sixth processes involved beating and sizing. For the former, workers laid the sheets on the *pitna*, holding them with one hand, and beat them with a mallet in the other hand so that they were softened and smoothed. For the purpose of sizing, however, the artisans prepared a fine paste of rice or wheat, and, using a soft brush, daubed it on the sheets that had been kept

Figure 6.1 Paper making in Patna in the early nineteenth century, showing the separation of paper from the mould, pasting on a wall with a brush and polishing on a wooden board

Source: Sketch by the author from the oil painting of A. W. Davis (1763–1822) made at the behest of the East India Company, originally displayed at Spink and Son Ltd, London.

beforehand on a large, smooth board. Finally, they were dried in the shade (or gentle sunshine), put under a press, glazed with *gila* (seeds of *Mimosa scandens*), shells or stone balls and bundled into quires after removing their edges. The paper was then ready for sale. Figure 6.1 depicts paper manufacturing at Patna in the early nineteenth century.

Among the raw materials that Sen mentions, old paper, gunnies and rags became more popular in the early 1870s (Table 6.1). It should have been motivated by their low prices. Jute also gained popularity in this period, especially in jute-growing districts, as its cultivation multiplied. It provided higher productivity, compared to other raw materials, which Table 6.1 confirms. The productivity of raw materials in Rajshahye and Bogra, where the use of jute was dominant, stood at 302 quires per maund and 320 quires per maund, respectively. It was only 45 quires per maund in Gya, and 71 quires per maund in Chittagong and Tirhoot, where old paper and rags were employed. It was slightly higher in Noakhally (153 quires per maund) and Dacca (200 quires per maund: Kerr 1874: 88), where *mesta* (an inferior variety of jute) was used, as also in Faridpore (108 quires per maund), where jute was used along with old paper.

Table 6.1 Paper-making districts in Bengal, 1872

District	*Raw materials*		*Production level(quires)*	*Production cost (Rs. per ream)*	*Selling price (Rs. per ream)*
	Type	*Amount (maunds)*			
Bankura	Waste paper, old gunny and rags	–	12,669	1.00	2.00
Howrah	Hemp, old gunny cloths, paper, linen.	–	NA	2.50	4.50
Jessore	Old paper	–	7,253	–	0.60
Murshidabad	Rotten gunnies, cotton, old paper	–	NA	1.50	2.20
Dinajpore	Jute	–	NA	–	–
Malda	Jute, old paper, rags	–	NA	1.40	2.40
Rajshahye	Old paper, jute, rags	1,060 (jute)	320,000	0.75	–
Pubna	Jute	–	NA	–	–
Rungpore	Jute	–	NA	1.88	–
Bogra	Jute	100	32,000	0.46	0.70
Darjeeling	Jute	–	NA	–	–
Jalpaiguri	Red jute	–	NA	1.75	2.50
Dacca	*Mesta*, hemp	–	NA	–	–
Mymensing	*Mesta*, old paper	–	NA	–	–
Faridpore	Jute, old paper	12	1,300	2.50	6.25
Backergunj	Jute, hemp	–	NA	–	–
Chittagong	Gunny, old paper, jute, *sunn*	300–400	25,000	3.09	–
Noakhally	*Mesta*	8.50	1,307	2.30	6.25
Purnea	Jute, *sunn*	130	10,000	–	–
Bhagalpur	Waste paper, old gunnies, jute, rags	–	NA	–	–
Gya	Hemp canvas	88	4,000	–	–
Tirhoot	Old gunnies	700	50,000	–	–
Shahabad	Old rags, jute	–	25,860	4.52	–
Cuttack	Hemp	–	NA	–	–
Balasore	Waste paper, rag, hemp	30	4,000	1.25[1]	1.42[1]

Notes: Units are converted at 1 ream = 20 quires = 500 sheets; in some places, however, the conversion rate of 1 ream = 10 quires is considered; 1: these figures are reported in quires; since they appear abnormally high figures (Rs. 25 and Rs. 28.40 per ream, respectively), we consider them in reams.

Source: Kerr (1874: 90).

By far, however, sunn hemp (*Crotalaria juncea*) was the best fibre for paper making in Bengal. But it was largely avoided. Quoting an authority in 1774, Watt notes that 'for paper-making "old ropes, cloths and nets, made from the *san* plant" were preferred to fresh fibre'. He adds, 'In a country teeming with fibres, it is surprising that the question of a good paper material has not been satisfactorily determined' (Watt 1908: 864–5). This may be explained by twin concurrent events, however: (i) that these fibrous plants grew in a scattered fashion over a wide region; and (ii) that transportation was underdeveloped in contemporary Bengal. Therefore, the high-yielding fibres, though plenty, were dear at production points, and hence unattractive to paper makers. 'Moreover,' Watt notes, 'as paper fibre, like esparto, must be fit for almost immediate immersion in the vats, paper-making can never pay the cost of separation and preparation, however simple and inexpensive' (ibid.: 865). That was why they avoided even fresh jute, notwithstanding its cheapness, but opted for 'jute waste' and 'jute cuttings'. Only in jute-producing belts were fresh jute fibres used, so as to gain from their cheapness as well as high productivity.

Table 6.1 also indicates the profitability in native paper making. From its last two columns the rate of profit is worked out at more than 100 per cent in Noakhally (171 per cent), Faridpore (150 per cent) and Bankura (100 per cent), where old paper and rag were mainly used. Profitability was low mainly in those places where jute was the primary raw material – such as Jalpaiguri (43 per cent) and Bogra (52 per cent). It was slightly higher where fresh jute or hemp was used along with waste materials, as in Howrah (80 per cent) and Malda (71 per cent). More detailed information about the cost of production in different districts, as also profits thereof, is available in Martin (1838). Table 6.2 gathers them together for a given unit of production (100 reams).

Certain adjustments are made in Table 6.2. First, the figures for Patna are given in the source for the production of seven reams of paper. For the sake of uniformity, those are converted corresponding to the production of 100 reams (that is, multiplying each entity by 100/7 = 14.28). Second, the sum of individual costs for Patna comes to Rs. 8 for seven reams in the source (Rs. 6 annas 31 pies 12); but it is reported at Rs. 7. It appears, however, that the cost of soda for this place (which was of 'impure' quality) is Rs. 4.76 per 100 *sers*, as against Rs. 1.92 per 100 *sers* in Shahabad and Rs. 2.50 per 100 *sers* in Saher. To retain the sum total, as reported in the source, I consider the cost of soda at Re 1 for 42 *sers* (that is, Rs. 2.38 per 100 *sers*), instead of Rs. 2 for 42 *sers*. This gives Rs. 14.28 for 600 *sers* of lime. Third, there is a discrepancy of Rs. 12 – annas 12 (i.e., Rs. 12.75) in the sum for Shahabad – Rs. 273 annas 10 pies 6 – as against the reported figure at Rs. 286 annas 6 pies 6. Since the cost of firewood is omitted in the source, Rs. 12.75 are added under 'Flour, firewood, etc.'.

Table 6.2 suggests, however, that various production ingredients constituted a higher proportion of cost when old paper, rags, etc. were used – such as in Patna (59.40 per cent), Shahabad (53.58 per cent) and Saher (51.69 per cent). *Per contra*, their cost share is only 28.20 per cent in the jute-using centre, Rungpore. This was mainly due to the fact that soda, a major ingredient in the former places, was not required to make pulp out of raw jute. The profitability is worked out at 25.42 per cent at Patna, 22.21 per cent at Shahabad and 12.53 per cent at Saher.

But the concept of profitability is trivial to an artisan. Traditional paper makers did not behave like capitalists, who exclusively focus on the rate of

Table 6.2 Costs of production and profitability in native paper making (in Rs. per 100 reams), early nineteenth century

Particulars	*Patna*	*Shahabad (Arwal)*	*Saher*	*Rungpore*
Ingredients				
Raw materials	28.57 (600 *sers* of old bags)	57.50 (2,620 *sers* of old bags)	62.00 (2,500 *sers* of old bags)	31.25 (500 *sers* of jute)
Soda	14.28 (600 *sers*)	45.00 (2,340 *sers*)	40.00 (1,600 *sers*)	Not required
Lime	14.28 (600 *sers*)	30.00 (2,340 *sers*)	24.00 (1,582 *sers*)	6.25 (300 *sers*)
Flour, firewood, etc.	2.07	20.94	46.25	14.06**
Subtotal	59.20	153.44	172.25	51.56
Labour costs				
Beating	25.00	80.00	100.00	71.87
Stirring*	7.14	25.00	28.00	34.38
Pasting, smoothing, drying, etc.	8.03	12.95	22.00	18.75
Cutting, packing	0.29	15.00	11.00	6.25
Subtotal	40.46	132.95	161.00	131.25
Total costs	**99.66**	**286.39**	**333.25**	**182.81**
Revenue	125.00	350.00	375.00	NA
Profit	25.34	63.61	41.75	-
Profitability (%) ((profit/cost) X 100)	25.42	22.21	12.53	-

Notes: The terms in parentheses represent the amounts of raw materials; * including working off the sheet; ** not including the cost of firewood.

Sources: Patna: Martin (1838: I, 33–4); Shahabad (Arwal): Martin (1838: I, 334); Saher: Martin (1838: I, 544); Rungpore: Kerr (1874: 89).

return from capital. Rather, as artisans, they were concerned about earnings from their skill and labour. To estimate their earnings, however, I consider after Martin (1838: I, 544) that each paper maker annually manufactured 100 reams, on average. In this case, their annual income comes to Rs. 25.34 in Patna, Rs. 63.61 in Shahabad and Rs. 41.75 in Saher. In practice, however, their earnings were higher than these figures, as they themselves carried out some of the jobs reported in Table 6.2, especially the work off the sheet (at Rs. 25 in both Shahabad and Saher: ibid.: 334, 544). Moreover, their family members also participated in production, and earned thereby. Martin, therefore, comments that, 'in fact, these people are in easy circumstances' (ibid.: 334).

The industry found its outlet mainly in local markets, although the major paper-manufacturing clusters catered also to the provincial market and outside. 'The principal places,' Sen (1836: 89) thus writes, 'where the paper is manufactured, as an article of commerce, …supply the whole of Bengal and a considerable portion of Upper Provinces and Eastern countries with that article.' His essay refers to 23 samples of Bengal's native paper along with their respective uses. Of them, five were used in native schools, three for printing, 12 in various documentations such as writing books, bills, drafts, etc., and three by grocers for packaging. From available sources, however, we are assured that those four market segments were extensively developed in contemporary Bengal. Adam (1868: 19–20) thus reports that, in the 1830s, there were about 100,000 'indigenous elementary schools' in Bengal, where students were taught for five years. Marshall (1988: 39) acknowledges that 'there were schools, at least in the larger villages, teaching elementary arithmetic and the rudiments of reading and writing'. Although the palm and plantain leaves were used in initial phases, Marshall writes, '[t]he last stage of this limited course of instruction is that in which the scholars are taught to write with lamp-black ink on paper, and further instructed in agricultural and commercial accounts and in the composition of letters' (ibid.).

Apart from indicating the use of paper in these schools, this evidence also testifies to the practice of keeping agricultural and commercial accounts in the contemporary society, and thus corroborates Sen's claim that native papers were used in documentation. In addition, printed books and instructions spread progressively across these schools from the early nineteenth century. In Calcutta, for example, 211 such schools were brought under the Calcutta School Society, formed in 1818–19. Out of them, 115 schools, with an enrolment of 3,828 students, 'received books from the School Society, and were examined and superintended by its officers and agents' (Adam 1868: 20). In fact, Bengal's institutional education received a stimulus from the sanction of Rs. 100,000 every year by the British Parliament in 1813. The sum was meant, according to the East India Company Act, for 'the revival and improvement of Literature, and the encouragement of the learned natives of India, and for the introduction and promotion of a knowledge of the sciences among the inhabitants of the British territories in India' (section 43, st. 53, Geo. III, chap. 155, quoted in Mahmood 1895: 22). The Act boosted institutional schooling in Bengal, and, hence, its paper industry, as the demand for paper was augmented both for writing and printing purposes. Last but not least, native paper was extensively used in grocers' outlets for packaging. Tavernier wrote in 1648 that 'throughout all the East tobacco in powder, and all drugs and other wares which can be so treated, are wrapped in white paper; this tends to the profit of the seller, who weighs the paper and the goods together. It is for this reason that so much paper is used in Asia, and it is the principal article of trade of the people of the provinces who send theirs even to Persia' (Tavernier 1889 [1648]: 231).

There is no estimation for Bengal's annual production of paper in the first half of the nineteenth century. To make an attempt to this end, we note in Table 6.1 that a production figure is available for 12 districts. But the reporting year is 1872, when native paper making was steadily declining. Their aggregate production is worked out at 493,389 quires, however – i.e., 41,116 quires per district. For 25 districts, then, the estimated output is 1,027,900 quires in

1872. The industry's decay in the middle of the nineteenth century may be comprehended by comparing these data with those available in Martin, which were collected between 1809 and 1813. The latter source informs us that, in Shahabad, annual production was 130,000 quires, since each paper maker annually manufactured 1,000 quires, and there were 130 paper makers in that district (Martin 1838: I, 489, 544). In contrast, its level of production was 25,860 quires in 1872 (Table 6.1) – only 19.89 per cent of that in the early nineteenth century. Again, relying on Martin, I estimate the annual output at 110,000 quires in Patna district (ibid.: I, 146), 96,000 quires in Bhagalpur (ibid.: I, 112) and 80,000 to 100,000 quires in Dinajpore (ibid.: II, 935), giving a district average at 98,667 quires. Table 6.1's district average (41,116 quires) is thus 41.67 per cent of this. Thus, our estimate is that, although the extent of decay was about 80 per cent in Shahabad, it was 58.33 per cent, on average, in Bengal. If we consider this average rate, the provincial level of output comes to 2,466,763 quires in the early nineteenth century.

To estimate the level of employment in this craft, we first note that, at the annual output level of 1,000 quires for each artisan, the number of paper makers comes to 2,466 in the early nineteenth century and 1,027 in 1872. For other workers, a contemporary source gives the employment structure for the manufacture of 40 quires of paper shown in Table 6.3.

Using this band of 45 workers, each paper artisan annually manufactured 1,000 quires. At this rate of employment, the number of workers is estimated at 111,004 in the early nineteenth century and 46,255 in 1872, corresponding to the estimated levels of production in the respective periods. Along with the number of paper makers, the figures are 113,470 and 47,282, respectively. The loss of employment is thus estimated at 66,188 around the middle of the nineteenth century, representing a 58.33 per cent fall. These estimations seem reasonable, since the census data confirm that the number of persons dependent on Bengal's paper making was 56,242 in 1891 (GOI 1903a: 493). Since the

Table 6.3 Employment in native paper making (for 40 quires), 1872

Nature of job	*Number of workers*
Lining	2
Drying	1
Cutting and washing fibres	2
Grinding	24
Washing	3
Taking up the layer	6
Brushing	3
Rubbing	2
Final cutting	2
Total	45

Source: Kerr (1874: 89).

ratio of actual workers and dependent people was 47:53 (ibid.: 488), the actual number of workers was 26,434 in that year. If our estimation is correct, it represents a 44.09 per cent fall from 1872 to 1891, as against our estimation of 58.33 per cent for the earlier period. The decaying process was accelerated in the following decade (1891–1901), as the number of dependent persons on native paper making was 12,230 in 1901, a decline of 78 per cent (GOI 1903a: 493). The actual number of workers in that year was just 5,748.

The decline of Bengal's native paper making is noticed in many contemporary documents. Kerr (1874: 89) thus writes, 'In Burdwan, where the finest quality of country paper was known to be made in 1832, the manufacture has now been entirely abandoned…' In 1880–1 it was reflected even in a country-level report, the Moral and Material Progress of India (P.P. 1882a: 64): 'The native paper manufactured in Hooghly and Burdwan is being rapidly superseded by English paper and the produce of the Bally Mills, near Calcutta.' A decade afterwards Collin noted it. Referring to Collin's report, Cumming (1908: 33) observes, 'There has been a further decadence since 1890 in the indigenous manufacture. Handmade paper is still produced at Hooghly district, principally at Mahanad Gosainmalpara, Neala and Ballidewanganj by a class of Muhammadans known as *kagjis*. They are fast dying out… The manufacture ceased five years ago at Nasriganj in Shahabad, and in Cuttack it has practically ceased.' Gupta (1908) also noticed the trend in 1907–8. Finally, we find Swan reporting in 1915, 'In 1908 Mr Cumming found that the indigenous manufacture of handmade paper was declining, and Mr Gupta reported that it had practically died out in Eastern Bengal. The decline has continued. In Hooghly district a few families of Kagazi Muhammadans [traditionally manufacturing paper] still follow the trade, but the majority have given it up' (Swan 1915: 10).

II

European ventures started emerging in Bengal's paper-making industry from the late eighteenth century. But their initial attempts struggled. Quoting a contemporary issue of the *Calcutta Chronicle* (1 April 1790), Shaw (1981: 36) tells us that the pioneer project, the Calcutta Paper Mill, was floated by Brown in 1790, to manufacture high-quality paper to cater to a few printing presses in Calcutta. But from the circumstantial evidence it appears that the project was short-lived. High-quality paper was not available in Calcutta at the start of the nineteenth century, when the Serampore Baptist Mission started printing religious scripts. In 1803 an associate of the mission reported that they had spent a large sum 'to procure a durable kind of paper, without which, the versions [of the New Testament in various Indian languages] would, in a few years, disappear, through the copies becoming a prey to insects, as was the case with all paper then made in India' (Marshman 1828: 126). Again, in 1806, William Carey, another associate, wrote, 'I am afraid that the work [English translation of the Hindu epic *Ramayana*] will be stopped for a want of paper to print on, unless our order by the *Medusa* frigate be soon fulfilled. I hope the paper will be of the best quality. The Society has been egregiously cheated in that article' (Carter 2000: 207).

The next European venture was that of William Jones, who set up a small-scale paper mill in Howrah in 1811. It presumably ran on mechanical devices, since its promoter had long experience in mechanics.[3] The project was designed to manufacture cartridge papers only, however, keeping in view the contemporary war demand. It was undoubtedly a technically viable project, since we find that, for the British expedition to Java that year, it met the entire demand for cartridge paper. But once the expedition was over and its war demand had subsided the unit faced the stereotypical crisis of a mono-product firm. Moreover, the East India Company's administration in India backtracked; instead of procuring its regular requirements domestically, the government fell back on imports from England. The venture therefore failed for the want of market.[4] Recalling the event, Marshman wrote in 1845, 'He [William Jones] was not encouraged to continue his exertions, for the Court of Directors had not then become alive to the importance of calling forth and improving the resources of the country.' He added, 'Down to that late period, India continued to be governed in a great measure upon the old colonial and selfish principle of the seventeenth and eighteenth centuries, of administering a colony solely for the benefit of the mother country, and fostering improvements only as far as they tended to promote that object.' He continued, 'The idea of governing the foreign possessions of Europe, and more especially those of England, on the enlarged principle of promoting their interest, though now reckoned among truisms, has been recognized and acted upon only within the present century' (Marshman 1845: 479). This is precisely the central hypothesis in this study. I adduce evidence to prove that traditional paper making, along with the initial European ventures, could not survive in Bengal under the adverse policies followed by the colonial authorities; later, when the British policies were changed, paper making was promoted.

In the meantime, however, the Baptist Missionary Society had been coming up with a paper manufacturing unit at Serampore (Hooghly). The guiding force was, indeed, William Carey.[5] The project was primarily intended for use by the Society in its printing press, replacing the so-called Patna paper, which it had been using for some years.[6] Although they were longer, and also whiter, than other local varieties, the Patna papers were fragile, damp-prone (Sen 1836: 92) and very often spoiled by insects. Therefore, for the sake of longevity, Carey subsequently settled on imported paper. But there he confronted 'its great cost, irregularity and delay in receiving supplies' (Khan 1961: 255). Captive paper manufacturing was then the only alternative. The work evidently started in 1805,[7] and production commenced in 1809. To meet the growing own-use requirements, it was expanded twice in quick succession, once in 1811 and then in 1814, when a treadmill was also installed (Chatterjee 1984: 40–4). It was driven by 40 people together working for local paper makers. The underlying technology was also of traditional origin, which Carey marginally modified by avoiding the use of 'conjee or rice-gruel' (Carey 1836: 87), so that insects would not be attracted. Production seems to have been in full swing from the outset, however. This is evident in the Society's stocktaking after the outbreak of fire in early 1812, which revealed that 'hundreds of reams' (Khan 1961: 242) of Serampore paper had been destroyed, along with 1,400 reams of imported paper.

Increasingly, however, working on the treadmill came to be regarded as inconvenient, especially on the question of economy – it was 'cumbrous and expensive'. Moreover, in the wake of the accidental death of a labourer working on the machine, 'the rest took a superstitious aversion to the wheel' (Marshman 1859: II, 224), giving rise to labour scarcity. The Society therefore abandoned the treadmill, and finally installed a 12 horsepower steam engine in 1820,[8] at a cost of about Rs. 20,000, inclusive of installation charges (Chatterjee 1984: 46). The entire affair (including its installation) was supervised by William Jones, who later supplied steam coal to this unit from his own collieries at Ranigunj. The steam engine was highly productive,[9] as was the entire paper-making project, into which £4,600 were invested in aggregate from 1809 to 1826.[10]

The mill was looked after by William Ward, however, a Baptist missionary who had long experience in printing and publication in England.[11] The Society also employed a paper engineer, J. Randall, from England in 1820 with generous compensation.[12] Mechanised paper making, under the supervision of European paper makers too, ensured the quality of what became popular as 'Serampore paper'. Regarding its production process, Carey (1836: 87) writes, 'We now make our paper by machinery, in which the pulp is let to run on a web of wire, and passing over several cylinders, the last of which are heated by steam: it is dried and fit for use about two minutes from its having been in a liquid state.' Further expansions took place in the following years, and by 1845 there were altogether three steam engines with an aggregate capacity of 50 reams of demy per day (Potts n.d.).

The periodic expansion of the Serampore Paper Mill suggests that it must have enjoyed market support. It manufactured both printing and cartridge papers. Printing papers were used in-house, and also sold in open markets. Serampore Press altogether printed 212,000 copies of books between 1801 and 1832, and much of its paper from 1809 to 1832 was sourced from the captive unit. Regarding its open market sales, we learn from a government document of 1842 that, in the Calcutta market, four varieties of country paper were available: Serampore paper, Bengal paper, Balasore paper and Arwully (Patna) paper. Serampore paper was thus distinguishable from other papers manufactured in lower Bengal. It was available in two varieties, royal and medium, priced respectively at Rs. 7 annas 14 and Rs. 6 annas 6 per ream ('Letter from T. H. Maddock, Secretary to Government of India, to Dr Campbell', in Anon. 1842: 217). On the other hand, the price of Bengal paper varied from Rs. 2 annas 8 to Rs. 6 annas 4 a ream, save for the superfine quality. Because of longer sizes (and, hence, greater weights), the Balasore and Arwully papers belonged to higher price brackets, at Rs. 20 and Rs. 13 per ream, respectively. The higher price of Serampore paper serves to confirm its popularity in the contemporary market. Khan (1961: 257) thus notes, 'There is evidence that Serampore paper acquired a great reputation… It was exported to other places.' Quoting a contemporary document, he underlines that from 1820 to 1865 Serampore was 'the one source of supply for local as distinguished from imported, and purely native hand-made paper'. Watt (1908: 866) also acknowledges the fame of the Serampore paper: 'The expression "Serampore Paper" is used all over India for a particular class of Native-made white paper.' The cartridge variety that the Serampore mill manufactured was sold mainly to the government, priced at Rs. 13 per ream in 1842. It is learnt that the cartridge paper which ignited the Sepoy Mutiny in India in 1857 was entirely supplied by the Serampore Paper Mill (Smith 1885: 245). The unit was closed in the early 1860s, however. A contemporary author notes that 'we well recollect seeing the silent and rusty machinery [of the Serampore Paper Mill] as far back as 1864' (Traill 1891: 330). Kerr (1874: 91) also confirms this in his report in 1872: 'Formerly there was a large mill at Serampore, which turned out printing and cartridge paper in enormous quantities, but it has now for some years been abolished.' Section IV delves into the underlying reasons for this.

Meanwhile, in 1841, there was a great experiment in manufacturing Nepali paper in Darjeeling. The driving force behind this project was Lord Auckland, the Governor General of India, who wished to set up 'a permanent factory, at this place [Darjeeling], for the supply of Stationery to the neighbouring stations of the plains' ('Letter of Dr Campbell, Supt. of Darjeeling, to T. H. Maddock, Secretary to the Government', in Anon. 1842: 216). The experiment was conducted by the district superintendent, Archibald Campbell, who also pioneered tea plantation in Darjeeling. The technology for Nepali paper was altogether different from what prevailed elsewhere in Bengal (for details, see Hodgson 1832: 8–11). As raw materials it used the inner bark of paper trees, which were abundantly available at high altitudes (including at Pucheem, 7,200 feet above sea level, near Darjeeling: 'Letter of Dr Campbell', in Anon. 1842: 211), and the ashes of oak wood (or the *bak* and the *oontees*, also widely available around Darjeeling). A solution was first prepared from these ashes, and the pieces of paper bark were poured therein to boil. Once softened after boiling, they were beaten in a stone mortar by an oak mallet, and then churned in a wide-mouthed vessel by a wooden instrument to prepare the pulp. This was then received in a 'paper frame' (with a bottom of cloth) through a sieve so that the unwanted matter could be collected in it; the aqua content of the pulp oozed through the cloth; and the pulp was uniformly spread onto the cloth via some gentle shaking. The paper, thus made, was dried near a large fire, and polished on a wooden board. The paper was then ready for sale. Interestingly, no sizing was required in this process. 'It would probably surprise the paper-makers of England, to hear that the *Kachar* Bhoteahs can make up this paper into fine smooth sheets of *several yards square*' (Hodgson 1832: 10, emphasis in original).

To carry out the experiment, Campbell recruited one paper maker, one assistant paper maker and three ordinary workers, all from Nepal, at the monthly wages of Rs. 10 for the paper maker and Rs. 8 for the rest. A paper manufactory was set up near his residence, with tools and implements made of locally available resources. In the first consignment, they manufactured 3,300 sheets (2 feet X 1½ feet) weighing 1 maund 7 *sers*. The cost of production was worked out at Rs. 25 annas 8 per maund, giving 96–120 sheets per rupee ('Letter of Dr Campbell', in Anon. 1842: 215). Noting that this cost was on the high side, Campbell commented, 'This result cannot be considered as more than an approximation to the cost by contract. Doubtless it could be made much cheaper under that system, or under more close supervision than I had it in my power to afford' (ibid.). From the viewpoint of quality, however, the experiment was successful; in Campbell's words, 'The Paper is however excellent of its kind' (ibid.).

The Governor General was indeed satisfied with the experiment, and urged it to be continued.[13] That the government was serious about the project can be gleaned from the fact that several specimen sheets were sent to a chemical engineer for further improvements, and also to the Serampore Paper Mill so that its commercial viability could be investigated (see the letter from Dr W. B. O'Shaughnessy to T. H. Maddock, 'On the Manufacture of Paper at Darjeeling', in Anon. 1842: 219). Drafting and printing papers apart, the government also considered ordering some special papers that would be convenient to use in government offices. Thus, for instance, it sought filtering paper, which, for the imported variety, 'costs 9 Rupees per ream, whereas it is understood that at Darjeeling it can be manufactured for about 3 rupees per ream'. The government also sought waterproof paper for use in post offices. 'The expenses of the preparation [of waterproof paper] is found to be a trifle, and the process so simple, that it may hereafter be done, it is hoped, by the Hill people themselves.' The document goes on to make clear, 'It is supposed by the Post Office authorities at Calcutta, that a great saving of expenses, as well as increased protection to the packets, may be secured by substituting for the wax cloth, costing 8 annas per yard, the prepared Darjeeling paper referred to' ('Letter from T. H. Maddock to Dr Campbell', in Anon. 1842: 218). But the project did not survive for long. Perhaps it was abandoned when the government decided to relinquish domestic paper in all government offices in India (to be discussed in section IV).

The last in this series was a large-scale paper mill that C. F. Harcourt set up at Ramkristopore (Howrah) in 1854 with captive water works. It manufactured sheathing paper, writing paper, packing paper and paste board. But this project was also short-lived. While narrating the story of this mill, an account of contemporary Howrah notes, 'The business flourished for the short span of three years, and then had to be given up, owing to the importation of foreign papers at low prices, the scarcity of materials, and failure of docks' (Banerjee 1872: 82).

III

A spate of successful investments followed in the early 1860s. It started with Messrs Borneo & Co., who set up a paper mill at Bally (Howrah) in 1861. Earlier there had been a sugar mill there, which the company had purchased from the Bagshaw and Company (ibid.: 96–7) and then converted it into a paper mill. All of its plant and machineries were bought from the Serampore Paper Mill. Subsequently, in 1867, it was registered as the Royal Paper Mill, a joint-stock company. It manufactured low-grade papers to cater to the needs of the local populace. The underlying logic is not difficult to understand. In the wake of the decay in traditional crafts and the closure of the Serampore Paper Mill, a vacuum was created in the market, which the company targeted. Raw materials were also readily available nearby. Because of its location in the milieu of jute mills, supplies of jute cuttings and rejects were guaranteed. These were used along with the waste paper, old gunnies and used ropes and rags that were plentifully available from the metropolitan habitats of Calcutta. Moreover, the Borneo Jute Mill operating in its neighbourhood under its own managing agency was a cheap source of raw materials. In 1872 the company produced 4,320 reams of paper using 1,300 maunds of raw materials (Kerr 1874: 90). The average price for its papers was Rs. 4.25 per ream, as against a cost of Rs. 2.72, so that profitability works out at 56.25 per cent.

The company's monopoly was lost in the following decades, however. Table 6.4 shows that, in 1882, the Titagurh Paper Mill was set up at Titaghar (the 24 Parganas), followed by two more large-scale units in the early 1890s: the Bengal Paper Mill at Ranigunj (Burdwan) in 1890 and the Imperial Paper Mill at Kankinara (the 24 Parganas) in 1893. In the meantime, three mills had already sprung up elsewhere in India: the Upper India Couper Mill at Lucknow in 1879, the Scindhia Paper Mill at Gwalior in 1883 and the Reay Paper Mill at Poona in 1885. There were two more mills in Bombay, but they were tiny in size and belonged to private enterprises. The table suggests two more points: first, this new-born industry manufactured a variety of papers that were used in printing, writing, wrapping, packaging and blotting, as well as cartridge paper; and, second, different types of raw material were used in the production process – a host of old and waste materials such as paper, gunnies, ropes and rags, on the one hand, and various fresh, fibrous materials from jute, hemp, rice and wheat straws, and *babui* and *munj* grasses, on the other. The industry sought to trade off between the quality and costs by altering the mix of raw materials, and adjusted the product mix to ensure the better utilisation of plant and machineries in fluctuating markets.

Table 6.5 outlines the industry's growth in India. A buoyant scenario is discernible in the table throughout the 1878–1903 period. Its capital base was extended from Rs. 232,083 in 1881 to Rs. 446,800 in 1891, and further to Rs. 5,922,000 in 1903, implying an average growth rate of 111.44 per cent per annum from 1881 to 1903. Likewise, its production increased from 8.12 million lbs in 1881 to 26.05 million lbs in 1891, and further to 43.63 million lbs in 1903, in quantity and from Rs. 1.20 million to Rs. 4.12 million, and further to Rs. 59.15 million, respectively, in value. These represent annual growth rates of 19.87 per cent and 219.50 per cent, respectively, for 1881 to 1903. In addition, the employment series is seen rising from 213 in 1878 to 2,633 in 1891 and further to 4,523 in 1903, with an underlying growth rate of 80.94 per cent per annum between 1878 and 1903. The last two decades of the nineteenth century thus represent the formative period of India's modern paper industry. Two more

Table 6.4 Modern paper mills in India, late nineteenth century

Name	*Year of establishment/ownership*	*Product mix*	*Raw materials*
Royal Paper Mill, Howrah	1867, joint-stock company	Printing and cartridge of sorts, badami, cream laid, writing, blotting, brown	Rags, grass, jute, hemp
Titaghur Paper Mill, Titaghur	1882, joint-stock company	White printing, badami, coloured, cartridge, foolscap, blotting, watermarked	Rags, grass, jute, hemp bagging, ropes, waste paper
Bengal Paper Mill, Ranigunj	1890, joint-stock company	Super badami, printing, writing, cartridge	Grass, rags, gunnies, waste paper, etc.
Imperial Paper Mill, Kankinara	1893, joint-stock company	White printing, badami, super badami, cream laid and wove, yellow wove, azure laid, white & brown cartridge, superior tub-sized, colour printing, blotting, brown, envelop brown	Babui grass, jute, rags, hemp, rope, gunnies
Upper India Couper Mill, Lucknow	1879, joint-stock company	Printing, brown, coloured blotting, white cartridge, cream & yellow wove, azure and cream laid, wrappers	Rags, jute and hemp ropes, gunnies, straw, waste paper, grass
Scindhia Paper Mill, Gwalior	1883, joint-stock company	NA	NA
Girgaum Paper Mill, Bombay	1862, private	Brown, white, blotting	Gunnies, rags, cotton
Mahamadbhai Jamaluddin Paper Mill, Bombay	1878, private	White	Rags
Reay Paper Mill, Poona	1885, joint-stock company	Writing, printing, blotting, brown	Wheat and rice straw, rags, gunnies, grass

Source: GOI (1899: 46).

Table 6.5 Growth of the paper industry in India, 1878–1903

Year	*Number of mills*	*Capital (Rs.)*	*Daily employment*	*Production*	
				Quantity (lbs)	*Value (Rs.)*
1878	1	NA	213[1]	2,201,646[2]	NA
1881	5	232,083	784	8,124,445	1,203,000
1882	4	241,100	832	7,595,240	1,160,040
1883	6	236,800	951	7,247,784	1,192,630
1884	5	216,800	956	9,796,041	1,411,500
1885	7	336,800	1,118	12,303,327	1,779,950
1886	7	336,800	1,437	16,160,788	2,327,940
1887	7	346,800	1,655	17,094,264	2,586,450
1888	7	346,800	1,687	18,363,665	2,684,430
1889	7	376,800	1,837	19,664,490	2,892,360
1890	7	376,800	2,085	20,447,079	3,288,750
1891	8	446,800	2,633	26,050,692	4,120,390
1892	8	492,200	2,465	26,451,549	3,873,620
1893	8	492,200	3,157	29,319,828	4,329,910
1894	9	612,200	3,544	34,231,577	5,039,240
1895	8	627,200	3,594	39,927,687	6,086,330
1896	8	627,200	3,613	40,707,589	5,871,160
1897	8	627,200	3,532	38,581,703	5,682,160
1898	8	627,200	4,187	42,181,500	6,106,460
1899	8	6,772,000	4,436	44,428,440	62,409,050
1900	8	7,022,000	4,871	45,940,591	62,517,480
1901	9	7,320,000	4,978	46,713,125	65,837,240
1902	8	7,320,000	4,865	46,654,883	64,383,190
1903	9	5,922,000[3]	4,523	43,633,870	59,147,990

Notes: 1: Estimated by the output–labour ratio of 1881; 2: this was the highest amount of production at the Royal Mill before 1880 (Liotard 1880: 22); 3: inclusive of £122,200, converted to rupees at £1 = Rs. 10.

Sources: 1881–99: GOI (1899: 463); 1900–3: GOI (1904: 368).

points are suggestive in the table. First, the yawning gap in the growth rates between the quantity and value series of production, as noted above, signifies that Indian mills must have improved the quality of their papers so that they fetched higher prices. The unit price is worked out at Rs. 0.15 per lb in 1881, Rs. 0.16 per lb in 1891 and Rs. 1.36 per lb in 1903, representing a price hike of more than nine times in about two decades. Technological breakthroughs should have underpinned this price gain. Second, certain phases were dominant in this growth process. Those were (i) 1878–81, (ii) 1884–6, (iii) 1890–1 and (iv) 1893–5, when the output rose annually by 1.97 million lbs, 3.18 million lbs, 5.60 million lbs and 5.30 million lbs, respectively. Thus, compared to the 1880s, the absolute growth of production accelerated in the first half of the 1890s.

Table 6.6 presents the industry's comparative growth scenarios between Bengal and India, and also among different firms in this province. From the

Table 6.6 Comparative growth of paper making between Bengal and India, 1893–1903

Year	*Production in lbs (value in Rs.)*						*Employment*					
	Royal	*Titaghur*	*Bengal*	*Imperial*	*Total for Bengal*	*India*	*Royal*	*Titaghur*	*Bengal*	*Imperial*	*Total for Bengal*	*India*
1893	10,133,760 (1,400,000)	7,717,588 (1,205,873)	3,429,440 (600,000)	–	21,280,788 (3,205,873) [72.58]	29,319,828 (4,329,910)	835	483	632	–	1950 [61.77]	3157
1895	9,775,200 (1,347,600)	8,313,654 (1,299,008)	5,600,000 (950,000)	8,230,774 (1,357,452)	31,919,628 (4,954,060) [79.94]	39,927,687 (6,086,330)	832	640	589	652	2713 [75.49]	3594
1896	9,756,000 (1,346,125)	7,824,730 (1,187,682)	5,600,000 (950,000)	8,104,663 (1,037,434)	31,285,393 (4,521,241) [76.85]	40,707,589 (5,871,159)	832	695	568	672	2767 [76.20]	3631
1897	8,616,956 (1,188,960)	7,472,600 (1,167,600)	6,000,000 (1,000,000)	8,628,480 (1,258,520)	30,718,036 (4,615,080) [79.62]	38,581,703 (5,682,160)	637	659	631	797	2724 [77.12]	3532
1898	10,156,944 (1,401,450)	7,784,992 (1,216,400)	6,250,000 (1,017,000)	9,080,860 (1,338,000)	33,272,796 (4,972,850) [78.88]	42,181,500 (6,206,460)	938	772	674	838	3222 [76.95]	4187
1899	10,610,920	8,028,160	6,420,000	9,994,880	35,053,960 [78.90]	44,428,440 (62,409,050)	1036	835	831	828	3530 [79.58]	4436
1900	10,752,000 (1,400,000)	9,324,835 (1,457,000)	6,212,080 (831,975)	10,124,800 (1,408,708)	36,413,715 (5,097,683) [79.26]	45,940,591 (6,251,748)	1157	886	925	869	3837 [78.77]	4871
1902	11,241,591 (1,464,000)	9,776,612 (1,527,595)	6,176,238 (675,526)	9,354,480 (1,376,301)	36,548,921 (5,043,422) [78.34]	46,654,883 (6,438,319)	1167	960	912	942	3981 [81.83]	4865
1903	9,256,514 (1,301,697)	9,277,184 (1,242,480)	10,736,320 (1,437,900)	6,460,556 (865,200)	35,730,574 (4,847,277) [81.89]	43,633,870 (5,914,799)	914	933	870	775	3492 [77.20]	4523

Note: Numbers in square brackets represent the percentile shares of Bengal in India's total production (in lbs) and employment.

Sources: 1893: GOI (1895: 383); 18945: GOI (1896: 419); 1896: GOI (1897: 425); 1897: GOI (1898: 452); 1898: GOI (1899: 462); 1899: GOI (1900: 436); 1900: GOI (1901: 361); 1902: GOI (1903b: 350); 1903: GOI (1904: 369).

figures for Bengal's and India's total production (columns 6 and 7, respectively) I work out that, in 1893, Bengal's production in lbs accounted for 72.58 per cent of the country-level figure. It moved upwards to 79.94 per cent in 1895, and 81.89 per cent in 1903. A similar trend is noticed in employment as well: Bengal's share was 61.77 per cent in 1893, but 75.49 per cent in 1895 and 77.20 per cent in 1903. Bengal thus heavily dominated Indian paper making.

The firm-level statistics for Bengal suggest that a competitive environment prevailed in the contemporary market, however. The table underlines that the four firms in this province were all almost equally strong, production-wise as well as employment-wise. Productions (in lbs) at the Royal, Titaghur, Bengal and Imperial Mills are found in the ratio of 1:0.85:0.57:0.84 in 1895, 1:0.75:0.60:0.94 in 1899 and 1:0.87:0.55:0.83 in 1902. The Royal Mill and the Bengal Mill thus belong to the upper and lower bounds of the scale, with the Titaghur and Imperial Mills operating neck and neck in between. In respect of employment too, a similar scenario prevailed. For the respective mills, the ratio stands at 1:0.77:0.71:0.78, 1:0.81:0.80:0.80 and 1:0.82:0.78:0.81 for the respective years. In 1903, however, the Bengal Paper Mill was the forerunner in output. The industry thus consisted of a few large-scale units with almost identical technology, and hence represented an oligopoly market. The resulting cut-throat competition undeniably cast favourably on quality and prices, which I discuss in Section IV. But the formation of a cartel was also not uncommon. Thus, the Stationery Department reports, 'It should be noted that the Indian mills have formed a combination to enhance the rates this year on account of the import duty, the fall in exchange, rise in the price of coal, and c., the result being that they all tendered at the same enhanced rates' (GOB 1896: 11). Bagchi (1972: 394) also notices such a cartel: 'The survival of the Titaghur Paper Mill and Bengal Paper Mill during the period 1901–14 also owed something to the fact that they began to co-ordinate their pricing and production policies from an early date, and the area of co-operation between the two companies included the supply of the basic raw material, viz. *sabai* grass.' Other oligopoly vices, such as closures and acquisitions, were also present. Thus, the Titagurh Paper Mill acquired the Imperial Paper Mill in 1903, which thenceforth ran as the Titagurh Paper Mill no. 2. Again, the Royal Paper Mill was closed down in 1907, which the Titagurh Paper Mill acquired afterwards. Its plant and machineries were distributed between the company's establishments at Titaghar and Kankinara.[14] These were indeed the outcomes of oligopolistic competition.

The industry never suffered from the dearth of capital or labour. All the paper-making units in Bengal were floated as joint-stock companies under the managing agency system (for the managing agents in Bengal's paper industry, see GOB 1893: ix, 8.). Their managing agents were involved in various business lines, and enjoyed the confidence of investors on both the Calcutta and Bombay stock exchanges, as also at London, so that a smooth flow of fund was always guaranteed. For 1898 the paid-up capital (inclusive of debentures) is reported at Rs. 1,222,000 for the Royal Paper Mill, Rs. 1,000,000 for the Titaghur Paper Mill, Rs. 950,000 for the Bengal Paper Mill and Rs. 1,200,000 for the Imperial

Paper Mill (GOI 1899: 462). The Royal Paper Mill was managed under Messrs George Henderson & Co.,[15] who looked after five more companies, two in jute and three in tea (Lokanathan 1935: 48). Similarly, the Titaghur Paper Mill was run under Messrs F. W. Heilgers & Co., who managed as many as 11 companies (of which eight were in coal and two in jute); the Bengal Paper Mill was under Messrs Balmer, Lawrie & Co., managing 12 companies (of which two were in coal and five in electricity and engineering); and the Imperial Paper Mill was under Messrs Jardine, Skinner & Co., having interests in 16 companies (four in jute, six in tea, four in coal and two in others). Because of technical sub-additivities in these production lines, they enjoyed scope economies in the form of lower overhead costs of management, and lower prices for raw materials such as jute cuttings and rejects, coal and electricity. These explain why the paper industry ran efficiently, and attracted public investment. Table 6.5 reveals that, at the country level, the industry mobilised Rs. 232,083 in 1881, Rs. 6,772,000 in 1899 and Rs. 7,320,000 in 1902. For Bengal, Bagchi (1972: 393) tells us that, on 31 December 1913, the paid-up capital (inclusive of debentures) amounted to as much as Rs. 4,585,000 for the Titaghur Paper Mill and Rs. 1,108,000 for the Bengal Paper Mill.

Nor did the industry face any labour problem. Its technology was highly capital-intensive, requiring fewer workers per unit of output. Table 6.6 shows that the industry's employment in this province was 1,950 in 1893, increasing to 3,492 in 1903, so that each worker produced 10,913 lbs and 10,232 lbs in the respective years. These are higher than the country-level productivity – 9,287 lbs and 9,647 lbs, respectively, for each worker. The industry ran on double shifts, however, 12 hours each, so that the utilisation of machinery was maximised and the overhead costs minimised, generating efficiency thereby. Although the double-shift operation called for two batches of workers simultaneously on the payroll, labour scarcity never cropped up. These are confirmed in Foley (1906). Noting that there were about 1,000 workers each at the Titaghur Paper Mill no. 1 and 2, and 700 to 800 workers at the Bengal Paper Mill, Foley (1906: 20–1) remarks, 'There was no scarcity of labour since Paper Mill machinery does not require many hands to keep it running, and there is a quantity of work connected with a Paper Mill that always makes it popular with labour.' The abundance of labour is also confirmed by the stationary state of wages for about two decades (ibid.: xxxi, appendix). The scarcity was felt only in respect of fitters, turners and mechanics in view of their potential for employment in other industries, especially in jute and engineering. Its recruitment policy resembled closely that of its sister concerns, however, where migratory workers dominated. Foley (ibid.: 21) thus noticed in 1906, 'At Titaghar and Kankinara the majority of the hands, and at Raniganj about half were imported from up-country.' The industry's wage structure should also be similar to that prevailing in the jute and engineering industries, since they competed in the labour market, especially for migratory workers.

The industry's initial phase of development was impeded by twin problems, however: marketing and raw materials. The former is discussed at length in

Section IV. But the question of raw materials seems perplexing in view of Bengal's abundance in fibrous plants. The problem did crop up, though, for the want of information, on the one hand, and the high railway freight charges, on the other. On the former question, the Royal Paper Mill once pleaded, 'We think a deal of valuable information [on paper-making fibres] might be collected if the Government would take the matter up, and instruct their officials in the various districts to make enquiries on the subject' (quoted in Liotard 1880: 6). While instructing the district-level officials pursuant to the memorandum, the government emphasised, '[T]he Governor General in Council had no doubt that great benefit was likely to result from careful and systematic enquiries on the part of district officials into the actual and possible resources of the country under this head.' Detailed information that the government gathered on that occasion and disseminated subsequently (Kerr 1874: 83–96) certainly promoted the interest of the industry.

Higher railway freight costs also got in the way of its early prosperity.[16] The average freight charge in Indian railways was evidently 10 pies per ton-mile for low-priced items such as plant fibres (first-class goods) in 1861–70 (Tiwari 1921: 433), juxtaposed to the average cost of hauling at only 1.13 to 1.28 pies per ton-mile on the East Indian Railway (ibid.: 458). Therefore, the paper mills, largely localised around Calcutta, could not profitably use raw materials from distant places. The only exception was the Bengal Paper Mill, which was set up at Ranigunj for the sake of raw materials from interior Bengal and its surrounding states, such as Bihar and Orissa (Bengal Paper Mill 1940: 1). Liotard (1880: 22) thus notes that the Royal Paper Mill 'on one occasion turned out as much as 1070 tons of paper in a year, and they would produce much more if they could obtain a sufficient supply of fibrous stuff at remunerative rates'. The government sought to remove this hurdle as well. We thus find the authority urging in 1883 that 'all rates…should…be fixed with due regard to…what the article would bear' (Tiwari 1921: 436). Again, in 1887, the Governor General in Council underlined that 'to protect the public and to prevent unreasonable charges on the part of the railway administrations, it is necessary for Government to impose restrictions as regards…the maximum rates for all descriptions of goods' (quoted in ibid.: 438). In view of such mounting pressures on railway companies, the average freight charge was curtailed to 5.895 pies per ton-mile in 1887 (ibid.: 433). In particular, special rates were sanctioned for low-price goods, including plant fibres (ibid.: 444). Certainly, these two state policies served the industry's interests in its nascent stage.

IV

Our research thus indicates that Bengal experienced the decay of its traditional paper making, and also the failures of a host of European ventures, in the first half of the nineteenth century, and its steady growth, based on modern technology and organisation, in the second half. I argue here that these conflicting trends are explained to a good extent by the contemporary store purchasing policies of the colonial administration. They led to swings in India's paper imports, and thus determined marketing opportunities for the domestic industry, indigenous and European alike. Before entering into those policy issues, let me review India's imports of paper during the second half of the nineteenth century. Appendix 6.1 presents import data for 1849 to 1914, which are plotted in Figure 6.2. Table 6.7 summarises these data.

Appendix 6.1 shows that, in 1849, India imported paper (including books) worth £112,761, a value which grew continuously for a couple of years thereafter. The import series in Table 6.7 is seen rising to £430,797 per annum in 1870–4, £662,365 per annum in 1880–4, and further to £924,787 per annum

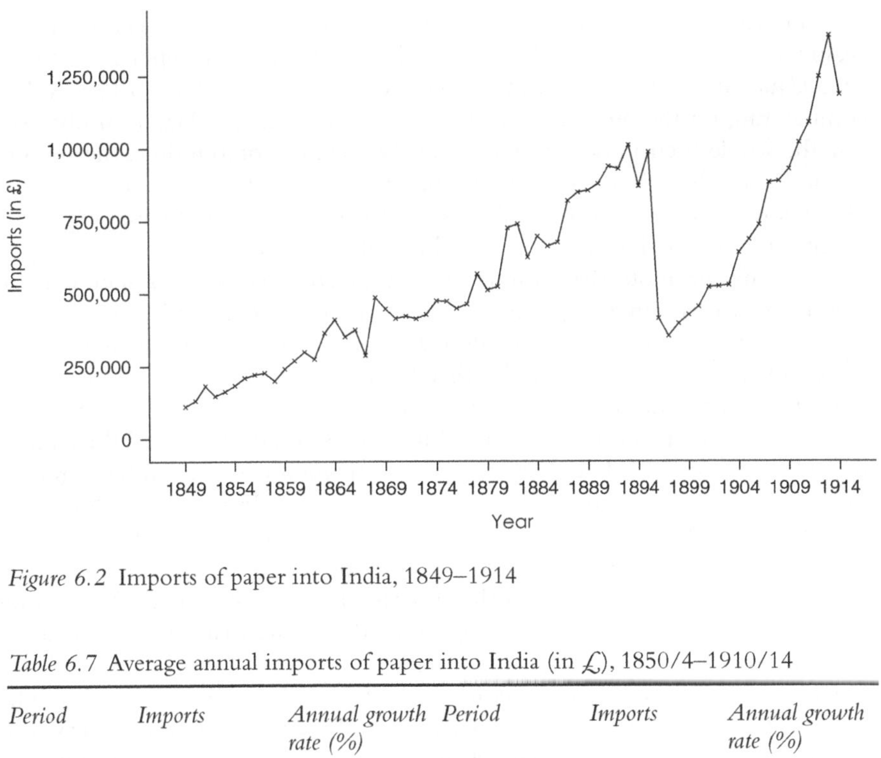

Figure 6.2 Imports of paper into India, 1849–1914

Table 6.7 Average annual imports of paper into India (in £), 1850/4–1910/14

Period	*Imports*	*Annual growth rate (%)*	*Period*	*Imports*	*Annual growth rate (%)*
1850–4	162,687	–	1885–9	772,501	3.33
1855–9	220,214	7.07	1890–4	924,787	3.94
1860–4	323,939	9.42	1895–9	515,295	(–) 8.86
1865–9	390,134	4.09	1900–4	534,310	0.74
1870–4	430,797	2.08	1905–9	824,051	10.84
1875–9	492,931	2.88	1910–14	1,185,611	8.78
1880–4	662,365	6.87			

Source: Appendix 6.1.

in 1890–4. The underlying annual growth rate is as high as 18.10 per cent for the 1849–93 period (Appendix 6.1). A steep downturn is noticed thereafter (Figure 6.2), reducing the series to £515,295 per annum in the 1895–9 period. A revival took place in 1905–9 onwards.

The upswing prior to 1862 is possibly explained by the tariff concessions of 1836. Under Act XIV of 1836 (P.P. 1840: 36), the import of papers was subject to 3½ per cent duty on British bottoms, and 7 per cent on foreign bottoms. Although it was enhanced to 10 per cent *ad valorem* (irrespective of the nationality of shipping) through Act VII of 1859 (GOI 1860: schedule A), it was repealed in 1861. A Royal Commission witness stressed in 1886 that, after the repeal of the paper duty in 1861, India's imports of paper increased largely from England, and to an extent from Germany and Belgium ('Evidence of G. Chater, Minutes of Evidence', in P.P. 1886: 8). Juxtaposed to such a soft tariff policy in British India, we find that the infant British paper industry was protected by high tariff barriers against France and Holland. The import duty in Britain was reportedly 20 per cent *ad valorem* in 1704, and 2d. to 10d. per pound between 1794 and 1801. While commenting on the protective tariff in Britain, Coleman (1958: 143) observes, 'On the whole, then, import duties averaged some three or four times the amount of the Excise duty.' From 1851 to 1856, however, Britain saw the construction of as many as 377 paper mills, and thus emerged as 'the greatest paper exporting country in the world in the middle of the century' (ibid.: 211).

To further promote British interests in India, the Secretary of State made it mandatory to use English paper in all government offices. This was executed through a Financial Department despatch (no. 218, of 27 December 1862), which reads as follows: all articles that Britain produced should be procured only through the Stores Department of India House, London. This provision was further tightened once the Stores Purchase Rules incorporated the administrative order in 1871. The interests of domestic industries were totally ignored in the absence of any provision for local purchase ('History of the Rules for the Supply of Articles for the Public Service in India, 1862–1918', in GOI 1920: 163). Only in contingency could domestic paper be purchased, and even then only under the vigilance of the superintendent of stationery. We are thus told with respect to 1871–2, 'The Superintendent states that the strictest care is exercised to avoid the necessity for local purchase, and that the selection of such articles as must be got is strictly confined to himself' (GOB 1873: 2). A similar statement is available for 1870–1 as well (GOB 1872a: 2): 'Although every possible care was taken to avoid, as much as possible, the necessity for local purchase by substituting articles available in store for similar articles required, there has been some slight increase in the expenditure under this head.'

The effects of the store purchase policy are discernible in Table 6.7. It demonstrates that India's imports of paper rose from £220,214 per annum in 1855–9 to £430,797 per annum in 1870–4, undergoing an annual average growth rate of 6.37 per cent. Bengal also witnessed the boom, as reflected in Table 6.8, whereby the series ascended from Rs. 1,027,020 in 1865–6 to Rs. 1,722,597 in 1870–1, suggesting an annual growth of 13.55 per cent.

Table 6.8 Imports of paper into Bengal (in Rs.), 1865/6–1900/1

Year	*Value*	*Year*	*Value*
1865–6	1,027,020	1883–4	1,136,902
1866–7	1,013,617	1884–5	1,032,322
1867–8	1,130,465	1885–6	669,760
1868–9	1,685,480	1886–7	633,415
1869–70	1,501,381	1887–8	821,157
1870–1	1,722,597	1888–9	774,342
1871–2	1,239,200	1889–90	629,637
1872–3	1,098,010	1891–2	698,683
1873–4	1,305,370	1892–3	632,849
1874–5	1,204,320	1893–4	581,124
1875–6	1,386,270	1898–9	444,327
1876–7	1,234,239	1899–1900	543,069
1877–8	1,158,168	1900–1	538,660
1878–9	1,284,071		

Sources: 1865–6: GOB (1869: xxix [for 11 months]); 1866–7: GOB (1869: xxii); 1867/8–68/9: GOB (1870: xxxvi); 1869–70: GOB (1871: xxv); 1870–1: GOB (1872b: cxix); 1871/2–75/6: GOI (1877: 56); 1876–7: GOB (1878b: cxliv); 1877/8–78/9: GOB (1880b: cxxviii); 1883/4–84/5: GOB (1886b: cxii); 1885/6–86/7: GOB (1888a: cxvi); 1887–8: GOB (1890a: cxx); 1888/9–89/90: GOB (1891a: cxx); 1891/2–92/3: GOB (1894b: cxvi); 1893–4: GOB (1895b: cxiv); 1898/9: GOB (1900: cxliv); 1899/1900–1900/1: GOB (1902: clii).

The second half of the nineteenth century thus began with twin curses for Indian paper making. A vast market belonging to the government was closed to it, on the one hand; and, on the other, imports were buoyed by the soft tariffs. These adversities precipitated the decay of Bengal's traditional paper making that I have discussed in Section I,[17] and also the decline of the Serampore Paper Mill in Hooghly and the Ramkristopore Paper Mill in Howrah, as discussed in Section II. As to the Serampore Mill, a contemporary biographer of William Carey comments, 'It stopped only when the Secretary of State for a short time ordered all official indents for stationery to be supplied from London, an unjust policy which has been denounced and given up as unfair to the native and local industries and to the tax-paying public' (Smith 1885: 245). A similar explanation is available for the Ramkristopore Paper Mill as well (Banerjee 1872: 82). Moreover, in view of the prohibitions on local purchases, the Royal Paper Mill came up with inferior-grade papers, as noted above, which local outlets sought.

The imperial design changed gradually after 1876, however. In that year the Secretary of State constituted a committee on India's stores purchase, and we find the committee recommending local purchases, and of local manufactures too, in some cases. Domestic interests were thus certainly subserved. But the interests of India's paper industry were largely ignored, as domestic writing paper was excluded thereof. According to the rules that followed, only European paper could be purchased, locally or in Britain, for drafting purposes, 'so as to secure uniformity and durability in public documents' ('History of the Rules for the Supply of Articles for the Public Service in India, 1862–1918', in GOI 1920: 164–5). For the industry, the only incentive was that other paper (especially printing paper) made inroads into government uses.

A further impetus followed when these rules were submitted to the Secretary of State for approval. He stressed in the approval note that 'the special attention of local Governments should be drawn to the importance of substituting local manufactures for European articles even at some temporary increase in cost' (ibid.: 165). This was reiterated in Finance Department resolution no. 3574, of 11 November 1880: 'The utmost encouragement consistent with true economy should be given to the supply of European articles by the local market; and whenever it is possible to do so even at some temporary increase of cost, articles of manufacture, or of indigenous origin should be substituted for European articles' (ibid.: 166). Further clarification followed in Finance Department resolution no. 185, of 10 January 1883: 'The Government is desirous to give the utmost encouragement to every effort to substitute for articles now obtained from Europe, articles of the bona fide local manufacture or of indigenous origin, and where articles of European and of Indian manufacture do not materially differ in price and quality, the Government would always be disposed to give preference to the latter' (ibid.: 167). A further clarification was this: 'There are many articles which may not be immediately obtained in the local market, but which can be made in the event of Government encouraging the manufacture' (ibid.: 168).

These policy reversals were reflected in Calcutta's Stationery Department. One of its documents notes, 'In May 1876 the Government of India inquired whether certain description of paper manufactured in Calcutta could not be substituted for similar paper indented for from England, so as to reduce the cost of future indents on the Secretary of State for India'(GOB 1878a: 6). Accordingly, 2,000 reams of various descriptions of paper were procured from the Royal Paper Mill. In the following year the department increased its intake, and issued them to various departments 'in lieu of the more expensive English papers' (GOB 1879: 3). A still higher intake took place in 1878–9, when local expenditures were almost doubled – from Rs. 78,838 in 1877–8 to Rs. 145,322 that year[18] – with a view to promoting the domestic industry. The department's report for 1878–9 (GOB 1880a: 3) records, 'It is in accordance with the policy of the Government that local manufacturers should be encouraged while a saving in cost is secured. Under recent orders this policy will receive a considerable development, and there is every reason to look for most satisfactory results from the new system.' The trend of local purchases accelerated in the following years, reaching Rs. 727,253 in 1879–80 and Rs. 904,955 in 1880–1. Government procurements then consisted mainly of printing papers, which were supplied to various government presses – Indian Printing, Bengal Printing, North Western Provinces and Oudh Printing, Central Province Printing, Assam Printing, Punjab Printing, British Burma Printing and Postal Press, Aligarh (GOB 1882: 2). The government also procured brown paper, blotting paper, yellow paper and envelopes locally.

Since the domestic stores were entirely procured from the Royal Mill (ibid.: 5), the company strived for better quality. Old machineries were all replaced by 1880–1 (ibid.), and better fibres were tried in production. A report for 1881–2 (GOB 1883: 4) thus remarks, 'The Company have... of late turned out a superior description of paper called "*munj* paper" which is a very fair substitute for English white cartridge paper.' It also entered into the writing paper market, as the paper's surface became 'sufficiently smooth to allow of its being used to a great extent for drafting purposes in the place of English paper' (ibid.). New enterprises in the industry further accelerated its technological progress, so that, by 1893, domestic papers successfully competed in all markets. According to a report for 1893–4 (GOB 1895a: 11), 'The paper turned out by the mills in this country was thus equal, and in some respects superior, to that turned out by the English mills.' Let me add that this trend was buttressed by a government order of July 1892, which forbade the use of English writing paper in all government offices (GOB 1894a: 2). A vast market was thus opened up to the domestic industry.[19] This is why, as noted earlier, the industry's growth rate accelerated in the early 1890s.

In addition to providing market support, the government also infused intra-industry competition through its supply orders. From 1876 to 1882 locally manufactured paper was procured exclusively from the Royal Paper Mill. This monopoly was lost with the award of trial orders to the Lucknow and Scindia Mills in 1883–4 (GOB 1885: 6), and regular orders thereafter (GOB 1886a: 4). In 1884–5 an order was also placed with the Titaghur Mill, where production had commenced a year earlier. Immense competition therefore followed. 'I have reasons to believe,' wrote the superintendent of stationery in 1884–5, 'that the provision of the paper will be efficiently as well as economically conducted by maintaining competition, while encouraging an enterprising industry in other provinces without injuriously affecting the long established Bally Mills Company' (ibid.: 5). The Bengal Paper Mill and the Imperial Paper Mill also received similar patronage from their inception, the former from 1890–1[20] and the latter from 1893–4 (GOB 1895a: 10). Table 6.9 displays the supply orders that several firms received from 1891/2 to 1899/1900. The competition that followed surely strengthened the industry. This is evident in a contemporary source (GOB 1887: 6): 'Healthy competition between the several mills has... contributed to great improvement in the quality of the paper as well as fairness in the price; and it is anticipated that... we shall in future be almost independent of supplies from Europe.'

In addition to intra-industry competition, foreign competition was also kept alive under a threat of policy reversals. In 1897–8, for example, the superintendent of stationery asked the mills to reduce their prices. 'I pointed out,' he reports (GOB 1899: 4), 'that, unless they did so, Government would have to revert to the practice of importing papers from home.' The threat finally yielded: '[T]he mills came to terms with us.'

The mounting government patronage is reflected in Table 6.10. It shows that the government's purchase of Indian paper increased from Rs. 242,100

Table 6.9 Paper delivered by different firms (in Rs.), 1891/2–1899/1900

Year	*Royal*	*Titaghur*	*Bengal*	*Imperial*	*Lucknow*	*Scindia*	*Total*
1891–2	458,980	669,348	239,053	–	125,792	128,731	1,621,904
1892–3	417,022	714,283	278,809	–	234,658	72,279	1,717,051
1893–4	371,531	638,237	373,939	–	248,062	83,002	1,714,771
1894–5	316,979	586,810	293,503	117,459	306,888	4,992	1,626,631
1895–6	320,848	469,379	315,523	222,065	469,104	–	1,796,919
1896–7	303,947	463,017	319,395	307,914	323,074	–	1,717,347
1897–8	359,258	558,751	360,970	341,970	386,770	–	2,007,719
1898–9	347,490	544,288	380,052	358,057	390,640	–	2,020,527
1899–1900	378,388	547,659	370,725	371,862	433,209	–	2,101,843

Note: '–' signifies that the mill in question did not deliver paper that year, either because it had not yet been set up or because it had been closed.

Sources: 1891–2: GOB (1893: i); 1892–3: GOB (1894a: i); 1893–4: GOB (1895a: i); 1894–5: GOB (1896: i); 1895–6: GOB (1897: i); 1896–7: GOB (1898: i); 1897–8: GOB (1899: i); 1898–9: GOB (1900: i); 1899–1900: GOB (1901: i).

Table 6.10 Government expenditures on local purchases of paper (in Rs.), 1880/1–1890/1

Year	*Indian paper*	*British paper*
1880–1	242,100	1,019,151
1881–2	271,138	1,022,335
1882–3	365,714	58,049
1883–4	442,320	32,569
1884–5	586,877	35,981
1885–6	670,592	24,483
1886–7	875,550	–
1887–8	872,182	–
1888–9	927,711	–
1889–90	1035,448	–
1890–1	1,367,514	–

Sources: 1880–1: GOB (1882: 12); 1881–2: GOB (1883: 12); 1882–3: GOB (1884: 12); 1883–4: GOB (1885: 12); 1884–5: GOB (1886a: 12); 1885–6: GOB (1887: 14); 1886–7: GOB (1888b: 5); 1887–8: GOB (1889: 5); 1888–9: GOB (1890b: v); 1889–90: GOB (1891b: v); 1890–1: GOB (1892: vi).

in 1880–1 to Rs. 875,550 in 1886–7 and further to Rs. 1,367,514 in 1890–1. *Per contra*, the local purchase of English paper declined from Rs. 1,019,151 in 1880–1 to only Rs. 24,483 in 1885–6, and thus became insignificant.

The patronage continued through 1914–15 (Table 6.11). Between 1907/8 and 1914/15 the government purchased Indian paper to the value of Rs. 3.37 to 4.08 million, as against the purchase of imported paper valued at from Rs. 1.23 to 2.88 million (taking purchases in India and Britain together). Imported articles thus constituted 27 to 41 per cent of total purchases. Moreover, a larger

Table 6.11 Government stores and private imports of paper into India (in thousand Rs.), 1907/8–1914/15

Year	*Government stores*					*Private imports*
	Imported paper purchased in Britain[1]	*Imported paper purchased in India*	*Total imported paper*	*Indian paper*	*Total*[2]	
1907–8	1,890	25	1,915 (31.91)	4,086	6,001	14,355
1908–9	1,860	25	1,885 (33.09)	3,811	5,696	13,650
1909–10	1,545	34	1,579 (31.91)	3,369	4,948	14,970
1910–11	1,455	22	1,477 (27.32)	3,930	5,407	16,560
1911–12	1,200	27	1,227 (25.44)	3,595	4,822	17,295
1912–13	1,740	20	1,760 (33.77)	3,452	5,212	20,760
1913–14	2,835	41	2,876 (44.38)	3,604	6,480	22,875
1914–15	2,340	123	2,463 (38.23)	3,979	6,442	18,390

Notes: 1: Converted from rupees at Rs. 15 = £1; 2: the terms in parentheses represent the percentage of imported paper in total government stores.

Source: GOI (1920: 236, appendix D).

proportion of these purchases were meant for Bombay and Madras, where Bengal paper mills did not like to venture. This is what a witness before the Stores Purchase Committee (1920) reported: 'The local manufacturers in Bengal did not on one occasion respond to calls for tenders from the Bombay Government, and were not generally anxious to do so at any time. The Bombay Government imported most of its requirements' ('Evidence of E. Daltry', in GOI 1920: 29). The same was reported for Madras as well (ibid.).

The growing uptake of stores from Indian manufacturers jeopardised the British paper interest. Table 6.7 shows that the growth rate of India's paper imports decelerated from the mid-1880s, and became negative from 1895 to 1899. In the case of Bengal, the fall is more discernible (Table 6.8). It nosedived from Rs. 1,136,902 in 1883–4 to Rs. 1,032,322 in 1884–5, and fell further to Rs. 444,327 in 1898–9. The trend of Table 6.7 survived to some extent in the late 1880s (and also revived after 1910: Table 6.11), however, since Bengal mills were not interested in the markets of Bombay and Madras.

The extent of the British discontent was reflected in the Royal Commission of 1886. A witness, John Evans, representing the Paper Makers' Association of England puts on record ('Minutes of Evidence', in P.P. 1886: 3) that 'in India mills have been started which have materially affected our exports to that country'. While explaining the reasons thereof, he emphasises, 'There is no doubt that it [the falling exchange rate] must have an effect. Many of the shipments to India, instead of realising what was anticipated, have produced far less than what the prices were when they were sent out. Owing to the fall in exchange any business transactions between this country and India have of late years been to a certain extent of a gambling character, so that you never know what you were going to receive in return' (ibid.: 7).

Without disputing the effect of the falling exchange rate for Indian currency, I argue that the comparative advantages of Indian paper mills contributed more to this success. For one thing, the paper that Britain exported to India was made of raw materials largely imported from this country, so that they involved two-way transportation costs. Competitiveness was curtailed thereby. A trade review for 1881–2 (GOI 1883: 44) thus underlines that Indian mills could easily compete with the low-grade imported paper, 'especially when it is considered that rags are now sent in considerable quantities from Calcutta and Bombay to England and the United States, and returned in paper, thus involving double freight'. The added advantage for Bengal was that 'the local labour is very [much] cheaper' (ibid.). Therefore, once the Bengal mills had been able to improve their quality, they prevailed over the British competition. A paper manufacturer in Hertfordshire, F. P. Barlow, narrated to the Royal Commission (P.P. 1886: 14), 'I…have seen the growth of paper mills there [in Calcutta] which has been going on very rapidly in the last five or six years. […] They are beginning to produce this year very good printing paper of the class of our cheap newspapers; a strong paper at a low rate.' He confessed, 'In India, he will be a very formidable competitor.'

British interests did not give up the market without resistance, however. Through the India Office in London, they sought time and again to manipulate government policy on the plea that British paper was cheaper than paper manufactured in Bengal. At the insistence of the India Office in 1880–1, the Calcutta Stationery Department undertook a comparative cost study between Indian and British paper. Table 6.12 contains the findings. For all varieties of paper reported in the table, the local supplies from the Royal Mill dominated. The table suggests that the price difference was more than Re 1 per ream for as many as 12 out of 31 varieties. The department's calculation (GOB 1882: 5) was that, in 1880–1, 'the extended use of Bally badami paper represents a saving of Rs. 54,668, as compared with the price of an equal quantity of English printing paper…and that together with brown paper, blotting paper, yellow paper, and envelopes, which are also supplied by the Bally Mill, the whole saving equals Rs. 59,617'. The imputed savings were Rs. 66,620 in 1881–2 (GOB 1883: 13), Rs. 80,707 in 1882–3 (GOB 1884: 13) and Rs. 61,283 in 1885–6 (GOB 1887: 13–14). To survive in competition, the British manufacturers then reduced their quotations, but the effort failed to yield any result. A report for 1890–1 (GOB 1892: 6) thus runs, 'There can be little doubt, I think, that the Indian paper now

Table 6.12 Comparative cost study between Bengal and British paper (in Rs.-annas-pice per ream), 1880–1

Description (quantity in reams)	*Price for Bengal*	*Price for British*	*Total savings*	*Description (quantity in reams)*	*Price for Bengal*	*Price for British*	*Total savings*
Bally badami				Super royal 60 lbs (100)	6–4–0	6–9–0	31–4–0
For general stock				Super royal 40 lbs (528)	4–2–8	4–6–0	110–0–10
Cartridge 45 lbs (19)	11–4–0	12–7–10	23–8–0	Super royal 30 lbs (15)	3–2–0	3–4–6	2–5–6
Royal 28 lbs (1,000)	4–3–8	5–11–0	1458–5–4	Double foolscap 24 lbs (200)	4–2–8	4–6–0	41–10–8
Royal 25 lbs (2,952)	3–12–5	5–1–3	3842–13–11	For census			
Royal 20 lbs (5,256)	3–0–4	4–1–0	5475–4–9	Super royal 40 lbs (44)	4–2–8	4–6–0	9–2–8
Super 28 lbs (700)	4–3–8	5–11–0	1021–9–0	Royal 32 lbs (920)	3–5–4	3–8–0	153–5–4
Double supper 56 lbs (1,000)	8–7–8	11–6–0	2916–10–8	Royal 30 lbs (213)	3–2–0	3–4–6	33–5–10
Demy 18 lbs (4,395)	2–11–5	3–10–6	4120–13–2	**Bally yellow**			
Double foolscap 28 lbs (1,000)	4–3–8	5–11–0	1458–5–4	For general stock			
Double foolscap 24 lbs (12,585)	3–10–0	4–14–0	15771–10–9	Royal 20 lbs (2,122)	4–6–0	5–0–10	1436–14–0
For census				Super royal 34 lbs (288)	7–7–0	8–9–5	331–8–0
Royal 20 lbs (17,474)	3–0–4	4–1–0	18202–4–2	Super royal 20 lbs (1,036)	4–6–0	5–0–10	701–9–6
Double royal 40 lbs (200)	6–8–0	8–2–0	416–10–8	Demy 15 lbs (686)	3–4–6	3–12–7½	348–7–1
Bally/Bengal brown				For census			
For general stock				Royal 20 lbs (40)	4–6–0	5–0–10	27–1–4
Brown 60 lbs (492)	6–4–0	6–9–0	153–15–3	For general stock			
Brown 16 lbs (100)	1–10–8	1–12–0	8–5–4	Bally white blotting demy 32 lbs (1,141)	7–10–8	8–4–9	719–7–1
Cartridge royal 50 lbs (146)	5–3–4	5–7–6	38–2–4	Bally white blotting demy 16 lbs (100)	3–13–4	4–2–4½	31–8–2
Cartridge royal 30 lbs (447)	3–2–0	3–4–6	382–6–8	Bally note envelope printed (190,045)	2–1–10	3–2–0	192–0–5
Super royal 120 lbs (315)	12–8–0	13–2–0	196–14–0	**Total**			59,617–7–1

Source: GOB (1882: 13).

supplied to the Stationery Office is as cheap, if not cheaper, than the English paper, and the price of the latter has apparently reached a minimum.'

The office of the Secretary of State raised the issue again in 1890–1, when the director general of stores placed fresh quotations for British paper in support of the argument that 'the paper could have been supplied cheaper from England' (ibid.). In the debate that followed, the central point was the question of quality. As to the fresh quotations, the Calcutta Stationery Department argued (GOB 1894a: 9), 'It is however very doubtful whether the India Office could really supply good paper at the prices quoted by the English contractors. [...] [T]he English Stationery Office has recently found it necessary to raise the prices of paper required for use in public offices, and applied for an extra grant of £20,500 for the purpose.' The apprehension was based on rampant adulterations in low-priced British paper, however. A contemporary issue of the *World's Paper Review* thus notes that 'experience has shown that the low-priced papers were largely adulterated, and complaints were common of their brittleness and deterioration' (quoted in ibid.). The evidence in point was the British blue-laid, 16 lbs foolscap, loft-dried paper, which was cheaper by nearly 50 per cent (13s. 6d. in 1883 and 7s. 4d. in 1891). But, on examination by advanced testing appliances in government laboratories, it was found to be adulterated with mechanical wood pulp. Therefore, the government promptly replaced the paper by a better variety of similar description at a price of 12s. 8d. There was a similar experience with the 'commoner printings' as well. Citing these incidents, the Calcutta Stationery Department stresses that 'the low-priced papers in the English market are unsuitable for official work and correspondence, and these are, I believe, the same class of papers for which the rates are quoted by the India Office' (ibid.: 10). For Indian paper, by contrast, high opinions were recorded: '[T]he Indian paper is not adulterated, being made from good rags and grass fibres, and the public service is supplied with a good substantial article at less price than at which it can be imported.' This was further confirmed in a conference held at Calcutta in 1893–4. One of its resolutions reads: 'Another point besides cheapness in favour of the country-made paper is the absence of adulteration in the materials used for its manufacture, and it has been brought to the notice of the Government that the cheap kinds of European papers, the price of which were quoted by the Secretary of State in competition with the Indian-made articles, have been condemned for office use in England' (GOB 1894b: 584).

The issue was further put on debate in 1896–7, when the Secretary of State called for a fresh comparative cost study. Calcutta's superintendent of stationery promptly replied: 'Experience has shown me that our ordinary Indian papers are of a far better quality, and also lower in price, than the English papers of a similar quality; and looking to the uncertainty which attends supplies from England, it was with some feeling of anxiety that I complied with this order' (GOB 1898: 12). The exercise he undertook confirmed his experience, however. But the director general of stores contested the underlying method of the comparative study, and, based on a revised method, he inferred that, out of

11 varieties, the British paper significantly dominated in eight, and the Indian paper only in one. Taking all varieties together, he claimed that there was 'a difference in favour of the former [European paper] on the stock obtained during the year, amounting to Rs. 86,233' (GOB 1901: 335). But the methodology erred in respect of the incidental charges on landing, storage and despatch, which were totally ignored. The superintendent of stores in Calcutta argued that, if those incidental charges were recognised, the balance turned to the favour of Indian paper by Rs. 47,721. Although, in six out of the 11 varieties, a loss of Rs. 61,846 was involved with domestic paper, his calculations indicate that 'almost the whole of the counterbalancing gain on the remaining five kinds is obtained on the single variety' (ibid.).

This gave rise to a policy dilemma. For the sake of economy, the government should award six supply orders to British manufacturers and five to Indian producers. This was what the British interests would insist on. But such a policy might ruin the domestic industry if, with the reduced government uptake, the firms could not attain the minimum economic scale.

Seized with this dilemma, the government constituted a committee in 1902 under J. E. O'Conor as the president. The committee noted that the Indian paper industry thrived on demand from various government departments as well as railways (for details, see Sen 1964: 35–6). Some of them were reeling from financial crises, managerial shortfalls, overproduction and high raw material prices. Their survival would be at stake if the government withdrew its patronage from certain lines of their product mix. And, if the industry sank altogether, government stores would become costlier. The committee, therefore, recommended procuring all the stores in India, which the government accepted (GOI 1902). The store purchase controversy, which had continued for a quarter of a century, was thus finally concluded.

V

This study underlines the fact that Bengal's medieval art of paper making prospered into the early nineteenth century on the basis of local raw materials, native manpower and the domestic market. Its estimated production stood at 2,466,763 quires per annum, and the level of employment at 113,470. This traditional industry started declining in the early 1860s, however, and had almost disappeared by 1914. From the late eighteenth century a number of European projects also came into being, but they failed to survive in the long run. The industry witnessed successful ventures after the early 1860s, however, but they were all large in scale, and by the close of the century there were four large-scale paper mills in Bengal, employing 3,492 persons. Their aggregate capital was Rs. 5.70 million in 1913. The replacement of the traditional industry by modern enterprises thus involved a loss of employment of 109,978 workers during the second half of the nineteenth century.

I have argued that the decay of traditional paper making was not a consequence of the emergence of modern paper-making enterprises. Rather, it was triggered by the influence of the soft import policy, as well as by the adverse store purchase rules. My investigations into the contemporary stores purchase rules indicate that the policy was later amended to bolster modern paper making in Bengal. The modern industry that thus emerged in Bengal enjoyed comparative cost advantages over its British counterpart.

Notes

1 For the debate on the introduction of paper technology into Europe, see Querol-Kroenberg (1974: 233–7); and Burns (1981). The technology was introduced in England in the sixteenth century – coinciding with the immigration of Huguenot refugees (Coleman 1958) – and in France in the fifteenth century (Jervis and Jones 1930).

2 Evidence indicates that, prior to Tsh'ai Lun, two varieties of paper prevailed: silk paper (using refuse silk from animal fibre) and *heh-ti (or neeh-ti)* paper (using bark cloth). Lun invented 'true paper' by using bark cloth (especially the bark of trees, raw hemp, and also old linen rags and fishing nets) but employing the silk paper manufacturing process (Dabrowski 2006).

3 Prior to this project, Jones worked for eight years in Calcutta as a mechanic. Ghosh (1997: 145) notes, 'Jones' extraordinary mechanical skill enabled him to set up a small paper works from which he furnished all the paper that was required.' He subsequently introduced mechanical coal mining in Bengal (Ray 2015: 470–1). We will see that he also assisted Carey in installing mechanical pulp making.

4 It was later purchased by Rustomjee, who converted it to a dyeing unit for cloth (Banerjee 1872: 80).

5 Carey's biographer notes that 'in the fifteenth and sixteenth centuries the district of Maldah in Bengal, a region where William Carey spent the first six years of his residence in India, had become a great centre for manufacturing this variety of paper, which was exported even then. It is more than possible that Carey, considering the erection of a press while still at Madnabadi, must have contemplated attaching a paper manufacturing unit to the printing establishment' (Khan 1961: 244–5).

6 The society's account from 1801 to 1807 shows that, in 1801–3, they printed 4,300 copies of different religious books containing 2,697,800 pages with Patna paper, and, in 1806 and 1807, 1,164 copies containing 3,990,000 pages with Bengal paper (Khan 1961: 262–5).

7 In that year Carey requisitioned the 'iron work of a paper mill…and a model' (quoted in Ghosh 1993: 169).

8 'This steam-engine, which may still be seen on the premises at Serampore, was the first ever erected in India, and excited almost as much interest as the first steam-boat, or the first railway. The natives crowded to see the "machine of fire", as they called it, which equalled the achievements of Vishwu-Kurmu, the architect of the gods. Gentlemen of scientific tastes, who had never had an opportunity of seeing a steam-engine, came to Serampore and studied its mechanism under the instructions of the engineer' (Marshman 1859: II, 225).

9 A Society document of 1826 made the point, 'With the exception of the steam engine, "(a small one of twelve horses' power for making paper,)" all the (moveable) property at Serampore would not fetch at the hammer a thousand pounds' (Marshman 1828: 166).

10 While justifying the Society's expenditure in this period, Marshman emphasised, 'In attempting to improve the paper so as to prevent its being devoured by insects, about £5000 have been expended, which attempt has now been happily crowned with success' (Marshman 1828: 159).

11 Marshman writes (1859: I, 95), '[H]e thus acquired an enlarged view of men and things, great facility of composition, and valuable habits of business, which proved of the highest advantage in his subsequent career at Serampore.'

12 Marshman (1828: 94-5) notes, 'As to Mr Randall, we constantly employed and paid him as our paper-maker... Indeed we have for these seven years past allowed his widow in England £50 annually, in consequence of the agreement we made with him.' He also received the expense of his passage from the Society.

13 The secretary to the government of India wrote to Campbell, 'I have been directed by the Governor General in Council...to express to you His Lordship's satisfaction, with the results of your interesting experiment in paper making.' He continued, 'The Governor General in Council desires, that you will continue your present course of experimental paper making till further notice, keeping in pay the manufacturers necessary for that purpose' ('Letter from T. H. Maddock to Campbell', in Anon. 1842: 216).

14 A contemporary document thus notes that 'the property [of the Imperial Mill] was acquired by the Titaghur Company... [W]ith the view of controlling production and of restricting competition, the Titaghur directors purchased the undertaking [the Bally Mills] and removed its two manufacturing machines to Titaghur and Kankinara' ('The City of Calcutta', in Playne 1917: 136).

15 This company was an associate of a multinational firm, the Borneo Company Ltd (Cox and Metcalfe 1998).

16 Regarding the importance of railway freight for the development of paper mills in India, Tiwari (1937: 283) observes, 'Raw materials like rags and grass are collected from distant centres with the result that the cost of transport forms a substantial part of the total cost. Again, the paper mills being largely localised in Bengal, railroad transport plays a prominent part in marketing the finished product. In view of these peculiar features of the industry, it would be no exaggeration to say that railway freight charges regulate the competitive capacity of the mills.'

17 Gadgil (1933: 45) thus notes: 'The glass and paper industries were also succumbing under the pressure of imported goods.'

18 'The large increase in the past year was chiefly caused by the purchase of paper manufactured at the Bally Mills, to the value of Rs. 55,003' (GOB 1880a: 3).

19 Traill (1891: 330) thus notes, 'The Local Mills manufacture Brown, Half Bleach or "Badami," White and Colored Printings, Blottings, & c. On these the mills find work enough and to spare, large orders being given by Government alone. In the first of these (Browns) they have driven Europe-made papers entirely out of the market; their Coloreds and Blottings meet with a limited demand; while their Printings are used freely, and are of fair quality.'

20 In 1890–1 the Stationery Department's report (GOB 1892: 6) emphasised, 'The recent establishment of the Bengal Paper Mills at Raneegunge by Messrs Balmer,

Lawrie and Company has increased the competition for Government patronage, and consequently a considerable reduction in the rates of all the Indian Paper Mills for the current year's supplies, has been effected.'

Bibliography

Adam, W. (1868) 'First Report on the State of Education in Bengal, 1835'. In Long, J. (ed.) *Vernacular Education in Bengal and Behar, Submitted to the Government in 1835, 1836 and 1838: With a Brief View of Its Past and Present Condition*, 214–17. Calcutta: Home Secretariat Press.

Al-Gharnati, A. H. (1979 [c. 1135]) *Tuhfat al-Albab wa Nukhbat al-I'jab*, Paris edn. Beirut: Dar al-Jabal.

Anon. (1842) 'Correspondence Relative to the Manufacture of Nipal Paper at Darjeeling, with Details as to Its Costs, Relative Value, Mode of Bleaching, and Rendering Water Proof', *Monthly Journal of the Agricultural and Horticultural Society of India* 1 (1), 210–21.

Bag, A. K. (1982) 'Technology in India in the Eighteenth-Nineteenth Century', *Indian Journal of History of Science* 17 (1), 82–90.

Bagchi, A. K. (1972) *Private Investment in India, 1920-1939*. Cambridge: Cambridge University Press.

Banerjee, C. N. (1872) *An Account of Howrah: Past and Present*. Calcutta (no pub.).

Bengal Paper Mill (1940) *Golden Jubilee Brochure: 1889-1939*. Calcutta: Bengal Paper Mill.

Burns, R. I. (1981) 'The Paper Revolution in Europe: Crusader Valencia's Paper Industry: A Technological and Behavioral Breakthrough', *Pacific Historical Review* 50 (1), 1–30.

Carey, W. (1836) 'On the Manufacture of Paper', *Transactions of the Agricultural and Horticultural Society of India* 2 (32), 87–8.

Carter, T. G. (2000) *The Journal and Selected Letters of William Carey*. Macon, GA: Smyth & Helwys Publishing.

Chatterjee, S. K. (1984) *William Carey and Serampore*. Serampore: Kartik Dutta Banik.

Coleman, D. C. (1958) *The British Paper Industry, 1495-1860*. Oxford: Clarendon Press.

Cox, H., and Metcalfe, S. (1998) 'The Borneo Company Limited: Origins of a Nineteenth Century Networked Multinational', *Asia Pacific Business Review* 4 (4), 53–69.

Cumming, J. G. (1908) *Review of the Industrial Position and Prospects in Bengal in 1908 with Special Reference to the Industrial Survey of 1890*. Calcutta: Bengal Secretariat Book Depot.

Dabrowski, J. (2006) 'Remarks on the Invention of True Paper by Cai Lun'. In *IPH Congress Book 16: Papers of the 28th International Congress of Paper Historians: Capellades – Montserrat, Barcelona, 5–8 October 2006*, 5–16. Birkeroed, Denmark: IPH.

Foley, B. (1906) *Report on Labour in Bengal*. Calcutta: Bengal Secretariat Book Depot.

Gadgil, D. R. (1933) *The Industrial Evolution in India in Recent Times*, 3rd edn. Oxford: Oxford University Press.

Ghori, S. A. K., and Rahman, A. (1966) 'Paper Technology in Medieval India', *Indian Journal of History of Science* 1 (2), 133–49.

Ghosh, A. (1993) 'Golak Chandra: India's Pioneer Innovator Technician', *Indian Journal of History of Science* 28 (2), 167–78.

Ghosh, A, (1997) 'Guru Jones: A Private Engineer in the Colonial Trap', *Indian Journal of History of Science* 32 (2), 139–59.

Gode, P. K. (1969) *Studies in Indian Cultural History*, vol. III. Poona: Prof. P. K. Gode Collected Works Publication Committee.

Gosavi, P. G. (1983) 'Did India Invent Paper?' *IPH Information* 17 (1), 7–12.

Gosavi, P. G. (1987) 'Quality of Ancient Indian Paper', *IPH Information* 21 (3), 103–11.

Gosavi, P. G. (2011) 'Paper Originated in India, Not in China', *IPH Paper History* 15 (2), 21.

Government of Bengal (GOB) (1869) *Annual Report on the Administration of Bengal, 1867–8*. National Library Archive, Calcutta.

Government of Bengal (GOB) (1870) *Annual Report on the Administration of Bengal, 1868–9*. National Library Archive, Calcutta.

Government of Bengal (GOB) (1871) *Annual Report on the Administration of Bengal, 1869–70*. National Library Archive, Calcutta.

Government of Bengal (GOB) (1872a) *Report on the Administration of the Stationery Department, 1870–1*. National Library Archive, Calcutta.

Government of Bengal (GOB) (1872b) *Annual Report on the Administration of Bengal, 1870–1*. National Library Archive, Calcutta.

Government of Bengal (GOB) (1873) *Report on the Administration of the Stationery Department, 1871–2*. National Library Archive, Calcutta.

Government of Bengal (GOB) (1878a) *Report on the Administration of the Stationery Department, 1876–7*. National Library Archive, Calcutta.

Government of Bengal (GOB) (1878b) *Annual Report on the Administration of Bengal, 1876–7*. National Library Archive, Calcutta.

Government of Bengal (GOB) (1879) *Report on the Administration of Stationery Department, 1877–8*. National Library Archive, Calcutta.

Government of Bengal (GOB) (1880a) *Report on the Administration of Stationery Department, 1878–9*. National Library Archive, Calcutta.

Government of Bengal (GOB) (1880b) *Annual Report on the Administration of Bengal, 1878–9*. National Library Archive, Calcutta.

Government of Bengal (GOB) (1882) *Report on the Administration of Stationery Department, 1880–1*. National Library Archive, Calcutta.

Government of Bengal (GOB) (1883) *Report on the Administration of Stationery Department, 1881–2*. National Library Archive, Calcutta.

Government of Bengal (GOB) (1884) *Report on the Administration of Stationery Department, 1882–3*. National Library Archive, Calcutta.

Government of Bengal (GOB) (1885) *Report on the Administration of Stationery Department, 1883–4*. National Library Archive, Calcutta.

Government of Bengal (GOB) (1886a) *Report on the Administration of Stationery Department, 1884–5*. National Library Archive, Calcutta.

Government of Bengal (GOB) (1886b) *Annual Report on the Administration of Bengal, 1884–5*. National Library Archive, Calcutta.

Government of Bengal (GOB) (1887) *Report on the Administration of Stationery Department, 1885–6*. National Library Archive, Calcutta.

Government of Bengal (GOB) (1888a) *Annual Report on the Administration of Bengal, 1886–7*. National Library Archive, Calcutta.

Government of Bengal (GOB) (1888b) *Report on the Administration of Stationery Department, 1886–7*. National Library Archive, Calcutta.

Government of Bengal (GOB) (1889) *Report on the Administration of Stationery Department, 1887–8*. National Library Archive, Calcutta.

Government of Bengal (GOB) (1890a) *Annual Report on the Administration of Bengal, 1888–9.* National Library Archive, Calcutta.

Government of Bengal (GOB) (1890b) *Report on the Administration of Stationery Department, 1888–9.* National Library Archive, Calcutta.

Government of Bengal (GOB) (1891a) *Annual Report on the Administration of Bengal, 1889–90.* National Library Archive, Calcutta.

Government of Bengal (GOB) (1891b) *Report on the Administration of Stationery Department, 1889–90.* National Library Archive, Calcutta.

Government of Bengal (GOB) (1892) *Report on the Administration of Stationery Department, 1890–1.* National Library Archive, Calcutta.

Government of Bengal (GOB) (1893) *Report on the Administration of Stationery Department, 1891–2.* National Library Archive, Calcutta.

Government of Bengal (GOB) (1894a) *Report on the Administration of Stationery Department, 1892–3.* National Library Archive, Calcutta.

Government of Bengal (GOB) (1894b) *Annual Report on the Administration of Bengal, 1892–3.* National Library Archive, Calcutta.

Government of Bengal (GOB) (1895a) *Report on the Administration of Stationery Department, 1893–4.* National Library Archive, Calcutta.

Government of Bengal (GOB) (1895b) *Annual Report on the Administration of Bengal, 1893–4.* National Library Archive, Calcutta.

Government of Bengal (GOB) (1896) *Report on the Administration of Stationery Department, 1894–5.* National Library Archive, Calcutta.

Government of Bengal (GOB) (1897) *Report on the Administration of Stationery Department, 1895–6.* National Library Archive, Calcutta.

Government of Bengal (GOB) (1898) *Report on the Administration of Stationery Department, 1896–7.* National Library Archive, Calcutta.

Government of Bengal (GOB) (1899) *Report on the Administration of Stationery Department, 1897–8.* National Library Archive, Calcutta.

Government of Bengal (GOB) (1900) *Annual Report on the Administration of Bengal, 1898–9.* National Library Archive, Calcutta.

Government of Bengal (GOB) (1901) *Annual Report on the Administration of Bengal, 1899–1900.* National Library Archive, Calcutta.

Government of Bengal (GOB) (1902) *Annual Report on the Administration of Bengal, 1900–01.* National Library Archive, Calcutta.

Government of India (GOI) (1860) *Acts Passed by the Legislative Council of India in the Year 1859.* Calcutta: Superintendent Government Printing.

Government of India (GOI) (1877) *Review of the Trade of British India with Foreign Countries, 1871/2–1875/6.* National Library Archive, Calcutta.

Government of India (GOI) (1883) *Review of the Trade of British India with Foreign Countries, 1881–2.* National Library Archive, Calcutta.

Government of India (GOI) (1895) *Financial and Commercial Statistics for British India, 1893–4.* National Library Archive, Calcutta.

Government of India (GOI) (1896) *Financial and Commercial Statistics for British India, 1894–5.* National Library Archive, Calcutta.

Government of India (GOI) (1897) *Financial and Commercial Statistics for British India, 1895–6.* National Library Archive, Calcutta.

Government of India (GOI) (1898) *Financial and Commercial Statistics for British India, 1896–7.* National Library Archive, Calcutta.

Government of India (GOI) (1899) *Financial and Commercial Statistics for British India, 1897–8*. National Library Archive, Calcutta.

Government of India (GOI) (1900) *Financial and Commercial Statistics for British India, 1898–9*. National Library Archive, Calcutta.

Government of India (GOI) (1901) *Financial and Commercial Statistics for British India, 1899–1900*. National Library Archive, Calcutta.

Government of India (GOI) (1902) *Letter from F.N. Baker, Finance and Commerce Department, Government of India, Commerce Department – Accounts & Finance, July 1902 – B*. West Bengal State Archives, Calcutta.

Government of India (GOI) (1903a) *Census of India, 1901*, vol. VI. Calcutta: Bengal Secretariat Book Depot.

Government of India (GOI) (1903b) *Financial and Commercial Statistics for British India, 1901–02*. National Library Archive, Calcutta.

Government of India (GOI) (1904) *Financial and Commercial Statistics for British India, 1902–03*. National Library Archive, Calcutta.

Government of India (GOI) (1920) *Report of the Stores Purchase Committee*. Simla: Government Central Press.

Gupta, G. N. (1908) *Survey of the Industries and Resources of Eastern Bengal and Assam*. Calcutta: Bengal Secretariat Book Depot.

Hannawi, A. A. (2012) 'The Role of the Arabs in the Introduction of Paper into Europe', *MELA Notes* 85, 14–19.

Hodgson, B. H. (1832) 'On the Native Method of Making the Paper, Denominated in Hindustan, Nipalese', *Journal of the Asiatic Society of Bengal* 1 (1), 8–11.

Hunter, D. (1939) *Papermaking by Hand in India*. New York: Pynson Printers.

Jervis, W. W., and Jones, S. J. (1930) 'The Paper-Making Industry in Somerset', *Geography* 15 (8), 625–9.

Kerr, H. C. (1874) *Report on the Cultivation of, and Trade in, Jute in Bengal and on Indian Fibres Available for the Manufacture of Paper*. Calcutta: Bengal Secretariat Book Depot.

Khan, M. S. (1961) 'William Carey and Serampore Books', *Libri* 2 (3), 197–280.

Liotard, L. (1880) *Memorandum on Materials in India Suitable for the Manufacture of Paper*. Calcutta: Home, Revenue and Agricultural Press.

Lokanathan, P. S. (1935) *Industrial Organisation in India*. London: G. Allen & Unwin.

Losty, J. P. (1983) 'Was India Really the Inventing Country of Paper?' *IPH Information* 17 (3), 108–10.

MacFarlane, N. (1987) *Handmade Paper of India*. Winchester, UK: Alembic Press.

MacFarlane, N. (1993) *A Paper Journey: Travels among the Village Papermakers of India and Nepal*. New Castle, DE: Oak Knoll Books.

Mahmood, S. (1895) *A History of English Education in India*. Calcutta: M. A. O. College (Aligarh).

Marshall, P. J. (1988) *Bengal: The British Bridgehead: Eastern India 1740–1828*. Cambridge: Cambridge University Press.

Marshman, J. C. (1828) *Statement Relative to Serampore*. London: Allen.

Marshman, J. C. (1845) 'Notes on the Right Bank of the Hooghly', *Calcutta Review* 4 (8), 476–520.

Marshman, J. C. (1859) *The Life and Times of Carey, Marshman, and Ward: Embracing the History of the Serampore Mission*, 2 vols. London: Longman, Brown, Green, Longman, & Roberts.

Martin, M. (1838) *The History, Antiquities, Topography, and Statistics of Eastern India*, 3 vols. London: W. H. Allen.
Mookerji, D. N. (1908) *Paper and Paper-Mache in Bengal*. Calcutta: Bengal Secretariat Book Depot.
Parliamentary Papers (P.P.) (1840) *Acts of the Government of India from 1834 to 1938 Inclusive*. London: Hansard.
Parliamentary Papers (P.P.) (1867) *Statistical Abstract Relating to British India, from 1840 to 1865*. London: HMSO.
Parliamentary Papers (P.P.) (1868) *Statistical Abstract Relating to British India, from 1857 to 1866*. London: HMSO.
Parliamentary Papers (P.P.) (1872) *Statistical Abstract Relating to British India, from 1862 to 1871*. London: HMSO.
Parliamentary Papers (P.P.) (1875) *Statistical Abstract Relating to British India, from 1865 to 1874*. London: HMSO.
Parliamentary Papers (P.P.) (1882a) *Statement Exhibiting the Moral and Material Progress and Condition in India during the Year 1880–1*. London: Hansard.
Parliamentary Papers (P.P.) (1882b) *Statistical Abstract Relating to British India, from 1871/2 to 1880/1*. London: HMSO.
Parliamentary Papers (P.P.) (1886) *Report of the Royal Commission on the Depression of Trade and Industry*, vol. 23. London: Hansard.
Parliamentary Papers (P.P.) (1893) *Statistical Abstract Relating to British India, from 1882/3 to 1891/2*. London: HMSO.
Parliamentary Papers (P.P.) (1896) *Statistical Abstract Relating to British India, from 1885/6 to 1894/5*. London: HMSO.
Parliamentary Papers (P.P.) (1900) *Statistical Abstract Relating to British India, from 1889/90 to 1898/9*. London: HMSO.
Parliamentary Papers (P.P.) (1907) *Statistical Abstract Relating to British India, from 1896/7 to 1905/06*. London: HMSO.
Parliamentary Papers (P.P.) (1908) *Statistical Abstract Relating to British India, from 1897/8 to 1906/07*. London: HMSO.
Parliamentary Papers (P.P.) (1919) *Statistical Abstract Relating to British India, from 1907/08 to 1916/17*. London: HMSO.
Parliamentary Papers (P.P.) (1920) *Statistical Abstract Relating to British India, from 1908/09 to 1917/18*. London: HMSO.
Playne, S. (ed.) (1917) *Bengal and Assam, Behar and Orissa: Their History, People, Commerce, and Industrial Resources*. London: Foreign and Colonial Compiling and Publishing.
Potts, E. D. (n.d.) *The Serampore Press and Its Printer*. William Ward, typed MS.
Querol-Kroenberg, F. (1974) 'The Arrival of Paper-Making in Europe'. In Sommerfeldt, J. R., Syndergaard, L., and Rozanne, E. (eds.) *Studies in Medieval Culture*, vol. IV, 233–7. Kalamazoo, MI: Western Michigan University.
Raitt, W. (1930) 'The Childhood of Papermaking, Kashmir, India', *Papermaker and British Paper Trade Journal*, February, 1.
Ramaseshan, S. (1989) 'The History of Paper in India up to 1948', *Indian Journal of History of Science* 24 (2), 103–21.
Ray, I. (2015) 'Dynamics of Bengal Coal Mining in the Nineteenth Century: Dissemination of Mineralogical Knowledge and Railway Networking', *Indian Economic and Social History Review* 52 (4), 463–99.
Roy, T. (2011) *The Economic History of India 1857–1947*, 3rd edn. New Delhi: Oxford University Press.

Sachau, E. C. (1910) *Alberuni's India: An Account of the Religion, Philosophy, Literature, Geography, Chronology, Astronomy, Customs, Laws and Astrology of India about AD 1030*, vol. I [containing the English version of Al-Beruni's *Kitab-ul-Hind*]. London: Kegan Paul, Trench, Trübner.
Sen, R. (1836) 'On the Manufacture of Paper Used by the Natives', *Transactions of the Agricultural and Horticultural Society of India* 2 (32), 88–93.
Sen, S. K. (1964) *Studies in Industrial Policy and Development of India (1858-1914)*. Calcutta: Progressive Publishers.
Shaw, G. (1981) *Printing in Calcutta to 1800*. London: Bibliographical Society.
Smith, G. (1885) *The Life of William Carey, D.D.: Shoemaker and Missionary*. London: John Murray.
Swan, J. A. L. (1915) *Report on the Industrial Development of Bengal*. Calcutta: Bengal Secretariat Press.
Tavernier, J. P. (1889 [1648]) *Travels in India* (trans. V. Ball), vol. I. London: Macmillan.
Tiwari, C. P. (1921) *The Indian Railways: The Historical, Economical and Administrative Aspects*. Ajmer: (no pub.).
Tiwari, R. D. (1937) *Railway Rates in Relation to Trade and Industry in India*. Calcutta: Longmans, Green.
Traill, D. M. (1891) 'Paper and Paper Making', *Indian Forester* 17 (8), 322–30.
Watt, G. (1908) *The Commercial Products of India*. London: J. Murray.

Appendix 6.1 Imports of paper (including stationery) into India (in £), 1849–1914

Year	*Imports*	*Year*	*Imports*
1849	112,761	1882	739,930
1850	132,370	1883	625,431
1851	183,751	1884	696,863
1852	148,734	1885	663,401
1853	164,008	1886	676,612
1854	184,570	1887	819,345
1855	210,181	1888	848,510
1856	221,500	1889	854,639
1857	227,701	1890	877,711
1858	200,093	1891	937,500
1859	241,596	1892	928,704
1860	269,804	1893	1,010,614
1861	299,508	1894	869,405
1862	274,988	1895	986,612
1863	364,612	1896	413,899
1864	410,782	1897	353,382
1865	352,318	1898	396,308
1866	375,381	1899	426,276
1867	288,140	1900	454,456
1868	486,978	1901	521,658
1869	447,851	1902	524,725
1870	414,851	1903	528,508
1871	422,145	1904	642,203
1872	413,959	1905	686,509
1873	428,003	1906	736,754
1874	475,027	1907	882,522
1875	472,963	1908	886,753
1876	448,618	1909	927,718
1877	463,354	1910	1,020,535
1878	567,991	1911	1,089,003
1879	511,728	1912	1,246,392
1880	523,739	1913	1,387,495
1881	725,860	1914	1,184,632

Sources: 1849–56: P.P. (1867: 46); 1857–66: P.P. (1868: 26–7); 1867–71: P.P. (1872: 18–19); 1872: P.P. (1875: 40–1); 1873–82: P.P. (1882b: 92–3); 1883–91: P.P. (1893: 208–9); 1892–94: P.P. (1896: 208–9); 1895: P.P. (1900: 205); 1896–1905: P.P. (1907: 148–9); 1906: P.P. (1908: 149); 1907: P.P. (1919: 156); 1908–14: P.P. (1920: 156–7).

7 Tea plantations

British capital, tribal labour and wastelands in the Himalayas

In historiography, the plantation economy is largely discussed in the context of dualism. Jones defines it as an organisation in which a handful of managers direct a large number of workers 'whose principal skill is to follow orders' (Jones 1968: 156). According to Beckford (1969: 322–3), it is an activity in which labour is drawn from the local reservoir to work under foreign capital and enterprise, and also to cater exclusively to the export market. Kooiman (1992: 53), therefore, emphasises, 'Handbooks on Asian history do not stop reminding us that plantations are not local plants, but foreign implantations.' The undertone in these writings is that the plantation economy should be studied from the colonial viewpoint so that various facets of their dual economies can be understood. That is perhaps why the plantation literature abounds with discussions on migratory labour – such as de Haan (1995), Evans (1995), Siddique (1995), Shlomowitz and Brennan (1990), Meyer (1990), Palmer (1986) and Baker (1961) – and entrepreneurship (for example, Palmer 1985a; Palmer 1985b; Mukherjee 1978; Mukherjee 1976; Stewart 1960; and Tharian 1984). Only a few studies deal with other aspects – such as Gupta (2001) and Gilboy (1934) on marketing. If plantations are treated as one of several other economic activities, however, it appears that they benefited colonising and colonised countries alike, and thus assume importance in the context of global economic history. Plantation crops – such as tea, coffee, indigo and sugar – could not be avoided in the Western culture in view of societal preferences for them. But they were highly land-intensive, which, *à la* Pomeranz (2000), western Europe avoided in order to escape the Malthusian-cum-ecological crisis (Ray 2015). Plantations in erstwhile colonies enabled European nations to obtain these crops without sacrificing their land resources. An added advantage was its role as a profitable vent for European surplus capital, as underlined by Wakefield (1849) (see also Robbins 1958). His line of argument – the so-called 'Wakefield system' – dominated contemporary policy making.[1] This tone of British interest is noticed in Siddique too. He writes, 'It was firmly held that in India there were ample opportunities for profitable investment in both fertile and uncultivated land to produce food and raw materials for the mother country [Britain]' (Siddique 1995: 89). The colony's interests, however, lay in the vast employment opportunities that plantations created for unskilled jobs.

If these arguments are true, we would expect the imperial government to actively promote plantations in colonies. Indeed, one of the primary thrusts in this chapter is to discuss how the colonial government in India sought to inculcate tea culture in this colony by way of wasteland distribution, the development of transport infrastructure, fiscal incentives, and so on. I also deliberate on the deployment of British capital and enterprise, as well as the employment of the local workforce, which subserved the British and Indian interests, respectively. The main focus of this study is on northern Bengal, where tea plantations grew up in three distinct regions – Darjeeling, the Dooars and the Terai – in the second half of the nineteenth century. The literature concentrates largely on the country-level experiences in general (for example, Griffiths 1967; Goradia and Sircar 2010; and Misra 1987), and on Assam (Sharma 2006; Roy 2011) in particular. North Bengal is grossly ignored.

There are five sections in what follows. Section I discusses the genesis of tea plantation in this belt, and also the trajectory of its growth between 1855 and 1914. Technological aspects are also discussed here in condensed form. Section II examines the issues relating to capital and labour. Section III analyses the behaviour of the global market that propelled its growth. In view of the inadequate data on the global distribution of tea from this region, I consider here Indian tea as a whole. There are two novelties in this section. First, it elaborates India's comparative advantages (both in terms of cost and quality) vis-à-vis its main rival, Chinese tea, which is nowhere discussed in the literature. Second, it critically examines the country-wise market diversification of Indian tea from 1871 to 1914. Section IV documents various promotional measures on the part of the colonial government, especially the grant of wastelands, the construction of road infrastructure, the development of railways and fiscal incentives. Section V concludes.

I

The genesis of tea plantations in India dates back to 1788, when Sir Joseph Banks noticed tea plants growing wild in the Cooch Behar (in present-day north Bengal) and Rangpore districts of Bengal. Notwithstanding his recommendation for patronising its cultivation,[2] there was no immediate interest, possibly because of the easy 'exchange and barter' of Chinese tea vis-à-vis the risk and labour involved in opening up plantations in Bengal (Chamney 1933: 31). In 1821, however, David Scott, Resident Agent to the Governor General, sent specimen tea plants to Calcutta, but, this time, the government botanist mistook them for the foliage of some other plant. Further analysis of a similar specimen, submitted by his successor, Francis Jenkins, removed the confusion, and the government botanist 'confirmed the first discovery of tea in India, by any European, as that made by Sir Joseph Banks in 1788' (ibid.). But opinions are divided as to the original habitat of tea. The majority believe its home to be China, whence it spread to Japan, Tonquin, Cochin China and Burma, and also to Assam and Cachar in India through the caravan route (Crawfurd 1869:199–200; Campbell 1869: 207–8; Weatherstone 1992: 2; Sarkar 1972: 2). But authors such as Baildon believe India to be its habitat.[3] A more scientific opinion is available in Wight (1959), who notices that this plant grows widely around the intersection of latitude 29° north and longitude 98° east, where several great south-east Asian rivers – the Yangtze Kiang, Mekong, Irrawaddy, Salween and Lohit – flow. Along these river courses tea plants grew in two axes: one from the north-east to the south-west, and the other from the north to the south. A 180° arc is formed in the south of the former axis, passing through south-east China, Indochina, north Burma and the Garo and Mizo Hills, ending up in the Sikkimese Himalayas. In these places, different races of tea were freely hybridised. Notwithstanding such differences in opinion, however, unanimity prevails in that tea first became a popular beverage in China (for tea drinking in China, see Okakura 1906: 25–44; and Walsh 1892: 9–28). As far back as in the ninth century, the Chinese government collected tax from it (along with salt), suggesting its great popularity among the people (Crawfurd 1869: 201).

In Bengal, tea plantation was initiated under state patronage. Its maiden success was evident in an experimental garden, set up in 1841 at Darjeeling town, under the district superintendent, Archibald Campbell. Its seeds came from another sub-Himalayan garden, located at Kumaon, and belonged to the Chinese genre. From Campbell's experiment the investors understood that Darjeeling was an ideal site for tea plantation. The plantation 'was quite successful as to its growth; and the quality was approved by an Assam planter, who visited the place in 1846' (P.P. 1862: 191). But investors' confusion loomed large on two grounds, delaying its commercial exploration for a decade (1846–55). First, the elevation of Darjeeling (around 7,000 feet above sea level) seemed unfavourable for any large-scale plantation. In the winter frosts killed the seedlings, and in the summer leaves would emerge gradually, slowing production. In fact, tea plants cannot survive at 7,500 feet above sea level. Second, transportation was a great challenge in contemporary Darjeeling. Modern means of transport were absent in the middle of the nineteenth century. Only porters and, to an extent, pack animals such as yaks (on contemporary transportations in hills, see Ray and Sarkar 2005: 9–10) could be employed for the purpose, involving uncertainty in the labour supply, not to mention exorbitant expenses.

In 1856, however, Captain Samler launched a commercial project, the Kursiong & Darjeeling Tea & Coffee Co. Ltd, with two plantations, one each at Kurseong and Darjeeling. It was followed by as many as 20 new plantations in quick successions, and by 1860 there were 21,865 acres of land in the possession of tea gardens, out of which 2,639 acres were planted. They reportedly turned out 62,240 lbs of leaves, employing 2,624 workers (P.P. 1862: 191). This, indeed, heralded the tea age in Bengal. According to a report covering 1859–60, 'Tea cultivation among the hills of Darjeeling is progressing in a considerable scale. Several hundreds of acres of land are now under cultivation' (P.P. 1861: 61). In the next quinquennium 11 more gardens were opened up, extending the plant area 3.72 times to 9,829 acres, and production 5.39 times to 335,481 lbs.

The following three years, 1866 to 1869, witnessed financial distress for the Indian tea industry as a whole. Among the various factors that contributed to the crisis, the crux was wild speculation, which contemporary literature describes as 'tea fever'. Taking advantage of the speculative psyche, a group of people set up gardens purely for quick sales, and many British investors bought their stocks without verifying any of the details. A contemporary author thus notes, 'Often in those days was a small garden made of 30 or 40 acres, and sold to a Company as 150 or 200 acres! I am not joking. It was done over and over again.' He continues, 'The price paid, moreover, was quite out of proportion to even the supposed area. Two or three lakhs of rupees (£20,000 or £30,000) have been often paid for such gardens, when not more than two years old, and 40 per cent, of the existing area, vacancies. The original cultivators "Retired", and the Company carried on' (Money 1878:7). Similar reports are available in district documents as well. 'The depression of the industry consequent on the collapse of so many concerns in 1866 was of course intensified by the ignorance of the general body of proprietors of tea shares, who...showed as much folly in their hurry to get out of tea as they had a few years before in their eagerness to undertake the speculation' ('Note', by J. W. Edger, in GOI 1873: ix). Planters were also inexperienced in many cases, devoid of any botanical knowledge on tea. The *Englishman's Overland Mail* of 1860 thus tells us that the industry recruited 'the boy fresh from school, who knew naught of agriculture, less, if possible, of horticulture' (quoted in Griffiths 1967: 105–6). Similarly, Money (1878: 2) points out that the managers were 'a strange medley of retired or cashiered Army and Navy officers, medical men, engineers, veterinary surgeons, steamer captains, chemists, shop-keepers of all kinds, used-up policemen, clerks, and goodness knows what besides!'. From the commercial viewpoint, however, the additional mistake was that, even in the presence of 60 to 70 per cent vacancies, the gardens were further extended under the 'tea fever' (ibid.: 5–6), so that overhead expenses soared.

Indeed, the financial distress caused industrial recession in certain regions, as in Gowalpara (in Assam) (GOB 1870: 192) and Sylhet (now in Bangladesh) (GOB 1869: 206). But there is evidence to confirm that the Darjeeling tea industry was not hard hit. The number of hill gardens, and also their acreage, fell in those years – for example, from 32 in 1865–6 to 24 in 1866–7, and from 9,829 acres to 7,986 acres, respectively (GOB 1868: 146). But 'this apparent retrogression', according to a source, 'was owing on the one hand to there having being little or no extension during the year, and on the other to cultivated lands of the poorer sort having been purposely allowed to relapse into jungle' (ibid.). Production did not show any recessionary symptoms, however; rather, it rose by 35,693 lbs in 1866–7. In the following year the area under cultivation was also extended, by 303 acres. What is more, Appendix 7.1 shows that, from 32 in 1865, the number of gardens increased to 39 in 1866 (mainly due to new gardens in the Terai), 40 in 1867, and further to 44 in 1868; and the level of output rose from 335,481 lbs in 1865 to 371,174 lbs in 1866 and further to 441,189 lbs in 1867. The gardens in the Terai, which started being developed from 1862, were also least affected. Perhaps only the projects in the pipeline suffered: 'In regard to the factories which have been closed, it is reported that no garden worth keeping up has been abandoned. The gardens which have been deserted are chiefly new ones, which were formed or were forming for the purposes of speculation, and the closing of these may be considered rather as an advantage than otherwise to the interests of *bona fide* tea planting' (GOB 1869: 205). Save for this period, however, the industry never met with serious setbacks right through to 1914.

Appendix 7.1 provides time series of land under cultivation, production, the number of gardens and employment. Data are not readily available for production in 1873 and 1874, and for acreage in 1883 and 1884. The former are estimated on the basis of the average productivity of land in 1872 and 1875 (namely 206.49 lbs per acre), and the latter by that in 1882 and 1885 (namely 213.55 lbs per acre). No attempt is made to estimate the missing figures for the number of gardens and employment. The widely varying size of gardens is likely to frustrate any estimation for the former. The latter estimation involves complexities, however, in that labour was employed not only for production but for the clearance of jungles as well, so that reliability suffers for any assumed relationship between employment and production, or between employment and land under cultivation. Appendix 7.1 is summarised in Table 7.1 (except for employment), showing annual average figures for five yearly intervals. For the intervals with missing figures on the number of gardens, the average is calculated based on available figures in respective intervals. Time series of production and acreage are plotted in Figure 7.1.

Steady-state growth is discernible in Figure 7.1 for both acreage and output. The line plotted for the former inclines more steeply than the latter, however (as implied by the widening gap between them), indicating high expectations for the industry's growth potentialities, whereby the extension of acreage went ahead of the production growth. Table 7.1 displays that, from 27 in 1860–4, the number of gardens increased to 62 in 1870–4 and 156 in 1875–9. A steeper rise in the latter quinquennium was primarily due to new plantations in the Dooars (belonging to the district of Jalpaiguri) after 1874. Production and acreage also reflected similar trends. During 1870–4 and 1875–9 the former rose from 2.85 million lbs to 5.43 million lbs, and the latter from 14,331 acres to 29,524 acres. For 1870–4 and 1910–14 as a whole the annual growth rate works out at 11.05 per cent for the number of gardens, 23.95 per cent for acreage and 59.78 per cent for production. Finally, in 1915, there were 300 tea gardens in Bengal over 161,300 acres of land, where 89.53 million lbs of tea were produced.

Tea plantations in Bengal were based on state-of-the-art technology, which generated comparative advantages in their favour. In contrast to the cottage organisation in China (for tea manufacturing in different countries, see Ibbetson 1912: 22–48), Bengal opted for the European model of large-scale plantations. Plantations were established on the slopes and valleys in hills, as also in the plains of the Terai and the Dooars, where sandy loam soils were available. Several streams flowing through these regions provided water for irrigation (for early plantations in Darjeeling, see Money 1878: 36–45). Unlike the practices in China, Bengal gardens were planted with, and also maintained using, scientific knowledge. Most of them had their own nurseries, so that healthy plants

Table 7.1 Tea statistics for Bengal (annual averages), 1860/4–1910/14

Year	*Gardens (number)*	*Area under cultivation (acres)*	*Production (lbs)*	*Exports from India*		*Imports into India*	
				Quantity (lbs)	*Value (Rs.)*	*Quantity (lbs)*	*Value (Rs.)*
1860–4	27	7,610	114,399	2,526,176	1,873,491	NA	1,379,168
1865–9	42	9,683 (5.44)	663,827	8,881,710	6,487,505	2,182,433	1,803,915
1870–4	62	14,331 (9.60)	2,852,684	18,625,148	15,654,056	1,745,718	1,825,050
1875–9	156	29,524 (21.20)	5,428,090	30,380,272	27,013,738	2,074,671	1,757,574
1880–4	211	40,310 (7.31)	8,426,913	55,904,642	37,455,026	3,012,079	2,335,934
1885–9	332	68,412 (13.94)	15,896,012	89,031,038	52,002,780	4,398,741	3,141,108
1890–4	365	95,619 (7.95)	24,771,091	120,243,378	64,444,182	6,231,957	4,418,422
1895–9	434	120,227 (5.15)	41,353,942	155,292,649	81,797,418	5,124,820	2,419,690
1900–4	398	135,121 (2.48)	46,393,258	194,549,576	81,478,078	3,881,974	1,357,348
1905–9	NA	139,392 (0.63)	59,073,573	231,786,711	74,026,613	3,704,191	1,285,024
1910–14	336	151,635 (1.76)	71,066,848	276,821,711	96,301,600	5,201,555	1,605,556

Notes: The terms in parentheses represent annual growth rates.

Sources: Appendices 7.1, 7.2 and 7.3.

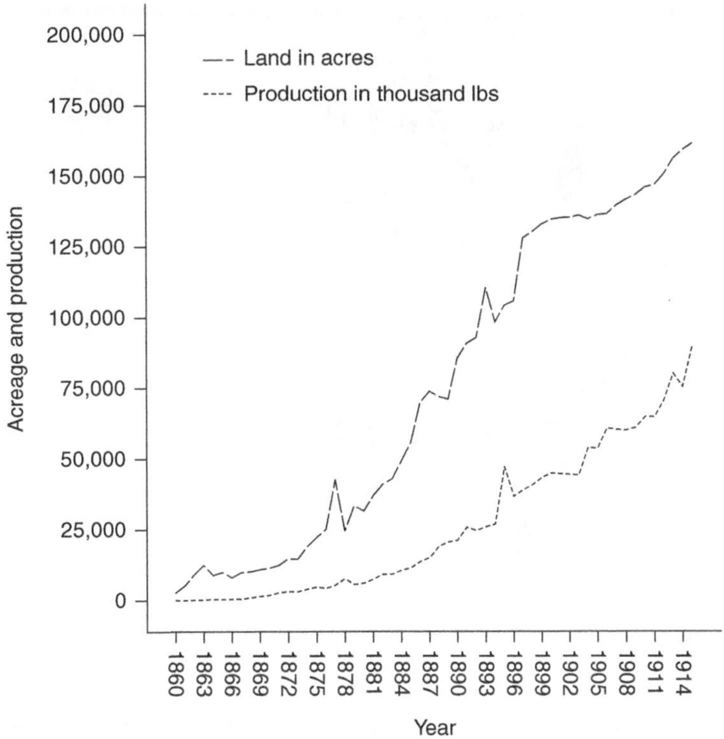

Figure 7.1 Growth of the tea industry in Bengal, 1860–1914

could be obtained. Scientific pruning was also followed at regular intervals to ensure their lateral growth. A nineteenth-century document estimates the cost of plantation for 100 acres of land at Rs. 5,000 in the first year, going up to Rs. 10,000 in the sixth (Money 1878: 82). For the purposes of processing, however, six young leaves were usually plucked (Figure 7.2). The youngest one was called 'flowery pekoe' ('a' in the figure), followed in order by 'orange pekoe' ('b'), 'pekoe' ('c'), 'souchong 1st' ('d'), 'souchong 2nd' ('e') and 'congou' ('f'). The latter four leaves were plucked, leaving their buds intact, at positions '1', '2', '3' and '4' in the figure, respectively, so that new shoots and leaves came out again. When only the former two were processed together, it showed pekoe tips, making white or pale yellow tea.

Tea manufacturing was highly mechanised in Bengal. It basically involved six processes: withering, rolling, oxidising, fermenting, drying and sorting (for nineteenth-century tea manufacturing in Darjeeling, see Anon. 1888: 59–65). Once reached at the factory, the leaves were immediately spread thinly on trays so that 20 to 50 per cent of the moisture was evaporated. This was done by means of powerful ventilating fans (the withering machine) generating dry,

Figure 7.2 A fully developed shoot of a tea plant
Source: Money (1878: 102).

warm air. The juice that the leaf cells contained was also concentrated in this process, enabling them to withstand the pressure of rolling. Rolling was done, again by machine, to burst the leaf cells so that the juice was coated on its surface. In this process, some of the organic acids, especially tannin, underwent partial oxidisation, whereby a part of the tannin became phlobaphene, glucose and gallic acids. They were again oxidised on a mechanical devise so that tannin was further converted into the aforesaid matters, minimising the astringent nature of the tea, and also generating an agreeable aroma thereby. Then followed the process of fermentation, in which the leaves were spread in layers under a cover of thin cloths, saturated with cold water. Finally they were dried, using machines for updraft drying, downdraft drying and automatic drying. Machinery was also used for sorting and packing (Wallis-Tayler 1900). Thanks to these mechanical devices, as we will shortly see, Indian teas dominated over the Chinese. They guaranteed better quality, and also minimised the cost of production. Thus, a report for 1889–90 confirms, 'In almost all the gardens machinery has been introduced for the purpose of manufacture, and as a consequence much time of labour and money are saved' (GOB 1891: 143).

II

Joint-stock companies largely dominated tea plantations in Bengal, though closely held companies and proprietorship firms were not altogether absent.

Table 7.2 Sterling tea companies in Darjeeling and Dooars, 1895–6

Company	*Year of establishment*	*Paid-up capital and debenture (£)*	*Land under cultivation (acres)*	*Dividend (%)*
Assam Dooars Tea Co.[1]	1894	100,000	1,206	-
British Darjeeling Tea Co.[2]	1895	75,000	1,469	-
British Dooars Tea Co.[3]	1894	33,500	1,200	-
Buxa-Dooars Tea Co.[4]	1895	50,000	789	-
Cachar and Dooars Tea Co.[5]	1895	160,000	1,351	8
Consolidated Tea and Land Co.[6]	1896	1,800,000	21,310	-
Darjeeling Co.[7]	1864	135,420	2,041	5½
Darjeeling Consolidated Tea Co.[8]	1896	120,000	2,159	-
Dooars Tea Co.[9]	1885	225,000	6,405	10 (and 2½% bonus)
Empire of India and Ceylon Co.[10]	1896	438,000	7,568	-
Lankapara Tea Co.[11]	1895	50,000	1,040	-
Lebong Tea Co.[12]	1862	65,656	1,546	10 (and 5% bonus)
Leesh Tea Co.[13]	1877	15,000	738	10
Meenglas Tea Co.[14]	1894	45,000	821	6
Singlo Tea Co.[15]	1895	210,000	3,573	8
Total		3,522,576	53,216	-

Source: Gow Wilson & Stanton Ltd (1897): 5 (for 1), 20–1 (for 2), 21–2 (for 3), 26–7 (for 4), 27–8 (for 5), 36–8 (for 6), 38–9 (for 7), 39–40 (for 8), 44–6 (for 9), 52–3 (for 10), 63–4 (for 11), 64–5 (for 12), 66 (for 13), 75 (for 14), 89–91 (for 15).

For 1895 a survey reveals that 15 sterling companies (i.e., those registered in London) worked in Bengal's tea plantation (Table 7.2). Time series of tea companies registered in Calcutta (the so-called rupee companies) are shown in Table 7.3.

A comparison between Tables 7.2 and 7.3 reveals that the level of investment in rupee companies stood at Rs. 11.90 million in 1895, as against Rs. 35.23 million (£3,522,576) for the sterling companies, so that the investment ratio between them comes to about 25:75. This corresponds to the ratio for India's overall tea plantations in 1930 (Buchanan 1934: 67). Even in the case of rupee companies, however, British capital dominated. Buchanan (1934: 59) thus observes, 'These [tea] companies were sometimes registered in India, in which case they might be either Indian or European owned, but more often they were British, registered in England.' Indian entrepreneurs evidently concentrated in the Dooars. But British capital dominated there as well. The Duars Committee (Monahan 1910: 1) estimates the aggregate nominal capital at £2,883,211 (i.e., Rs. 28,832,110) for sterling companies, and Rs. 1,706,250 for Indian-owned gardens, in 1904. The latter thus shared only 5.59 per cent.

Table 7.3 Rupee joint-stock companies operating in Darjeeling and Dooars, 1885–1905

Year	*Companies (number)*	*Area under plough (acres)*	*Paid-up capital (Rs.)*	*Return on capital (%)*	*Dividend (%)*	*Capital/ acre (Rs.)*
1885	37	19,500	9,595,911	8.82	7.28	492.10
1886	37	17,000	9,640,511	4.87	4.07	567.09
1887	40	18,000	9,829,242	4.73	4.62	546.07
1888	39	19,000**	9,482,438	7.00	6.34	499.07
1889	40	20,000	10,425,118	5.35	5.12*	521.26
1890	39	21,839	9,874,955	2.60	2.91*	452.17
1895	43	28,642	11,896,069	9.90	6.50	415.34
1896	42	31,656	11,834,400	8.68	7.58	373.84
1897	36	25,470	9,728,000	5.35	4.16	381.94
1898	35	26,225	9,036,000	6.99	6.09	344.56
1899	32	24,234	8,458,500	10.06	8.01	349.03
1900	36	27,055	9,428,975	2.58	3.03	348.51
1901	31	21,835	7,740,875	4.40	2.11	354.52
1902	30	21,768	7,836,475	4.39	1.94	360.00
1903	32	23,029	8,321,235	7.05	3.34	361.34
1904	34	24,798	8,854,825	6.14	5.12	357.08
1905	33	24,511	8,659,900	7.92	5.70	353.31

Notes: * Weighted average of dividends in Darjeeling and Dooars companies divided by their respective numbers of companies; ** estimated by the simple average of 1887 and 1889.

Source: ITA (1906): 204 (for 1885–90), 293 (for 1895–1905).

The rupee companies generally operated on smaller scales. Their average size varied between Rs. 243,000 and Rs. 281,000, as against Rs. 2,348,384 for sterling companies (Tables 7.2 and 7.3), suggesting that the latter was about ten times larger than the former, on average. In terms of acreage also, they belonged to the lower end – 450 to 757 acres per garden, as against 3,548 acres for a sterling company. Again, in respect of capital intensity, we find that, compared to the capital per acre of land of Rs. 661.94 for sterling companies in 1895, it stood at Rs. 567.09 for rupee companies in 1886, further falling to Rs. 452.17 in 1890, Rs. 415.34 in 1895 and Rs. 353.31 in 1905. Thanks to the economies of scale generated by larger sizes, as well as the higher capital intensity, the sterling companies could provide higher dividends: 9.28 per cent in 1895 (as calculated from data in Table 7.2), as against 6.50 per cent for rupee companies in that year (Table 7.3).

From the investment levels in rupee and sterling companies in 1895 – Rs. 415.34 per acre and Rs. 661.94 per acre, respectively – average investment comes out at Rs. 599.68 per acre, when weighted by their respective levels of investment. Using this as a norm, I estimate total investment in Bengal's tea plantation at Rs. 62.48 million in 1895 (for 104,197 acres; see Appendix 7.1). It rises to Rs. 81.03 million for 1900–4, Rs. 83.59 million for 1905–9 and Rs. 90.93 million for 1910–14. These estimates suffer from an upward bias, however, since lands in excess of what those joint-stock companies owned (namely, for 1895, 104,197 – 81,858 = 22,339 acres, or 21.44 per cent) were held by privately owned companies and proprietorship firms, for which investment per acre should be low.

Although Bengali entrepreneurs took interest in the pioneer tea company in India,[4] their presence was later noticed only at Jalpaiguri. Started with a proprietorship garden by Rahim Buksh in 1877, Bengali enterprises flourished rapidly in the following decades. Gathering information from contemporary sources, Mukherjee (1976: 506) reveals that the number of Indian-dominated joint-stock companies, which was only six in 1882–91, increased to 64 in 1911–20. He further informs us that, out of 163 Indian-owned tea companies in north-east India in 1933, as many as 88 belonged to Jalpaiguri-based Bengali entrepreneurs, who hailed mainly from the professional (legal) and service classes.

Major employment opportunities were created in plantations. Appendix 7.1 shows that the level of employment was just 2,624 in 1860, but rose to 8,000 in 1870 and 12,361 in 1872. Through a peak at 140,313 in 1893, it finally stabilised at around 130,000 in the mid-1910s. The series underwent violent fluctuations at times, especially in the 1890s. Good harvests in the recruiting areas reduced the supply of labour; and their number proliferated in the event of droughts and famines (Monahan 1910: 21, 24). On the demand side, recruitment was driven by the pace of jungle clearance in newly set up gardens, or else by the extension of cultivation in existing ones.

Appendix 7.1 displays the number of permanent and temporary workers in aggregate, not as separate entities. The latter figure was significant, however. In 1899, for example, their respective numbers were 21,049 and 17,127 in Darjeeling, and 43,928 and 26,655 in the Dooars (GOB 1901: 160), so that the ratios between them were in the order of 1:0.81 and 1:0.61. In 1900 these figures stood at 21,333 and 18,822 for Darjeeling and 47,258 and 29,391 for the Dooars (GOB 1902: 111), yielding ratios of 1:0.88 and 1:0.62, respectively. Temporary workers were preferred, however, on three grounds. First, they were instrumental in economising labour costs, as the gardens never provided them with accommodation, medical facilities or the other fringe benefits that permanent workers customarily enjoyed (Monahan 1910: 27–38). Second, such recruits acted as a cushion to adjust the level of employment with demand fluctuations in the product market (Buchanan 1934: 71–2). Third, temporary workers were gainfully deployed in some seasonal jobs – especially for the clearance of jungle and weeds, and also for the collection of fuel in the winter (Anon. 1888: 71; Arbuthnott 1904: 2).

Bengal's employment scenario differed significantly from that in Assam, however, where, for the safeguard of migratory workers, the government intervened. Similar to the practices in Assam, plantations in Darjeeling and the Dooars also depended on migratory workers, as there had previously been scanty human settlement in those places. But labour coercion was never heard of. Steady immigration from Nepal resolved the labour issue for Darjeeling: 'The Darjeeling planters do not labour under the same disadvantages as those of Assam and Cachar in respect of want of labourers, coolies being almost always obtainable from the adjacent hill territory of Nepal' (P.P. 1861: 61). Indeed, Sir Jung Bahadoor's administration in Nepal assured peace and tranquillity across the society, so that its population proliferated (Edger 1873: xxiv). Consequently, the land–man ratio was so depressed 'that the land can no longer find food for them all' (O'Brien 1883: 73), and, hence, there was an outward movement of labour. It certainly called for an improved transportation system for the movement of both labour and food[5] – a prerequisite that was largely satisfied, as we will see shortly, under state patronage. Moreover, there was no legal prohibition on this cross-border labour movement from either country (GOI 1873: 17). About 96 per cent of the labour force in the hills belonged to this community (Dash 1947: 118). There were also Lepchas from Sikkim who worked in the gardens (Anon. 1888: 70–7).

In the Dooars as well, human settlements were few and far between. The only tribe residing there, the Mech, had migrated elsewhere before development took place. The Rajbangsi who lived nearby never worked in fields, though they 'may thatch or take a contract for huts' (Arbuthnott 1904: 1). Learning from the Assam experiences, however, the Dooars planters depended on migratory labour from Chota Nagpur, Sonthalia, Chaibassa and Nepal. The Arbuthnott Committee, set up to ascertain working conditions in the tea plantations, revealed that, for 67 gardens (accounting for two-thirds of the land), 52 per cent of the workers had migrated from Chota Nagpur, 21 per cent from Sonthalia, 7 per cent from Chaibassa and 20 per cent from Nepal (ibid.: 1–2). Among immigrants, tribal people such as the Uraons, Mundas and Santhals dominated (Dash 1947: ch. 3).

Labour laws were conspicuously absent in Bengal, which sharply contrasted with what prevailed in Assam. In many cases, after completing their contracts in Assam, workers willingly joined the Dooars workforce (Arbuthnott 1904: 2), suggesting that a better working environment should have prevailed there. In fact, the Dooars planters preferred free labour to work with. In a representation to the lieutenant governor in 1888, the Dooars Planters' Association (ITA 1889: 65) submitted, 'The opposition and abuses caused by the Arkuttees and Professional Recruiters having become so prevalent, we would consider the retention of a special officer appointed by the government as almost a necessity to guard the interest of Free Labourers proceeding from Chota Nagpore to the Julpigoree and Darjeeling Districts.'

The conventional theory of wage does not work for the plantation economy, especially in Bengal. It was initially low, and remained so even in the phase of the industry's explosive growth. In 1873 the monthly wage rate in Darjeeling was Rs. 5.50 for males (and also for strongly built women), Rs. 4.50 for females and Rs. 3 for children. The respective rates were Rs. 5, Rs. 4 and Rs. 2.50 in the Terai (GOI 1873: 18). These wage rates continued for a couple of decades. From Bengal Proceedings (General), October 1900, Iftikhar-ul-Awwal (1979: 52) quotes the rate at Rs. 5.50 to 6.00 for males and Rs. 4.50 for females, in Darjeeling, and Rs. 6 and Rs. 4.31, respectively, in the Dooars. According to the Arbuthnott Committee (1904: 4), the rate was Rs. 6 for males, Rs. 4.50 for females and Rs. 2.50 for children in 1904. Iftikhar-ul-Awwal (1979: 53) confirms that these wages continued through 1914, however.

Although low-level wage stagnation appears inconsistent in an industry's expansionary phase, it is a historical datum for tropical mining and plantations.[6] To account for the event, however, the historiography relies heavily on demand-side factors, especially the planters' perception that the low productivity among immigrants hailing from the subsistence economy was commensurate only with a low wage rate. The planters also believed what the backward-bending labour supply curve suggests: a lower wage attracts more labour, and vice versa.[7] To keep wages low, three strategies are identified on the planters' side: (i) the formation of planters' cartel (formal and informal); (ii) the introduction of the 'superintendent' system (Iftikhar-ul-Awwal 1979: 55[8]); and (iii) restrictions on the inter-garden mobility of labour. Indeed, planters were largely organised under the Indian Tea Association (ITA), which sought to regulate the wage rate. Thus, the proceedings of the ITA in 1884 (ITA 1885: 6) note, 'The attention of the General Committee was drawn to the high rates which were in some cases paid for labour on garden in the Dooars, as compared with those ruling in other Tea Districts, the effect being that coolies were induced to leave one garden for another on which those high rates prevailed.' The association accordingly recommended that 'some joint action might be taken on the part of those interested'. There were also district-level associations – such as the Dooars Planters' Association and Darjeeling Planters' Association– which issued labour rules to curb competition in the labour market (see, for Dooars labour rules, Arbuthnott: 40–2; and, for Darjeeling labour rules, Anon. 1909: 626). These measures certainly reduced the mobility of labour, and kept wages in check.

My point of disagreement, however, is that these demand-side restrictions, if implemented stringently, should have led to the scarcity of labour in the long run. But, save for some stray incidences,[9] Bengal plantations never suffered from a scarcity of labour. The Labour Enquiry Commission (GOB 1896: 51) thus observes, 'With regard to the question of the labour-supply to the tea districts of Jalpaiguri and Darjeeling the Commission is of the opinion that very little action on the part of the Government is, at present, necessary.' Therefore, we need to account for why the supply of labour was abundant at low wages.

My argument is that the supply of labour did not suffer at low wages since the workers continued their relations with the subsistence economy. For a couple of decades the majority of them worked at a stretch for about three years, and then retired to the subsistence sector with their accumulated savings. A contemporary planter thus shares his experiences: '78 [coolies] proceeded on a visit to their homes and 38 were sent to recruit… [T]he majority of the 78 would not return. A few might, but others, friends and relatives, would return in their stead' (Arbuthnott 1904: 6). Their home visits were also frequent every year, especially on the eve of the harvest season, and they returned only 'after the harvest is over' (ibid.). The connection between the wage economy and the subsistence economy, as these pieces of evidence suggest, signify that the plantation wage did not represent a return from permanent full-time employment but an income in addition to workers' claims on the subsistence economy. This explains, *à la* Myint, why migrant workers were willing to accept low wages in Bengal plantations. In later years, however, the workers increasingly settled in and around the plantations. But, in these cases, the garden authorities mostly provided them with land for subsistence cultivation,[10] so that the relation between wage and subsistence economies continued, perpetuating low wages in the long run.

III

Indian tea never ventured seriously into the domestic market. This is evident in its limited domestic sales, and with high volatilities at that, from 1885 to 1914, as estimated in Table 7.4. The estimation underlines that domestic sales rose steeply from 1.60 million lbs per annum in 1885–9 to 7.06 million lbs per annum in 1890–4 but sank steadily thereafter to 1.96 million lbs in 1900–4. Further revival brought it to 7.43 million lbs in 1910–14. Contemporary reports confirm these estimates; for example, domestic sales stood, according to ITA reports, at 1½ million lbs for 1883 (ITA 1884: 19) and 1887 (ITA 1887: 86), and, according to government sources, 4½ million lbs for 1895–6 (P.P. 1897: 109) and 5¼ million lbs for 1896–7 (P.P. 1898: 116). Oscillations are distinct in percentile shares as well, which moved between 1 and 6 per cent, suggesting that foreign outlets should have absorbed more than 94 per cent. According to a contemporary document, 'It is only by the influence of the distress that follows overproduction, that India will become, again and again, the scene of determined efforts to develop the consumption of tea by her people' (ITMEC 1905: 176).

Table 7.4 Annual domestic consumption of Indian tea (in million lbs), 1885/9–1910/14

Period	*Production*	*Exports*	*Domestic consumption (production – exports)*
1885–9	90.63	89.03	1.60 (1.76)
1890–4	124.89	117.83	7.06 (5.65)
1895–9	158.87	152.95	5.92 (3.73)
1900–4[1]	196.51	194.55	1.96 (1.00)
1905–9	238.39	231.78	6.61 (2.77)
1910–14[2]	284.25	276.82	7.43 (2.61)

Notes: The terms in parentheses represent domestic consumption as a percentage of production; 1: excluding 1904; 2: excluding 1914.

Sources: Production: GOI (1914: 10–11); exports: Appendix 7.2.

These statistics should not be interpreted as suggesting a trivial domestic market, however. Rather, India contemporaneously possessed a vast domestic market, which China mainly supplied. Import statistics, as presented in Table 7.1, indicate that, in 1860–4, India's imports stood at Rs. 1.38 million per annum. They rose to Rs. 1.80 million in 1865–9, representing 2.18 million lbs in quantity. The series rose steadily through 1890–4 – at 6.23 million lbs per annum in quantity, and Rs. 4.42 million in value – indicating growing domestic demand. But it went largely unnoticed. Only from 1895–9 onwards did imports decline.

Indeed, the proceedings of the Indian Tea Association confirm the planters' apathy towards the domestic market. It is true that its first chairman stressed, and promised to continue, 'the work of the Tea Syndicate in endeavouring to extend the sale of Indian tea in India itself, where there is a practically unlimited market for cheap teas, if they can be brought within reach of the poorer class of natives' ('Speech of Mr Inglis', in ITA 1882: 42). But no effort followed. Again, in 1895, the Assam branch of the association reiterated the importance of the domestic market. But the chairman, H. S. Ashton (ITA 1895: 3), emphasised, 'On the whole, I think it was shown that the natives can get tea if they want it, but that for the most part they only want it either as a luxury or when they can get it for nothing.' He argued, 'In America the people have means but no taste, and in India taste but no means, and our commercial enterprise will do better expending its forces upon the first of this unfortunate combination than upon the second.' This was, according to Lord Curzon, the Viceroy of India, an erroneous strategy.[11] On his advice, the Indian Tea Markets Expansion Commission (ITMEC) was set up in 1901 to promote tea drinking in India.

From the beginning, however, the industry targeted the British market. Thanks to the Chinese monopoly, though, Indian tea received mixed reactions at the debut sale at London: 'Ladies, particularly those of mature age and judgement, ...were enthusiastic in their praises of the new tea, but many of the lords of creation...compared it somewhat irrelevantly to chopped straw, and some pleased to display their facetiousness by observing that a mixture of gunpowder [a variety of green tea: Walsh 1892: 74] was wanted to make it go off' (reported in *The Asiatic Journal*, and quoted in Ibbetson 1912: 42). Indian tea was therefore able to penetrate there only very slowly, supplying no more than about 25,000 lbs in 1854.

Such reactions are well understood in the tea market, since a taste for it is not a natural one but is 'acquired'[12] through habit. Once 'acquired', though, as was the case with Chinese tea in mid-nineteenth-century Britain, it enjoys a strong brand affiliation. Therefore, Indian tea was greatly disliked (Walsh 1892: 166). To break this barrier to entry, Indian planters initially went for retailing pure Indian tea, which, they believed, had a better flavour, and was also stronger, than its rival. But tea connoisseurs in Britain did not accept it. A contemporary author notes, 'It did not avail to tell John Bull it was better Tea, that it was far stronger, that it was in no way adulterated; for he simply shook his head, the flavour was different to what use had made him familiar, and he would none of it' (Money 1878:172).

Grocers, however, noticed that the inferior Chinese tea, when blended with the Indian, made it stronger, and thus fetched higher prices. Later on, such blending was found capable of enriching all varieties of Chinese tea, and thus, by 1870, it had become a custom. It is evident that '[l]ittle by little the custom of so mixing became very general, so much so that it may almost be said to-day [1870] that if Indian teas cannot be purchased pure, no more can Chinese' (ibid.). The English palate was thus gradually 'educated' to the flavour of Indian tea, initially in a blended form, and finally in pure. The time lag in this educating process explains why Chinese tea dominated the British market for more than a decade after Indian tea's arrival in London. Table 7.5 shows that it was only after 1869 that India dominated the British tea market.

There were several competitive advantages for Indian tea. One of them was surely its quality. In respect of quality, Indian tea had become so popular in Britain by 1865 – thus receiving such an 'extraordinarily high price' – that Chinese vendors started taking up Indian names for their wares. The October 1865 issue of the *Produce Market Review* points out, 'In some instances the Chinese had recourse to the puerile device of calling their tea by the name of "Assam Pekoe Souchong" of course with the praise-worthy object of obtaining Assam prices for China tea' (quoted in Ibbetson 1912: 43). Subsequently, Darjeeling tea was an added feather in the cap. According to a government report of 1861, 'The small samples of tea hitherto prepared here [in Darjeeling] have been very satisfactory; and though the plantations may still be said to be in their infancy, the superintendent of Darjeeling confidently anticipates that the Darjeeling teas will soon rank with the very highest class of Indian teas' (P.P. 1861: 61).

Better technology, as well as superior organisation, ensured its quality. Cultivation and manufacturing were organised jointly in Bengal, and of course using mechanical devices on a large scale. This ensured better command over different production processes – a *sine qua non* from the viewpoint of quality – generating, at the same time, both scale and scope economies. In contrast, these activities were segregated in contemporary China, and confined to tiny scales, with mechanical devices totally absent. Ibbetson (1912: 23) notes, 'The methods and apparatus employed by the Chinese in the manufacture of their teas are extremely simple. [...] A large portion of the tea is prepared in the humble cottages of the peasants... The drying pans and furnaces in these places are of very primitive construction.' The quality aspects were, therefore, grossly neglected. A nineteenth-century British consul at Foochow observes, 'There is apparently no desire on the part of the natives [in China] to improve the manufacture of their teas; ...the same carelessness is displayed in picking, packing, and shifting of the teas that has been for so many years induced to bring the name of China tea into dispute' (quoted in anon. 1906: 4).

Chinese tea also suffered from adulteration at various levels. For brighter appearance, its green teas were often 'painted' with gypsum and copper. 'They poison the herb to gratify the ridiculous tastes of Europe and America for bright green, just as many of our pickle-makers poison the pickle. [...] They never think of drinking this tea themselves' (Chamney 1933: 22). Foreign articles – such as iron filings and silica – were also mixed up for the sake of a gain in weight, as is evident in a sample test at the auction centre at Mincing Lane, London, in 1882. The test detected 'injurious, and in some cases, even poisonous, matters' in Chinese teas, 'while in the Indian exhibits placed under the same test, "not one case of adulteration" was recorded' (Baildon 1882: 25). Another form of adulteration was what was called 'mixture' – that is, the addition of sloe, liquorice and ash tea leaves. This is evident in a local journal: '[A]ll around the settlement, in every open space, large quantities of what is termed… "the mixture" lie exposed to the sun at noon-day… [T]here are the establishments, well known to the police, where the mixture is fired, loaded, packed, sold and despatched for shipment.' The report continues, 'Whether the mercantile result be intended to astonish the palates of old ladies in London or Glasgow, or to pass as genuine Souchong with skippers who have little knowledge of tea, we know not; but the fact remains, that the trade thrives well, and pays' (quoted in Baildon 1882: 24–5). The addition of these odd substances must surely have damaged the standing of Chinese tea on the global market.

Cost-wise as well, Indian tea enjoyed the competitive edge. In 1848 Ball estimated the cost price of Chinese (black) tea at 27 tales per picul (that is, 1s. 7d per lb), involving 12 tales for cultivation and processing, 1.3 tales for packing, 3.9 tales for transportation, 3 tales as different charges at Canton and 6.8 tales as profit for Hong merchants. For ocean transportation and high overhead costs (and profits), the East India Company claimed about 33 tales per picul, so that its selling price was about 60 tales per picul (or 3s. per lb) in London (Ball 1848: 353–4). Even if teas were manufactured at 10d to 11d a lb in a congenial environment, and the intermediary costs were reduced after the abolition of monopoly trade practices in Canton (including the opening up of five ports to foreigners), Ball's estimation was that they could not be offered below between 1s. 2d and 1s. 4d a lb in London (Ball 1848: 357–8). On the other hand, for the late 1840s, his estimate for the cost price of Assam tea at London was 10½d per pound. Again, according to Anon. in 1888, Darjeeling tea could be offered at Rs. 20.50 a maund (that is, 10d per lb) in London, which included the costs of cultivation, manufacturing, packaging, conveyance and various overhead expenses (Anon. 1888: 100). Thus, notwithstanding almost equal manufacturing costs between Chinese and Indian tea, the former was dearer in view of various trade customs and internal conveyances.

These comparative advantages enabled Indian tea to rapidly multiply its market share in Britain. Table 7.5 shows that its share was only 31.94 per cent in 1866 but jumped to 51.46 per cent in 1869, curbing the supremacy of the Chinese supply. Although it was declining in share, the British market for China grew through 1879, albeit at a slow pace. Side by side there prevailed a high rate of growth for Indian tea – annually at 21.81 per cent from 1869 to 1879. This trend might be partly explained by its growing re-export from Britain. But a more significant factor was the steep rise in its per capita consumption, which, though as low as 0.03 lbs in 1711 and 0.57 lbs in 1780, became 1.25 lbs in 1840, 3.50 lbs in 1865, 5 lbs in 1890 and as high as 6.47 lbs in 1912 (Ibbetson

Table 7.5 Sales of tea from different countries in the British market (in million lbs), 1866–92

Year	*Indian tea*	*Chinese tea*	*Ceylon tea*	*Total*	*Year*	*Indian tea*	*Chinese tea*	*Ceylon tea*	*Total*
1866	45.84	97.68	–	143.52	1880	438.36	114.49	–	552.85
	(31.94)	(68.06)		(100)		(79.29)	(20.71)		(100)
1867	63.60	104.63	–	168.23	1881	483.36	111.72	–	595.08
	(37.81)	(62.19)		(100)		(81.23)	(18.77)		(100)
1868	77.46	99.34	–	176.80	1882	504.96	114.46	–	619.42
	(43.81)	(56.19)		(100)		(81.52)	(18.48)		(100)
1869	107.16	101.08	–	208.24	1883	590.00	111.78	–	701.78
	(51.46)	(48.54)		(100)		(84.07)	(15.93)		(100)
1870	135.00	104.05	–	239.05	1884	642.17	110.84	–	753.01
	(56.47)	(43.53)		(100)		(85.28)	(14.72)		(100)
1871	139.56	109.45	–	249.01	1885	656.78	113.51	3.27	773.56
	(56.05)	(43.95)		(100)		(84.90)	(14.67)	(0.43)	(100)
1872	166.56	111.00	–	277.56	1886	684.20	104.23	6.26	794.69
	(60.01)	(39.99)		(100)		(86.10)	(13.12)	(0.78)	(100)
1873	202.16	111.67	–	313.83	1887	831.12	90.51	9.94	931.57
	(64.42)	(35.58)		(100)		(89.22)	(9.72)	(1.06)	(100)
1874	185.28	118.75	–	304.03	1888	862.10	80.65	18.55	961.30
	(60.94)	(39.06)		(100)		(89.68)	(8.39)	(1.93)	(100)
1875	232.20	122.11	–	354.31	1889	960.00	61.10	28.50	1049.60
	(65.54)	(34.46)		(100)		(91.46)	(5.82)	(2.72)	(100)
1876	257.40	123.36	–	380.76	1890	1019.62	57.53	35.52	1112.67
	(67.60)	(32.40)		(100)		(91.64)	(5.17)	(3.19)	(100)
1877	278.52	132.26	–	410.78	1891	989.42	52.29	51.23	1092.94
	(67.80)	(32.20)		(100)		(90.53)	(4.78)	(4.69)	(100)
1878	367.44	120.65	–	488.09	1892	1095.28	34.48	63.10	1192.86
	(75.28)	(24.72)		(100)		(91.82)	(2.89)	(5.29)	(100)
1879	340.92	126.34	–	467.26					
	(72.96)	(27.04)		(100)					

Notes: '–' indicates a nil entry; the terms in parentheses represent the shares of different countries in the total.

Source: ITA (1892: 290).

1912: 15–16; for 1865 and 1890, Walsh 1892: 240). Explosive growth was thus evident in British per capita consumption once Indian tea had entered the market.

From the early 1880s, however, the Chinese market shrank volume-wise as well. From 126.34 million lbs in 1879 it fell to 113.51 million lbs in 1885, as against a sharp rise from 340.92 million lbs to 656.78 million lbs for the Indian. To account for these abrupt changes, contemporary sources often pointed to the aggressive market campaign launched by Indian planters under the aegis of the Calcutta Tea Syndicate from the late 1870s, culminating with the formation of Indian Tea Association in 1881 ('Speech of Mr Inglis', in ITA 1882: 42). The campaign was so vigorous that sales were often described as 'forced' sales: '[T]here is not the slightest doubt but that the check which the consumption of China tea appears to have sustained in England is entirely due to the *forced* use of India and Ceylon teas in that country and her dependencies...' (Walsh 1892: 242, emphasis in original). But a more crucial factor was that, under competitive pressures, Indian planters steadily reduced their costs of production. For ten companies involved in Indian tea plantations, the accounting figures indicate that the London price of tea fell, on average, from 1s. 9¼d per lb in 1878 to 1s. 6d in 1881, 1s. 2¼d in 1884 and further to 1s. in 1886 (White 1887: 741). In response, the average cost price (including sale charges) in London was curtailed from 1s. 5d to 1s. ½d, 11½d and 9½d, respectively, so that profitability was never lost.

Their costs were minimised in several ways. In the first place, there were economies of scale – acquired through extending cultivation, as well as through takeover and merger – which reduced the cost of management and supervision (evidently by 1d per lb: White 1887: 742), and also handling charges in Calcutta, since the marginal cost of handling was much lower than the average cost. Second, growing mechanisation, especially the introduction of labour- and fuel-saving machinery, as discussed above, reduced manufacturing costs. Third, packaging costs fell in this period by more than 50 per cent, internal conveyancing costs by more than 33 per cent and ocean freight charges by about 45 per cent (ibid.). For the 1878–86 period as a whole, average profit works out at 3¼d per lb. Since each penny of profit per pound represented 3 per cent net profit in a well-organised plantation, their average dividend payout stood at around 9 per cent – a satisfactory return in the contemporary market. While Indian planters thus survived in the phase of falling prices, it was not so for the Chinese. Unable to withstand competition through cost economy, China increasingly supplied inferior tea for low-price markets 'until her produce is... thoroughly discredited' (White 1887: 741).

Devaluation of the Indian currency provided additional support in this phase. The global silver market was evidently glutted after the early 1870s on account of the withdrawal of major currencies (including the pound sterling) from the silver standard. In London, for example, bar silver was quoted at 59.75d per ounce in March 1873 but only 46.93d in December 1885 – a fall of 21.46 per cent. Consequently, the silver-based Indian currency depreciated against the pound sterling. The exchange rate evidently fell from 1s. 11.12d per rupee in 1873 to 1s. 9.64d in 1875–6, 1s. 7.95d in 1880–1 and further to 1s. 6.25d in 1885–6 (O'Conor 1887: 87). These represent a 21.06 per cent devaluation, which significantly counterbalanced the falling price of Indian tea in pound sterling (43.53 per cent from 1878 to 1886, as stated above), since the costs of production, expended in rupee, became cheaper in pound sterling terms.

From the mid-1880s, however, India confronted a new challenge: a challenge from Ceylon, where tea plantation had been coming up rapidly. Its growth was indeed staggering at the outset. Despite beginning in 1867, only 2,720 acres had been taken into plantation by 1877. But momentum was built up thereafter, bringing the total to 170,000 acres of land in 1887 and 350,000 acres in 1897 (Ibbetson 1912: 38). Since British planters were also helming this development, opting for similar organisations and practices to those in India, tough competition followed. Table 7.5 shows that Britain imported 3.27 million lbs of Ceylonese tea in 1885, which went up to 63.10 million lbs in 1892. Even so, it was confined to a market segment of about 5.30 per cent, however, as against about 92 per cent for India.

The global distribution of Indian tea, as displayed in Table 7.6, underwent significant changes in the last quarter of the nineteenth century. For about a decade and a half the British market for Indian tea expanded rapidly: from 17.58 million lbs per annum in 1871–5 to 92.04 million lbs per annum in 1885–9, with an underlying annual growth rate of 30.25 per cent. Accordingly, Britain's market share in Indian supplies rose from 88.02 per cent to 93.63 per cent. Although the market expanded thereafter – rising to an annual level of 204.12 million lbs in 1910–14 – its market share fell steadily to 73.13 per cent in 1910–14, suggesting that Indian teas should have been strengthening elsewhere. Table 7.6 indicates that, during this period, Russia came into prominence after the United Kingdom, followed by Canada and Australia, respectively. Their shares work out in the order of 10.38 per cent, 3.82 per cent and 3.55 per cent in 1910–14. Evidence indicates that Indian planters concertedly created these markets to compensate for the falling price trend in British outlets (GOI 1879: 32).

Outside the United Kingdom, Indian planters first identified Australia as a prospective market, where extensive campaigns were undertaken in two successive world trade exhibitions – one at Sydney in August 1878, the other at Melbourne in October 1880. According to a contemporary source, 'The exports of Indian tea to Australia rose within 12 months [of the Melbourne exhibition] from next to nothing to 2 million of lbs a year' (Edward Buck, commissioner for the government of India at the Melbourne Exhibition, 'Note on Indian Tea in Continental Europe', in ITA 1905: 166). Table 7.6 indicates that, on average, Australia directly imported 54,000 lbs a year in 1880–4, which rose to 2.92 million lbs in 1885–9 and 9.82 million lbs in 1910–14. But this expansion took place only in high-end markets without making any dent in the Chinese monopoly in inferior teas. Australia's intake of Chinese tea was 24.13 million lbs in 1888–9, as against less than 3 million lbs for Indian tea

Table 7.6 Market distribution of Indian tea (in thousand lbs), 1871/5–1910/14

Country	*1871–5*	*1880–4**	*1885–9***	*1890–4*	*1895–9*	*1900–4*	*1905–9*	*1910–14*
United Kingdom	17,581	54,108	92,045	110,863	138,094	163,191	175,738	204,117
	(88.02)	(88.29)	(93.63)	(92.20)	(88.92)	(83.88)	(75.82)	(73.73)
Australia	56	54	2,924	5,069	6,879	7,736	8,935	9,824
Canada	–	–	33	126	960	5,904	10,268	10,581
United States	37	350	104	111	1,291	1,856	2,112	2,471
Russia	–	–	–	–	520	5,029	16,504	28,738
Persia	461	–	664	2,217	3,411	2,704	980	679
Turkey	14	–	–	479	2,109	3,542	3,216	3,046
Germany	–	–	–	–	450	711	–	511
Others	1,825	6,773	2,541	1,378	1,579	3,871	14,034	16,855
Total	19,974	61,285	98,311	120,243	155,293	194,544	231,787	276,822

Notes: '–' signifies a negligible amount; the terms in parentheses represent the percentage share of the United Kingdom in the total; * average for1882, 1883 and 1884; ** average for 1887, 1888 and 1889.

Sources: 1871–5: GOI (1876: 112); 1880–4: GOI (1886: 48); 1885–9: GOI (1891: 32); 1890–4: GOI (1896: 33); 1895–9: GOI (1899: 29) and GOI (1901: 19); 1900–4: GOI (1905: 18) and GOI (1906: 26); 1905–9: GOI (1909: 38) and GOI (1912: 52); 1910–14: GOI (1914: 14–16) and P.P. (1918b: 524–6).

(GOI 1890: 35–6). In fact, Australia demanded inferior tea in bulk, which India could not provide (GOI 1905: 24). 'Quality in tea is hardly yet appreciated [in Australia] except by a select few... [so that] Indian tea...has not been able to find its way in considerable quantity' (GOI 1896: 34). Ceylon grabbed the opportunity, however, and expanded its business rapidly.

Indian planters also targeted North American markets, especially the United States and Canada. The US market could not grow appreciably, however, and in 1910–14 still stood at an average of only 2.47 million lbs per annum. The underlying reason was that India competed only in the black tea market, which constituted only 32 per cent in 1899–1900 (GOI 1901: 18), leaving the vast markets for oolongs, Japans and greens, where Chinese and Japanese teas dominated. In contrast, there was rapid progress in Canada, where the annual intake exceeded 10.50 million in 1910–14. These figures represent direct exports from India, however, not the total consumption of Indian tea, as re-exports were frequent from other countries. Thus, for example, Britain re-exported 908,743 lbs of Indian tea to the United States and 823,207 lbs to Canada in 1895 (GOI 1897: 35); and 902,619 lbs and 905,597 lbs, respectively, in 1896 (GOI 1898: 35). Again, in 1898 the United States received 882,000 lbs of Indian tea from Hong Kong (GOI 1900: 35).

Behind this development India's aggressive campaigns are also in evidence. Under the aegis of ITA, planters campaigned vigorously at the Chicago Exhibition, held in 1893, which contributed to a 47.30 per cent rise in exports – from 1,482,311 lbs in 1892 to 2,137,600 lbs in 1893 (jointly for the United States and Canada). This is confirmed in a speech by the ITA chairman (ITA 1894: 3) – it 'is without doubt largely due to our exhibit at the Chicago World's Fair' – and also in a government report (GOI 1895: 33): 'The occurrence of the World's Fair at Chicago was made the occasion of well-directed efforts to push Indian tea in the States, with...promising results.' The task was initially entrusted to an agent, but he failed to promote the taste for pure Indian tea, as it was blended with the Chinese and the Japanese. We thus find ITA resolving in 1888 that 'we must go direct to the consumer, and that suitable blends of pure Indian tea, or such tea as can be drunk without being blended, should be offered for sale by our own agencies in small packing' (ITA 1888: 88). With this objective in view, ITA floated the Associated Tea Planters Ltd with a paid-up capital of £50,000, for 'establishing Markets in the United States of America and in Canada for the sale of Tea grown on Plantations in East Indies' (Watson 1889: 64). This strategy brought the desired results, especially in Canada (Table 7.6).

For India, however, Russia emerged as the most important outlet outside Britain. From only 520,000 lbs per annum in 1895–9, Indian exports soared to16.50 million lbs per annum in 1905–9, and further to 28.74 million lbs in 1910–14 (Table 7.6). This trend should not be interpreted as reflecting a sudden rise in Russia's domestic consumption, however. Russians had been connoisseurs of Indian tea for a long time,[13] but took it mainly via Persia, and also through Afghanistan[14] and Turkey,[15] to some extent. Persia, for example, imported an average of 2.2 million lbs of Indian tea per annum in 1890–4 and 3.4 million lbs per annum in 1895–9. Although it was partly meant for domestic consumption (GOI 1896: 33), a significant portion was re-exported to Russia. This trade route altered greatly after the introduction of a new custom regulation in the Russian Empire on 13 January 1895, however. Under the new regulation, a higher duty was imposed on Indian tea imported overland from Persia and Afghanistan through the Khanate of Bokhara (for details, see 'Report of Her Majesty's Consul at Batum on "Transit of Tea"', in GOI 1897: 35–6). What it was promoting was the sea route through Batum, via Port Said and Alexandria, to different Russian ports. For Indian tea, the custom duty was not charged at Batum but at Askabad or at Bokhara, at 6 rubles 60c. per pood[16] of 36 English lbs for inferior tea, and at 14r. 40c. for higher grades – and in Russian paper currency too. Teas from other places were taxed at 21r. in gold at Batum, however. These measures promoted Russian trade in Indian green tea by as much as 800 tons through this new route between 13 January and 31 December 1895. Later the preferential treatment was also sanctioned for the Trans-Siberian Railway route through Dalny and Port Arthur. Moreover, a two-way steamer service was introduced between Calcutta and Vladivostok to save transhipment costs at Colombo (GOI 1909: 37).

Russia also imported Indian tea from the United Kingdom, Germany and China. From the United Kingdom, for example, it imported 8.25 million lbs in 1906 (P.P. 1908a: 105), 3 million lbs in 1908 (P.P. 1910: 45), 6.50 million lbs in 1909 (P.P. 1911: 44) and 5 million lbs in 1910–11 (P.P. 1912: 47). Government reports for these years also underline Russia's import of 'a large but unknown quantity via China'. Moreover, a large amount of trade – for example, through the Trans-Siberian Railway via Dalny and Port Arthur (4.90 million lbs in 1903–4), as also overland trade through Kashmir (2 million lbs in 1903–4) – was not reported as direct exports to Russia, but shown under the headings 'China Treaty Ports' and 'Kashmir', respectively (P.P. 1905: 112).

IV

India's tea plantations owe much to imperial governance. At the instance of Lord William Bentinck, Governor General of India, the Tea Committee was set up in 1836 to steer its development, and we find its efforts culminating in a series of experimental gardens, for which tea seedlings and expert tea makers were imported from China (P.P. 1858: 32). Many such experimental gardens in Assam were subsequently handed over to a private enterprise, the Assam Tea Company, in 1840 (see note 4). Bengal also received similar patronage. We have seen that the superintendent of Darjeeling first set up an experimental garden in Bengal, followed by two more such gardens in the lower valley of Lebong, one by the civil surgeon, Dr J. R. Withecombe, and the other by Major James Arden Crommelin of the Engineers, by 1852. These pilot projects motivated Bengal's tea plantations under private enterprise. Since the Chinese seeds responded well to Darjeeling's soil, the government also distributed them free of cost among budding entrepreneurs (for the distribution of tea seeds among private enterprises, see P.P. 1863b: 3–8).

Once investors were thus inspired, two important issues concerned the government: land and transportation. Since the price of land crucially affects the cost of plantations, thanks to its high land intensity, the government adopted liberal rules in 1855 (the so-called 'old' rules) for the distribution of wastelands in Bengal (Edger 1873: x–xvi; Fielder 1869: 30–1). In Darjeeling alone, about 250,000 acres of wasteland belonged to the government in 1859–60 (ibid.: 32). The 'old' rules plotted wastelands (each plot admeasuring no less than 500 acres) and leased them for 99 years. One-fourth of the area was granted perpetually rent-free for the development of roads and fuel woods, while the remaining three-fourths were exempted from rent for the first 15 years. For the remaining 84 years the annual rent was charged at a variable scale: 4½d per acre for the first ten years, and 6d per acre for the next 74. A time-bound schedule was stipulated for the development of the land: its one-eighth segment to be developed within five years, one-fourths within ten years, one-half within 20 years and three-fourths within 30 years; otherwise, the grant was liable to be rescinded. A district document of 1873 reveals that, out of 64 gardens in Darjeeling, 16 gardens were run under the 'old' rules, covering an area of 22,020 acres.

The 'old' rules suffered from a major drawback, however, in that there was no restrictive clause on the financial capacity of a lessee. Reckless land jobbing, therefore, followed. 'People took up land which they were unable to make use of, hoping either that they might dispose of it to advantage before the time for inquiry [as to the clause of land utilisation] arrived, or that they might be allowed to commute the leasehold [in the future] ...on favourable terms' (Edger 1873: xii). In fact, local officials initially verified individual cases, but the practice soon discontinued in view of the government's promotional outlook, as also under mounting pressure from the speculators (ibid.: xi).

To remove this drawback, Lord Canning's administration adopted a new set of rules (the so-called 'fee-simple' rules) on 17 October 1861, which the Secretary of State approved on 30 August 1862 with a major modification. The modification was that, in place of Lord Canning's proposal for fixed-price sale (at Rs. 2.50 to Rs. 5 per acre), the approval provided for auction sales at an upset price of Rs. 2.50 per acre, payable in instalments over ten years. There was also a provision for lease, whereby the Board of Revenue was entrusted to determine its terms and conditions in consultation with local authorities. For Darjeeling, however, the lease was sanctioned for ten years, with a rent holiday for the first two years and a rent of 6 annas per acre thereafter (GOB 1868: 51).

The 'fee-simple' rules, as they were formulated and executed, demonstrated the lenient attitude of the imperial government. In the first place, no ready money was required to purchase land, or to take it on lease, so that less capital was initially involved. Second, although leases under the 'old' rules continued in the absence of any retrospective effect of the 'fee-simple' rules, the latter contained a provision for the redemption of leasehold land into perpetual ownership on payment of the present value of its future rents. In 1863–4 79 plots

(18,248 acres), held under the 'old' rules, were thus commuted in Darjeeling (GOI 1866: 315). Third, quite a large number of applications were submitted to acquire wastelands under Lord Canning's resolution of 17 October 1861, which was widely publicised. A source tells us that 'every acre of culturable land in the District [Darjeeling Hills settlement] has been applied for' (GOB 1863: 60). The 'fee-simple' rules provided that these applications, if duly registered, should be processed accordingly. A compassionate outlook on the part of the local administration is evident in this: '[O]n this liberal principle several applications for grants [under Lord Canning's resolution] in Darjeeling, which had been somewhat irregularly admitted by the Local Officers, were nevertheless held to be *bona fide* arrangements' (GOB 1864: 27). They were subsequently exempted from the auction clause of the 'fee-simple' rules. Fourth, for the collection of fuel, the gardens were entitled for lease at a subsidised rate, one-half of the district prices (GOB 1874: 78), which certainly reduced their overhead costs. Finally, planters were entitled to partly surrender their plots, so that they could downsize their holdings for the rationalisation of costs. This provision was very useful during the crisis of 1866–9. In 1863–4 16 plots of land (13,517 acres) were held in Darjeeling under the 'old' rules and 41 plots (37,962 acres) under the 'fee-simple' rules (GOI 1866: 315). Land under leasehold ownership amounted to 38,239 acres (66 plots), and that under perpetual ownership stood at 46,982 acres (51 plots), in 1868–9 (GOB 1870: xxxiii). In Jalpaiguri 370 plots (23,774 acres) were leased out in 1868–9, which rose to 439 (26,996 acres) in 1875–6 (GOB 1877: 62).

The auction clause of the 'fee-simple' rules attracted severe criticism from the planters' community, however. In many cases a prospective entrepreneur might have searched out a plot of land in the midst of dense forest but then failed to secure it at auction, by not being the highest bidder. Money (1878: 3) thus concludes, 'The only fair rules for the sale of waste lands were those of Lord Canning, which the Secretary of State at home, who could know nothing of the subject, chose to modify and upset.' Another bone of contention was that the auction sales hiked land prices in Darjeeling to as high as Rs. 30 an acre, as it was for some plots in 1862–3 (GOB 1864: 27). In that year the average price works out at Rs. 17 an acre. Pointing to the role of speculation in these price hikes, a contemporary report (GOB 1874: 77) notes, 'During the last few years many cases have come to light, especially in the Darjeeling Hills, where large tracts of land suited for tea have been taken up by local speculators at the minimum price, or on lease-hold tenure, and then sold in small lots at enormously advanced price to *bona fide* planters, who were thus crippled at the outset.' The upset price was subsequently increased to Rs. 10 an acre for Darjeeling, however, though it was Rs 8 for Assam, Cachar and Sylhet, and Rs. 6 for Chittagong (GOB 1874: 78). While describing these evils of the wasteland policy, a government official pointed out in 1873 (GOI 1873: xv), 'The cardinal error, which misled the able and well-meaning administrators whose action did so much injury to the industry they meant to foster, seems to have been an idea that they were bound to work on some general principles of economical or political science of universal application, instead of finding out what were the actual conditions under which the tea industry would have to be carried on in Bengal, and shaping their policy accordingly.'

Again, both the 'old' rules and the 'fee-simple' rules suffered from inadequate provisions for land survey and its demarcation. Whatever mild provisions had been there in the original 'fee-simple' rules were subsequently removed through Act no. XXIII of 1863. Contemporary evidence confirms that this amendment took place 'in consequence of the [planters'] pressure brought to bear on Government on this matter' (ibid.: x). Several types of malpractice followed as a result, however . In addition to grabbing land much in excess of the grant, there is evidence that some leased-out plots had no real existence but had 'been sold by the original applicants at the rate of 10 shillings per acre to tea companies formed in London' (Edger 1873: xii). There were also cases in which the plots were earmarked without verifying ground realities so that forest lands – even the land beyond British territory – were treated as wastelands (GOB 1873: 144). Planters also occupied many settled lands, evicting the *ryots* with the tacit approval of the government.[17] Such events occurred even where hill tribes had been gathering their livelihoods for decades together awaiting for final settlements.[18] The Act of 1863 had no provision for remedy, save for that the government would financially compensate the sufferers (GOI 1873: x). Since the local people in Darjeeling were thus evicted from land, or compelled to pay high rents for grazing and firewood, 'they in their turn had taken lawless revenge by burning down tea-houses' (GOB 1873: 77). These evils are summed up in an early 1870s document: 'There was no efficient provision made for the survey and demarcation of the leaseholds, or for the protection of native interests. These omissions have had very grave results in Darjeeling, the only district in which much land has been taken up on this tenure; for there is much uncertainty about grant boundaries in this district, and the interests of cultivating occupants have been sacrificed in many instances' (Edger 1873: xv).

The drawback was subsequently removed in special rules, known as the *ad interim* rules, issued by the lieutenant governor of Bengal in 1871. It was stipulated that 'the Collector was in each case to verify the facts and circumstances before he sold a plot of waste, and was not to content himself with leaving claimants or objectors to come forward, – a practice under which ignorant aborigines and others had been deprived of the lands they held' (GOB 1873: 144; GOI 1873: xvi).

This analysis thus emphasises that land speculation took place in Bengal because of the government's overzealous outlook for the promotion of plantations. In addition, the interests of local people suffered significantly. But one should appreciate these policies as instrumental to the development of a vast tract of wasteland in this province, and, hence, the rapid growth of its tea plantations. While describing the appalling conditions of local people under previous rules, the lieutenant governor also underlined this welfare implication. He said, 'If the hill people have no definite property in particular land, they have at any rate a right to live somewhere.' But he also said at the same time, 'Whatever injustice has been hitherto done in ousting them has, the Lieutenant-Governor hopes, been compensated by the facilities which they have for employment in the tea gardens.' He noted, 'The people of Nepalese race (now the majority of the population of the Darjeeling Hills) readily avail themselves of this means of livelihood to the benefit of all parties under a system of free labour' (GOB 1873: 79).

The state also developed the transportation system in Darjeeling, which was crucial to the burgeoning tea plantations. Means of communication were virtually absent in the hills when the king of Sikkim ceded them to East India Company administration in 1835. There were only a few narrow tracks through forests, with cane bridges at places to cross hilly torrents. It was then largely uninhabited; no more than 20 families were there when Campbell became the district's first superintendent in 1839 (O'Brien 1883: 15). Hence, the question of road development had never cropped up. For trade and personal trips, Sikkim developed southward communications towards Tibet. Darjeeling's linkage with the port town of Calcutta was all the more tedious, taking five to six days in transit.

The government constructed the Old Military Road (now called the Pankhabari Road) between 1839 and 1842 linking Darjeeling with Siliguri. But its steepness prevented any wheeled traffic, and, hence, involved a high cost of conveyance: Rs. 2 per maund between Pankhabari and Darjeeling (Dash 1947:179–80). The government, therefore, constructed a cart road in this route (it still has the same name: the Hill Cart Road) with a gradient varying from 3 in 100 to 1 in 18, along with 300 bridges, which involved a total cost of Rs. 775,000. It was opened up to traffic from Darjeeling to Kurseong (19½ miles) in 1864 and up to Siliguri (an additional six miles) in 1869 (ibid.: 181). Meanwhile, for Calcutta-bound traffic, the Ganges–Darjeeling Road (126 miles) was constructed, at a cost of Rs. 1,468,000, from the Karagola Ghat (opposite Sahebganj, enjoying railway connectivity with Calcutta) to Siliguri via Purnea, Kisanganj and Titaliya (ibid.: 180). These arterial roads provided transport links between Darjeeling and Calcutta.

There were two types of feeder roads in the district: garden roads (privately constructed and maintained by garden authorities: Bald 1922: 100–7) and roads under the local administration. I have already discussed the government assistance to the former. For the movement of traffic between the garden roads and the Hill Cart Road, the district administration constructed several linkages. Of the more prominent ones, let me cite the Tista Valley Road (18½ miles long, running from Sivok to Sikkim and Tibet via Rangpo, and to Kalimpong and Tibet via the Rishi Road), the Pashok Road (17 miles, connecting the Tista with the Hill Cart Road at Jorebungalow), the Rangit Road (17½ miles, running from Darjeeling to the Tista via the river Rangit), the Simanabasti–Dudhiajhora Road (22¾ miles, running from Simanabasti to Dudhiajhora) (Dash 1947: 182–4), the Darjeeling–Toungloo Road (31 miles, connecting them via Goompahar and Jore Pookri) and the Toungloo–Phaloot Road (20 miles, connecting them via Sendukphoo) (O'Brien 1883: 39–40).

Many tea gardens were scattered alongside these roads, while short-distance roads were there for other businesses.

Although the road infrastructure was improved for a number of years, the means of transport basically remained primitive as well as expensive. For Calcutta-bound traffic, the East Indian Railway extended its service from Calcutta to Sahebganj in 1860, where a ferry service was available on the Ganges. But the journey from Karagola (opposite to Sahebganj) to Darjeeling was exasperating – by bullock cart from Karagola to Siliguri, and by horse-driven cart from Siliguri to Darjeeling. In 1878, however, the North Bengal State Railway launched its service on a metre-gauge line (156 miles) from the Manihari Ghat (connecting to Sahebganj) to Jalpaiguri via Rangpur, which was subsequently extended up to Siliguri. Siliguri thus got railway linkages with Calcutta. To connect Darjeeling with Siliguri, the Darjeeling Himalayan Railway opened up traffic between Siliguri and Kurseong in 1880, and between Kurseong and Darjeeling in 1881, covering a distance of 51 miles by a 2 foot narrow-gauge line. It ran along the Hill Cart Road – though diversions were frequent in search of easier alignments – at an average gradient of 1 in 29. In addition to this main line, there were two branch lines: the Siliguri–Kisanganj branch and the Tista Valley branch. The former ran west from Siliguri and served the tea gardens in the Terai. The latter went north-east along the Bagrakot Road to Sivok, and then followed the course of the Tista through Gielle Khola so that tea gardens in the Kalimpong Hills could be served. The government assisted this railway by providing land free of cost, and also the right to use the existing Hill Cart Road. Moreover, it guaranteed gross receipts at Rs. 200,000 per annum (GOI 1918: 165). The hill gardens at Darjeeling thus got railway facilities from the early 1880s.

Transportation was equally hazardous in the Dooars before the advent of railways. The existing roads (mostly non-metalled: Ray 1998: 10–11) were badly maintained ('Letter from the Assistant Secretary, Indian Tea Association, to the Secretary, Financial Department, Government of Bengal, dated 24 August 1888', in ITA 1889: 86)[19] and the ferry services inadequate. The latter were crucial in this region, given the presence of several fast-flowing streams with dangerous currents. The Dooars Planters' Association thus put on record in 1888, '[A]s to the Ferries a Manager reports that he went all the way to Jalpaiguri to see the Roads and Ferries for himself. At the Chel river directly below Dam Dim he found that there was only one Government boat to do all the work of the District and he learnt that not fewer than 100 carts were there at one time waiting to be crossed over, his own Teas being kept there 5 days as well as those of others' (ibid.). These problems disappeared, however, once the Bengal Dooars Railway had opened up 37 miles in 1894 and, with its extensions, 154 miles by 1903 (ITA 1894: 167–8). Its main line ran from the Barnes Ghat to Mal, its eastern branch from Lataguri to Ramshai and its western branch from Mal to Dam Dim, with a further extension from Mal to Madarihat. All these areas were dotted with tea gardens. These lines were finally linked up with the Eastern Bengal Railway at Lalmonirhat, giving them connectivity with the

Calcutta-bound rail network. For this railway project the government again provided land free of cost, and guaranteed a 5 per cent net profit on capital expenditure through the District Board of Jalpaiguri (ibid.: 166).

The Darjeeling Himalayan Railway charged freight at 1.36 to 2.56 pies per maund in the Tista Valley and Kisanganj sectors. The rates were higher for the Siliguri–Darjeeling section: 2.96 to 4.96 pies per maund uphill and upwards of 1.8 pies downhill. Possibly the Company's monopoly explained this price discrimination, which Darjeeling planters always complained of. 'The fact however remains that for many years the railway had practically a monopoly of the handling of the import and export trade of Darjeeling town and the hill areas of the District and the only competition they had to face was bullock cart traffic which was only appreciable in the Tista Valley and in the Terai' (Dash 1947: 193). A source informs us that, in Darjeeling, railway traffic amounted to 47,000 tons in 1909–10, whereas there was not a single ton of road traffic (ibid.: 194). In fact, in Bengal's long-distance tea traffic, railways dominated even over the river transport. In 1901–2, for example, Bengal gardens despatched 518,923 maunds of tea to Calcutta (worth Rs. 12,983,050) by rail, as against only 3,730 maunds (Rs. 214,291) by river (GOB 1903b: 59).

The tea plantations also received fiscal patronage. In addition to the relief in rent, as discussed above, the government never imposed custom duty on tea (GOB 1873: 147). Nor was the income from tea plantations brought under the purview of the Indian Income Tax Act of 1886 (Griffiths 1967: 557–76). Moreover, at the behest of Indian Tea Association in 1903, a tea cess was introduced at ¼ pie a pound for providing financial assistance towards the promotion of foreign markets (ITA 1903: 7–8). The fund thus created was handed over to an autonomous committee, and the government acted merely 'as a revenue collecting agency' (GOI 1914: 7). Soft fiscal policies in Britain also benefited the Indian plantations. In 1852 tea attracted an import duty of 2s. 1d a pound. It was reduced to 1s. 5d in 1862, 6d in 1865, and further to 4d in 1890, greatly increasing the per capita consumption of tea. The rate was raised twice from 1900 to 1904, however: by 2d per pound in 1900, as a war tax, and by a further 2d per pound in 1904. It must have caused hardship to Indian planters (Rees 1904: 1–9), but, through the effective persuasion of the Bengal government, the additional duty was annulled in 1905. In this respect, the ITA chairman noted (ITA 1905: vi), '[T]he heavy burden on our industry has been reduced by 2d. per lb, and we were undoubtedly greatly assisted in our protests by the powerful influence of Lord Curzon, who throughout his Viceroyalty has taken an active and sympathetic interest in the welfare of our industry.'

V

This study thus underlines the fact that the state promoted the development of tea plantation in Bengal during the second half of the nineteenth century, by way of the distribution of wastelands, the development of transportation (both railways and roadways) and soft fiscal policies. It subserved the British interest by creating a profitable vent for British capital. Together with a little share of indigenous capital, it amounted to Rs. 90.93 million per annum between 1910 and 1914. There were altogether 300 tea gardens in 1915, with a plough area of more than 161,000 acres. Bengal was the beneficiary as a result, as substantial employment opportunities – about 133,350 in 1915 – were created in these plantations. Their aggregate level of production stood at about 90 million lbs in 1915. Foreign sales dominated their outlets, however. The lion's share went to the United Kingdom, leaving insignificant, though rising, proportions for Russia, Canada and Australia from the early 1890s. In all these countries China had enjoyed a monopoly in the past. Indian tea became dominant in all of them, however, on the strength of its comparative advantages, in terms of both quality and price.

Notes

1 A British parliamentary debate thus emphasised, 'A larger field for the employment of capital, a greater vent for our manufacturers, a wider range for our shipping, are the objects we should aim at' (quoted in Ambirajan 1978: 45).

2 Bank wrote to the company directors, 'They [tea plants] may certainly be cultivated with success in the Northern Parts of the Province of Behar Rungpoor and Coosbeyhar [Cooch Behar] for instance where the Latitude and the Cooling influence of the neighbouring mountains of Bhutan give every reason to expect a climate eminently similar to the Parts of China in which good black Teas are at Present manufactured' (quoted in Griffiths 1967: 34). Note that, by carving out the northern part of erstwhile Rangpur, the Jalpaiguri district was formed in 1869. The Dooars belonged to this region.

3 Baildon's conjecture is based (i) on the Chinese mythologies that from the eyelashes of a Buddhist devotee (who was an Indian prince) named Dharma grew tea bushes in China; and (ii) on the authority of Kaempfer that the tea plant was introduced in Japan by a person named Dharma. He concludes that 'it is possible, and even very probable, that the plant was brought to the notice of the Chinese by Dharma, just as it was to that of the Japanese by the same person' (Baildon 1882: 9).

4 In February 1839 the Bengal Tea Association was formed, with a capital Rs. 1,000,000 (2,000 shares of Rs. 500 each), to take lease of the government's experimental gardens in Assam. Members of the Carr, Tagore & Co. owned 475 shares. In the same month the Assam Tea Company was formed in London, with £500,000, for the same purpose. On 30 May 1839 the former was merged with the latter, and it was referred to as the Calcutta Committee (Kling 1966: 44). There were five Indian members in the Calcutta Committee, including Dwarkanath Tagore, Prasanna Kumar Tagore and Motilal Seal (Mukherjee 1976: 488f.).

5 The administrative report (GOB 1862: 142) thus noted that 'hill-men chiefly from Nepal were preferred to coolies imported from the plains, and that a greater influx of labour from Nepal could be secured if the supply of food in Darjeeling could be increased and the price lessened by improving the means of communication'.

6 Myint (1980: 44) observes that 'these [low] wages tended to stick at their initial level in spite of the rapid expansion in the production of the mining and plantation'.

7 According to Anon. (1888: 71–2), 'The coolies are too well paid in Darjeeling, and if they were paid a lower rate, they would turn out to work better.'

8 Under the superintendent system, a number of neighbouring gardens jointly employed a superintendent to ensure a given scale of wage amongst them, and also to restrict inter-garden labour movement (Iftikhar-ul-Awwal 1979: 55).

9 Anon. (1888: 72) thus notes, 'There may be a few gardens where the labour supply is scarce, through being close to Darjeeling or the manager being disliked, or in unhealthy situations where it is necessary to pay highly…'

10 'In these gardens one finds number of coolies who have become practically permanent residents. They have been living on the same plots of land for a number of years, and have a house superior to the average found in coolie lines, with a well-cultivated plot of land of their own on the garden property' (Arbuthnott 1904: 6).

11 'The anomaly of tea growers striving for markets thousands of miles away, while making no effort to capture that lying at their door, formed the subject of strong remark by His Excellency Lord Curzon' (ITMEC 1905: 176).

12 'Tea is an acquired taste' (Money 1878: 172). He clarifies that it means 'not only that the adult who had never tasted Tea would not like it when first offered to him, but also that, with those who consume it regularly, any Tea that differs in flavour from what is habitually drunk is not realised' (ibid.).

13 'Its development dates from the discovery that Indian dust gives a greater strength to "tablet" tea than Chinese' (GOI 1909: 37). In fact, Russia imported brick tea from China by 8 million lbs in 1907, 'in which Indian dust has been blended' (ibid.).

14 Indian exports to Afghanistan were diverted to Persia in the late 1880s due to 'the extortionate dues charged in that country on tea from India in transit to countries beyond making the continuance of that route unprofitable' (GOI 1891: 32–3).

15 Indian tea 'shipped to European Turkey was intended partly for Russian consumption and partly for Azarbizan in North Persia which it reaches by way of Trebizond' (GOI 1900: 35).

16 A Russian unit of weight equivalent to 16.38 kg, or 36.11 lbs.

17 This was perhaps due to the contemporary perception about wastelands. While analysing the influence of John Locke's theory of property on India's wasteland policies, Whitehead (2010: 92) notes, 'Since the revenue settlements and private property rights did not apply to the hill areas, such lands were deemed to be still wastelands [in the Lockean sense], occupying a "natural state" inhabited by wild tribes who wandered at will and appropriated the fruits of their labour in common. They were also often regarded as outlaws.'

18 Thus, a report for 1872–3 underlines, 'During the past year very close inquiries have been made into the waste land affairs of Darjeeling. It has been turned out that the rights of the occupiers in the Darjeeling Hills had been in very many cases wholly ignored; ryots belonging to the tribes which had held those hills long before the British came to India, had been treated as mere squatters, whose land could be sold over their heads as waste. In one lot a thousand acres of some of the best cultivated land in the Darjeeling district, with villages and families thereon, had been sold as Government waste land to a local speculator. In another some scores of acres of cardamom gardens, a kind of cultivation which involves much labour and expense, had been sold as waste, without reference to, or consideration for, the ryots who owned the gardens' (GOB 1874: 79).

19 In this connection, J. N. Stuart, the ITA chairman, remarked in his AGM speech (ITA 1894: 3), 'I believe the matter of roads and communications generally throughout the Dooars is the most pressing point for the Committee to take up, and I feel that if the matter is put properly before the Lieutenant-Governor, he will do the utmost that the fund at the disposal of the Government will allow.'

Bibliography

Ambirajan, S. (1978) *Classical Political Economy and British Policy in India*. Cambridge: Cambridge University Press.

Anon. (1888) *Notes on Tea in Darjeeling by a Planter*. Darjeeling: Scotch Mission Orphanage Press.

Anon. (1906) 'Tea: The Injustice of the High Duty' [written by a member of *The Times* advertising staff from information supplied by the Anti-Tea-Duty League, etc.]. London: Times Office.

Anon. (1909) 'Labour Rules'. In *Indian Planters' Gazette and Sporting News*, 8 May.

Arbuthnott, J. C. (1904) *Report on the Conditions of Tea Garden Labour in the Duars of Bengal, in Madras, and in Ceylon*. Shillong: Assam Secretariat Printing.

Baildon, S. (1882) *The Tea Industry in India*. London: W. H. Allen.

Baker, C. (1961) 'A Note on Nguru Immigration to Nyasaland', *Nyasaland Journal* 14 (1), 41–2.

Bald, C. (1922) *Indian Tea: Its Culture and Manufacture*, 4th edn. Calcutta: Thacker, Spink.

Ball, S. (1848) *An Account of the Cultivation and Manufacture of Tea in China*. London: Longman, Brown, Green, & Longman.

Beckford, G. L. (1969) 'The Economics of Agricultural Resource Use and Development of Plantation Economies', *Social and Economic Studies* 18 (4), 321–47.

Buchanan, D. H. (1934) *The Development of Capitalistic Enterprise in India*. New York: Macmillan.

Campbell, A. (1869) 'Note on the Late Mr. Crawfurd's Paper on the Migration of Coffee, Tea, etc.', *Transactions of the Ethnological Society of London* 7, 207–9.

Chamney, M. (1933) *The Story of the Tea Leaf*. Calcutta: New Indian Press.

Crawfurd, J. (1869) 'On the History and Migration of Cultivated Plants Producing Coffee, Tea, Cocoa, etc.', *Transactions of the Ethnological Society of London* 7, 197–206.

Dash, A. J. (1947) *Bengal District Gazetteers: Darjeeling*. Calcutta: Bengal Secretariat Press.

De Haan, A. (1995) 'Migration in Eastern India: A Segmented Labour Market', *Indian Economic and Social History Review* 32 (1), 51–93.

Edger, J. W. (1873) 'Note'. In Government of India *Papers Relating to the Tea Industry in Bengal*, i–xxviii. Calcutta: Bengal Secretariat Press.

Evans, B. (1995) 'Constructing a Plantation Labour Force: The Plantation–Village Nexus in South India', *Indian Economic and Social History Review* 32 (2), 155–76.

Fielder, C. H. (1869) 'On the Rise, Progress, and Future Prospects of Tea Cultivation in British India', *Journal of the Statistical Society of London* 32 (1), 29–37.

Gilboy, E. W. (1934) 'Time Series and the Derivation of Demand and Supply Curves: A Study of Coffee and Tea, 1850–1930', *Quarterly Journal of Economics* 48 (4), 667–85.

Goradia, P., and Sircar, K. (2010) *The Saga of Indian Tea*. Vadodara: Contemporary Targett.

Government of Bengal (GOB) (1862) *Annual Report on the Administration of Bengal for 1860–1*. National Library Archive, Calcutta.

Government of Bengal (GOB) (1863) *Annual Report on the Administration of Bengal for 1861–2*. National Library Archive, Calcutta.
Government of Bengal (GOB) (1864) *Annual Report on the Administration of Bengal for 1862–3*. National Library Archive, Calcutta.
Government of Bengal (GOB) (1865) *Annual Report on the Administration of Bengal for 1863–4*. National Library Archive, Calcutta.
Government of Bengal (GOB) (1866) *Annual Report on the Administration of Bengal for 1864–5*. National Library Archive, Calcutta.
Government of Bengal (GOB) (1868) *Annual Report on the Administration of Bengal for 1866–7*. National Library Archive, Calcutta.
Government of Bengal (GOB) (1869) *Annual Report on the Administration of Bengal for 1867–8*. National Library Archive, Calcutta.
Government of Bengal (GOB) (1870) *Annual Report on the Administration of Bengal for 1868–9*. National Library Archive, Calcutta.
Government of Bengal (GOB) (1871) *Annual Report on the Administration of Bengal for 1869–70*. National Library Archive, Calcutta.
Government of Bengal (GOB) (1873) *Annual Report on the Administration of Bengal for 1871–2*. National Library Archive, Calcutta.
Government of Bengal (GOB) (1874) *Annual Report on the Administration of Bengal for 1872–3*. National Library Archive, Calcutta.
Government of Bengal (GOB) (1877) *Annual Report on the Administration of Bengal for 1875–6*. National Library Archive, Calcutta.
Government of Bengal (GOB) (1878) *Annual Report on the Administration of Bengal for 1876–7*. National Library Archive, Calcutta.
Government of Bengal (GOB) (1879) *Annual report on the Administration of Bengal for 1877–8*. National Library Archive, Calcutta.
Government of Bengal (GOB) (1881) *Annual Report on the Administration of Bengal for 1879–80*. National Library Archive, Calcutta.
Government of Bengal (GOB) (1891) *Annual Report on the Administration of Bengal for 1889–90*. National Library Archive, Calcutta.
Government of Bengal (GOB) (1894) *Annual Report on the Administration of Bengal for 1892–3*. National Library Archive, Calcutta.
Government of Bengal (GOB) (1895) *Annual Report on the Administration of Bengal for 1893–4*. National Library Archive, Calcutta.
Government of Bengal (GOB) (1896) *Report of the Labour Enquiry Commission*. Calcutta: Bengal Secretariat Press.
Government of Bengal (GOB) (1897) *Annual Report on the Administration of Bengal for 1895–6*. National Library Archive, Calcutta.
Government of Bengal (GOB) (1900) *Annual Report on the Administration of Bengal for 1898–9*. National Library Archive, Calcutta.
Government of Bengal (GOB) (1901) *Annual Report on the Administration of Bengal for 1899–1900*. National Library Archive, Calcutta.
Government of Bengal (GOB) (1902) *Annual Report on the Administration of Bengal for 1900–01*. National Library Archive, Calcutta.
Government of Bengal (GOB) (1903a) *Annual Report on the Administration of Bengal for 1901–2*. National Library Archive, Calcutta.
Government of Bengal (GOB) (1903b) *Report of the Rail-borne Traffic of Bengal for the Year 1901–02*. National Library Archive, Calcutta.

Government of Bengal (GOB) (1905) *Report of the Rail-borne Traffic of Bengal for the Year 1903–04.* National Library Archive, Calcutta.

Government of Bengal (GOB) (1908) *Annual Report on the Administration of Bengal for 1906–7.* National Library Archive, Calcutta.

Government of Bengal (GOB) (1909) *Annual Report on the Administration of Bengal for 1907–8.* National Library Archive, Calcutta.

Government of Bengal (GOB) (1910) *Annual Report on the Administration of Bengal for 1908–9.* National Library Archive, Calcutta.

Government of Bengal (GOB) (1914) *Annual Report on the Administration of Bengal for 1912–13.* National Library Archive, Calcutta.

Government of Bengal (GOB) (1916) *Annual Report on the Administration of Bengal for 1914–15.* National Library Archive, Calcutta.

Government of Bengal (GOB) (1917) *Annual Report on the Administration of Bengal for 1915–16.* National Library Archive, Calcutta.

Government of India (GOI) (1866) *Annals of the Indian Administration for 1864–5*, vol. IX. National Library Archive, Calcutta.

Government of India (GOI) (1872) *Annals of the Indian Administration for 1870–1*, vol. XV. National Library Archive, Calcutta.

Government of India (GOI) (1873) *Papers Relating to the Tea Industry in Bengal.* Calcutta: Bengal Secretariat Press.

Government of India (GOI) (1876) *Review of the Trade of British India with Foreign Countries during 1870–1 and 1874–5.* National Library Archive, Calcutta.

Government of India (GOI) (1878) *Review of the Trade of British India with Foreign Countries for 1876–7.* National Library Archive, Calcutta.

Government of India (GOI) (1879) *Review of the Trade of British India with Foreign Countries for 1877–8.* National Library Archive, Calcutta.

Government of India (GOI) (1885) *Review of the Trade of British India with Foreign Countries for 1884.* National Library Archive, Calcutta.

Government of India (GOI) (1886) *Review of the Trade of British India with Foreign Countries for 1884–5.* National Library Archive, Calcutta.

Government of India (GOI) (1887) *Review of the Trade of British India with Foreign Countries for 1885–6.* National Library Archive, Calcutta.

Government of India (GOI) (1890) *Review of the Trade of British India with Foreign Countries for 1888–89.* National Library Archive, Calcutta.

Government of India (GOI) (1891) *Review of the Trade of British India with Foreign Countries for 1889–90.* National Library Archive, Calcutta.

Government of India (GOI) (1895) *Review of the Trade of British India with Foreign Countries for 1893–4.* National Library Archive, Calcutta.

Government of India (GOI) (1896) *Review of the Trade of British India with Foreign Countries for 1894–5.* National Library Archive, Calcutta.

Government of India (GOI) (1897) *Review of the Trade of British India with Foreign Countries for 1895–6.* National Library Archive, Calcutta.

Government of India (GOI) (1898) *Review of the Trade of British India with Foreign Countries for 1896–7.* National Library Archive, Calcutta.

Government of India (GOI) (1899) *Review of the Trade of British India with Foreign Countries for 1897–8.* National Library Archive, Calcutta.

Government of India (GOI) (1900) *Review of the Trade of British India with Foreign Countries for 1898–9.* National Library Archive, Calcutta.

Government of India (GOI) (1901) *Review of the Trade of British India with Foreign Countries for 1899–1900*. National Library Archive, Calcutta.
Government of India (GOI) (1903) *Review of the Trade of British India with Foreign Countries for 1901–2*. National Library Archive, Calcutta.
Government of India (GOI) (1905) *Review of the Trade of British India with Foreign Countries for 1903–4*. National Library Archive, Calcutta.
Government of India (GOI) (1906) *Review of the Trade of British India with Foreign Countries for 1904–5*. National Library Archive, Calcutta.
Government of India (GOI) (1909) *Review of the Trade of British India with Foreign Countries for 1907–8*. National Library Archive, Calcutta.
Government of India (GOI) (1912) *Review of the Trade of British India with Foreign Countries for 1910–11*. National Library Archive, Calcutta.
Government of India (GOI) (1914) *Report on the Production of Tea in India in the Calendar Year 1913*. Calcutta: Superintendent Government Printing.
Government of India (GOI) (1918) *Bombay, Baroda and Central India Railway System Corrected up to 31 March, 1918*. Calcutta: Superintendent Government Printing.
Gow Wilson & Stanton Ltd (1897) *Tea Producing Companies of India and Ceylon*. London: A. Southey.
Griffiths, P. (1967) *The History of the Indian Tea Industry*. London: Weidenfeld & Nicolson.
Gupta, B. (2001) 'The International Tea Cartel during the Great Depression, 1929–1933', *Economic History Review* 61 (1), 144–59.
Ibbetson, A. (1912) *Tea: From Grower to Consumer*. London: Sir Isaac Pitman & Sons.
Iftikhar-ul-Awwal, A. Z. M. (1979) 'Supply of Labour to Bengal Tea Industry, 1900–1939', *Bangladesh Historical Studies* 4, 49–63.
Indian Tea Association (ITA) (1882) *Annual Report*. Calcutta: ITA.
Indian Tea Association (ITA) (1884) *Annual Report*. Calcutta: ITA.
Indian Tea Association (ITA) (1885) *Annual Report*. Calcutta: ITA.
Indian Tea Association (ITA) (1886) *Annual Report*. Calcutta: ITA.
Indian Tea Association (ITA) (1887) *Annual Report*. Calcutta: ITA.
Indian Tea Association (ITA) (1888) *Annual Report*. Calcutta: ITA.
Indian Tea Association (ITA) (1889) *Annual Report*. Calcutta: ITA.
Indian Tea Association (ITA) (1891) *Annual Report*. Calcutta: ITA.
Indian Tea Association (ITA) (1892) *Annual Report*. Calcutta: ITA.
Indian Tea Association (ITA) (1893) *Annual Report*. Calcutta: ITA.
Indian Tea Association (ITA) (1894) *Annual Report*. Calcutta: ITA.
Indian Tea Association (ITA) (1895) *Annual Report*. Calcutta: ITA.
Indian Tea Association (ITA) (1903) *Annual Report*. Calcutta: ITA.
Indian Tea Association (ITA) (1905) *Annual Report*. Calcutta: ITA.
Indian Tea Association (ITA) (1906) *Annual Report*. Calcutta: ITA.
Indian Tea Markets Expansion Commission (ITMEC) (1905) 'Final Report of the Commissioners'. In Indian Tea Association *Annual Report*, 176–82. Calcutta: ITA.
Jones, W. O. (1968) 'Plantations'. In Sills, D. L. (ed.) *International Encyclopaedia of the Social Sciences*, vol. XII, 156. New York: Macmillan.
Kling, B. B. (1966) 'The Origin of the Managing Agency System in India', *Journal of Asian Studies* 26 (1), 37–47.
Kooiman, D. (1992) 'Plantations in Southern Asia: Indigenous Plants and Foreign Implantations', *South Asia* 15 (1), 53–79.

Meyer, E. (1990) 'Aspects of the Sinhalese–Tamil Relations in the Plantation Areas of Sri Lanka under the British Raj', *Indian Economic and Social History Review* 27 (2), 165–88.

Misra, B. (1987) 'Quality, Investment and International Competitiveness: Indian Tea Industry, 1880–1910', *Economic and Political Weekly* 22 (6), 230–8.

Monahan, F. J. (1910) *Report of the Duars Committee*. Shillong: Eastern Bengal and Assam Government Press.

Money, E. (1878) *The Cultivation and Manufacture of Tea*, 3rd edn. Calcutta: Thacker.

Mukherjee, S. (1976) 'Emergence of Bengali Entrepreneurship in Tea Plantation in a Bengal District, 1879–1933', *Indian Economic and Social History Review* 13 (4), 487–512.

Mukherjee, S. (1978) 'Changing Control in Some Selected Tea Producing Companies of Jalpaiguri Town', *Social Scientist* 6 (11), 57–69.

Myint, H. (1980) *The Economics of the Developing Countries*. Bombay: B. I. Publications.

O'Brien, R. D. (1883) *Darjeeling: the Sanitarium of Bengal, and Its Surroundings*. Calcutta: W. Newman.

O'Conor, J. E. (1887) 'Note on the Effect of a Low Rate of Exchange on the Indian Export Trade'. In Government of India *Review of the Trade of British India with Foreign Countries for 1885–6*, 51–88. National Library Archive, Calcutta.

Okakura, K. (1906) *The Book of Tea*. London: G. P. Putnam's Sons.

Palmer, R. (1985a) 'White Farmers in Malawi: Before and after the Depression', *African Affairs* 84 (335), 211–45.

Palmer, R. (1985b) 'The Nyasaland Tea Industry in the Era of International Tea Restrictions, 1933–1950', *Journal of African History* 26 (2), 215–39.

Palmer, R. (1986) 'Working Conditions and Worker Responses on Nyasaland Tea Estates', *Journal of African History* 27 (1), 105–26.

Parliamentary Papers (P.P.) (1858) *Memorandum of the Improvements in the Administration of India during the Last Thirty Years*. London: Hansard.

Parliamentary Papers (P.P.) (1861) *Moral and Material Progress and Condition of India for the Year 1859–60*. London: Hansard.

Parliamentary Papers (P.P.) (1862) *Moral and Material Progress and Condition of India for the Year 1860–1*. London: Hansard.

Parliamentary Papers (P.P.) (1863a) *Moral and Material Progress and Condition of India for the Year 1861–2*. London: Hansard.

Parliamentary Papers (P.P.) (1863b) *Reports Made to the Government on the Extension of Tea Plantations in India*. London: Hansard.

Parliamentary Papers (P.P.) (1867) *Statistical Abstract Relating to British India, from 1840 to 1865*. London: HMSO.

Parliamentary Papers (P.P.) (1869) *Moral and Material Progress and Condition of India for the Year 1867–8*. London: Hansard.

Parliamentary Papers (P.P.) (1873a) *Moral and Material Progress and Condition of India for the Year 1871–2*. London: Hansard.

Parliamentary Papers (P.P.) (1873b) *Statistical Abstract Relating to British India, from 1862 to 1871*. London: HMSO.

Parliamentary Papers (P.P.) (1876a) *Statistical Abstract Relating to British India, from 1865 to 1874*. London: HMSO.

Parliamentary Papers (P.P.) (1883a) *Moral and Material Progress and Condition of India for the Year 1881–2*. London: Hansard.

Parliamentary Papers (P.P.) (1883b) *Statistical Abstract Relating to British India, from 1872/3 to 1881/2*. London: HMSO.

Parliamentary Papers (P.P.) (1884) *Moral and Material Progress and Condition of India for the Year 1882–3*. London: Hansard.
Parliamentary Papers (P.P.) (1888) *Moral and Material Progress and Condition of India for the Year 1886–7*. London: Hansard.
Parliamentary Papers (P.P.) (1889) *Moral and Material Progress and Condition of India for the Year 1887–8*. London : Hansard.
Parliamentary Papers (P.P.) (1893a) *Moral and Material Progress and Condition of India for the Year 1891–2*. London: Hansard.
Parliamentary Papers (P.P.) (1893b) *Statistical Abstract Relating to British India, from 1882/3 to1891/2*. London: HMSO.
Parliamentary Papers (P.P.) (1894) *Moral and Material Progress and Condition of India for the Year 1892–3*. London: Hansard.
Parliamentary Papers (P.P.) (1895) *Moral and Material Progress and Condition of India for the Year 1893–4*. London : Hansard.
Parliamentary Papers (P.P.) (1897) *Moral and Material Progress and Condition of India for the Year 1895–6*. London: Hansard.
Parliamentary Papers (P.P.) (1898) *Moral and Material Progress and Condition of India for the Year 1896–7*. London: Hansard.
Parliamentary Papers (P.P.) (1899a) *Moral and Material Progress and Condition of India for the Year 1897–8*. London: Hansard.
Parliamentary Papers (P.P.) (1899b) *Statistical Abstract Relating to British India, from 1888/9 to 1897/8*. London: HMSO.
Parliamentary Papers (P.P.) (1900a) *Moral and Material Progress and Condition of India for the Year 1898–9*. London: Hansard.
Parliamentary Papers (P.P.) (1900b) *Statistical Abstract Relating to British India, from 1889/90 to 1898/9*. London: HMSO.
Parliamentary Papers (P.P.) (1902) *Moral and Material Progress and Condition of India for the Year 1900–1*. London: Hansard.
Parliamentary Papers (P.P.) (1905) *Moral and Material Progress and Condition of India for the Year 1903–4*. London: Hansard.
Parliamentary Papers (P.P.) (1906) *Moral and Material Progress and Condition of India for the Year 1904–5*. London: Hansard.
Parliamentary Papers (P.P.) (1907) *Statistical Abstract Relating to British India, from 1896/7 to 1905/06*. London: HMSO.
Parliamentary Papers (P.P.) (1908a) *Moral and Material Progress and Condition of India for the Year 1906–7*. London: Hansard.
Parliamentary Papers (P.P.) (1908b) *Statistical Abstract Relating to British India, from 1897/8 to 1906/07*. London: HMSO.
Parliamentary Papers (P.P.) (1910) *Moral and Material Progress and Condition of India for the Year 1908–9*. London: Hansard.
Parliamentary Papers (P.P.) (1911) *Moral and Material Progress and Condition of India for the Year 1909–10*. London: Hansard.
Parliamentary Papers (P.P.) (1912) *Moral and Material Progress and Condition of India for the Year 1910–11*. London: Hansard.
Parliamentary Papers (P.P.) (1914) *Statistical Abstract Relating to British India, from 1904/05 to 1912/13*. London: HMSO.
Parliamentary Papers (P.P.) (1918a) *Statistical Abstract Relating to British India, from 1907/08 to 1916/17*. London: HMSO.

Parliamentary Papers (P.P.) (1918b) *Tables Relating to the Trade of British India with British Possessions and Foreign Countries for 1916–17*. London: Hansard.

Parliamentary Papers (P.P.) (1919) *Statistical Abstract Relating to British India, from 1908/09 to 1917/18*. London: HMSO.

Pomeranz, K. (2000) *The Great Divergence: China, Europe, and the Making of the Modern World Economy*. Princeton, NJ: Princeton University Press.

Ray, I. (1998) *Road Planning for Economic Development*. New Delhi: Classical Publishing.

Ray, I. (2015) '"The Great Divergence" Revisited: The Case of Bengal in Early Modern Times', *Economic History of Developing Regions* 30 (2), 125–56.

Ray, I., and Sarkar, R. (2005) 'Reconstructing Nineteenth-Century Trade Routes between Bhutan and Assam: Evidences from British Political Missions', *Journal of Bhutan Studies* 13 (Winter), 1–30.

Rees, J. D. (1904) 'Tea and Taxation', *Imperial and Asiatic Quarterly Review and Oriental and Colonial Record* 18 (35), 2–10.

Robbins, L. (1958) *Robert Torrens and the Evolution of Classical Economics*. London: Macmillan.

Roy, S. (2011) 'Historical Review of Growth of Tea Industries in India: A Study of Assam Tea'. In L. Chun-Hua and Z. Ming (eds.) *International Conference on Social Science and Humanity*, vol.V, 166–70. Singapore: IACSIT Press.

Sarkar, G. K. (1972) *The World Tea Economy*. New Delhi: Oxford University Press.

Sharma, J. (2006) 'British Science, Chinese Skill and Assam Tea: Making Empire's Gardens', *Indian Economic and Social History Review* 43 (4), 429–55.

Shlomowitz, R., and Brennan, L. (1990) 'Mortality and Migrant Labour en Route to Assam, 1863–1824', *Indian Economic and Social History Review* 27 (3), 313–30.

Siddique, M. A. B. (1995) 'The Labour Market and the Growth of the Tea Industry in India: 1840–1900', *South Asia* 18 (1), 83–113.

Stewart, N. R. (1960) 'Tea: A New Agricultural Industry for Argentina', *Economic Geography* 36 (3), 267–76.

Tharian, G. K. (1984) 'Historical Roots of the Crisis in the South Indian Tea Industry', *Social Scientist* 12 (4), 34–50.

Wakefield, E. G. (1849) *A View of the Art of Colonization, with Present Reference to the British Empire; in Letters between a Statesman and a Colonist*. London: John W. Parker.

Wallis-Tayler, A. J. (1900) *Tea Machinery and Tea Factories*. London: C. Lockwood & Son.

Walsh, J. M. (1892) *Tea: Its History and Mystery*. Philadelphia: Henry T. Coates.

Watson, W. L. (1889) 'Report of the Sub-committee on the American Market for Indian Tea'. In Indian Tea Association *Annual Report*, 59–65. Calcutta: ITA.

Weatherstone, J. (1992) 'Historical Introduction'. In Willson, K. C., and Clifford, M. N. (eds.) *Tea: Cultivation to Consumption*, 1–23. London: Chapman & Hall.

White, J. B. (1887) 'The Indian Tea Industry: Its Rise, Progress during Fifty Years, and Prospects Considered from a Commercial Point of View', *Journal of the Royal Society of Arts* 35, 733–54.

Whitehead, J. (2010) 'John Locke and the Governance of India's Landscape: The Category of Wasteland in Colonial Revenue and Forest Legislation', *Economic and Political Weekly* 45 (50), 83–93.

Wight, W. (1959) 'Nomenclature and Classification of the Tea Plant', *Nature* 183 (4677), 1726–8.

Appendix 7.1 Tea statistics for Bengal, 1860–1915

Year	Gardens (number)	Land (acres)	Production (lbs)	Employment	Year	Gardens (number)	Land (acres)	Production (lbs)	Employment
1860	21[1]	2,639[1]	25,425*	2,624[1]	1888	324[32]	71,841[32]	18,950,822[31]	–
1861	30[2]	5,152.5[2]	27,983[3]	4,819[3]	1889	340[32]	70,968[32]	20,497,857[34]	–
1862	–	9,102[4]	40,446[4]	7,447[4]	1890	–	85,573[33]	21,070,453[34]	–
1863	32[6]	12,344[5]	126,439[5]	6,098[5]	1891	356[35]	90,815[33]	25,690,346[35]	–
1864	25[6]	8,813[6]	351,700[6]	–	1892	367[35]	92,852[33]	24,492,851[36]	131,698[37]
1865	32[7]	9,829[8]	335,481[8]	–	1893	368[37]	110,510[38]	25,806,399[39]	140,313[37]
1866	39[9]	7,986[8]	371,174[8]	–	1894	370[40]	98,345[41]	26,795,407[42]	81,971[40]
1867	40[9]	9,765[10]	441,189[10]	–	1895	398[40]	104,197[43]	47,171,891[40]	89,838[40]
1868	44[10]	10,068[10]	851,549[10]	7,073[10]	1896	–	105,707[44]	36,652,000[44]	–
1869	55[11]	10,769[11]	1,319,743[11]	7,622[11]	1897	–	128,067[44]	38,951,000[44]	–
1870	60[12]	11,325[12]	1,704,136[12]	8,000[12a]	1898	–	130,241[45]	40,726,000[45]	–
1871	63[12b]	12,305[14]	2,665,821[12]	9,536[12b]	1899	469[46]	132,923[45]	43,268,817[46]	84,769[46]
1872	–	14,639[15]	3,000,000[16]	12,361[17]	1900	418[47]	134,572[45]	44,850,628[47]	116,794[47]
1873	–	14,503[18]	2,994,724**	–	1901	405[47]	135,129[48]	44,623,074[47]	109,070[47]
1874	–	18,881[19]	3,898,738**	–	1902	393[49]	135,200[50]	44,416,956[49]	101,266[49]
1875	121[18]	22,162[18]	4,610,758[18]	–	1903	376[49]	136,000[50]	44,189,630[49]	102,994[49]
1876	132[18]	25,028[18]	4,181,622[18]	–	1904	–	134,704[50]	53,886,000[50]	–
1877	163[20]	42,652[20]	5,284,049[20]	–	1905	–	136,153[51]	53,570,740[51]	–
1878	173[21]	24,417[21]	7,525,980[21]	–	1906	–	136,484[51]	60,688,193[51]	–
1879	189[21]	33,359[21]	5,538,040[21]	–	1907	–	139,516[51]	60,216,558[51]	–
1880	200[22]	31,558[22]	5,978,079[22]	–	1908	–	141,553[51]	59,971,647[51]	–
1881	209[22]	36,968[22]	7,403,293[23]	–	1909	–	143,254[51]	60,920,725[51]	–

(continued)

Appendix 7.1 Cont.

Year	*Gardens (number)*	*Land (acres)*	*Production (lbs)*	*Employment*	*Year*	*Gardens (number)*	*Land (acres)*	*Production (lbs)*	*Employment*
1882	225[24]	40,938[24]	9,088,796[25]	–	1910	–	145,868[51]	64,674,243[51]	–
1883	–	42,862**	9,153,104[26]	–	1911	–	146,756[51]	64,653,923[52]	–
1884	–	49,222**	10,511,291[27]	–	1912	374[52]	150,497[51]	70,524,169[52]	124,412[52]
1885	–	55,698[28]	11,422,894[29]	–	1913	–	156,002[51]	80,108,705[53]	129,580[54]
1886	–	69,810[30]	13,610,682[29]	–	1914	297[53]	159,054[53]	75,373,201[53]	130,438[53]
1887	–	73,741[30]	14,997,805[31]	–	1915	300[55]	161,300[55]	89,526,057[55]	133,341[55]

Notes: * Considering that 90,108 lbs of green leaves yielded 36,808 lbs of tea in 1863 (GOB 1865: 98), and 62,240 lbs of leaves were plucked in 1860 (P.P. 1889: 115), this figure is obtained; ** estimated.

Sources: 1: P.P. (1862: 191); 2: P.P. (1863a: 310); 3: GOB (1863: 60); 4: GOB (1864: 82); 5: GOB (1865: 98); 6: GOB (1866: 141); 7: GOB (1868: 146); 8: P.P. (1869: 50); 9: GOB (1869: 207); 10: GOB (1870: 191; for acreage, the figure is deduced from (a) the acreage at 10,068 in 1869, and (b) the rise in acreage at 303 acres, as in the present source; 11: GOB (1871: 124); 12: GOB (1873: 232); 12a: de Haan (1995: 57); 12b: GOB (1873: 392); 13: GOI (1872: 380); 14: P.P. (1873a: 33); 15: GOB (1874: 20); 16: GOB (1874: 21); 17: GOI (1873: 18); 18: GOB (1878: 147–8); 19: O'Brien (1883: 54); 20: GOB (1879: 160–1); 21: GOB (1881: 180); 22: P.P. (1883a: 76); 23: ITA (1884: 65); 24: P.P. (1884: 196); 25: ITA (1884: 18–19); 26: ITA (1885: 44); 27: ITA (1886: 107–108); 28: P.P. (1888: 105); 29: ITA (1887: 88); 30: P.P. (1889: 115); 31: ITA (1889: 39); 32: GOB (1891: 392); 33: P.P. (1894: 98); 34: ITA (1891: 188); 35: GOB (1894: 371); 36: ITA (1893: 271); 37: GOB (1895: 152); 38: P.P. (1895: 99); 39: ITA (1894: 257); 40: GOB (1897: 138, 143); 41: P.P. (1898: 116); 42: ITA (1895: 246); 43: P.P. (1899a: 122); 44: P.P. (1900a: 114); 45: P.P. (1902: 122); 46: GOB (1900: 356); 47: GOB (1903a: 306–7); 48: P.P. (1905: 111); 49: GOB (1905: 507); 50: P.P. (1906: 111); 51: GOI (1914: 10–11); 52: GOB (1914: 60, 66); 53: GOB (1916: 67, 73); 54: GOI (1914: 13); 55: GOB (1917: 67).

Appendix 7.2 Exports of tea from India, 1855–1914

Year	*Amount(lbs)*	*Value(Rs.)*	*Year*	*Amount(lbs)*	*Value(Rs.)*
1855	–	405,040[1]★	1885	69,666,116[12]	48,971,770[12]
1856	–	630,750[1]★	1886	80,557,329[12]	48,831,430[12]
1857	–	1,210,610[1]★	1887	89,982,346[12]	53,024,460[12]
1858	–	533,310[1]★	1888	99,339,868[12]	54,731,370[12]
1859	–	605,330[1]★	1889	105,609,533[12]	54,454,870[12]
1860	–	1,277,710[1]★	1890	110,194,819[12]	55,042,930[12]
1861	1,473,270[2]	1,302,803[2]★	1891	123,158,069[12]	62,838,700[12]
1862	2,253,773[2]	1,781,280[2]★	1892	112,788,626[13]	62,923,480[15]
1863	2,920,232[2]	2,202,820[2]★	1893	120,149,407[14]	65,858,350[15]
1864	3,457,430[2]	2,802,840[2]★	1894	122,872,885[16]	75,557,450[15]
1865	4,998,360[3]	2,190,440[3]	1895	130,372,544[16]	76,648,890[15]
1866	6,936,843[3]	3,593,577[3]	1896	150,421,245[17]	81,315,480[15]
1867	8,789,344[4]	6,853,205[4]	1897	151,452,000[18]	80,053,560[15]
1868	11,434,002[4]	9,421,473[4]	1898	157,471,000[18]	80,048,040[15]
1869	12,250,000[5]	10,378,830[2]★	1899	175,038,000[18]	90,921,120[18]
1870	17,750,000[6]	11,205,170[2]★	1900	190,305,000[18]	95,509,301[18]
1871	17,124,508[7]	14,484,673[7]	1901	179,685,000[18]	81,494,893[18]
1872	17,789,911[8]	15,776,907[8]	1902	183,710,931[17]	60,152,000[18]
1873	19,324,235[8]	17,429,256[8]	1903	207,159,793[19]	85,579,327[19]
1874	21,137,087[8]	19,374,292[8]	1904	211,887,158[19]	84,654,867[19]
1875	24,361,599[8]	21,664,168[8]	1905	214,223,788[20a]	64,153,000[20]
1876	27,784,124[8]	26,074,251[8]	1906	233,653,637[20a]	73,697,000[20]
1877	27,925,400[9]	26,201,400★	1907	227,621,657[20a]	76,704,000[21]
1878	33,656,715[9]	30,618,670[9]★	1908	233,961,538[20a]	74,758,000[22]
1879	38,173,521[10]	30,510,200[10]	1909	249,472,934[20a]	80,821,065[24]
1880	46,413,510[11]	30,542,400[11]	1910	254,392,416[23]	84,502,000[25]
1881	49,255,342[12]	36, 628,590[12]	1911	260,862,382[23]	88,529,000[25]
1882	58,233,345[12]	37,388,420[12]	1912	278,601,489[23]	88,646,000[25]
1883	60,473,113[12]	41,342,210[12]	1913	289,518,833[23]	105,566,000[26]
1884	65,147,899[12]	41,373,510[12]	1914	300,733,434[27]	114,265,000[26]

Note: ★ Converted at £1 = Rs. 10.

Sources: 1: P.P. (1867: 52–3); 2: GOI (1876: lxxvi); 3: GOB (1868: xxx) (for 1865–6, 11 months' figures are given); 4: GOB (1870: xxxvii); 5: GOI (1872: 380); 6: GOB (1874: 20); 7: GOB (1874: ci); 8: GOI (1878: 49); 9: P.P. (1883b: 100–3); 10: GOI (1885: xli); 11: GOI (1886: 49); 12: P.P. (1893b: 216–19); 13: GOB (1894: 25); 14: P.P. (1893a: 207); 15: P.P. (1900b: 212); 16: GOB (1897: 162); 17: GOI (1914: 17); 18: GOI (1903: 22); 19: GOI (1909: 38); 20: GOB (1908: 80–1); 20a: P.P. (1914: 160–1); 21: GOB (1909: 79); 22: GOB (1910: 80); 23: GOI (1914: 15); 24: average exports for 1908–12 were reportedly Rs 83,451,213 in GOB (1916: 73); this, along with exports during 1908–12 (excepting 1909), gives this figure; 25: GOB (1914: 60, 66); 26: GOB (1916: 67, 73); 27: P.P. (1919: 165).

Appendix 7.3 Imports of tea into India, 1855–1915

Year	*Quantity (lbs)*	*Value(Rs.)*	*Year*	*Quantity (lbs)*	*Value(Rs.)*
1855	–	1,017,120[1]★	1886	4,214,342[6]	3,242,600[6]★
1856	–	1,201,780[1]★	1887	3,623,872[6]	2,604,180[6]★
1857	–	1,113,430[1]★	1888	4,767,004[6]	3,179,370[6]★
1858	–	1,027,090[1]★	1889	5,382,851[6]	3,636,810[6]★
1859	–	2,726,830[1]★	1890	4,770,008[6]	3,251,410[6]★
1860	–	1,642,820[1]★	1891	6,353,017[6]	4,431,610[6]★
1861	–	1,049,640[1]★	1892	6,022,883[7]	4,433,360[8]★
1862	–	969,180[1]★	1893	7,687,757[7]	5,729,060[8]★
1863	–	1,745,960[1]★	1894	6,326,122[7]	4,246,670[8]★
1864	–	1,488,240[1]★	1895	7,407,703[7]	4,931,830[8]★
1865	1,778,513[2]	1,257,440[1]★	1896	7,847,832[7]	3,456,130[9]★
1866	2,606,291[2]	1,863,100[3]★	1897	3,515,013[10]	1,419,910[10]★
1867	1,971,467[2]	1,345,527[3]★	1898	3,650,442[10]	1,232,960[10]★
1868	2,526,840[2]	2,533,640[3]★	1899	3,203,111[10]	1,057,620[10]★
1869	2,029,054[2]	2,019,870[3]★	1900	4,949,633[10]	1,691,420[10]★
1870	1,668,567[2]	1,665,220[3]★	1901	3,204,467[10]	1,069,290[10]★
1871	740,552[4]	1,140,550[4]★	1902	3,848,357[10]	1,373,200[10]★
1872	2,025,129[4]	2,025,130[4]★	1903	3,672,833[10]	1,388,820[10]★
1873	2,465,770[4]	2,465,760[4]★	1904	3,734,579[10]	1,264,010[10]★
1874	1,828,571[4]	1,828,590[4]★	1905	3,799,272[10]	1,223,290[10]★
1875	1,701,473[4]	1,699,820[4]★	1906	2,683,875[10]	1,076,659[10]★
1876	2,771,204[5]	2,475,660[5]★	1907	3,910,714[11]	1,515,640[11]★
1877	1,755,300[5]	1,401,100[5]★	1908	4,447,506[11]	1,437,540[11]★
1878	2,323,033[5]	1,906,110[5]★	1909	3,679,587[11]	1,171,990[11]★
1879	1,822,345[5]	1,305,180[5]★	1910	4,625,327[11]	1,383,380[11]★
1880	2,534,518[5]	2,120,620[5]★	1911	6,611,816[11]	1,953,910[11]★
1881	2,845,212[6]	1,996,910[6]★	1912	4,521,310[11]	1,396,900[11]★
1882	2,751,085[6]	1,930,520[6]★	1913	4,772,532[11]	1,524,090[11]★
1883	3,055,170[6]	2,376,140[6]★	1914	5,476,790[11]	1,769,500[11]★
1884	3,874,412[6]	3,255,480[6]★	1915	6,202,146[11]	2,253,630[11]★
1885	4,005,637[6]	3,042,580[6]★			

Note: ★ Converted at £1 = Rs. 10.

Sources: 1: P.P. (1867: 46–7); 2: P.P. (1876a: 32–3); 3: P.P. (1873b: 18–19); 4: GOI (1876: lxii); 5: P.P. (1867: 92–5); 6: P.P. (1893b: 208–11); 7: P.P. (1899b: 219); 8: P.P. (1900b: 204–5); 9: P.P. (1907: 148–9); 10: P.P. (1908b: 150–1); 11: P.P. (1918a: 156–7, 158–9).

8 Major industries in 1858–1914

A summary

The present chapter summarises the major findings of industry-wise analysis under four headings: (i) the state of major industries around 1914; (ii) capital and entrepreneurs; (iii) land and labour; and (iv) market and government policies. These form the subject matter in the four sections that follow. For topical interest, I elaborate certain general aspects of the contemporary industrial economy that have only been adumbrated in the texts – such as the managing agency system, in section II; the migration of labour, in section III; and fiscal policies, in section IV. Section V concludes, with a brief discussion on basic changes in the industrial landscape of Bengal during this phase of reindustrialisation.

I

The present study identifies five industries in Bengal that underwent rapid progress during the second half of the nineteenth century. Those are: coal mining; iron smelting and its downstreams; jute processing; paper making; and tea cultivation. In coal mining, as many as 151 joint-stock companies had arisen in Bengal by 1916, along with a large number of tiny firms of proprietorship type. Since only eight such companies ventured outside this province, Bengal surely boasted of its coal mining, with output standing at 15 million tons in 1914. Jute processing and tea cultivation also accommodated a large number of firms. In the former, there were 67 modern mills in 1914–15, with 789,236 spindles and 37,541 looms. For 1908–9 their aggregate production is reported at Rs. 183.50 million. In tea cultivation, there were 300 gardens in 1915, with 161,300 acres of land, where the level of production was about 90 million lbs.

Paper making and iron smelting were then only in their infancy, though the signs of prosperity were distinct. By the turn of the nineteenth century four large-scale paper mills had been set up as joint-stock ventures. Later, two of them were acquired by a third. In 1903 the industry's total production amounted to about 36 million lbs, projecting Bengal as the paper-making hub in the country, with a production share of about 81.89 per cent. As to iron smelting, a different scenario prevailed. A series of early ventures failed, for one reason or another. Finally, the Bengal Iron and Steel Company survived, with installed capacities in 1907 for 520,000 TPA of pig iron, 25,000 to 30,000

TPA of castings and 20,000 TPA of steel. In tandem, a host of engineering industries arose. In 1911 there were 12 large-scale foundries and 15 smaller ones, four arms and ammunition factories, six dockyards and nine engineering workshops. With the setting up of these units the province became a major centre for engineering industry in the country, accounting for 41.27 per cent of total employment. Apart from railway workshops (where the rest of India accounted for 70.37 per cent of total employment), Bengal dominated – in foundries (63.66 per cent), arms and ammunition (57.66 per cent) and dockyards (57.23 per cent).

Three of these industries – iron smelting, paper making and jute processing – had reigned in Bengal prior to British rule. Village artisans (and also tribal people, as in iron smelting) carried out these industries at the cottage scale, using primitive technology. Their tools and implements were also manufactured and maintained in the villages. In some cases, their products were later proved excellent (such as iron), and were even exported to Western countries in the middle of the nineteenth century (such as jute goods). But the technologically innovative products of Britain impaired their financial viability during the colonial age. They achieved a resurrection in the second half of the nineteenth century, however, on modern rails, fighting against the competition from British industries.

One of the primary reasons for this industrial prosperity was the natural resources that were bequeathed to this province. Because of its climate and soils, Bengal was the main jute-producing country globally, and thus enjoyed enormous advantages in this line of production. The seams of coal and iron ore available in Bengal were not inferior in quality to those deposited elsewhere, and were certainly abundant in quantity. Bengal was also rich in various types of fibrous plants that were suitable for paper manufacturing. Moreover, on its northern fringes, soil textures, climatic parameters and the volume of rainfall were ideally suited for tea plantations.

The industrial structure in Bengal, as it had emerged by 1914, should have guaranteed its further industrial prosperity. This was mainly due to coal mining and iron smelting, which provided the basic ingredients for modern industries. No less important was jute processing, which supplied packaging materials for various consumer and industrial goods. The development of these industries gave Bengal a competitive edge for further economic development.

II

British capital underpinned Bengal's reindustrialisation in the second half of the nineteenth century. Contemporary accounts from Britain suggest that this flow of capital was augmented under imperial patronage. Jenks (1938: 225) writes, 'English politicians had promised English businessmen an income on behalf of the Indian ryot. And drawing hope largely from the promise, something like one hundred and fifty million pounds of British capital were invested in India between 1854 and 1869.' He estimates that, out of this, about £20 million was earmarked for industries such as tea cultivation, jute manufacturing and commercial banking. The trend was further accelerated after the opening of the Suez Canal in 1869, which slashed transit times between London and Calcutta and, hence, allowed an early realisation of profits (Knowles 1924: 316–7; Waters 1926: 97; Bose 1954: 23–4).

Entrepreneurial functions in this period were largely carried out under a novel organisational instrument: the managing agency system.[1] Prior to this period – especially from the late eighteenth century onwards, when East India Company servants were debarred from commercial activities – finances were organised under the so-called agency houses. Those houses collected funds from government officials and invested in cross-sector activities, in production (especially indigo cultivation), trading and banking (Webster 2006: 746; Tripathi 1971: M61). Their collapse during the economic depression of 1829–34 heralded the managing agency system in Bengal. Although it was pioneered by a Bengali entrepreneur (Kling 1966; Webster 2006: 750–1),[2] British capital and enterprises heavily dominated this form of organisation. It gave rise to 'gentlemanly' capitalists in London, who were heavily involved in Bengal's industrial adventures. Webster (2006: 761) notes, 'There can be no doubt that the London East India agency houses were part of the gentlemanly capitalist nexus in the City. Their involvement in schemes to channel British capital to India and the east were precisely those activities that Cain and Hopkins regard as central to "gentlemanly capitalism".' The trend was perpetuated after the British financial crisis of 1847–8, especially after the reforms that followed the demise of the East India Company in 1858. These events contributed to 'a new institutional framework [the managing agency system] …which facilitated a substantial increase in the export of capital to Britain's "jewel in the crown", and other parts of the east' (Webster 2006: 760).

The managing houses performed multidimensional tasks. They promoted joint-stock companies, provided them with initial capital and supported their infancy. While exposing them to the public, they retained their controlling shares and ran their management on commission. Since each managing house thus managed a large number of firms, it acquired specialisation in different fields of management, and thus enjoyed the benefits of Adam Smith's division of labour (Smith 1937 [1776]: 3–12). Moreover, the firms they controlled were vertically and horizontally integrated, generating both scale and scope economies and, hence, a high degree of efficiency.

This novel organisation carried out Bengal's industrial development during the second half of the nineteenth century. The industrial capital that was generated in the process was not insignificant for a provincial economy. In coal mining there were 151 joint-stock companies in 1916 with nominal capital of Rs. 83.36 million, and in jute processing in 1914–15 14 joint-stock companies owning 67 mills in which Rs. 85.73 million had been invested. In tea cultivation, there were two types of companies: sterling companies and rupee companies, of which there were 15 and 43, respectively, in 1895. Total investment in this industry works out at Rs. 90.93 million at the close of the study period. Because of their late start, however, iron smelting and paper making had lower levels of investment: Rs. 7.00 million, in 1907, and Rs. 5.69 million, in 1913, respectively. On the downstream side of iron smelting a number of joint-stock companies were also involved. Nine such companies had an aggregate paid-up capital of Rs. 9.75 million in 1911. Thus, in aggregate, industrial capital in the modern sector comes to Rs. 282.46 million by the close of the study period. This excludes the capital of myriad tiny units that ran contemporaneously in different lines of production.

Alongside the British capital, the managing agencies mobilised funds from the Bengali community as well, especially from the landed aristocrats and big traders. In his pioneering work on the asymmetric information theory in economics, Akerlof explains the participation of Indian capital in British managing houses by his 'lemon principle'. His logic is that, by virtue of their 'honest' dealings, those houses attracted 'the savings of rich landlords' who had 'a fear to invest in ventures controlled by other communities' (Akerlof 1970: 498). Bengali entrepreneurs also participated independently in this development process, albeit on a modest scale. Their presence was felt mainly in coal mining and the tea plantations. In coal mining, Dwarkanath Tagore was one of the pioneer entrepreneurs who set up the Bengal Coal Company, the largest firm in the industry. The second largest concern, located at Searsole, was also owned by a Bengali entrepreneur. In fact, out of 37 collieries in 1859, ten were held indigenously. The number increased to 40 in 1897. Two points should be noted, however. First, indigenously held mines were tiny in size; and, second, their enterprises ran largely on promoters' capital; joint-stock companies constituted only about 10 per cent of them.

In tea plantations as well, Bengali entrepreneurs became involved in their country's first ventures, but the industry's development in the province was nurtured exclusively through British capital. The presence of Bengalis was later noticed only at the Dooars in Jalpaiguri. The first Bengali enterprise was set up there in 1877, but numbers swelled in the following decades. There were only six Indian-dominated joint-stock companies in 1882–91, rising to 64 in 1911–20. Out of 163 Indian-owned tea companies in north-east India in 1933, as many as 88 belonged to Jalpaiguri-based Bengali entrepreneurs. In the latter category there were reportedly 128 directors, which included only three Europeans and six Marwaris. The domestic entrepreneurs hailed mainly from the professional and service classes, however, rather than from the mercantile community and landed aristocracy.

Bengali entrepreneurs also participated in the downstream industries of iron smelting, but, as with other industries, they were confined to smaller undertakings. We have noted eight such firms in Howrah's iron works and dockyards. This district also accommodated 16 small engineering firms in 1901, indigenously held, that manufactured various engineering products. The presence of indigenous entrepreneurs is also noticed in Watson (1907: 46), where we find about 149 such firms operating in and around Calcutta.

III

On the supply side, Bengal possessed abundant land and labour around the middle of the nineteenth century. Even the land-intensive activities, such as tea cultivation and coal mining, never suffered from a shortage of land. The Darjeeling Hills, which had once belonged to the Kingdom of Sikkim, were ceded to the East India Company in 1835. Largely under forest and 'practically uninhabited' (Dash 1947: 38), only 100 people resided there in 1839, increasing to 10,000 in 1852 under state initiatives (ibid. 39). Therefore, surplus land was abundant. In the Darjeeling Hills alone about 250,000 acres of wasteland belonged to the government in 1859–60, where tea bushes were subsequently planted. A government report for 1871–2 (GOB 1873: 143–4) thus stresses, 'The land was so abundant that there could be no difficulty in amply supplying all the wants of *bona fide* tea planters without doing injustice to any man.' A similar story holds good for the Dooars as well. The western Dooars, where tea gardens later clustered, had been annexed from the Kingdom of Bhutan in 1865. The region ran along the northern extremities of Jalpaiguri district for about 85 miles, covering an area of about 475 square miles (Monahan 1910: 1). It was also sparsely populated, and entirely belonged to the government. These lands were also provided to tea planters.

The minerals – coal and iron ores – were deposited in the western fringe of the province, especially in Ranigunj and the Rajmahal Hills. The surface of this tract was undulating, with isolated peaks in short and low ranges. The soils were ferruginous with hard beds of laterite, giving rise to dense forests. Agriculture was least practised, and, hence, human settlements were few and far between. Hunter (1876: preface) writes, 'Instead of a wealthy and well-educated population of Hindus and Muhammadans, the western tract is comparatively thinly inhabited by races or castes of a less advanced type, and into whose constitution the aboriginal or semi-Hinduized element strongly enters.' For the purposes of mining, these lands were provided under lease, or under the *zemindari* system. William Blanford (1865: 26) reports that '[t]he surface of the field was formerly covered with jungle, which has now [in 1852] been cleared nearly throughout'. On the question of land, therefore, mining was never constrained.

The other industries, notably jute processing, paper making and engineering, were clustered around Calcutta, where, during the second half of the nineteenth century, the scarcity of land was never felt. Even in 1880, as de Haan (1997: 919) points out, 'the area north of Calcutta was a "jungle", an area with swamps and marshes and a few scattered villages'. Modern mills exploited this advantage, however. We thus find that, whereas the Dundee jute mills struggled in multi-storied buildings with acute shortages of space as well as water, the Calcutta mills afforded spacious office accommodation and comfortable factory sheds, often stretching over several acres of land. The Victoria Mill, for example, had a land area of about 40 acres, which no Dundee mill could even dream of. These were quite astonishing to managers and foremen hailing from Dundee. Moreover, European officials working in various industries around Calcutta were provided with residential quarters with 'tennis courts' and 'spacious lawns' (Buchanan, 1934: 245).

The abundance of labour was another point of advantage. Because of Bengal's traditional skill in jute processing and paper making, modern mills in these industries gathered workers from within the province, at least in their early phase of development. As to the former, Rungta (1985: 116) tells us, 'The supply of labour came mainly from the population living within walking distance of the Mills (say, about five miles). [...] [T]he supply seems to have been sufficient, except during the monsoons.' For coal mining as well, miners were employed from nearby villages. In the case of iron smelting, I have already mentioned that the traditional sector supplied the labour force to its initial ventures.

With the rapid industrial progress, the local reservoir of labour was exhausted, however, and a steady stream of immigration followed. There were three contemporary circuits of migration passing through the neighbourhood of Calcutta. By virtue of their location, the modern industries in the neighbourhood of the city drew labour from all these circuits, with the jute mills dominating therein. A survey among 70,000 jute workers in 1895 revealed that about 50 to 60 per cent of them had migrated from North-Western Provinces and Bihar. Migrations also took place from Andhra Pradesh and Orissa. The literature suggests that various socio-economic and political factors – such as the scarcity of land, low rural wages and repression in their places of origin – underpinned migrations in nineteenth-century Bengal.

Migratory workers also dominated coal mining, especially after the onset of the railway age. They consisted mainly of the Santhals, an aboriginal tribe, hailing from Chota Nagpur, and the Santhal Parganas of Bihar. They were strong-built, courageous and hard-working, so highly suitable for mining. Thanks to their emotional attachment to landholdings, they could be easily attracted to mining by a piece of leasehold land. As they migrated with their families and claimed lower wages for other family members, the industry gained thereby. In addition, there was Muslim immigration from the Manbhum district of Bihar, as also from within the province – who worked in masonry, boring and coal cutting – as well as up-country workers, the Beldars, working in quarries. The pace of the migrations accelerated after fresh excavations at Jheria in the 1890s.

Migratory workers dominated tea plantations from the outset, as there were few human settlements in the Darjeeling Hills and the Dooars. Their origins varied, however. Workers in the former came mainly from the adjacent hill territory of Nepal, which constituted about 96 per cent of its labour force. There were also Lepchas from Sikkim, who worked in the Darjeeling gardens. The Dooars planters depended on migrations from Chota Nagpur, Sonthalia, Chaibassa and Nepal, however. For 67 gardens in the Dooars (accounting for two-thirds of the land area), 52 per cent of the workers had reportedly migrated from Chota Nagpur, 21 per cent from Sonthalia, 7 per cent from Chaibassa and 20 per cent from Nepal (Arbuthnott 1904: 1–2). Among immigrants, tribal people such as the Uraons, Mundas and Santhals dominated.

Wage rates were relatively high in the modern industries. In coal mining, hewers' monthly wages stood at Rs. 5.52 in 1859, which increased to Rs. 16.56 in 1895, and further to Rs. 18.69 in 1906. Moreover, they usually worked along with other family members, and thus enjoyed higher family income. Thus, along with his wife and two children, a miner could earn more than Rs. 9 a month in 1860. In iron smelting, an unskilled worker got Rs. 8.12 per month, and it was still higher for skilled labour. The monthly wage structure in jute mills was like this: for a male worker, Rs. 14 in winding, Rs. 21 in weaving and Rs. 11 in sewing (that is, Rs. 15.33 on average); for a female worker, Rs. 11 per month in sewing; and, for a child, Rs. 12.04 per month in spinning. For a family with two sons and one daughter, their family income thus stood at Rs. 68 per month in 1906. A similar wage structure should prevail in the paper mills as well, as they competed with each other in the labour market, especially for migratory workers. Wages were on the low side in the tea plantations, however. The monthly rate in 1900 was Rs. 5.50 to 6.00 for males and Rs. 4.50 for females, in Darjeeling, and Rs. 6 and Rs. 4.31, respectively, in the Dooars. Moreover, those rates remained the same for a couple of decades. Since all family members used to participate in plantations, decent livelihoods were ensured. From the evidence of large-scale migrations, however, we can be sure that these wage rates were much higher than those prevailing in neighbouring states, and also elsewhere in Bengal, including its agriculture and fisheries sector.

IV

From the marketing viewpoint, the emerging industries may be divided into two groups: (i) jute processing and tea (which relied largely on the global market); and (ii) coal mining, iron smelting and its downstreams, and paper making (which depended mostly on domestic sales). All these industries rose in prominence on the strength of their comparative cost advantages.

The Calcutta jute mills enjoyed comparative advantages mainly from two sources: jute crops in their vicinity; and cheap labour. The contemporary freight rate between Calcutta and London was Rs. 1.48 per maund. Taking raw jute from Bengal and sending finished products back thus involved Rs. 2.96 a maund. At least at this level the prices of Bengal jute products should be less than those of Dundee goods in India's domestic market as well as in the markets of the Far East. Even in the British market, Calcutta mills could dominate because of the high freight costs between London and Dundee, which stood at about Rs. 0.49 a maund. The cost price of Bengal jute goods involved a transport cost of Rs. 1.48 per maund to London, whereas the similar cost for Dundee products to London aggregated to Rs. 2.46 per maund. Again, compared to Dundee mills, the wage rate in Calcutta was cheaper at least by 48 per cent in spinning and 46 per cent in weaving. The Bengal jute mills thus had the edge from the cost point of view over their Dundee counterparts.

In tea, Bengal competed against China in the international market. Tea cultivation and manufacturing were organised jointly in Bengal, using mechanical devices to a large extent as well. In contrast, these activities were segregated in contemporary China, and confined to tiny scales, with mechanical devices totally absent. Cost-wise as well, Indian tea enjoyed a competitive edge. In 1848 Ball estimated that, in a very congenial situation, Chinese (black) tea could not be offered below 1s. 2d to 1s. 4d a lb in London, as against 10d per lb for Darjeeling tea. Moreover, in the declining phase of global prices from the mid-1870s, Bengal planters minimised their costs in several ways: economies of scale, mechanisation, lower packaging costs and lower conveyance expenses. Instead of pursuing any such measures, the Chinese planters opted for inferior teas to survive in competition. In addition, the continuing devaluation of the Indian currency helped Indian planters to combat falling prices.

In coal mining, Bengal had to compete against Britain in the domestic market. In the second half of the nineteenth century the Indian coal market had been growing rapidly, but it was under a British monopoly. On the strength of their comparative cost advantages, the Bengal mines surmounted the challenge following the development of the railways. Whereas, in 1858–60, the average price for British coal was Rs. 18.11 a ton at Calcutta, the tonnage price of Ranigunj coal was Rs. 7.75, which gave it an efficiency-adjusted price of Rs. 10.08. This price differential ensured Bengal coal a stronghold in Bengal, as well as in north India. But it could not successfully venture into the Bombay market. The opportunity came about subsequently on account of great cuts in railway freight charges between Ranigunj and Bombay in the 1880s and 1890s, and a steep rise in the domestic price of British coal after 1884–5. As against a price well above Rs. 20 a ton for British coal in Bombay, Ranigunj coal could be sold there at Rs. 14.74 per ton, suggesting an efficiency-adjusted price of Rs. 19.16. As a result, by the turn of the century Bengal coal dominated the entire domain of India's domestic market. It could also successfully venture into the global market, especially in South and South-east Asia.

In paper manufacturing too Bengal enjoyed a marketing edge. Contemporary documents indicate that, compared to the products from Britain, Bengal mills turned out an equal, and in some cases superior, quality of paper. Cost-wise also, Bengal paper competed successfully. For paper used in government offices, a detailed cost comparison between the two confirms the cheapness of Bengal paper – by Rs. 66,620 in 1881–2, Rs. 80,707 in 1882–3 and Rs. 61,283 in 1885–6. A similar scenario prevailed in iron smelting, where Bengal enjoyed cost advantages over Britain in the Calcutta market. For production in the Damuda Valley, Oldham puts the cost figure at £2.88 a ton, as against £3.76 in south Wales, giving a cost margin of £0.88 a ton in favour of Bengal. Of course, the former involved additional costs of freight and insurance for importing machinery from abroad. But these were more than compensated for by the freight charges (20s. a ton), insurance (2 per cent) and duty (5 per cent) that British iron had to bear in Calcutta.

Turning to the question of government policies towards modern industries, my analysis suggests that the adverse industrial policies that had prevailed in the early colonial period were largely annulled under later administrations, especially after the assumption of power by the Crown in 1858. We have seen that the growth of coal mining was delayed in Bengal by about seven decades for the want of a congenial industrial environment. Its development potential was unleashed only after the effective implementation of two major policies, which had been adopted under East India Company rule but not pursued vigorously until 1858 and the rule of the British Crown. One was the prospecting for coal on behalf of a government organisation, the Geological Survey of India. The knowledge thus gathered gave investors confidence as to the viability of coal mining in Bengal, and helped them shape their business strategies. An equally important policy move was the construction of railways in India, which supported coal mining in two ways: (i) directly, as a bulk consumer, it augmented its demand; and (ii) indirectly, it did so by providing easy access to distant markets.

Government assistance was all the more important for the development of tea cultivation in Bengal. The first tea garden was opened in Darjeeling by a district administrative official. This had demonstration effects among private capitalists. Simultaneously, Darjeeling's transport network, both railways and roads, was developed for the sake of its cost-effective linkage with the port town of Calcutta. For the plantations in the Dooars as well, similar facilities were made available. What is more, the government provided wastelands at both locations at favourable terms.

In respect of iron smelting (and also its downstreams) and paper making, my finding is that early state policies, especially the store purchasing rules, were inimical to the development process. This was particularly so in view of the fact that, as a bulk buyer for these products, the government refused to buy them, and their financial viability was at stake. Only from the mid-1870s onwards, when this discriminatory policy was progressively removed, did these industries prosper.

Fiscal policies from 1859 also supported industrial development in the colony. Act VII of this year increased import duties for a considerable number of articles, from 5 to 20 per cent, though they were reduced to 10 per cent by Act X of 1860 in view of a falling off in revenue (P.P. 1861: 17). Moreover, machinery of all kinds, and conveyances and carriages of every description, were included in the free import list, and tea and coffee in the free export list. The custom tariff table for 1870–1 (P.P. 1872: 25–6) shows that there was no import or export duty on the following items: arms, ammunition and military stores, articles for engineering purposes, machines and machinery, coal and coke, and paper. Bengal's engineering industry, coal mining and paper making could, therefore, develop in a laissez faire environment. Domestic protection was in place for jute processing and tea plantations, however; there was no export duty on jute goods (both raw and manufactured) and tea, but a 7½ per cent import duty on both of them.[3] Furthermore, the government introduced tea cess at 1/4 pie a pound in 1903 for the promotion of Indian tea in foreign markets.

V

Three points should be highlighted by way of conclusion. First, Bengal's reindustrialisation between 1858 and 1914 drastically changed the industrial landscape that had prevailed in the territory for centuries. The earlier industries, especially cotton textile, silk textile and indigo dye manufacturing, had spread across the province, suggesting a pattern of regionally balanced industrial development. Only salt making and ship building were in specific areas, the former concentrated along the coastal belt, the latter in and around Calcutta. The 1858–1914 industrial development localised the development process in three corners of the province, however, leaving a vast central tract undeveloped. Tea plantations were concentrated in the northern fringe, coal mining in the western corner, and others in and around Calcutta. These regions thus assumed the character of what Marshall (1890: 332–6) calls 'industrial districts' (see also Harrison 1992 for a review of the concept). Various advantages were, indeed, associated with this, but the larger part of the province sank into backwardness. The second issue relates to the dominance of migratory workers in the modern industries, which altered the character of industrial labour in Bengal. While the artisans and workers in its age-old industries had hailed entirely from the local populace, the modern industries employed workers from neighbouring provinces, such as Bihar and Orissa, and also from far-off places in south India.

A further point of dissimilarity can be found in the direction of capital movements and their underlying causes. The former epoch witnessed a great exodus of capital from Bengal, which was engineered by various extra-economic factors – such as the payment of tribute to Delhi prior to British rule, and the Company's control over state revenues thereafter. The flow was reversed in the latter epoch, a move motivated solely by market forces. Bengal's comparative cost advantages in various lines of production attracted British capitalists to venture into the province.

Notes

1 Gregory (1962: 90–4) points to the similarity of South African mining with the Asian managing agency system. Turrell and Van-Helten (1986: 269) discuss the differences between them, however. Tomlinson (1981: 46 fn 12) suggests that the Japanese *zaibatsu* firms imitated the Indian system.

2 In fact, Carr, Tagore & Co. was the first managing agency house in Bengal to undertake six joint-stock companies.

3 The import duty on jute was later withdrawn.

Bibliography

Akerlof, G. A. (1970) 'The Market for "Lemons": Quality Uncertainty and the Market Mechanism', *Quarterly Journal of Economics* 84 (3), 488–500.

Arbuthnott, J. C. (1904) *Report on the Conditions of Tea Garden Labour in the Duars of Bengal, in Madras, and in Ceylon*. Shillong: Assam Secretariat Printing.

Blanford, W.T. (1865) 'On the Geological Structure and Relations of the Raniganj Coal Field, Bengal', *Memoirs of the Geological Survey of India* 3 (1), 1–195.

Bose, S. K. (1954) *Capital and Labour in the Indian Tea Industry*. Bombay: All India Trade Union Congress.

Buchanan, D. H. (1934) *The Development of Capitalist Enterprise in India*. New York: Macmillan.

Dash, A. J. (1947) *Bengal District Gazetteers: Darjeeling*. Calcutta: Bengal Secretariat Press.

De Haan, A. (1997) 'Unsettled Settlers: Migrant Workers and Industrial Capitalism in Calcutta', *Modern Asian Studies* 31 (4), 919–49.

Government of Bengal (GOB) (1873) *Annual Report on the Administration of Bengal for 1871–2*. National Library Archive, Calcutta.

Gregory, T. (1962) *Ernest Oppenheimer and the Development of Southern Africa*. Oxford: Oxford University Press.

Harrison, B. (1992) 'Industrial Districts: Old Wine in New Bottles?', *Regional Studies* 26 (5), 469–83.

Hunter, W.W. (1876) *A Statistical Account of Bengal*, vol. IV. London: Trübner.

Jenks, L. H. (1938) *The Migration of British Capital to 1875*. London: Jonathan Cape.

Kling, B. B. (1966) 'The Origin of the Managing Agency System in India', *Journal of Asian Studies* 26 (1), 37–47.

Knowles, L. C. A. (1924) *The Economic Development of the British Overseas Empire*, 3 vols. London: George Routledge & Sons.

Marshall, A. (1890) *Principles of Economics*, vol. I. London: Macmillan.

Monahan, F. J. (1910) *Report of the Duars Committee*. Shillong: Eastern and Assam Government Press.

Parliamentary Papers (P.P.) (1861) *Moral and Material Progress and Conditions of India for the Year 1859–60*. London: Hansard.

Parliamentary Papers (P.P.) (1872) *Statistical Abstract Relating to British India, from 1862 to 1871*. London: HMSO.

Rungta, S. (1985) 'Bowreah Cotton and Fort Gloster Jute Mills', *Indian Economic and Social History Review* 22 (2), 109–37.

Smith, A. (1937 [1776]) *An Inquiry into the Nature and Causes of the Wealth of Nations*. New York: The Modern Library.

Tomlinson, B. R. (1981) 'Colonial Firms and the Decline of Colonialism in Eastern India, 1914–47', *Modern Asian Studies* 15 (3), 455–86.

Tripathi, D. (1971) 'Indian Entrepreneurship in Historical Perspective: A Re-interpretation', *Economic and Political Economy* 6 (22), M59–M66.

Turrell, R.V., and Van-Helten, J. J. (1986) 'The Rothschilds, the Exploration Company and Mining Finance', *Business History* 28 (2), 181–205.

Waters, C. M. (1926) *A Short Survey of the Economic Development of England and the Colonies (1874–1914)*. London: Noel Douglas.

Watson, E. R. (1907) *A Monograph on Iron and Steel Work in the Province of Bengal*. Calcutta: Bengal Secretariat Book Depot.

Webster, A. (2006) 'The Strategies and Limits of Gentlemanly Capitalism: The London East India Agency Houses, Provincial Commercial Interests, and the Evolution of British Economic Policy in South and South East Asia 1800–50', *Economic History Review* 59 (4), 743–64.

9 Deindustrialisation in the nineteenth century

A myth or a reality?

'Deindustrialisation' is one of the most debatable issues in Indian historiography (see Morris et al. 1969). It centres on twin foci. First: did deindustrialisation take place in nineteenth-century India? Second: if so, was it the British rule in the subcontinent that was responsible for the event? The empirical studies that have so far been undertaken to this end are less convincing to prove (or disprove) the occurrence of the event. Against this background, this chapter seeks (i) to bring together available empirical studies on the issue and (ii) to provide empirical evidence on this matter in respect of Bengal from 1757 to 1914. The evidence is discussed on the basis of industry-level data. My previous work (Ray 2011) estimates the loss of employment in five major industries between 1757 and 1857. These are juxtaposed against the gain in employment in five modern industries from 1858 to 1914 to arrive at a final judgement. The loss of employment in three of the industries – iron smelting, jute processing and paper making – that had earlier prevailed in the traditional sector but declined afterwards is also accounted for. A further objective of this chapter is to examine whether, in view of Bengal's experiences from 1757 to 1914, the dominant hypotheses explaining the occurrence of deindustrialisation are valid.

For topical interest, the discussion begins with a search for the genesis of the debate. Deindustrialisation was simply a noise in India around the middle of the nineteenth century, which subsequently grew into widespread cries and protests during the nationalist movement. It came back into academia thereafter, especially in the 1960s, generating the debate. Some historians attribute it to colonial discriminations that thwarted the country's economic development in the early modern age (Dutt 1940). Side by side, counter voices are raised, alleging that the hypothesis stems from extra-economic value judgements (Das 1959; Robb 1981). Interestingly, both 'nationalist' as well as 'Marxist' (or 'neo-Marxist') writers hold that British policy caused a decline in artisan industries, thus creating a paradox, since the 'moderate' nationalist leaders in India did not

This is a revised version of 'The Myth and Reality of Deindustrialisation in Early Modern India', in Chaudhary, L., Gupta, B., Roy, T., and Swamy, A. (eds.) *A New Economic History of Colonial India*, chapter 4, Routledge, London and New York, 2016. Reproduced with the permission of the copyright holders and the publishers, Routledge.

subscribe to Marxian philosophy. The present chapter also seeks to settle these issues of Indian economic historiography. My approach is this. By way of a search for the genesis of the debate, I first seek to answer the question: was the hypothesis initially formulated on the basis of relevant and adequate data and information? Or was it deduced otherwise? My investigation in this respect also helps us understand why the 'nationalist' analysis falls into line with the Marxian.

The plan of the chapter is this. Section I analyses the origins and antecedents of the hypothesis, and discusses at length Marx's deliberation on the issue that has greatly influenced the literature for more than a century and a half. It also analyses the pioneer views of India's moderate nationalist leaders on the subject to ascertain their similarities with the Marxian concept, and to identify the significance of the event in the country's nationalist movement. I argue here that its significance in India's 'moderate' nationalism gives a specific connotation to the term. Section II gathers together various empirical studies that seek to prove (or disprove) the occurrence of the event during the colonial period. Section III presents the findings of my previous work on the loss of industrial employment in Bengal from 1757 to 1857, and also the net gain in industrial employment from 1858 to 1914 that the present study suggests. Finally, section IV discusses the dominant hypotheses of deindustrialisation in the literature, particularly the views of neo-Marxian writers such as Frank (1996) and Wallerstein (1986), in which deindustrialisation is believed to have been an event in the formation of the capitalist world economy. The terms-of-trade hypothesis, as proposed by Morris (1963), is also analysed here. This section examines the validity of those hypotheses in view of the experiences of Bengal during the 1757–1914 period. Section V concludes.

I

The genesis of the debate on the Indian experience goes back to Marx's writings (Marx 1853). Not only did he kick off a debate that has been continuing for more than a century and a half, but he also bequeathed certain methodological tools to the ensuing debate. To understand these spirits of the debate I need to discuss at length Marx's deliberations on India's deindustrialisation in the nineteenth century. In his stylised Indian society, there was agriculture totally dependent on government public works, especially irrigation, as well as an industrial economy almost exhaustively constituted of the cotton textile industry, which was export-oriented. Exporting textiles brought in precious metals to satisfy the Indians' great desire for gold and silver jewellery. Marx believed that the textile industry was so extensive that it defined the contemporary social fabric: 'The hand-loom and the spinning-wheel, producing their regular myriads of spinners and weavers, were the pivots of that society' (ibid.). In this stylised economy, the decline of textiles would cause a collapse of the entire society. Since the textile industry was export-based, Marx explains its decline with reference to British trade policies. On the basis of trade statistics, he contends that 'England began with driving the Indian cottons from the European market; it then introduced twist into Hindostan, and in the end inundated the very mother country of cotton with cottons' (ibid.). Simultaneously, British rule also brought an end to India's agricultural prosperity by neglecting public works. Marx writes, 'Those family-communities [villages] were based on domestic industry, in that peculiar combination of hand-weaving, hand-spinning and hand-tilling, which gave them self-supporting power.' But, he continues, 'English interference having placed the spinner in Lancashire and weaver in Bengal, or sweeping away both Hindoo spinner and weaver, dissolved these small semi-barbarian, semi-civilised communities, by blowing up their economical basis, and thus produced the greatest, or to speak the truth, the only social revolution ever heard of in Asia' (ibid.).

The subsequent debate on India's deindustrialisation inherits three crucial aspects of this analysis. First, the term is defined to connote a state of industrial decline in a country that resulted from imperial policies. Although this is implicit in pioneering works in Indian economic history (such as Dutt 1901), Roy (2000) makes it explicit. We will shortly see that this underlying connection between the decline of industries and colonial rule anticipated the 'nationalist' version of deindustrialisation. Second, the Marxian surmise that the cotton textile industry accounted for all industrial activity in India appears to have been implicitly accepted in the literature, since detailed discussion on any other industry is absent in it. It is true that, because of its pioneer role in the British Industrial Revolution, the cotton textile industry has its own place of prominence in global economic history. But India's case for deindustrialisation should not be confined to this industry alone, as there were other important manufacturing industries in contemporary India. Third, the methodological shortcoming of assessing the decline of an industry by trade statistics, which Marx adopted in his stylised analysis of India, is also inherited in the literature (for example, Desai 1971). Morris (1963) raises doubts as to the interpretation of the textile import figures. Larger imports, he argues, might cater to higher domestic demand, or else be re-exported overland, without damaging domestic industry. Additionally, the extent to which the decline of exports adversely affected the industry depended on the export share of its output. These methodological issues underlie the legacy of Marx's deliberations on the subject.

The conjectural relationship between colonial rule and industrial decline brought deindustrialisation into focus in India's nationalist movement during the last three decades of the nineteenth century and into the twentieth. A number of authors – for example, Digby (1901) and Dutt (1901) – gathered additional data to corroborate the proposition that British trade policies destroyed Indian industries. Some moderate nationalist leaders, Naoroji in particular, gave a further explanation for the hypothesis on the basis of the drain theory (for a discussion, see Ganguli 1965). He explained how 'the internal drain' mopped up resources from the countryside to the capital city, giving rise to 'the external drain'. According to him, the drain of resources from India stood at more than £500,000,000 during 34 years in the second half of the nineteenth century

(Naoroji 1901: 35). He argued that India's deindustrialisation during the colonial period was an outcome of the drain of savings. To corroborate this line of causation he refers to John Stuart Mill, who emphasised that it is the stock of capital, rather than the demand for commodities, that sets the limit for industrial development of an economy (ibid. 55). 'The demand for commodities,' he quotes from Mill, 'determines the direction of labour, but not the more or less of the labour itself, or of the maintenance or payment of the latter. These depend on the amount of the capital…' (ibid.). It therefore logically follows that, once a substantial drain of capital from India was evident, there must have been deindustrialisation. He further strengthens his argument by another of Mill's dictums: that good governance cannot promote industries under the scarcity of capital.[1]

But an apt question at this stage is: why were the moderate nationalist leaders so preoccupied with deindustrialisation? It appears that the concern arose out of their worries about the mass incidence of absolute poverty across the country. In fact, Naoroji pointed out that there was a vicious circle between deindustrialisation and mass poverty, which was created and perpetuated by the drain of wealth. 'Poor India,' he writes, 'has not even to support its absolute want, even were the whole production employed in supporting labour… [S]aving, and therefore addition to capital…, [is] altogether out of [the] question… [But] there is actual continuous yearly abstraction from this scanty production…so the candle burns at both ends – capital going on diminishing on the one hand, and labour thereby becoming less capable, on the other, to reproduce as much as before' (Naoroji 1901: 56). Growing poverty was its inevitable consequence. This conjugation between deindustrialisation and mass poverty gave rise to the political significance of the event. In his presidential address of the Indian National Congress (INC) in 1895, Surendranath Banerjea thus noted, 'Ours is a political organisation; but we cannot overlook considerations which affect the development of our industries and our manufactures. The economic condition of a people has an intimate bearing upon their political advancement' (see Zaidi 1985: 257).

This still begs the question: why were the moderate nationalist leaders in India so concerned about the mass poverty? This question is especially pertinent in view of the fact that the majority of the moderate nationalist leaders belonged to the urban privileged class, and overlooked the plight of the poor on many occasions. Citing some such instances, Seth (1999: 105) observes that 'the Congress in these early years was either uninterested in or opposed to government measures purportedly directed at protecting and improving the lot of rural cultivators or urban workers'. It is possible, then, that the moderates had a specific agenda. They believed that, since deindustrialisation was the cause of mass poverty, its eradication warranted extensive industrial development in the country, and that such development necessarily called for the Indianisation of the civil service and a responsible government. These latter reforms were the basic agenda of the moderate nationalism in India (Banerjea 1925: 126). Gopal Krishna Gokhale thus emphasised, 'It is with me a firm conviction that unless you have a more effective and more potent voice in the government of your own country, in the administration of your own affairs, in the expenditure of your own revenues, it is not possible for you to effect much in the way of industrial development' (see Karve and Ambekar 1962: 178). The Congress also adopted a resolution at its 1886 session underlining the relationship between the introduction of representative institutions and the question of poverty (Zaidi and Zaidi 1976: 138).

This tone underlies the concept of deindustrialisation that dominated Indian historiography. Thus, focusing more on the political antecedent of the term, Roy (2000) calls deindustrialisation a theory, constituted of four propositions: (i) traditional industries declined in a colony; (ii) the decline was initiated by technological obsolescence in the domestic economy; (iii) it was sustained by colonial policies; and (iv) the development of modern industries could not compensate for the economic loss resulting from the decline of traditional industries. Such a concept poses some problems for empirical application, as it does not deal with (i) colonial industry that was not traditional, (ii) a decline not triggered by technological obsolescence but by discriminatory colonial policies and (iii) a decline triggered by technological obsolescence but not sustained by discriminatory policies. These alternative events did occur in nineteenth-century India, however. For example, the ship-building industry, which had been developing in Bengal on the basis of European technology since 1780, was destroyed during the colonial period (case (i)); the decline of the salt industry in Bengal was not initiated by any technological obsolescence (case (ii)); and the decline of the cotton textile industry in Bengal since the mid-1820s was not sustained by any discriminatory colonial policies on the part of Britain (case (iii)) (Ray 2011: 171–205, 131–70, 52–87). In view of these issues, we need to redefine the concept.

It is clear from this discussion of the origin of the term that its basis in India embodies contemporary values that took shape in a colonial setting and even blurred market forces. This drawback carries on into the post-colonial literature. Robb (1981: 512) notes, 'If the first point about the debate [on deindustrialisation] in 1968 is thus its continuity with the past, the second is the obvious one that it called for a methodology that is anti-historical: the threat that certain conclusions are ideologically unacceptable displays more heat than wisdom.' These two components of the composite definition – colonial policy and industrial decline – are not conceptually linked: if colonial policies are found oppressive to industries, one should not conclude that there must have been industrial decline; nor should one deduce from an empirical finding on industrial decline that the colonial rule was oppressive. Evidence shows that, in nineteenth-century Bengal, the silk textile industry survived even under discriminatory policies while the indigo dye industry declined even when the government supported it (Ray 2011: 88–132, 206–44). Thus, an adverse policy is neither a necessary nor a sufficient condition for deindustrialisation to occur – because there could be market forces that ensure the survival or decline of an industry. Therefore, for the sake of clarity, we should distinguish the causal factors carefully. It is one thing to ask if a decline took place; it is another to ask why the decline took place.

This critique leads me to offer the following definition: deindustrialisation is a state of affairs whereby (i) there was a downfall of an industry, and (ii) the industry's downfall was not compensated for by the growth of a modern industry in the same line of production. This is empirically easier to test, because it is a definition constructed in the framework of industry studies. By contrast, the existing literature seeks to study the question of deindustrialisation in a framework of the inter-sectoral transfer of jobs. This is difficult to test, because India's nineteenth-century sources are not able to provide the requisite support to that end (see also Simmons 1985: 604).[2] It is also a more value-free definition in terms of causal factors. A specific industrial decline may have been caused either by market forces (for example, technological obsolescence), or by discriminatory colonial policies, or both. Studying the problem in this framework would leave least scope for value judgement.

II

The post-colonial literature is dominated by the explanation for the occurrence of India's deindustrialisation, but has not investigated enough whether the event took place at all. This is often acknowledged even explicitly. Thus, Wallerstein (1986: PE34) notes, 'The debate over the empirical characterisation will go on for a long time, since we are still very poor in accumulated data on which to base our judgement.' Perlin (1983: 53) also notes 'the lack of any serious regional monographs on textile industries, in the 17th or 18th centuries, of a kind long legion in the European historiography'. This is indeed the underlying tone in the greater body of the literature.

Empirical evidence on India's deindustrialisation falls broadly into two categories: (i) inter-sectoral studies, based on employment or output criteria: and (ii) industry studies (see Appendix 9.1 for a full list of empirical studies). Most works in the former category are based on census data relating to industrial workers. The very first work in this class was by Clark (1957: 515), who reconstructs the census data for 1881, 1901, 1911, 1921 and 1931 and reports that the number of workers belonging to manufacturing (including electricity and gas), mining and construction activities as a proportion of the total workforce fell from 34.7 per cent to 22.2 per cent, 16.8 per cent, 15.5 per cent and further to 14.6 per cent, respectively, confirming deindustrialisation. But a number of drawbacks are subsequently noticed in his methodology. In the first place, the 'general labour' category that Clark considers as representing industrial workers in fact included many agricultural labourers. Since the practice was discontinued afterwards, serious discrepancies cropped up. Second, there was a discrepancy in respect of 'sellers'. Earlier censuses, particularly those in 1881 and 1891, treated them as industrial workers, but the later ones did not. Third, the enumeration of female workers involved a reporting problem. In many cases women working part-time in domestic industries, and even in other commercial establishments, were reckoned as industrial workers. Removing female workers altogether, Thorner and Thorner (1962: 70–7) rework the census data for 1881 and 1931 and arrive at a different conclusion from Clark's. Although the raw data display a fall from 21.1 million in 1881 to 12.9 million in 1931 (ibid.: 72), the filtered data show that the number of manufacturing workers stagnated at around 14.8 million between those periods (ibid.: 76).

Chattopadhyay (1975) also works on the census data but avoids the earlier censuses because of the disputed data. His study corroborates deindustrialisation on the basis of the following findings: (i) the incidence of industrial workers in the total population fell from 5.94 per cent in 1901 to 4.50 per cent in 1931; and (ii) the share of such workers in the total workforce declined from 8.73 per cent to 6.65 per cent in the same period. In another study, he deals with the presidency of Bengal and also its three provinces separately (Chattopadhyay 1981). His calculations reveal the occurrence of deindustrialisation in the Bengal Presidency as well as in the provinces of Bihar and Orissa, but not in the Bengal province. In particular, he finds: (i) that, for the presidency of Bengal as a whole, the number of male industrial workers dropped from 1.88 million in 1901 to 1.71 million in 1931; (ii) that their number fell from 0.63 million to 0.51 million in Bihar and from 0.25 million to 0.21 million in Orissa, in the same period; and (iii) that the data set shows different behaviour for the province of Bengal: the number of male manufacturing workers there increased from 0.99 million in 1901 to 1.25 million in 1921; for 1921–31, a sharp downward trend is noticed in the series, but Chattopadhyay attributes it to the contemporary Great Depression.

The greatest drawback to these census-based studies is that they seek to trace an event in a period when the event may have already finished. If India's deindustrialisation, as is sometimes suggested, took place in the late eighteenth century and the early nineteenth, the censuses, which started only in 1881, would not capture the effects fully. To avoid this problem, Bagchi (1976) compares the census data of 1901 with Buchanan Hamilton's data collected between 1809 and 1813 for Gangetic Bihar (the present-day districts of Patna, Gaya, Shahabad, Monghyr, Bhagalpur and Purnea). Under the assumption that each spinner supported one other person, his study indicates that the population dependent on industry fell from 21.6 per cent[3] to 8.5 per cent, and that, activity-wise, the rate of decline was highest for spinners, from 10.3 per cent to 1.3 per cent, as against a fall from 2.3 per cent to 1.3 per cent for weavers, and from 9 per cent to 7.2 per cent for other industrial workers (ibid.: tabs. 1–5). India's nineteenth-century deindustrialisation is thus made evident. But it is not clear to what extent Gangetic Bihar represented the presidency of Bengal, let alone India, which hosted a number of manufacturing industries at the beginning of the nineteenth century. Further, the census data of 1901 lack comparability with those of Buchanan Hamilton with respect to the definitions of various working categories, as pointed out by Vicziany (1979). In addition, the quality of Buchanan Hamilton's data is severely questioned in the literature (Roy 2006: 123).

The employment yardstick that these studies have adopted for the measurement of deindustrialisation is also a bone of contention. In particular,

Krishnamurthy (1976) argues that the falling employment level was not necessarily a phenomenon of deindustrialisation, but might represent growing capital intensity in the prevailing technology. Extending this argument, Roy (2000) contends that the capital intensity might have increased owing to the replacement of domestic production by wage work within the organisation of small-scale industries. Referring to Sivasubramonian's data on the rising proportion of income in secondary industries,[4] he observes that 'what we see in census and income statistics is the beginning of a large-scale substitution of labour by machinery within India. [...] We see also strong signs that in fact real incomes increased within small industry as well' (ibid.: 129–30).

Bairoch (1982) follows a different approach, based on an estimated time series of world manufacturing output from 1750 to 1938. His estimation indicates that India's share in world manufacturing output was as high as 24.5 per cent in 1750, next only to China's 32.8 per cent (see Simmons 1985: 600). While the latter improved its share to 33.3 per cent in 1800, the former was displaced to 19.7 per cent in that year. It fell further to 17.6 per cent in 1830, 2.8 per cent in 1880 and 1.4 per cent in 1913. A continuous process of deindustrialisation is thus suggested for India under colonial rule. But this study has also attracted criticism on various grounds. Apart from the speculative nature of these estimates, the study suffers from a logical failing in that, in the face of rising manufacturing output in the rest of the world, India's declining share does not necessarily confirm the event of deindustrialisation. Moreover, non-traded manufacturing goods, which the study does not account for, dominated Indian industries in the eighteenth and nineteenth centuries.

In the industry-level studies, I should first refer to Clingingsmith and Williamson (2008), who evaluate the case of the cotton textile industry in a framework of the sectoral terms of trade. The study is based on a neo-Ricardian model consisting of three sectors, grain (G), agricultural commodity exports (C) and textiles (T), with labour as the only mobile input across them, costing a nominal wage rate (w). While grain is not traded, textiles and agricultural commodities are globally traded at P_T and P_C, respectively. Additionally, the grain wage is defined as w/P_G (= 1), and the own wages in textiles and agricultural commodities as w/P_T and w/P_C, respectively. For 1760–1860, the study suggests strong deindustrialisation on the basis of the empirical evidence that there was a spectacular rise in the own wage in textiles (w/P_T) due to the fall in P_T and a rise in w. While the former is explained by the contemporary technological innovations, the latter is deduced from the steady surge of P_G upwards, as evident in the estimation, under the assumption that $w/P_G = 1$. Indeed, these statistics also suggest unfavourable terms of trade (P_G/P_T) for textiles, confirming strong deindustrialisation. Weak deindustrialisation is also evident in the estimated statistics, which show that the inter-sectoral terms of trade between textiles and agricultural commodities (P_C/P_T) moved strongly in favour of the latter. The validity of these conclusions, however, hinges on two crucial assumptions made in the study: the Ricardian-type assumption of constant real wage, $w/P_G = 1$, which helps to establish a rising nominal wage rate (w) from an increasing trend of the grain price P_G; and the underlying assumption that adverse terms of trade for industries is a sufficient condition for deindustrialisation. The latter theoretical construction belongs to the partial equilibrium analysis, which cannot explain a real-world event such as deindustrialisation. In a general equilibrium framework, one should recognise, for example, whether the adverse terms of trade for textiles led to price reductions for inputs, especially for raw cotton. The data estimation, especially the use of some proxy variables, also casts doubt on these conclusions.

For the textile industry, Harnetty (1991) and Twomey (1983) also confirm nineteenth-century deindustrialisation. Harnetty does so on the grounds that, in contrast to its entire share of the domestic market in 1801, the industry could retain only a 23 per cent share in 1900–1, leaving 66 per cent for imported goods and 11 per cent for mill-made products (Harnetty 1991: 508). For the Central Provinces, where his study concentrates, he notices that imports of those goods shot up from 22,881 maunds to 104,945 maunds from 1863/4 to 1887/8, whereas exports of country-made cloths moved downwards from 60,352 maunds to 30,241 maunds in the same period (ibid.: 464). He also gathers evidence of perpetual decline in the industry's profitability and wage rate, and concludes: 'Clearly, by the late nineteenth century the handloom weavers, especially the more skilled ones, had experienced a decline in living standards which reflected the decline of the industry in the face of competition from mill-made cloth' (ibid.: 470). His confirmation of the event is subject to some qualifications, however (see Frisof 2008: 28–30).

Twomey (1983: 49, 52), for his part, estimates that the industry's export-related employment in India fell by 300,000 from 1790 to 1830, of which Bengal shared about 81 per cent, and that the overall reduction of employment in the industry stood at 3.6 million from 1850 to 1880. But these estimates involve speculation in respect of the output of hand-spun yarn, the growth of population and per capita income and the coefficient relating cloth production to employment.

Guha (1972) substantiates India's deindustrialisation in cotton textiles using the consumption of raw materials as a yardstick for the measurement of production. According to his estimates, the net availability of cotton yarns (including the imported and machine-spun varieties) fell from 419 million lbs in 1850 to 240 million lbs in 1870, and further to either 184 or 221 million lbs in 1900, showing the waning of the industry. Habib (1985) supports this finding, citing Harnetty's data that the British import of raw cotton from India rose from 145 million lbs in 1855 to 443 million lbs in 1872. He observes, 'Unless the Indian per capita cotton production also increased on such a dramatically high scale, the per capita availability of cotton within the country must have undergone an enormous decline' (ibid.: 364 fn). But McAlpin (1974 and 1975), as referred to in Habib (1985: 364 fn), denies such an increase in per capita cotton acreage in India during that period. Roy (2006) points out, however, that, notwithstanding the usefulness of his methodology, his estimates suffer from several weaknesses.

III

My previous work (Ray 2011) discusses five major manufacturing industries in Bengal during the early colonial rule, namely cotton textiles, silk textiles, indigo dye, salt manufacturing and ship building. Tracing the pre-colonial roots for each of them, the study seeks to assess their performances from 1757 to 1857, identifying the roles of market forces and state policies therein. The summary statistics on employment, as reported in it, are shown in Table 9.1.

The table demonstrates that, far from encountering deindustrialisation, Bengal enjoyed industrial prosperity between 1795 and 1829, when the level of employment in the five major industries went up in aggregate by almost 2 million people. This was due to the prosperity of the pre-colonial industries, such as cotton and silk textiles as well as salt manufacturing, on the one hand, and the emergence of new industries, such as ship building and indigo dye manufacture, on the other. Bengal's industrial decay started in the early 1830s, however, and extended into the following decades. The aggregate fall in the employment level was to the tune of 2.15 million through 1860, which must have caused devastation in the contemporary society. Cotton textiles displayed the highest reduction (1,263,240), followed by indigo dye (837,199) and salt manufacturing (63,923).

On the basis of Table 9.1 I have constructed Table 9.2, to display the swings in these industries between 1795/9–1825/9 and 1825/9–1855/9.

For the evaluation of the employment effects of the free trade policy, the discussion should start from 1795, since private trade began to flourish only after the partial demonopolisation of 'the Eastern trade' in 1793. In view of successive annulments of the barriers to trade, the post-1793 period witnessed the effects of the technological revolution in Britain working through to this colony. For a couple of years, however, Bengal's major industries could successfully compete in the global market, and they consolidated their position. For example, its export business in indigo dye, cotton textiles and silk textiles prospered through 1829, leading to gains in employment (Table 9.1). But, after that, they could not withstand global competition, and declined. Therefore, the period from 1795 to 1859 should be studied as a whole to assess the impacts of technological advancement abroad (*pari passu* with the effects of the free trade policy) on the industrial economy of Bengal. That is, the loss of employment from 1825/9 to 1855/9 should be read with the gain in employment from 1795/9 to 1825/9. If these two periods are juxtaposed, as I have done in Table 9.2, the loss of employment during the later period appears to have been balanced to a good extent by employment gains in the former period, reducing the net loss to only 203,575. My industry-wise estimations show that, from 1795/9 to 1855/9, the net loss was highest for cotton textiles (383,193), followed by salt manufacturing (30,731). Only silk textiles and indigo dye behaved differently. The former did not enter into the decaying phase till 1860; and the latter, though it had started decaying, was not extinct by the end of this period.

Table 9.1 Changes in annual employment scenario in Bengal, 1795/9–1855/9

Year	*Silk*	*Cotton**	*Salt*	*Ship building*	*Indigo dye*	*Total employment (excluding cotton)*	*Change in employment (including cotton)*
1795–9	88,775	179,905	88,020	928	460,080	637,803	–
1800–4	84,040	198,931	90,303	4,508	522,478	701,329	(+) 262,457
1805–9	97,255	141,798	108,567	2,400	833,419	1,041,641	(+) 482,110
1810–14	155,536	126,745	113,639	5,400	868,826	1,143,401	(+) 228,505
1815–19	158,109	210,128	114,655	5,589	994,757	1,273,110	(+) 339,837
1820–4	202,242	145,589	123,785	2,341	1,040,878	1,369,246	(+) 241,725
1825–9	219,267	56,856	121,212	1,429	1,364,060	1,705,968	(+) 393,578
1830–4	188,460	–21,616	149,887	1,074	1,230,295	1,569,716	(-) 157,868
1835–9	237,786	–53,573	93,947	1,626	1,146,199	1,479,558	(-) 143,731
1840–4	232,730	–181,250	98,861	2,443	1,387,171	1,721,205	(+) 60,397
1845–9	227,670	–221,108	90,504	0	1,054,268	1,372,442	(–) 569,871
1850–4	211,227	–317,480	59,044	0	596,865	867,136	(–) 822,786
1855–9	233,271	–468,213	57,289	0	526,861	817,421	(–) 517,928

Note: * These figures represent changes in employment opportunities.

Source: Ray (2011: 252).

Table 9.2 Changes in employment in major industries, 1795/9–1825/9 to 1825/9–1855/9

Industry	*Employment gain (+), 1795/9–1825/9*	*Employment loss (−), 1825/9–1855/9*	*Net gain (+) / loss (−), 1795/9–1855/9*
Silk textiles	(+) 130,492	(+) 14,004	(+) 144,496
Cotton textiles	(+) 880,047*	(−) 1,263,240	(−) 383,193
Salt manufacturing	(+) 33,192	(−) 63,923	(−) 30,731
Ship building	(+) 501	(−) 1,429	(−) 928
Indigo dye manufacturing	(+) 903,980	(−) 837,199	(+) 66, 781
Total	(+) 1,948,212	(−) 2,151,787	(−) 203,575

Note: * The change in employment in cotton textiles for 1795–9 is not included, since this figure represents the change in 1795–9 compared to the previous period.

To assess the effects of British rule on these industries, we should begin our analysis from 1757, when the East India Company took on the bulk of the administration of Bengal's economic affairs. In the early decades of its rule the Company vigorously carried out export business from Bengal, which promoted its industries and created large employment opportunities. Moreover, modern ship building and indigo dye manufacturing started under British rule. Therefore, we should avoid altogether the employment effect of the ship-building industry, as it was extinct by 1859, and take only the (+) 526,861 (instead of the (+) 903,980 in column 2 of Table 9.2) for indigo dye manufacturing that prevailed in 1855–9 (omitting the (–) 837,199 in column 3 of Table 9.2 from the calculations). We should also consider the additional employment of 179,905 for cotton textiles in 1795–9 (as noted in column 3 of Table 9.1). This reverses the balance sheet, since the employment gain comes out at 1,750,497, set against the loss of 1,313,159, indicating a gain of 437,338 for the period from 1757 to 1859 as a whole. This excludes the augmentation of employment in cotton textiles between 1757 and 1795 (Ray 2011: 58).

Employment data for the period from 1858 to 1914, as obtained in this study, are summarised in Table 9.3.

The modern industries that arose in this period generated substantial employment – 236,294 in jute processing, 132,500 in coal mining and 130,000 in tea cultivation – which, along with the other two industries, gives additional employment of 562,286. But some of these industries that had earlier prevailed in Bengal's traditional sector offered much greater employment opportunities – about 638,000 in jute processing, 280,000 in iron smelting and 111,000 in paper making. Therefore, notwithstanding considerable industrial growth from 1858 to 1914, there is a net loss of employment by 466,718 in Table 9.3.

Thus, if 1829–30 is taken as the cut-off year for discussion, the loss of employment comes to 2.15 million for the period from 1829 to 1859, and, together with that in traditional industries from 1858 to 1914, 3.18 million.

Table 9.3 Changes in employment in Bengal's major industries, 1858–1914

Industry	*Employment gain in modern sector*	*Employment loss in traditional sector*	*Net gain (+) / loss (−)*
Coal mining	132,500	–	(+) 132,500
Iron smelting and downstream	60,000	280,000	(−) 220,000
Jute processing	236,294	638,000	(−) 401,706
Paper making	3,492	111,004	(−) 107,512
Tea cultivation	130,000	–	(+) 130,000
Total	562,286	1,029,004	(−) 466,718

Accounting for the gain of employment in modern industries at 562,286, the net loss of employment from 1829 to 1914 works out at about 2.62 million. The net loss is found at 670,293 for 1795 to 1914, however, which represents the effects of the technological revolution in Britain and its free trade policy. If the period from 1757 to 1914 is recognised with a view to examining the impact of colonial rule, it comes only to 29,380. Therefore, the judgement on Bengal's deindustrialisation issue hinges on the selection of the base year.

Reading the question of deindustrialisation in these time dimensions removes certain controversies that prevail in the empirical literature, especially those focused on Bengal. My empirical findings broadly agree with Bagchi (1976), that deindustrialisation is confirmed for the Gangetic Bihar for 1809/13 to 1901. This area belonged to the province of Bengal in the early nineteenth century, where the traditional industries such as cotton and silk textile manufacturing, jute processing, iron smelting, paper making and indigo dye manufacturing thrived. In view of my findings on them, it transpires that there should be massive deindustrialisation in that region during the nineteenth century. My findings also concur with what Chattopadhyay (1981) concludes: that, in the province of Bengal, the number of workers increased from 1901 to 1921. The argument is that Bengal's modern industries, which I have discussed in this study, emerged only in this province. In addition, by 1901 the decaying process of traditional industries was virtually complete in this part of the presidency, so that the effects of deindustrialisation could not be traced in a study that begins in 1901.

IV

The neo-Marxian school of thought seeks to situate deindustrialisation as an event in the formation of the capitalist world economy. There is little agreement on how and when the event occurred (Brewer 1990; Limqueco and McFarlane 1983). But most of them acknowledge the drain of wealth in the context of India's incorporation into the world capitalist system. Marx referred to it as the plunder of Bengal, which, according to the neo-Marxians, represented one of the constituents of the primitive accumulation in the 'metropolitan' centres of world capitalism. For peripheral countries, it represented the phase of decapitalisation, which, as Luxemburg (1951 [1913]: 373–6) points out, might have been ushered in by way of taxation as well. In line with Marx's own discourse on India's industrial decline, however, authors such as Frank (1978) and Wallerstein (1986) believe that British policies motivated the formation of world capitalism. Frank thus points out that capitalism was set up by the successive annulments of various protectionist policies of mercantilism in Britain under the philosophy of laissez faire. The process began in 1774 with the withdrawal of import prohibitions on Indian cotton textiles in England, was consolidated through the modification of the East India Company monopoly charter in 1793 and the ending of the charter on India trade in 1813, and culminated in the repeal of the Corn Laws in 1846 and Navigation Laws in 1849. With these, as Frank (1978: 75) remarks, 'British industrialists won the battle to institute free trade – and to enshrine it as a natural scientific law...' Not only did the metropolitan policies thus institute the first stage of capitalism, but they were equally effective in the subsequent stages. The following two stages of capitalism witnessed a large-scale capital accumulation involving a vast expansion of world trade. With support from suitable policy designs, the latter brought about deindustrialisation in the periphery and industrialisation at the centre, and thus heralded such an international division of labour that a dependent relationship was forged between the core and the periphery.

Wallerstein also points out that deindustrialisation was the starting point of world capitalism. He relates, 'The famous or notorious "general process of deindustrialisation" in India was, of course, very much a part of this qualitative economic change' (Wallerstein 1986: PE30). But he does not concur that the free trade policy that Britain pursued after its industrial excellence totally explains India's deindustrialisation. A host of restrictive policies, sometimes coercive, are identified instead. In the first place, the monopsonistic power of the East India Company in particular, and that of British traders in general, weakened the bargaining position of Indian artisans, and reduced them to 'wage workers'. This destroyed the traditional entrepreneurial skill of the society, leaving decision making at the behest of the British entrepreneurs. Obviously, British interests were subserved in the process. Second, contrary to its proclaimed policy of free trade, Britain adopted restrictive trade practices regarding the importation of Indian textiles, and thus severely curtailed their export outlets in that country. Similar setbacks loomed large in other foreign markets as well, as Britain imposed higher tariffs on Indian textiles that were carried on foreign bottoms and were destined for markets such as the United States, Holland, Denmark, Sweden and Portugal. While these restrictive trade policies crippled the export vents of Indian products, there were also several discriminatory acts from the colonial administration that hit domestic industries in India hard and directly. In sum, Wallerstein also emphasises state policies (though not the free trade policy) as an explanation for India's deindustrialisation.

Since deindustrialisation is not a market-driven outcome in the neo-Marxian analysis but an outcome of various state policies, the motives behind those policies need to be identified. To this end, Wallerstein (ibid.) argues, 'No doubt, in this heyday of British cotton textiles, during which the British sought to eliminate or limit the competition everywhere, with some considerable success, the elimination of Indian competition, first of all in Britain, second of all in continental Europe and North America, and finally to a significant extent in India itself, was only one element (perhaps even a secondary one) in a larger British strategy within the capitalist world-economy.' The crucial one, he points out, was the replacement of domestic crops such as foodgrains by the cash crops that the world market demanded. It should be noted that deindustrialisation performed two tasks simultaneously: first, it created a vast colonial market for the British products; and, second, it channelled the colonial supply of raw materials to British industries. The changes in the cropping pattern in Indian agriculture perpetuated the second process, and thus broke down the previous economic self-sufficiency not only at the village level but at the regional level too. According to Wallerstein (ibid.), 'This is precisely what one means when one says it entered into the social division of labour of the capitalist world-economy, wherein self sufficiency was (and is) to be found essentially only at the level of this whole world-system.'

Once India was incorporated into the world capitalist system it became subject to a dependent relationship with the 'core' capitalist country: Britain. On the basis of the theory of unequal exchange (Emmanuel 1972), Frank (1984) argues that this core–periphery relationship gave rise to exploitation, which initiated and perpetuated the emergence of underdevelopment in peripheral countries such as India.

These neo-Marxian explanations of deindustrialisation seem inadequate for the case of Bengal from 1757 to 1914. For one thing, they totally ignore reindustrialisation in this colony during the second half of the nineteenth century, whereby a series of modern industries sprang up. Contrary to their allegation that the laissez faire doctrine inculcated deindustrialising effects, three of its major industries – engineering, coal mining and paper making – grew up in an environment in which there was no import/export duty. Nor was there any record of decapitalisation for this period. Our analysis suggests *per contra* that, in Bengal's joint-stock ventures, at least Rs. 282.46 million had been invested by 1914. Again, without disputing the neo-Marxian surmise that the erstwhile artisans were eliminated from entrepreneurship during the first half of the nineteenth century, I argue that it does not necessarily suggest that entrepreneurs were altogether missing in the second half. The British capitalists took up the challenge, and carried out reindustrialisation.

Second, our empirical evidence does not corroborate the view that adverse colonial policies perpetuated deindustrialisation. My previous study on Bengal for 1757 to 1857 indicates that there were indeed discriminatory policies towards cotton and silk textiles, salt manufacturing and ship building. But the former two industries survived the discrimination. Moreover, the contemporary government promoted indigo plantations in this colony during that period. For the period from 1858 to 1914, the present study underlines the industry-friendly outlook of the colonial administration. Prospecting for coal was undertaken by the government to demonstrate its techno-economic viability in Bengal. The administration also initiated and promoted the construction of railways, thus ensuring its further development. In tea cultivation, the maiden venture took place at the behest of the government, which also inspired investors; distributed wastelands at favourable terms; and developed both roadways and railways for the ease of transportation. In the case of paper-making and engineering industries, adverse policies had certainly been there at the beginning, but they were repealed progressively, heralding a more congenial environment.

Third, I agree when the neo-Marxian writers argue that Bengal's cropping pattern changed in this period, with the introduction of cash crops. But it also promoted Bengal's industrial interest; the development of modern jute processing is the evidence in this respect.

The core thesis in this study is that the pivotal aspect in the course of an industrial economy – its progress or regress – was the dictum of comparative cost advantages, which determined the strength of market forces. In fact, the mainstream writers in this field, Morris in particular, also seek to explain India's nineteenth-century deindustrialisation by contemporary market forces. But, instead of seeing comparative cost advantages as the driving force, Morris (1969: 606–8) considers movements in the terms of trade between industries and agriculture as explaining the event.

According to the terms-of-trade hypothesis, the Industrial Revolution generated two effects in the international commodity market. On the one hand, the technological and institutional innovations that initiated the Industrial Revolution significantly reduced the cost prices of various manufacturing products, and also their market prices, by introducing mechanical principles, alternative energy sources and a better form of organisation. On the other hand, there was a steady multiplications of firms in various industries using more and more raw materials from agriculture, so that their prices soared internationally. The movement of international terms of trade in favour of agricultural commodities during the nineteenth century is evident in the British terms of trade between 1801–10 and 1841–50, which shows that the ratio of the country's export prices (representing the prices of manufactured goods) to import prices (representing the prices of industrial intermediaries, food and other primary products) fell by about 40 per cent (Imlah 1952). Indian industries could not respond adequately to these changes because of the scarcity of entrepreneurs in the society, the stubborn attitude of the people towards any departure from traditionality, and their 'otherworldliness', signifying a deep attachment on the part of the people to spirituality rather than the materialistic world (Morris et al. 1969: 606–8; see also Morris 1967 for a discussion). Indian industries could not, therefore, reduce costs enough during the phase of globalisation. They gained instead by increasing the supply of industrial raw materials from agriculture, such as raw cotton, raw silk and raw jute. The changing international terms of trade between industries and agriculture was thus reflected in India's domestic terms of trade between them, reallocating the country's resources and causing deindustrialisation (see also Williamson 2008: 374).

But this hypothesis also fails to explain the case of Bengal, as some of its important arguments are not empirically acceptable. In the first place, since Bengal's reindustrialisation between 1858 and 1914 was based on the advanced technological knowledge of Britain, Bengal's new industries also employed mechanical principles and inorganic energy sources. Their organisational structures were also not inferior. Second, there was no dearth of entrepreneurs in the contemporary society, as British entrepreneurs took an interest in Bengal, mobilising capital from both Britain and India. Moreover, their industrial activities generated demonstration effects among indigenous entrepreneurs, who undertook tea cultivation, coal mining and engineering works, albeit on a small scale. Hence, the traits of 'traditionality' or 'otherworldliness', as alleged by Morris, should not be levelled against people in the contemporary society of Bengal. In fact, Tripathi (1971: M62) notes that 'the impact of the superior business outlook of the foreigners on the Indians must be analysed in the context of the material changes that were simultaneously taking place'. He underlines that the effects of the Western ideas and new education in Bengal 'encouraged the non-commercial classes to look at the opportunities for gain more sympathetically and meaningfully' (ibid.).

Based on the analysis of 13 major industries in Bengal from 1757 to 1914, this study arrives at the following hypothesis: deindustrialisation was largely an outcome of the interplay of market forces that were generated by comparative cost advantages among trading countries. This explains the decay of Bengal's five industries in the traditional sector (cotton textiles, silk textiles, jute processing, iron smelting and paper making) and the growth of five industries in the modern sector (coal mining, iron smelting and its downstreams, jute processing, paper making and tea cultivation). Only two industries (salt manufacturing and ship building) decayed in the face of discriminatory policies, and one (indigo dye manufacturing) on account of administrative failings. Thus, the policy discriminations explain only 2.06 per cent of the total fall in industrial employment in Bengal.[5] In fact, policy discrimination was present for a host of other industries, especially prior to 1858 and also for some years afterwards (particularly for engineering and paper making). But their comparative advantages counterbalanced the adverse effects of the discrimination, enabling them to survive till their comparative benefits had been eroded (as in the case of cotton and silk textiles). Market forces became more explicit in the second half of the nineteenth century, when adverse state interventions were totally absent. Instead, many promising state policies were put into practice, with some more on the horizon, taking shape through the Indian Industrial Commission (1916–18) (GOI 1918).

V

Two issues are emphasised here by way of conclusion. First, Bengal's industrial landscape witnessed a triangular conflict of interests in the second half of the nineteenth century, involving British capitalists in British industries, British capitalists in Bengal industries and Bengali capitalists. Whenever there was conflict in industrial matters between Britain and India, the latter two groups united together and fought jointly against the former. In fact, British capitalists working in Bengal often sought favourable state policies, which ultimately subserved the economic interests of Bengal between 1858 and 1914. My discourse presents many such instances – such as the amendment of the store purchasing policies for the benefit of the paper-making and engineering industries, the distribution of wasteland and the promotion of export markets for tea plantations, and lenient Factory Acts that served the interests of the Calcutta jute mills. In these cases, the British capitalists in Bengal and the domestic capitalists made joint representations to the colonial administration, but met with stubborn resistances from the British capitalists in the United Kingdom. Similar conflicts also broke out between British capitalists working in Bengal and indigenous capitalists, and they fought each other. In fact, there were parallel associations for them in different industries – for example, the Indian Tea Association (ITA), representing British capitalists, and the Indian Tea Planters' Association (ITPA), representing Indian capitalists in the tea plantations, and the Indian Mining Association (IMA) and the Indian Mining Federation (IMF), respectively, in coal mining (Kidron 2001: 8).[6] At the apex level, there were the Bengal Chamber of Commerce and Industries (BCCI) and the Bengal National Chamber of Commerce and Industries (BNCCI) for the respective interest groups (for their centenary reviews, see Tyson 1953; and Palit 1999).

Second, Bengal's industrial decay in traditional lines had more devastating effects in the society than those our statistics project. Traditionally, artisans and industrial workers hailed exclusively from the local populace, and the contemporary society greatly benefited. But the modern industries that sprang up from 1858 to 1914 depended largely on migratory workers from neighbouring states, and also from far-off regions. Such workers even dominated unskilled jobs (such as porters) in the tertiary sector, which the modern industries gave rise to. Therefore, the erstwhile artisan families, and the families of industrial workers, crowded the agricultural sector, which languished in a state of backwardness. Economic slowdown thus ensued, and Bengal's welfare suffered.

Notes

1 Mill noted, 'There can be no more industry than is supplied by materials to work up, and food to eat. Yet in regard to a fact so evident, it was long continued to be believed that laws and governments, without creating capital, could create industry' (quoted in Naoroji 1901: 55).

2 Simmons (1985: 604) notes, 'The nineteenth-century – and of course the earlier – landscape, however, is still very bleak, and if we are compelled to rely upon either

the simple backward extrapolations of Heston or the somewhat heroic guestimates of Angus Maddison, the present outlook is far from promising and with few signs of improvement on the immediate horizon.'

3 Bagchi reports it mistakenly at 18.6 per cent. See Clingingsmith and Williamson (2008: 219, tab. 2 fn 'a').

4 Sivasubramonian (1997) shows that this proportion increased from 12.7 per cent to 16.9 per cent from 1900/5 to 1942/7, indicating the country's industrialisation.

5 This is based on the fall of employment in salt manufacturing and ship building (65,352), on the one hand, and that in all industries from 1825/9 to 1855/9 (excepting silk) (2,137,783), along with iron smelting, jute processing and paper making (1,029,004).

6 Simmons (1976: 213) writes, 'In fact, one of the main reasons behind the establishment of the wholly indigenous trade association (IMF) in 1913 was a clash of interest between the Indian and European branches of the [coal-mining] industry in the matter of the distribution of scarce wagon capacity.'

Bibliography

Bagchi, A. K. (1976) 'De-Industrialisation in Gangetic Bihar 1809–1901'. In Das Gupta, A., and De, B. (eds.) *Essays in Honour of Prof. S. C. Sarkar*, 499–522. New Delhi: People's Publishing House.

Bairoch, P. (1982) 'International Industrialization Levels from 1750–1980', *Journal of European Economic History* 11 (1/2), 269–333.

Banerjea, S. (1925) *A Nation in Making: Being the Reminiscences of Fifty Years of Public Life*. Bombay: Oxford University Press.

Brewer, A. (1990) *Marxist Theories of Imperialism: A Critical Survey*. London: Routledge.

Chattopadhyay, R. (1975) 'De-Industrialisation in India Reconsidered', *Economic and Political Weekly* 10 (12), 523–31.

Chattopadhyay, R. (1981) 'Trend of Industrialisation in Bengal, 1901–1931', *Economic and Political Weekly* 16 (35), 1425–32.

Clark, C. (1957) *The Conditions of Economic Progress*, 3rd edn. London: Macmillan.

Clingingsmith, D., and Williamson, J. G. (2008) 'Deindustrialisation in 18th and 19th Century India: Mughal Decline, Climate Change, Climate Shocks and Britain's Industrial Ascent', *Exploration in Economic History* 45 (3), 209–34.

Das, M. N. (1959) *Studies in the Economic and Social Development of Modern India, 1848–56*. Calcutta: Government Printing.

Desai, M. (1971) 'Demand for Cotton Textiles in Nineteenth Century India', *Indian Economic and Social History Review* 8 (4), 337–61.

Digby, W. (1901) *'Prosperous' British India: A Revelation from Official Records*. London: Unwin.

Dutt, R. C. (1901) *The Economic History of India under Early British Rule*, vol. I: *From the Rise of the British Power in 1757 to the Accession of Queen Victoria in 1837*. London: Kegan Paul, Trench, Trübner.

Dutt, R. P. (1940) *India Today*. London: Victor Gollancz.

Emmanuel, A. (1972) *Unequal Exchange: A Study of the Imperialism of Trade*. New York: Monthly Review Press.

Frank, A. G. (1978) *Dependent Accumulation and Underdevelopment*. London: Macmillan.

Frank, A. G. (1984) *Critique and Anti-Critique: Essays on Dependence and Reformism*. New York: Praeger.

Frank, A. G. (1996) 'India in the World Economy, 1400–1750', *Economic and Political Weekly* 31 (30), PE50–PE64.

Frisof, D. (2008) 'Deconstructing De-Industrialization: R. C. Dutt, M. D. Morris and Interpreting Nineteenth Century Indian Economic History', *Brown Journal of History* 2 (spring), 21–32.

Ganguli, B. N. (1965) *Dadabhai Naoroji and Drain Theory*. New York: Asia Publishing House.

Government of India (GOI) (1918) *Report of the Indian Industrial Commission, 1916–18*. Calcutta: Superintendent Government Printing.

Guha, A. (1972) 'Raw Cotton of Western India, 1750–1850', *Indian Economic and Social History Review* 9 (1), 1–41.

Habib, I. (1985) 'Studying a Colonial Economy – without Perceiving Colonialism', *Modern Asian Studies* 19 (3), 355–81.

Harnetty, P. (1991) '"Deindustrialization" Revisited: The Handloom Weavers of the Central Provinces of India, c. 1800–1947', *Modern Asian Studies* 25 (3), 455–510.

Imlah, A. H. (1952) 'British Balance of Payments and Export of Capital, 1816–1913', *Economic History Review* (new series) 5 (2), 208–39.

Karve, D. G., and Ambekar, D. V. (eds.) (1962) *Speeches and Writings of Gopal Krishna Gokhale*, vol. I. London: Asia Publishing House.

Kidron, M. (2001) *Foreign Investments in India*, reprint edn. London: Routledge.

Krishnamurthy, J. (1976) 'De-Industrialisation Revisited', *Economic and Political Weekly* 11 (26), 964–7.

Limqueco, P., and McFarlane, B. (1983) *Neo-Marxist Theories of Development*. Hastings: Croom Helm.

Luxemburg, R. (1951 [1913]) *The Accumulation of Capital* (trans. A. Schwarzschild). New York: Modern Reader Paperbacks.

Marx, K. (1853) 'The British Rule in India', *New-York Daily Tribune*, 25 June, available at www.marxists.org/archive/marx/works/1853/06/25.htm.

McAlpin, M. B. (1974) 'Railroads, Prices, and Peasant Rationality: India 1860–1900', *Journal of Economic History* 34 (3), 662–84.

McAlpin, M. B. (1975) 'Railroads, Cultivation Patterns, and Foodgrain Availability: India 1860–1900', *Indian Economic and Social History Review* 12 (1), 43–60.

Morris, M. D. (1963) 'Towards a Reinterpretation of Nineteenth-Century Indian Economic History', *Journal of Economic History* 23 (4), 606–18.

Morris, M. D. (1967) 'Values as an Obstacle to Economic Growth in South Asia: An Historical Survey', *Journal of Economic History* 27 (4), 588–607.

Morris, M. D., Matsui, T., Chandra, B., and Raychaudhuri, T. (eds.) (1969) *Indian Economy in the Nineteenth Century: A Symposium*. Delhi: Indian Economic and Social History Association.

Naoroji, D. (1901) *Poverty and Un-British Rule in India*. London: Swan Sonnenschein.

Palit, C. (1999) *Growth of Commerce and Industry in Bengal*. Calcutta: Bengal National Chamber of Commerce and Industry.

Perlin, F. (1983) 'Proto-Industrialisation and Pre-Colonial South Asia', *Past and Present* 98 (1), 30–95.

Ray, I. (2011) *Bengal Industries and the British Industrial Revolution*. London: Routledge.

Robb, P. (1981) 'British Rule and Indian "Improvement"', *Economic History Review* (new series) 34 (3), 507–23.

Roy, T. (2000) 'De-Industrialisation: Alternative View', *Economic and Political Weekly* 35 (17), 1142–7.

Roy, T. (2006) *The Economic History of India, 1857–1947*. New Delhi: Oxford University Press.

Seth, S. (1999) 'Rewriting Histories of Nationalism: The Politics of "Moderate Nationalism" in India, 1870–1905', *American Historical Review* 104 (1), 95–116.

Simmons, C. P. (1976) 'Indigenous Enterprise in the Indian Coal Mining Industry, c. 1835–1939', *Indian Economic and Social History Review* 13 (2), 189–218.

Simmons, C. P. (1985) '"De-industrialization", Industrialization, and the Indian Economy, c. 1850–1947', *Modern Asian Studies* 19 (3), 593–622.

Sivasubramonian, S. (1997) 'Revised Estimates of the National Income of India, 1900–1 to 1946–7', *Indian Economic and Social History Review* 34 (2), 113–68.

Thorner, D., and Thorner, A. (1962) *Land and Labour in India*. Bombay: Asia Publishing House.

Tripathi, D. (1971) 'Indian Entrepreneurship in Historical Perspective: A Re-Interpretation', *Economic and Political Weekly* 6 (22), M59–M66.

Twomey, M. J. (1983) 'Employment in Nineteenth-Century Indian Textiles', *Exploration in Economic History* 20 (3), 37–57.

Tyson, G. (1953) *The Bengal Chamber of Commerce and Industry, 1853–1953: A Centenary Survey*. Calcutta: Bengal Chamber of Commerce.

Vicziany, M. (1979) 'The Deindustrialization of India in the Nineteenth Century: A Methodological Critique of Amiya Kumar Bagchi', *Indian Economic and Social History Review* 16 (2), 105–43.

Wallerstein, I. (1986) 'Incorporation of Indian Subcontinent into Capitalist World-economy', *Economic and Political Weekly* 21 (4), PE28–PE39.

Williamson, J. G. (2008) 'Globalization and the Great Divergence: Terms of Trade Booms, Volatility and the Poor Periphery, 1782–1913', *European Review of Economic History* 12 (3), 355–91.

Zaidi, M. A. (ed.) (1985) *Congress Presidential Addresses*, vol. I. New Delhi: Indian Institute of Applied Political Research.

Zaidi, M. A., and Zaidi, S. (eds.) (1976) *The Encyclopaedia of the Indian National Congress*, vol. I. New Delhi: S. Chand.

Appendix 9.1 Various empirical studies on India's deindustrialisation

Author	*Nature of study*	*Publication year*	*Reference period*	*Study area*	*Measurement yardstick*	*Findings*
Clark	Inter-sectoral framework	1950	1881–1911	India	Employment level (census data)	Evidence of deindustrialisation
Thorner and Thorner	Inter-sectoral framework	1962	1881–1931	India	Employment level (census data)	No evidence of deindustrialisation
Chattopadhyay	Inter-sectoral framework	1975	1901–1931	India	Employment level (census data)	Evidence of deindustrialisation
Chattopadhyay	Inter-sectoral framework	1981	1901–1931	Bengal Presidency	Employment level (census data)	Evidence of deindustrialisation
				Bihar and Orissa	Employment level (census data)	Evidence of deindustrialisation
				Bengal Province	Employment level (census data)	No evidence of deindustrialisation
Bagchi	Inter-sectoral framework	1976	1808–1901	Gangetic Bihar	Employment level (data of Buchanan Hamilton and census data)	Evidence of deindustrialisation
Bairoch	Inter-sectoral framework	1982	1750–1938	India	Manufacturing output (own estimation)	Evidence of deindustrialisation
Clingingsmith and Williamson	Industry-level framework	2008	1760–1860	India	Relative prices (secondary source)	Evidence of deindustrialisation
Harnetty	Industry-level framework	1991	1800–1947	Central Provinces of India	Employment level and number of looms (secondary source)	Evidence of deindustrialisation
Twomey	Industry-level framework	1983	1790–1830	India	Trade-induced employment level (own estimation)	Evidence of deindustrialisation
Guha	Industry-level framework	1972	1850–1900	India	Raw material consumption (secondary source)	Evidence of deindustrialisation

Source: See text.

Index

Note: All numbers in **bold** refer to tables, in *italics* to figures.

For Product Safety Concerns and Information please contact our
EU representative GPSR@taylorandfrancis.com Taylor & Francis
Verlag GmbH, Kaufingerstraße 24, 80331 München, Germany